BLESSED EVENTS

PRINCETON STUDIES
IN CULTURAL SOCIOLOGY

——————————EDITORS——————————

Paul J. DiMaggio

Michèle Lamont

Robert J. Wuthnow

Viviana A. Zelizer

*Origins of Democratic Culture: Printing, Petitions,
and the Public Sphere in Early-Modern England*
by David Zaret

*Bearing Witness: Readers, Writers,
and the Novel in Nigeria*
by Wendy Griswold

Gifted Tongues: High School Debate and Adolescent Culture
by Gary Alan Fine

Offside: Soccer and American Exceptionalism
by Andrei S. Markovits and Steven L. Hellerman

Reinventing Justice: The American Drug Court Movement
by James L. Nolan, Jr.

*Kingdom of Children: Culture and Controversy
in the Homeschooling Movement*
by Mitchell L. Stevens

Blessed Events: Religion and Home Birth in America
by Pamela E. Klassen

BLESSED EVENTS

RELIGION AND HOME BIRTH IN AMERICA

Pamela E. Klassen

PRINCETON UNIVERSITY PRESS   PRINCETON AND OXFORD

Library of Congress Cataloging-in-Publication Data

Klassen, Pamela E. (Pamela Edith), 1967–
Blessed events : religion and home birth in America / Pamela E.
Klassen.
p. cm. — (Princeton studies in cultural sociology)
Includes bibliographical references and index.
ISBN 0-691-08797-0 (alk. paper) –
ISBN 0-691-08798-9 (pbk. : alk. paper)
1. Childbirth at home—Religious aspects. 2. Religion and culture.
I. Title. II. Series.
BL619.K53 2001
291.1'783—dc21   2001019852

This book has been composed in Galliard

Printed on acid-free paper.∞

www.pup.princeton.edu

Printed in the United States of America

10 9 8 7 6 5 4 3 2 1

for Magdalene and Isabel

_____

the muscle and the bone gave way
and then I saw your face
now I'm a true believer in the existence of grace
    —Cate Friesen, *"flesh and bone"*

Contents

Motherhood Issues

THIS BOOK explores how women in the United States give religious meaning to the act of childbirth. It is at once a portrayal and a commentary on how contemporary women—from a wide range of religious identities—reflect upon and practice the sacred in their procreative lives. Childbirth, the process of one body becoming two (or more), is an act of creation that leaves echoes in a woman's body and memory. In addition to this intimate sphere of body and memory are more public attempts to make meaning from childbirth. Medical and legal discourses, advice books, and even the cautionary tales of experienced women shape cultural perceptions of birth. Spanning the intimate and the public, childbirth has assumed a place alongside similarly politicized "motherhood issues" ranging from abortion to teen pregnancy. Over the past century North Americans have debated the meanings and practices of childbirth in the context of a society grappling with what it is to bear and raise children in a feminist, or at least feminist-influenced, age. These debates are not motherhood issues in the conventional sense of that phrase—that is, issues that bring forth only sanguine truisms or taken-for-granted agreement. Though without the media profile of other reproductive issues, childbirth has provoked impassioned controversy as many birthing women have critiqued and refused the model of medicalized birth that has become dominant in North America. The rise of midwifery care in hospitals, birthing centers, and homes testifies to the burgeoning success of these women's efforts to transform childbirth.

The varied movements to reform childbirth in North America are not only about politics—they are not only about who holds the power in birth. They are also fundamentally about the meaning of birth to a woman's life and the life of her family and community. Since the early days of the post–World War II natural-childbirth movement in North America and the beginnings of the post-1960s home-birth movement, the luminaries of these movements—people like Dr. Grantly Dick-Read, author of *Childbirth Without Fear*, and midwife Ina May Gaskin, author of *Spiritual Midwifery*—have insisted that childbirth contains religious and spiritual meaning. They, and the women who have taken their books to heart, have viewed childbirth as a religious or spiritual process capable of provoking transformation for women, men, and babies alike.

Home-birthing women are an important part of this movement for childbirth reform, while also being part of a wider impulse in their culture that critiques the presuppositions of biomedicine—that is, the models of the body and medicine based on Western understandings of physiology. These women insist that birth is more than a biomedical event by asserting that in addition to being a physiological process, birth is also a religious and spiritual occasion. In their dual positions as childbirth reformers and critics of biomedicine, home-birthing women are what I call "postbiomedical bodies"—bodies that continue to rely on some aspects of the dominant biomedical model while simultaneously adopting very different models drawn from religion or from alternative therapies.

Given the breadth of childbirth reform, many more women than home-birthers might consider birth to be a religious event and might inhabit postbiomedical bodies, but my choice to look at home birth in particular allows an important vantage point on the fusion of religion and childbirth. Biomedical interpretations of the physical process of birth have largely supplanted the explicitly religious discourse that surrounded childbirth in previous centuries, especially as it moved from the home to the hospital. In contemporary home birth, however, religious discourse has enjoyed a resurgence. The variety of religions women draw from to make meaning of their births mirrors the great variety in North American religion more generally. Those who find home birth a rich source of religious meaning include both feminist and traditionalist Christians and Jews, followers of Goddess spirituality, and women who find "spirituality" in more informal ways. This religious diversity in the midst of a particular, minority choice of childbirth provokes a host of questions about how such ideologically diverse women think about and experience their bodies, their homes, and their religious convictions.

While considering the interrelationship between childbirth and religion I want to keep in mind two themes. First, I watch for ways that feminist and traditionalist approaches to childbirth collide and conjoin. While some feminists have been decidedly hostile to the idea that childbirth could be a source of female empowerment, others have fought for the reform of childbirth practices as just such a source of empowerment. These latter feminists, however, would not want to claim that bearing children is a necessary goal in every woman's life, as some traditionally—or newly orthodox—religious people might insist. In between the extremes of those viewing childbirth as oppression versus childbirth as destiny are both feminists and traditionalists trying to make meaning from childbirth.

A second theme running throughout the book is that of "agency" and its limits, as women make therapeutic choices about their bodies with the help of religious understandings—decisions that are often in contrast to the dominant biomedical culture. What emerges is a complex picture of how childbirth and religion can both allow and threaten agency as it is commonly conceived in North America; namely, as the freedom of "rational" actors to choose. Both childbirth and religion can inspire moments when the body exerts its will most forcefully—moments that become opportunities for disruption of one's everyday habits of thinking and action, at times even in spite of one's conscious choices.[1] Just as choices in childbirth practices are limited by physical necessities and contingencies despite the variety of methods available today, so too are religious practices limited by cultural inheritances despite the freedom of choice offered by the contemporary "spiritual marketplace." For example, a secular, Euro-American woman newly embracing Native spirituality or Orthodox Judaism can never erase her past in the hopes of achieving a newly "authentic" identity—she will be a hybrid of what she was and what she seeks to become. Some would argue that the limits inherent in physical and cultural embodiment are not limits to agency at all, especially when "getting religion" or giving birth. Instead, they may be harbingers of a different and particular kind of agency accessible through different faculties than rational consent.

Feminist and traditionalist women alike claim that the childbearing body is a begetter of profound meaning. Regardless of their perspectives they insist that women have a vital role in defining and embodying that meaning; they are not content to consider birth and maternity either irredeemably sullied by long-held patriarchal projections or hopelessly disenchanted by medical procedure. As I explore the commonalities and differences among these diverse women, I argue that an analysis of contemporary home birth accomplishes three related goals: illustrating the continued importance of religion as a source for challenging biomedical models of the body, questioning and broadening the category of what and who counts as "religious," and establishing the enduring power of childbirth to foster religious reflection and initiate religious practice.

I have many people to thank for helping me to write this book. First, I am deeply grateful to all the women who welcomed me into their homes and told me their stories. I am especially grateful to the woman whom I call here Simone Taylor, who invited me to attend the birth of her second child. All of these women graciously gave of their time and selves, as they recounted their stories of childbirth with joy, humor, and poignancy. I also wish to thank the many midwives who offered their perspectives on the meanings of home birth, including Louise Aucott, Rebecca Hamilton, Rondi Anderson, Hilary Monk, Chris Sternberg, Nancy Wainer Cohen, and other midwives to whom I promised anonymity. Dr. Joseph Cohn helpfully offered the perspective of a physician.

Many friends and colleagues have offered advice and support at various stages of this project. Karen McCarthy Brown has watched as this book grew from its beginnings as an idea and has generously offered her considerable insight and encouragement. Her example of feminist scholarship and mentoring has sustained me on many occasions. Leigh Schmidt also read this work in its early stages as a dissertation and was a careful and supportive advisor. As well, Emily Martin offered a welcome "outside" reading of the dissertation that I hope I have put to good use. Doug Arava, Talal Asad, Robbie Davis-Floyd, Ron Grimes, Charles Hirschkind, Robert Orsi, and Janelle Taylor all read versions of some of these chapters and have spurred me to think in some new directions. Lynn Davidman and Mary-Jo Neitz both read the entire manuscript and gave me encouragement and wise counsel. Arlene Macdonald provided excellent research assistance in the final stages. My dealings with the people at Princeton University Press have been most enjoyable. In particular, Ian Malcolm has been an insightful reader and a personable editor and Joan Hunter was a careful and astute copy editor. I thank them all for their hard work. Courtney Bender, Cynthia Eller, Bob Gibbs, Leigh Gibson, Marie Griffith, Chris Hiller, Nina-Marie Lister, Anne Merideth, Vanessa Ochs, Ruth Richardson, and Val Steinman provided both friendship and critical commentary, a combination I truly value.

I wrote this book while participating in several supportive communities that I wish to thank, including the Center for the Study of American Religion at Princeton University and the Department for the Study of Religion and Victoria College at the University of Toronto. At Princeton, Anita Kline and Robert Wuthnow were particularly supportive of my work. The temporary communities offered by the Louisville Institute Dissertation Fellowship symposium and the After the Body Conference at Manchester University, in the United Kingdom, were also important for me as I worked on the book. The Canada/U.S. Fulbright Program, Drew University, the Social Sciences and Humanities Research Council of Canada, and the Louisville Institute for the Study of American Religion all provided necessary funding during my graduate studies. As well, the University of Toronto's Connaught Fund and the Victoria College Conference Travel Fund have allowed me to present some of this work at conferences. Victoria College also funded the preparation of the index. I gratefully acknowledge the support of all these institutions.

I thank Cate Friesen for permission to quote from her song "Flesh and Bone," from her album *Joy's Disorder* (1999). I also thank the University of Chicago Press for permission to reprint chapter 6, which was published in an earlier version as "Sacred Maternities and Post-Biomedical Bodies" (© 2001 by The University of Chicago. All Rights Reserved.) in *Signs: A Journal of Women in Culture and Society* 26, no. 3, and *The Scottish Journal of Religious Studies* (now *Culture and Religion*) for permission to reprint chapter 7, which was published in an earlier version in Volume 19, no. 1, of that journal.

For both ordinary and extraordinary daily sustenance I thank my family and friends. In particular, Maggie MacDonald has given both literal and figurative labor support to me as a scholar and a mother and has made both vocations much more enjoyable. My brother Joel Klassen has helped me in many ways, by caring for my children, by transcribing many of my interview tapes, and by encouraging me to consider the implications of scholarship. I am also grateful to my father John Klassen and his partner Vicki Sharp for their support of my research and my family. My mother, Susanna Klassen, has cared for my children and for me with great generosity and love, enabling me to work. John Marshall has tirelessly read many drafts of this book, giving me the benefit of his critical acumen, patience, and love, and has gracefully shared with me the joys and labors of raising our children. Finally, I would never have started this book were it not for my daughter Magdalene, who was its first inspiration, and I might never have finished it were my daughter Isabel not such a delightful, contented baby. This book is for both of them.

BLESSED EVENTS

1

Procreation Stories: An Introduction

> Unlike death, its only competitor as an essential
> human experience, birth has an involved witness
> who lives to tell the story, a birthing woman. Her
> experience is of universal importance, because it is
> she who is caught up in that elemental activity,
> childbirth, with hurricane intensity. And it is her
> story that is rarely, if ever, told.
>   *Carol H. Poston, 1978*

IN A CHILD's blue wading pool decorated with dolphins and fish, Simone
Taylor, a small woman with the strong body of a runner and short blonde
hair, sat naked in about six inches of warm water, hands on her pregnant
belly. She reclined into the lap of her husband, David, and rested the back
of her head on his shoulder. As he held her, she closed her eyes, and took
advantage of a lull in her body's rhythms. Simone was giving birth in the
living room of her two-bedroom apartment with the help of David and
two midwives, who knelt beside the pool. I stood by with a video recorder
and two cameras, taking pictures of the birth at her request.

With the next contraction, Simone shifted from David's lap to her hands
and knees, hoping the change in position would give her some relief from
the weight of her uterus. She erupted with a deep and forceful groan. The
midwives responded with a chorus of, "Open, open, open, open." The
contraction subsided and she reclined once more into David's lap. One
of the midwives poured more warm water into the pool, as I held some
watermelon close enough to Simone's mouth for her to take a few bites.
She ate, leaned back, and waited with eyes closed, thinking to herself as
she told me later, "I could wait forever. I don't really want to do this!"

Next to Simone's powerful groaning, the quiet of waiting was palpable.
We all kept still as Simone prepared herself for the effort of birth, and as
her baby waited to continue its descent through her birth canal. The next
contraction brought Simone to her hands and knees again. Her low groan
became a higher-pitched scream, as she cried out, "Owwww! No, I can't
do this, God! Make it stop!"

"You can do it; open, open, open, open," the midwife chanted. "Your
baby's almost here."

With the ebbing of the contraction, Simone rested once more against David. "I'm being a wimp," she lamented. "No, you're not," we all replied at once. I added, viscerally remembering my own pain just one year earlier, "You're being totally brave."

For the rest of her labor, Simone stayed in David's arms. During the next contraction the baby's head crowned and Simone's perineum stretched wide. "Aieee!" she cried. "Please make it stop!"

"Open, open, open," the midwives repeated gently.

"I'm tearing!" Simone insisted.

"No, you're not, you're stretching," the midwife reassured her as she supported Simone's widening perineum with her hands. "Your baby is almost here."

With another great cry and push from Simone, the baby's head emerged into the midwife's waiting hands. "The baby's head is born," the midwife said calmly. "One more great big push." Simone, eyes closed, reached down to touch her baby's head. We waited again for Simone to push the rest of the body out with another contraction. The baby, halfway between the world and its mother's womb, waited too.

Then, with a low moan and some forceful grunts, Simone pushed the rest of her baby out. As the midwife placed the wet and wrinkled baby, still attached to its thick, pulsing cord, on Simone's chest, the baby gave forth a lusty cry, announcing its presence to the world. Covered with a blanket and capped with a hat, the baby nestled in Simone's arms as David spoke gently: "Hello, baby! Hello, baby! It's good to see you!" Stopping himself, he laughed and said, "Wow!"

Simone lay back exhausted and closed her eyes. After a few minutes, while David delighted in his new daughter and the family dog came over for a look, Simone roused herself. "Ten fingers, ten toes?" she asked.

"She's beautiful, a blue-ribbon baby," the midwife enthused.

"Look at those eyes," Simone murmured. "I think I'm going to start having fun in a few minutes," she said with a smile. Simone began to examine her new baby and marveled at her newborn's resemblance to her older child. "Anna," she declared to her baby, "you are so beautiful. We're going to have a great life together."

After David cut and tied the cord, Simone delivered the placenta. One of the midwives then helped Simone out of the wading pool and into the shower, while the other midwife dressed Anna and swaddled her. Freshly showered with a clean T-shirt on, Simone crawled into bed. The midwife snuggled Anna up next to her, and Simone began to nurse her baby. Still wearing the "good karma" earrings she had carefully put on at the start of her labor, Simone looked rosy-cheeked and a little bewildered as she gazed at her newborn child. A few minutes later, Simone's mother brought Leah, Simone's four-year-old daughter, back home. With a look of wonder, Leah walked into the bedroom and saw her newborn sister. She promptly climbed into bed with her mother and father and reveled in holding her new sister, bundled in blankets, just half an hour out of her mother's womb.

More than twenty years ago Carol Poston could write, quite accurately, that women's stories of childbirth were "rarely, if ever, told."[1] This is not the case today, thanks in part to feminism and to a growing alternative childbirth movement. Women are telling their birth stories—to their children, to their friends, to writers, scholars, and television producers, and, in their own books, to the wider world. My story of Simone's birth and this book as a whole join a panoply of other voices, women's and men's, telling stories of childbirth.[2]

Over the course of researching this book, I have listened as women told me of seemingly unrelenting pain, overwhelming joy, unsettling fear, and gritty determination. I have had a particularly childbirth-attuned ear and eye, listening and watching for any references to childbirth in the culture around me, and storing these pieces of the wider story of childbirth in North America in file folders, on scraps of paper, and in my mind. Perhaps two of the most famous births during this time were those experienced by pop icon Madonna and by the mother of the first surviving septuplets, Bobbi McCaughey, both of whom gave birth by cesarean section in the hospital. While in part driven by celebrity and the extraordinary, the media frenzy surrounding both of these very different birthing women also showed the power of childbirth to capture the imaginations and attentions of North Americans. Most interestingly for me, however, the media coverage often highlighted these women's religiosity—Madonna's "turn to the East" in the wake of her daughter's birth and Bobbi McCaughey's Evangelical Christian faith and supportive church community both attracted much media interest, albeit mostly of an uncritical sort.[3]

In this book I take the analysis of the link between religion and childbirth much further than the brief, popular accounts of "celebrity" or "extraordinary" births. Working with the childbirth stories of "ordinary" women like Simone, I ask questions about how women interpret and create the meanings of childbirth in their own lives—how they make sense of the pain, evolve evocative metaphors for their birthing bodies, and sometimes find transformative power in their procreation. For all of the women I have met in the course of this research, childbirth is not simply a life-crisis moment that comes and goes. Birth sticks with a woman, remaining in her bones and her flesh as an embodied memory long after the baby has left her womb. And for all of the women I met, those embodied memories were either immediately or gradually woven into religious meanings, whether from the perspective of an Evangelical Christian, a Reform Jew, a Goddess feminist, or a "not-so-religious" woman.

Guiding my inquiry into the religious meanings these women attribute to childbirth are the two issues I referred to earlier: one, tensions between feminist and traditionalist appraisals of the symbolic meaning of birth, and two, the kinds of agency afforded to or denied women as they derive religious meanings from childbirth. More specifically, considering these issues leads me to ask the following: What does home birth, a woman-centered movement struggling to return birth to the home and to women's control, mean in practice for women's gender and religious identities? Does this supreme valuing of women's roles as birthers and nurturers define women solely as procreators and caretakers, or does it open up new realms of cultural and social power for women? Asking these questions while being attuned to the significance of religion not only allows me to explore new understandings of what it means to practice religion in contemporary America, but also challenges both feminist and traditionalist interpretations of motherhood and childbearing women.

As a scholar of religion, I understand the word "religion" to be embedded with meaning on many levels. In contemporary America, perhaps the most popular understanding of religion lies in its contrast with "spirituality." In this usage, religion is age-old tradition, encrusted with hierarchy, institutionalization, and meaningless ritual. Spirituality, on the other hand, is thought to be a more immediate, accessible, personal relationship with God (or another deity), sometimes encountered through meaningful ritual. Though these are not my own definitions of religion and spirituality (as will become apparent in chapter 4), I realize they have a powerful hold over contemporary discourse about religious or spiritual matters. At this point, I do not want to choose one word over another at the risk of obscuring my arguments, or worse, misrepresenting the stories of the women in these pages. For some women, giving birth evoked "spiritual" responses that they drew from eclectic sources. Others interpreted their births within more traditional religious doctrines or allusions. What these women shared, despite their different sorts of religious or spiritual allegiances, was the desire to situate birth within realms of meaning beyond the biological act itself. In all cases, they worked with their bodily experiences of birth in imaginative and empowering ways, becoming creative visionaries. As I will show, all of these women did this creative, imaginative work at the margins of traditions, collecting scraps of ritual, metaphor, and, in some cases, literal objects, to bring meaning to the process of birth and its aftermath.

Religions have long used birth, a rite of passage we all pass through in one form or another, as a central metaphor to express the hope and potential of recreating the self, and in some cases, society.[4] Many religions have mythical birth stories at their root; earthly women give birth to supernatural gods or holy men, but never become quite as powerful as their sons. Ironically, given the fruitfulness of the idea of birth to many religious systems in terms of divinely wrought immaculate conceptions, being born again, and enduring cycles of death and rebirth, in Western religions women's actual experiences of birth have been sorely ignored and underritualized.[5] In this study I shift this meaning-making gaze in a different direction. I ask not how religious traditions have ritualized birth or used it to make sense of human existence, but how birthing women use religion to make sense of their births, and how in turn they draw on birth to make meaning in their lives.

Though I would argue that no birth is ordinary, in one important way the stories that I tell here are themselves extraordinary, at least in the context of North America on the cusp of the second millennium, when most women give birth in the hospital. All of the women I write about have chosen to give birth at home, some with midwives or doctors in attendance, and others with no one but their husbands. Their choices are rooted in diverse motivations, some explicitly and doctrinally religious, others more diffusely so. But they all share at least one commitment in common, namely that childbirth is not a disease but a natural process that healthy women, left to their own devices, are good at. While many women who give birth in the hospital would share this commitment, these home-birthing women have pushed their convictions one step further in their decision to birth at home. Their subtle shifting of the language of birth reflects these convictions about birthing, as they replace the conventional phrase "to give birth" with the more active "to birth," a linguistic gesture that I replicate at times throughout the book as a way to focus attention on the action of childbirth.[6]

The stories of women like Simone are important in their own right, but are also important for North American society more generally. Their forceful questioning of the ways increasingly expensive and invasive medical technologies manipulate human bodies—especially at the beginnings of human life—is rooted in a concern not only for physical integrity, but for the integrity of the spirit. Their insistence that physical pain in childbirth need not always be interpreted as suffering that requires obliteration through drugs is grounded in an embodied conviction that pain can also generate propitious forms of power, and in some cases, community. For these women, a society that supports a woman's choice to give birth at home and supports her caregivers would learn to honor the sensations and process of childbirth. Through extending this support, society might come to a more profound respect of the diversity of physical and social experiences, and a deeper realization of what slim threads of commonality might tie us together as human beings.

In choosing to write about women like Simone, I intend this book to speak to several audiences at once, some of which may overlap. First, I hope scholars in religion, women's studies, anthropology, and cultural studies will find contemporary childbirth to be a fascinating site for the interplay of religion, gender, and the biological and symbolic body. In the case of home birth, where in certain states women must break the law in order to give birth at home with their chosen caregiver, this interplay includes the law, as women challenge the authority of the state over their childbearing bodies. Direct-entry midwives, those who do not undertake nursing training but instead train in midwifery schools or by apprenticeship to another midwife, are the objects of most of the state laws that declare midwife-attended home birth illegal. In the year 2000, direct-entry midwives were illegal in nine states and legal but not able to obtain licensure in seven states, including New Jersey.[7] Operating in an underground economy, without access to payment from medical insurance, direct-entry midwives are nevertheless attractive to some women, whether because of their more intimate style of care or because they will attend births that certified nurse-midwives, their professionally legitimate cousins, cannot attend, such as a home birth after a woman has had a previous cesarean section.

I also write with a more general audience in mind of women and men who are interested in contemplating the meanings of childbirth, whether in their own lives or in the wider culture. Included in this audience are the women about whom I write. Some of these women have responded directly to me after reading an earlier version of this work, and I have taken their comments into consideration in writing this book. In every case, I hope that my renditions of these significant events in these women's lives ring true to their own experience, even if they may not always be in agreement with my interpretations.

Meeting the Women: Some Comments on Method

I met the women in this book through a variety of channels, including through midwives (who first asked their clients if I could call), postpartum gatherings at a midwife's house, flyers posted in another midwife's office, a midwifery study group, and most commonly, referral from women I had already interviewed. As such, I do not present their stories as representative of all birthing women, or even of all home-birthing women. They are a group of particular women whose voices come together because of my efforts to gather stories, and in some cases, their willingness to share their networks of friends with me.[8] Though I was careful not to solicit only self-identified religious women—for example, my flyer made no reference to religion—inevitably after an interview in which I had asked questions about religion, some women directed me to friends who they thought had particularly spiritual birth stories. As well, since I had told the midwives who referred me to women about my interests, and had introduced myself as a graduate student in religion, they also pointed me to women they thought of as religious or spiritual. However, I was also careful to interview women who claimed no religious affiliation at all, or who claimed that birth had little to do with their religious background. Significantly, in talking with me, these women did speak of religious practices or spiritual interpretations tied to their births. Therefore, though the group I ended up speaking with might be more religious than a random group of home-birthing women, they were a very diverse group religiously speaking, with a wide range of perspectives and levels of religious commitments. As well, their religious interpretations of birth correspond with a persistent theme in home-birth literature that depicts childbirth as an important spiritual experience.

Many of the women agreed to meet with me after only talking with me on the phone, but usually in these cases I mentioned a specific person who had given me their name. Due to the illegality of direct-entry midwifery (midwives who have trained either as apprentices or in nonnursing midwifery schools) in many northeastern states, several women were initially suspicious of me until I could show that I had the support of their direct-entry midwives. In several cases I was asked whether I was "pro– or anti–home birth," especially by women who had employed direct-entry midwives or who had birthed unassisted. When I could respond that I too had given birth at home, albeit with certified nurse-midwives, these women agreed to speak with me.[9]

For all but one of the forty-five interviews, I traveled to the woman's home, and spoke with her for between one and a half and four hours (in the exceptional case, the woman came to my home). In two cases, I interviewed a woman before and after her home birth, and in another case I interviewed a woman twice.[10] The interviews took place in two northeastern states over the course of two years in 1995–96. During this time I also interviewed four midwives, three of whom were certified nurse-midwives, with licenses to practice at home and hospital privileges. One was a direct-entry midwife, who had trained by apprenticeship and was unlicensed and illegal, and thus unable to accompany her clients to hospital. These interviews and many more informal conversations with other midwives, both licensed and unlicensed, helped me to gain helpful technical and contextual information. In addition to interviews, more observational fieldwork shaped my understanding of the home-birth movement. I attended a number of home-birth-related events, such as postpartum gatherings organized by direct-entry midwives, at which their clients who had given birth in the past month met to talk about their births and introduce their babies. I sat in on office hours at a certified nurse-midwife's office, talking about my project with clients, and visited a "midwifery study group" attended by direct-entry midwives, labor assistants,[11] interested women, and one medical student. I also attended a daylong "healing workshop" on childbirth issues led by a nationally known home-birth activist. One woman, Simone Taylor, whose baby's birth I described above, did me the honor of inviting me to take pictures at the birth.[12] Throughout, I traveled in a world peopled mostly by women; a woman's husband might occasionally pop in during an interview, especially if it was the evening, but for the most part the gatherings I went to, the offices I frequented, and the homes I visited were overwhelmingly women's places.

Given the diversity of sites I traveled among, it is difficult to circumscribe the "field" of my research. I did not have to go farther than a three-hour drive to meet my "informants," but I did find myself in what I considered alien environments within the familiarity of my assumed home ground. As a white, Canadian woman in my late twenties with an ambivalent relationship to my Mennonite background, meeting women of such religious diversity was both exhilarating and intimidating for me. Entering an Old Order Amish woman's home with its typically large and impeccably kept kitchen, with no sign of electricity anywhere, usually made me nervous, and very conscious of my car, my clothes, and my questionable piety. These concerns eased, however, upon meeting a woman like Mary Rose Erb, who I first saw driving handily up her driveway in a smart, black, horse-drawn buggy as I waited outside her house with my daughter. Mary Rose warmly welcomed me into her home, apologized for making me wait, and then proceeded to give me thoughtful and direct answers to my questions as we sat around her kitchen table. We chatted about our children's sleeping and nursing habits long after my "questions" were answered, while her four-year-old daughter amused my eleven-month-old with a doll in a cape dress.

Crossing the threshold of a Pentecostal woman's home prompted similar bouts of nerves, in anticipation of inquiries about my spiritual state. With some women, like Janet Stein, these inquiries eventually did arise. While I was perched on the doorstep of her town house about to leave, Janet asked me whether I was a Christian, and I stumbled out something about being in a state of questioning. She quickly handed me a pamphlet the size of my palm that pointed the way to salvation with Jesus Christ, and seemed content that at least I was undecided. On a second visit to her house, however, she did not inquire again, and was happy simply to continue her witness in the form of telling me her life story. Other women inquired about my religious identity, and while many wanted to know more about Mennonites, none was so directly concerned with my current spiritual state as Janet.

My feelings of being an outsider, however, were not limited to my meetings with women who differed from me religiously. Instead, even at gatherings where I might have felt more culturally at home in some ways— like an underground midwifery study group peopled with aspiring lay midwives, lesbian holistic healers, and self-proclaimed feminists—I was conscious of being something of an outsider. Once when I was about to leave a meeting of the midwifery study group, one of the leaders of the group called me back into the circle of women to ask me which midwives had attended my baby's birth. When I replied with the names of the midwives, whom everyone there knew were certified nurse-midwives, the group chuckled, not entirely sympathetic to the licensed CNMs, given their own illegal status as direct-entry or aspiring midwives. Earlier that afternoon, when I had mistakenly brought a bowl of meat-filled tortellini salad to the study group's potluck meal and told a vegetarian it was filled with cheese, I was mortified, and chastised when I informed her of my error, one bite too late. And in that anti-immunization crowd, I made no mention of my choice to have my daughter immunized. My lifestyle choices—choosing CNMs, eating meat, immunizing my child—once made visible, subtly distinguished me from this group of women who otherwise were much more similar to me than Pentecostal or Amish women. Revealing and concealing different aspects of myself, while not always a conscious and rarely a calculated maneuver, was an ever-present part of my interactions with all of the women I met—as it is with every human encounter.[13]

My musings about my relative position vis-à-vis the various women I encountered are in part driven by concerns that have occupied many ethnographers. In at least the last fifteen years, ethnographers have increasingly questioned their methods and claims to authority, especially in a "globalizing" world where the subjects of ethnographies are often also their readers. Feminist ethnographers have been particularly concerned with issues of responsibility and accountability, as they consider the political consequences of their work for women who may be placing themselves in personally awkward or threatening situations as a result of their willingness to talk about their lives.[14] While the women in my study had little awkwardness in talking about birth, there were other parts of their "procreation stories,"[15] such as their stories of abortion, that did bring them to hesitate, whisper, and sometimes cry. Unlike abortion, childbirth stories are set on more acceptable terrain. Though childbirth is politically contested and some women recount their experience in the genre of the "horror story," women (at least middle-class, married, heterosexual women) are not condemned for giving birth, but celebrated.[16] For the most part, <u>talking about birth made these women feel good</u>.

Much of their ease with talking about home birth stemmed from their knowledge that I had made the same choice. Between-women discussions of motherhood—from choice of birthplace to mode of child rearing—can be enlivening, but they can also be fraught with tensions. Women make many choices about bearing children. Some choose not to mother, some face infertility and may choose among adoption and fertility treatments, some choose hospital birth or scheduled cesarean sections, while others stay at home to give birth. In possibly two of the most charged of choices, some opt for bottle feeding while others breast-feed, and some stay at home to care for their children while others make use of various arrangements of child care.[17] In the specific context of childbirth, some women undergo circumstances that obviate choice altogether, such as experiencing premature labor or placenta praevia, two situations demanding a hospital birth. When women who have made different choices are in conversation, the specter of judgment can loom heavily. Even among women who have made similar choices, these judgments may be made, as I found when women who had given birth with direct-entry midwives made comments about home birth–certified nurse-midwives being "mini-obstetricians."

My proximity to home birth <u>was both an important reason why I was successful in finding so many women eager to speak with me</u>, and a cause for caution. If I had not given birth, I would not have been surprised to find women giving me less birth story and more birth advice, and I probably would have asked different questions. I also would have understood less of what women meant when they spoke of physical sensations such as contractions and the urge to push. Certainly, women experience childbirth in many different ways, but having done it oneself, the other's experience is both more viscerally and mentally comprehensible. In many situations, especially with the Amish women with whom I had the least in common (despite my Mennonite heritage), the fact of my motherhood offered the opportunity for much of our discussion. On the many occasions that my daughter accompanied me, she often broke the ice in the way that only babies can, with her ready smiles and babble. And on the occasions when I would breast-feed her during an interview, I always sensed approval, and even a sort of intimate solidarity. I was not just a <u>scholar talking to these women—I was a lactating, mothering woman, someone, in many ways, just like them.</u> The connections forged around children and childbirth in my interactions with such religiously, if not culturally, diverse women were the elemental ground of what became one of my larger arguments—that shared values around childbirth can form the basis for alliances between what might otherwise seem intractably different women.

This difference calls forth caution on my part. In my analysis, I have tried to avoid eliding differences while being entranced by the potential of the "intimate solidarity" enjoined by childbirth. In significant ways, I was not just like these women. Just because we shared a way of giving birth did not mean that we also held interpretations of that experience in common. Encountering different perspectives on the experience of childbirth from such a variety of women, my interpretation of my own birth has changed many times—I have alternately seen my own naïveté, good luck, strength, and prejudices. Although, for example, I think that I would never plan to give birth unassisted, while interviewing women who did I began to feel it was not such an outlandish choice.

Perhaps the biggest difference between me and many (not all) of the women was my feminism. This came out most clearly in differing attitudes to marriage, in which several women, including Evangelical Christians and an Orthodox Jew, thought that wives should be submissive to their husbands. Another difference, which in some cases reflected this view of marital relationships, related to choices about child care. Most of the women, both feminist and nonfeminist, felt that babies needed their mothers to be their primary caretakers in the early years. During the course of my interviews, my husband and I shifted from sharing the care of my daughter between us to putting her in part-time day care. I felt myself in the position of being between the two worlds of stay-at-home mothers and "working" mothers, but more fully on the way to the latter.[18] In some ways, however, many of the women saw me as a blank slate—or perhaps a mirror—because I too had given birth at home. Whereas for me going to their homes and talking to them was working (albeit in a very congenial mode), many women seemed to see it simply as talking. Several commented freely on how they thought young children needed to be at home with their mothers, without pausing to worry about offending me even when my daughter was not with me.[19]

The interviews I engaged in were loosely structured and often entailed much give and take between the other woman and me.[20] There are both strengths and weaknesses in my approach. Interviewing 45 women allowed me to see greater diversity among women who chose home birth, especially in terms of religion. It has also meant, however, that with the exception of several women whom I met repeatedly at several home-birth-related events, I did not have the time to establish a deeper level of intimacy and repeated opportunities for reflection that more in-depth life-history work allows. While diversity in religious approaches to home birth was one of the primary interests I held upon embarking on this project, I have often wished that I had the time to meet with more of these women on an ongoing basis.[21]

Despite being complete strangers at the start, most women were very willing to speak with me and were quite forthcoming once we began talking.[22] Speaking with them in their homes as their children played—and my baby sometimes joined in—was most often very enjoyable, with most of the women offering me tea, snacks, or sometimes lunch. Most seemed very comfortable with discussing the physical details of birth, though a few preferred euphemisms like "down there" for "vagina."[23] Ironically, given the critique of medicalization shared by most of the women, many of them also seemed at ease with the biomedical terminology of birth—talking, for example, of the stations of engagement, the stages of labor, and Braxton-Hicks contractions.[24] Part of this ease stemmed from their generally high levels of self-education regarding childbirth, but it was also a sign of the implicit (and partial) hegemony of medical models of birth even within the alternative-birth movement. As I will discuss in the following chapters, the language of birth is a hybrid of medical terminology, metaphors of nature, and religious allusions.

These women's comfort with talking about birth partly stemmed from the knowledge most women had of the political nature of their choice to give birth at home. Many women were eager to talk to me with the hopes that scholarly attention would correct the many misrepresentations they felt home birth has suffered. They wanted to tell their stories to convey the message that home birth is safe and satisfying for the mother, baby, and family. How a woman tells the story of her birth, however, and the role religion has in that telling, has a great deal to do with her present circumstances. If she has just recently emerged from giving birth, her tale is likely to be filled with more raw detail and less overarching meaning. If she has ten years between her and the pains and joys of birth, she may have gradually crafted a birth narrative based in reflection and remembering that has sifted some of that raw detail into a story with more portable kernels of meaning.[25] Many of the women suggested that the deeper meaning of their babies' births only came to them with sustained reflection and distance from the physicality of the event, and for some women, changes in their religious life changed the meanings of these births. Throughout this study then, a certain provisionality must be granted to the tales I tell: this is what birth meant for these women in the context of a conversation with me, then a Euro-American graduate student in her late twenties, with a young daughter who was born at home. Nevertheless, though their stories may well be different now or when told to a different listener, our talking was filled with detailed narratives and considered reflections that have provided me with very rich sources to ponder.

My version of the results of that talking, this book, has the potential to offend those women who so generously told me their stories, and this gives me pause. Despite my personal commitment to women's right to choose where and with whom to give birth, I do not restrain myself from critique in this study of home birth. The primary focus of my critique is the unquestioned use of the heavily loaded (and cultured) term "natural"—a powerful legitimator of both biomedical and midwifery approaches to childbirth.[26] I approach the slippery notion of the natural with the assumption that birth is a profoundly cultured act, so that any reliance on its naturalness by home-birthing women is itself an act of cultural fashioning. Home-birthing women are refusing the dominant cultural way of birth in North America. They are resisting what might be called a biomedically shaped version of "habitus"—the socially formed body that seems "natural" and that allows persons to act within their culture without needing to think twice.[27] But in resisting the "second nature" that has made giving birth in the hospital seem like the normal thing to do, home-birthing women are invoking another reworked, resistant, and encultured view of nature.

Understanding this view of nature calls for sustained reflection on women's birthing bodies and the layers of history and social distinctions embedded in their practices of childbirth. Practice, in Karen McCarthy Brown's succinct definition, "refers to [the] ongoing work of individuals and communities in creating, adjusting, and maintaining meaning in their worlds."[28] Brown emphasized the role of the memory-laden, mindful body in this never-ending work. The bulk of my reflection, however, is based on women's ways of *talking* about birth, and as such I am primarily accessing the practices of home birth through discourse, or through talk about what I have called "embodied memory." In so doing, seeking the "true meaning" of childbirth is not my aim. As Paula Treichler warned, "The word *childbirth* is not merely a label, provided us by language, for a clear-cut event that already exists in the world; rather than describe, it *inscribes*, and makes the event intelligible to us. We cannot look *through* discourse to determine what childbirth 'really' is."[29] I endeavor to show how the intimate and seemingly natural bodily act of birth is constructed, even in its least "interventionist" form, and how religion is a vital and creative source for this construction. I also insist that these constructions do not float only in the realm of ideas, but are naturalized into women's bodies, often in unpredictable ways. Considering women's stories of home birth with both sympathy and scrutiny allows me to analyze these naturalized bodies in a way that suggests both the potential hazards and the triumphs of women reclaiming birth.

In what follows, then, I have tried to balance many parts of myself in analyzing the stories these women told me, and in shaping the context in which I develop this analysis. This book first germinated in my own process of preparing to give birth at home, as I read all manner of childbirth advice books with implicit (or sometimes explicit) prescriptions for how to do it "right." That the home-birth texts I read were especially laced through with religious or spiritual language prompted me to think about what significance religion and spirituality might have for home-birthing women themselves. What at first was going to be a dissertation on another rite of passage—weddings—quickly became a study of childbirth, as I explored the seemingly never-ending variety of religious interpretations of birth. My ongoing concern to juxtapose these home-birth stories with religious studies and feminist theory, seeing where they connect and where they collide, is the main way that my particular perspective reasserts itself in these pages. My commitment to healthy, fulfilling birth practices is another. Though I realize that globally there are many barriers to safe and satisfying childbirth, and that not all women are going to desire the same kind of experience, my goal here is to show that individuals and societies make implicit and explicit choices in their ways of birth. These birth choices, like many others, are premised on complex mixtures of privilege, sacrifice, and self-interest. Rarely made with complete freedom and always embedded in social, economic, cultural, and bodily contexts, these choices nonetheless demand careful consideration.

The chapters that follow this one interpret the relationship of religion and home birth from a range of perspectives, always coming back to the questions of how do feminists and traditionalists draw symbolic meaning from the bodily experience of birth, and what sorts of agency does this meaning entail. Chapter 2 provides a broad contextual base for understanding the home-birth movement in North America. I sketch a brief history of changing childbirth practices in North America, with especial attention to the significance of religion, and draw a demographic picture of who is turning to home birth. I also show how and why childbirth has come to interest scholars as part of a wider fascination with reproductive politics at the turn of the millennium. The third chapter then delves into the controversy and debate surrounding home birth, suggesting that much of this debate stems from competing notions of risk and contrary understandings of what is ethical. I analyze how risk, responsibility, and fear of death combine to make home birth a profoundly religious or spiritual experience for these women, while also making it a practice berated or even demonized by many. This leads me in chapter 4 to compare how different understandings of religion and spirituality affect women's interpretations of birth, and conversely how experiences of childbirth shape their very diverse religious lives. Just what do women consider to be religious or spiritual in the context of childbirth, and what sorts of transformations of the self and society do these considerations imply?

The next three chapters then focus on increasingly localized sites: the home, the body, and the pain of childbirth. Here I trace how these women

interpret home, body, and pain both as ideas and as tangible realities encountered in new ways in childbirth. Exploring the meanings of home
allows me to investigate how home is counterposed to the hospital and to
analyze the kinds of religious bricolage that women undertake in their
domestic spaces. Throughout, my exploration is informed by feminist critiques of domesticity that have worked to expose the seemingly natural
link between women and the home. Focusing in chapter 6 on the bodies
inhabiting these homes or, more specifically, the bodily metaphors that
these women employ in asserting that birth is a "natural" process, permits
me to explore my twin themes of the symbolic languages and the embodied agency evoked by birth. In the final chapter, I discuss the variety of
approaches that home-birthing women take to the bodily pain of birth,
including enduring it, surmounting it, and transforming it into pleasure.
I explore the thorny question of finding power in pain, whether through
explicitly religious interpretations or not, and demonstrate how for some
women experiencing the pain of birth elicits visionary creativity.

In my epilogue, I conclude with reflections on the politics of motherhood in North America, and consider what the home-birth movement
reveals about these negotiations over maternal power. In an increasingly
"biocapitalist" world, what significant cultural meaning can a small minority of women who choose to give birth at home without drugs or high-
tech equipment entail? According to many of these women, they are
changing the consciousness of the world one baby at a time, and perhaps,
two parents at a time, as they strive for births that are gentle, respectful,
and blessed events.

2

Cultural Contexts of Home Birth

WHO ARE THE WOMEN who choose home birth, how do history and culture shape their choices and stories, and what do their stories mean? While most of this book is concerned with answering these questions through attending carefully to specific women's voices, in this chapter I answer these questions in broad strokes. I draw a bird's-eye view of the home-birth movement through a number of different angles. First I describe the demography of home birth in the United States—for example, who is choosing it, where they live, and what the regional cultural influences are that support their decisions. Then I lay out some of the conditions for the contemporary resurgence of home birth by briefly telling a history of childbirth practices in America, focusing especially on religion. Finally, I set home birth within the wider context of other studies, mostly anthropological, that have inquired into the meaning of childbirth. These three circles of inquiry into the demography, history, and anthropology of childbirth overlap to provide a range of procreation stories that shape both academic and popular understandings of childbirth in the United States.

In the preceding chapter, I borrowed Faye Ginsburg's phrase "procreation stories" to signify the often complex paths of women's reproductive lives. In this chapter, I apply it to broader narratives of childbirth and the wider overlapping contexts in which the meanings of home birth are made. The importance of attending to the larger contexts of birth in the United States is not only academic, since many birthing women who choose midwifery care are well informed about the history and politics of childbirth. Particularly given the profile of home-birthers as generally well-educated, middle-class women, it is not surprising that they are avid readers, at least when it comes to birth. All the women I interviewed (except for some of the Amish women) were familiar with at least some of the historical, anthropological, and popular studies of birth that I draw upon here. These books played a role in shaping their views of home birth, and are as much a part of the "field" of home birth as they are tools for understanding that field. Consequently, before laying out my interwoven circles of inquiry, I briefly discuss the significance of reading to women's development of their own procreation stories.

The women in my study were generally highly educated (except for the Amish women, who attended school until eighth grade). Several had medical training as veterinarians, nurses, chiropractors, or clinical assistants, and one woman was an epidemiologist. The few women who did not go to college went to alternative higher education (like Christian Science nurses' training or a community college) or considered themselves self-taught regarding issues of health and healing. Even the Amish women read Amish newsletters about "family life" and pregnancy and childbirth books loaned to them by their midwives. Of those women who were not Amish, many claimed to be voracious readers and often cited books as the first place they found out about home birth. The majority of the homes I visited during my interviews bore out these claims, with shelves in the living room filled with books, and often a woman could point to the part of the shelf where her well-thumbed pregnancy and birth books lay. As well, a midwife's office frequently doubled as a lending library, housing further reading resources such as the classics in home-birth literature complete with psychedelic covers, and the more recent, tamer coffee-table versions of home-birth tomes.[1]

Reading is an important way that middle-class women develop their interest in and knowledge of alternative ways of childbirth. Especially in the last forty years, as birth control access and technology improved and abortion was legalized, "pregnancy and birth became, at least for the medically advantaged, a chosen and cherished experience."[2] Similarly to their making other life choices, middle-class women have sought to educate themselves about "facts" or alternatives in birth. Accordingly, the number of books about childbirth has blossomed, representing many perspectives—from countercultural to hypermedical.[3] Just like the book market for women in general, the market for books about pregnancy and childbirth is large and seemingly impossible to saturate.[4]

Where women had once gained most of their knowledge about childbirth from female kin or friends, already by the late nineteenth century they increasingly had turned to books.[5] In the nineteenth century, most of the advice literature directed to mothers also was written by mothers, as "collections of homespun wisdom based in large measure on common sense and practical experience."[6] But with urbanization, industrialization, and a declining birth rate, medical, governmental, and psychological "experts" took over the role of counselor, writing texts presented as "scientific tracts" and based on a "professional rather than a parental relationship."[7]

Alternative-birth literature reversed this pattern, but with a twist, as the earliest critics of obstetrical care were male obstetricians themselves, while later commentators have almost all been women—midwives, childbirth educators, and activists.[8] These later authors usually offered their advice to women as mothers themselves, and often included numerous birth stories written by women in their own voices.[9] However, some also presented their expertise as anthropologists, midwives, or childbirth educators, and exploited medical perspectives and even methodologies for their own purposes.[10] In the process, they "domesticated" medical forms of knowledge for the benefit of home birth.

Though getting information through reading is clearly important to a woman's decision to give birth at home,[11] it is not the only factor in her choice. In a study of women choosing between hospital and home birth, Carol Shepherd McClain found that women giving birth at the hospital made their decisions based mostly on knowledge gained from books. Women choosing home birth, however, not only relied on books, but also based their decisions on "concrete knowledge" achieved through social networks of friends. By this she meant "knowledge gained vividly from observation and participation," such as going to the birth of a friend's baby and discussing pregnancy and childbirth in detail with friends.[12] Many of the women in my study had previous knowledge of home birth whether through observation or via stories of the births of friends' or family members' children before electing that route on their own. With this concrete knowledge in mind, however, reading books and attending childbirth education classes still remained important ways these women prepared themselves for birth.

Several of the books women mentioned to me were classic advice books of the alternative childbirth movement, from British obstetrician Grantly Dick-Read's pathbreaking *Childbirth without Fear*, first published in the United States in 1944, to the 1975 book *Spiritual Midwifery*, written by Ina May Gaskin and the Farm midwives. More recently, in 1991, Sheila Kitzinger, the prolific British anthropologist and childbirth activist, published an elegantly laid out how-to book, entitled *Home Birth*. Though the women in my study did not always remember the names of the books they had read, these three books, along with a few others, were most frequently mentioned when I asked them about books they had read in preparation for childbirth.

Reading within the limited selection of home-birth advice books (at least when compared with the number of advice books based on the medical model), women encounter a diversity of perspectives from a movement with many leaders who share some views and who would debate others. Filled with assumptions and prescriptions about gender, sexuality, and the significance of birth to a woman's identity, these books—even those one might consider to be "secular"—are also remarkably consistent in their portrayal of birth as a religious or spiritual event. Reading is a critical process, and I cannot suggest all the ways these women might have read these books. But as I turn to a discussion of the "big picture" of home birth, it is important to remember that many of the women in my study are aware of this big-picture view as well, although, as will become clear, their perspectives may be somewhat different from my own.

Home-birthing Women: Who Are They?

I use the phrase "home-birthing women" throughout this book, but within that phrase lie some differences that need spelling out. While most home-birthing women would very likely share a commitment to ensuring women's access to giving birth at home with appropriate caregivers, they do not all take the same path to that commitment. Even though the number of American women who give birth at home every year is only around 1 percent of birthing women (in 1994 that meant around 40,000 women), this minority has some significant strands of diversity within it— one of the most pronounced being religious diversity.[13]

Any attempt to draw a demographic portrait of home-birthing women is made difficult by at least three factors. First, the failure of birth certificates to distinguish (until recently) between planned and unplanned home birth, and second, the unwillingness of some home-birthing parents to disclose on a birth certificate who attended their child's birth, for fear of legal action against a direct-entry midwife. Finally, a small number of home-birthing parents refuse altogether to secure birth certificates for their children immediately after birth.[14] However, some patterns can be sketched in comparing a woman who gives birth at home to the average U.S. childbearing woman. According to a 1995 study, a home-birthing woman is more likely to be older, to be having a second or subsequent child, and to have less formal education. She is somewhat more likely to be married and white, and less likely to smoke or drink alcohol while pregnant. She is more likely to begin her prenatal care later, and is less likely to receive certain prenatal tests, like ultrasound or amniocentesis. She is also less likely to be diagnosed with a prenatal medical risk condition or obstetric complication. She is more likely to be attended during childbirth by someone other than a physician or certified nurse-midwife; for example, by a direct-entry midwife or by her husband or a friend. Finally, the health of her baby at birth is likely to be better than that of the average baby born in the United States.[15]

In addition to this larger comparison with all childbearing women, a more focused comparison can be drawn showing that women having home births cluster in two groups. The first group is "older or more formally educated mothers who are likely to prepare themselves prenatally for a home birth." The second is made up of "those who are younger or have less formal education for whom home birth may be a result of lack of planning or other manifestation of problems with health care access."[16] When race is added to these distinctions, the effects of poverty and racism in limiting access to health care are more clearly evident. Euro-American home-birthers have more formal education and better birth outcomes than Euro-American women generally, and African-American home-birthers tend to have less formal education and poorer birth outcomes than African-American women in general.[17]

These statistical differences between Euro-American and African-American women's home-birth experiences show that though the alternative-birth movement often considers itself progressive, or even "revolutionary," as one woman asserted to me, it has been so for a particular minority of women. The statistics on home birth, along with the statistics on infant and maternal morbidity and mortality in general, demonstrate that African-American women must still struggle harder for accessible health care of good quality than most of their Euro-American counterparts. Struggling for basic access puts some African-American women in a position very different from those who are struggling to avoid medical models of care. In these circumstances, according to anthropologist Gertrude Fraser, many African-American women find it difficult to "untangle the web of domination in order to take back what is good and whole and useful in their own medical [midwifery] traditions. Instead they turn to progress with the blessing of their elders, while affluent members of the dominant culture turn with nostalgia to the vestiges of a world view taken completely out of its cultural context."[18] Ironically, Fraser found that traditional African-American midwives, if they still attend any births, usually do so for middle-class Euro-American women "who are able to choose freely, confident that they and their offspring will be afforded the best that midwifery and science has to offer."[19]

Fraser may overstate the confidence of Euro-American women in medical care,[20] but she does isolate an important inequity in the birth experience of Euro- and African-American women. Women giving birth at home who must be transported to the hospital often experience chastisement or disrespect from medical authorities for their eschewing of a medicalized birth. But Euro-American women are much more likely to know that they have adequate insurance that will both pay for their hospital stay and grant them the access to health care that they need, and they are much less likely to suffer from racism in the hospital environment. Choice is often rooted in privilege, and feeling free to choose where, how, and with whom to give birth is no different.[21]

Regional studies like Fraser's have shown the importance of local culture to the fate and character of midwifery and home birth in different geographical regions. For example, the Latina tradition of *parteras* (midwives) in the Southwest, the African-American tradition of "grand-midwives" in the South, and the countercultural centers of childbirth activism on the Pacific Coast and in Tennessee have all shaped home birth in the United States in distinct ways.[22] Older traditions of home birth lasted longest in the South and Southwest, but not only because of deeper cultural traditions. Lay midwives also persisted because of a racist medical system in which the medical profession "feels greater responsibility for the births of white and middle class patients while it considers alternative care-providers acceptable for less attractive clients."[23] In part, traditions of midwifery lasted longer among African-American and Hispanic women because of indifference to their childbearing needs from much (but not all) of the medical and hospital establishments.[24]

The newer forms of home-birth midwifery are most common in the West and the Southwest, where childbirth activists and midwives successfully lobbied their state governments to reactivate old midwifery legislation, or to newly legalize direct-entry midwifery. Direct-entry midwives (the majority of whom attend home births, with some working at birth centers) have also made significant inroads in some northeastern states, such as Pennsylvania and Vermont.[25] The Northeast in general, however, is a predominantly medicalized region, at least as far as childbirth is concerned. While nurse-midwifery is legal, most nurse-midwives work in hospitals, and do not attend home births. Direct-entry midwifery is illegal or requires a permit that is no longer available in most northeastern states, including New York and New Jersey.[26] At the time I was doing my research, women in New Jersey who wanted a home birth had the choice of only two practices, one being a certified nurse-midwife home-birth practice and the other a direct-entry midwife practice. In addition to legal restraints and the practical difficulties that result from them, home birth may be less common in the Northeast because its folk traditions of religion and medicine are less distinct when compared to those of the Southwest or South. (Pennsylvania would be an exception here, with its large Mennonite and Amish populations.) As well, countercultural subcultures (whether those of hippies or survivalist Christians) are not as prominent in the Northeast as in the Pacific Coast area or the Southwest. Like women elsewhere, however, women in the Northeast have rediscovered home birth in the past thirty years. While many of these women root their choices in notions of a long-standing tradition of midwifery, most of those views of tradition are not tied to distinct, living, or directly remembered traditions with common cultural and religious moorings. Women in the Northeast thus apply their diverse religious traditions to their births on a more individual basis, making for a less distinct birthing culture than in other regions.[27]

Turning specifically to my own study, the women generally fit within the cluster of Euro-American married women with formal education. Two of the 45 women were African-American and one was Hispanic. One of the 45 women was divorced and remarried, one was divorced, and another was in the process of separating from her husband. Several women held advanced degrees, and most had at least some college education. All but one of the women had planned to give birth at home. Of the eighty planned home births among the 45 women, the birth attendants divided evenly between direct-entry midwives and certified nurse-midwives, with another two births being attended by doctors, and three women giving birth unassisted by any professional caregiver.[28]

In terms of class, the women and their husbands spanned a range of occupations and incomes, from a husband who was an electrician making $20,000 per year to one who was a software designer making more than $100,000 per year, but for the most part they were middle class. More than three-quarters of the women cared for their children at home, and about a third of these women also worked part-time at jobs that ranged from assisting in their husband's chiropractic office to being veterinarians. Six women had full-time employment, all in professional occupations such as teaching, nursing, ministry, or chiropractic.

All of these women's reasons for choosing home birth fit within Judith Rooks's description of a "cluster of related reasons" for American women's choice of home birth. These included being able to have control over the circumstance of their births; supportive caregivers and environments; avoidance of routine interventions in hospital birth (like episiotomies, epidurals, and fetal monitoring); family involvement in the birth; and lower cost. Another significant reason, according to Rooks and the women in my study, was the desire to "experience the beauty and spiritual potential of a simple, natural, birth."[29] What this spiritual potential entails, however, is not necessarily simple. Though in terms of class and race these women were somewhat homogenous, religiously they were very diverse—at least within the scope of Christianity, Judaism, and Goddess or "New Age" religions.[30]

Several scholars have acknowledged the importance of religion to women choosing home birth, although, as Judith Rooks put it, "there are no data to quantify it."[31] Perhaps the significance of religion to home birth (and to other social or cultural issues) is particularly difficult to quantify because, methodologically, religion is a slippery category to analyze. One regional study in 1977 comparing 60 women across different birth sites found home-birthing women to be less religious than hospital-birthing women, when religiosity was defined as affiliation with an organized religion.[32] Levels of religiosity change with broader definitions, however, as a national study of 675 home-birthing couples found that almost half of the couples surveyed considered "spiritual beliefs" to be important to their choice of home birth. Another 9 percent felt "cultural beliefs" were important.[33] The glossing of religion as a prevalence of "spiritual" concerns is a common way to address (or dispense with) the significance of religion to home-birthing women.[34] Often, the particular content of this spirituality is not further explored, or several religious traditions are lumped together without detailed consideration of their similarities or differences.[35]

Robbie Davis-Floyd's otherwise excellent analysis of both home- and hospital-birthing women is an example of how the way one defines "spirituality" or "religion" can affect one's analysis. The only women Davis-Floyd categorized as understanding birth as a process of "spiritual growth" were those who gave birth at home.[36] For Davis-Floyd this spirituality was synonymous with a "holistic" framework that sought mind-body and mother-baby integration and was "based on systems theory, which assumes the fundamental interconnectedness of all things."[37] While this definition may discount the understandings of "spiritual growth" held by some of the women who gave birth in the hospital, it also misses differences among home-birthing women's understandings of spirituality. For example, Davis-Floyd described advocates of home birth as allies in holism with supporters of homeschooling, environmentalism, and alternative health practices, but specifically distinguished between "religious fundamentalist homeschoolers" and "wholistic homeschoolers."[38] In my research this distinction did not always seem well founded. Women who embrace home birth come from a wide range of religious and political perspectives.[39] I spoke with "fundamentalist" homeschoolers and "holistic" homeschoolers who chose home birth for some of the very same reasons.

That the minority and very politicized practice of home birth attracts to it such a diversity of religiously inclined people is one of the main enigmas I address in the chapters that follow. As such, my study does not "quantify" the significance of religion to home birth, but explores the various qualities of this relationship. I explicitly address what other researchers of home birth have described as a "hard-to-define level of self-awareness" that is shown in women's attention to the interaction between religion and the body and in their concern about good health and nutrition.[40] I found this self-awareness lodged within a variety of religious allegiances, cutting across stereotypical views of liberal and conservative in the United States. Through a variety of circuitous paths, women arrived at some similar understandings of embodiment, self, and birth. All of these women's paths are set within the controversial historical terrain of childbirth in America, sometimes consciously, and sometimes not.

Religion and the History of American Childbirth

Looking with a historical lens, the religious meanings invested in childbirth in North America are everywhere apparent. A seventeenth-century woman in labor in New England, fearing for her life in the midst of her pain, called on God to keep her safe, and an eighteenth-century midwife in Maine considered in part that "serving others was her way of serving God."[41] Several prominent women in American religious history have had specific links to childbirth, both practical and theological. Anne Hutchinson, the seventeenth-century woman who was expelled from her Puritan church for preaching that God freely granted salvation if one had faith, was also a midwife. Ironically, her supporters used her midwifery skills as evidence of her piety, while her detractors believed that these skills, and her giving birth to a deformed baby, proved her intimacy with Satan.[42] Even when female religious leaders have advocated celibacy, some have infused childbirth with religious significance, albeit a negative kind. For example, the eighteenth-century founder of the Shakers, "Mother" Ann Lee, whose four children died in infancy, thought childbirth was an experience of "terror" from which women needed to be saved.[43] Nevertheless, she frequently used the metaphor of childbirth to explain religious experience, including her own conversion.[44] By contrast, almost two hundred years later, Dorothy Day, leader of the twentieth-century Catholic Worker Movement, credited her blissful experience of giving birth and loving her baby with bringing her to the final step of becoming a Catholic. She wrote: "No human creature could receive or contain so vast a flood of love and joy as I often felt after the birth of my child. With this came the need to worship, to adore."[45]

As these and less prominent women show, throughout four centuries many American women have viewed childbirth as a bodily process capable of purveying religious messages and effecting religious transformation. Even though their official traditions did not necessarily nurture the religious significance of childbirth, they found birth deeply transforming on their own. As historian David Hall suggested about religious life in early New England, "Life crises (rites of passage) and especially childbirth may explain why people moved from merely 'formal' Christianity to critical self-searching, and why women were more likely to be church members. It is surely not coincidental that Anne Hutchinson put her questions about assurance of salvation to women undergoing childbirth."[46] The women in my study are heirs—some directly, some not—to this critical self-searching brought about through the bodily transformation of birth. Their introspective search is embedded within larger political and cultural understandings of the meanings of maternity and the maternal body. Setting this self-searching within the transformation from "social childbirth" to medicalized birth over the course of the last two centuries, while paying special attention to religious influences, provides a helpful background for my later consideration of contemporary women's lives.[47]

In the eighteenth century, women began to cede only part of the birth process to doctors, as birth remained in the home, and women retained control over the rituals of "social childbirth." The minority who turned to doctors in the home placed "the body in the hands of men, the spirit in the company of women."[48] By the nineteenth century, however, those women who strove to plan their childbirth experience were less likely to understand childbirth as "God's plan in action or God's judgement on the adequacy of their prayerful preparation for the event, as had many of their seventeenth-century sisters."[49] The shift of childbirth from the home to the hospital, and away from social childbirth, was a gradual process beginning in the nineteenth century and reaching its peak in the mid-twentieth century.[50] Doctors had already overtaken midwives in many urban areas by the mid-nineteenth century, as middle- and upper-class women became convinced of the superiority of a doctor's skills—namely, his use of tools like forceps and anesthesia.[51] While midwives continued to attend the majority of births until the 1920s, their clientele gradually became poorer, less educated, and more likely to be recent immigrants or African-Americans, a social profile that fit many midwives as well.[52]

In the early twentieth century, middle- and upper-class women began to heed their doctors' advice to give birth in the hospital—a place of supposed efficiency, safety, and the latest technology. The few poor women and unwed mothers who had been giving birth in charitable "lying-in" hospitals at the end of the nineteenth century had already led the way, whether by choice or by coercion.[53] Hospital birth was considered more efficient, both for the doctor and for the woman whose social networks had crumbled under the strain of urbanization and industrialization, leaving her without a wide net of people to depend on for help with the birth, her other children, and her housework. In some cases, even her husband might be away at work far from home.[54] The contention that birth was safer in the hospital, however, was often not the case for either affluent or poor women. Even the renowned obstetrician Joseph B. De Lee reluctantly agreed in the 1930s that due to rampant infection, "home delivery, even under the poorest conditions, is safer than hospital delivery."[55] Obstetricians, long ridiculed by other doctors as inferior because of their all-female clientele and the questionable status of their specialty as a "science," were often poorly trained and ill supervised, and eager to intervene in the birth process.[56] Working in the hospital did little to abate the negative effects of their interventions, as the germs that caused puerperal fever (which resulted in death before the introduction of antibiotics in the 1930s and 1940s) thrived as a result of such interventions as forceps, inductions, and cesarean sections.[57]

The two models of childbirth, one of a disease necessitating surgical intervention and the other of a physical process needing attentive waiting, not only differentiated obstetricians from midwives, but also distinguished among obstetricians. While some obstetricians of a less interventionist bent have always persisted, obstetricians with a more "activist ideology" have dominated the field.[58] The view that "the hospital was to become a laboratory and school around which the profession of obstetrics might be upgraded and organized" served to forward the activist ideology.[59] Medicalization also encouraged the narrowing of meanings attributed to women's birthing bodies, which came to be seen primarily as reproductive machines, or, more narrowly still, as material for the obstetrical laboratory. Ironically, with this atrophy of meaning came the overdetermined meaning of the physician's role, as "physicians increasingly began to claim medical authority over all decisions—moral, ethical, religious, social, economic, even political—relating to childbirth."[60] The rise of hospital births, then, contributed to the decline of religious authority—whether that of a tradition or an individual's faith—in matters of childbirth.[61]

This decline was not immediate, however, as in the case of Jewish maternity hospitals. At the turn of the century, when these urban hospitals tried to attract Jewish women away from home births attended by traditional female (and Jewish) midwives, and to the hospital, they often used the very medium of religion to do so. As an 1892 report of the Jewish Maternity Hospital of Philadelphia stated: "The birthing mother 'will not be obliged to break the Dietary Laws' . . . and will be treated as though she were surrounded by her own kith and kin."[62] Portraying hospital birth as modernized and safer but with the same social and religious support networks as home birth was a successful strategy, as Jewish women led the way in the shift to hospital birth among immigrant groups in America.[63]

The situation of African-American midwives in the South shows a different side of the success of medical over religious authority—one in which the economic and educational resources of the community did not allow the same blend of medical and religious practice effected in the Jewish case. As anthropologist Gertrude Fraser has shown, by the mid-twentieth century the "new secular medical authority" largely derailed the "spiritual authority" that buttressed the work of African-American midwives in rural Virginia.[64] In their relationship with medical and state authorities, however, midwives were not entirely opposed to making use of the benefits of medical care that had long been denied them and their clients, as long as they could continue to work within their tradition of "creative improvisation."[65] In Fraser's analysis, midwives were not initially threatened by medical regulation but instead saw it as potentially beneficial in keeping with the "history of syncretic medical and religious practice in Afro-American communities."[66] In the end, however, African-American midwifery traditions of "mother wit" and notions of the body infused with religious meaning were overwhelmingly obscured in later generations of women, according to Fraser.[67]

Taking several steps beyond the tentative collaboration that African-American midwives sought in selectively valuing some medical approaches to birth, many Euro-American women, both as patients and doctors, embraced the medical model that saw pregnancy and birth as pathological.[68] Affluent women who actually had choices about what sort of birthing care they desired were especially active in demanding that doctors find ways to render birth less painful, regardless of the level of intervention. The "twilight sleep" movement of the 1910s was a case in point, as upper-middle-class feminists demanded that doctors in the United States adopt this German practice in which women were drugged so that their minds would not remember the pain of birth. Their bodies, however, felt the pain as they thrashed about in darkened rooms, ensconced in a specially designed version of a straitjacket.[69]

Race and class conditioned the accessibility of feminist-driven childbirth reforms like twilight sleep. Poor women used to manual labor were considered less needy of pain-relieving childbirth methods, because of their supposed higher tolerance for pain.[70] Furthermore, the real benefit of twilight sleep in the eyes of the elite was that the prospect of painless childbirth would encourage the sensitive, white, upper-middle-class woman to have more children, thus ensuring a "better race for future generations."[71] Though different mixtures of pain-relieving anesthestics soon replaced the specific method of twilight sleep, the drugged birth had won converts among both doctors and birthing women alike.[72] Between the wars, hospital birth grew in both popularity and accessibility, as pain-relieving drugs were increasingly available only in hospitals and not at home, and as clinics made medical care available to poorer women. After World War II, hospitals expanded at the same time that government regulations and doctors had driven most midwives out of practice except in the rural South, and fewer doctors would agree to attend home births.[73]

In the midst of this shift to drugged birth in the hospital, some doctors advocated alternatives. British obstetrician Grantly Dick-Read was the most celebrated of the early "natural childbirth" doctors. In his 1944 U.S. edition of *Childbirth without Fear*, Dick-Read argued that the practice of drugging women in labor was depriving them and their babies of a fundamental experience. He advocated his specific method of natural childbirth as a way women could be fully sentient and aware at their births.[74] Dick-Read's method centered around what he called the "Fear-Tension-Pain Syndrome," in which fear of childbirth, brought on by negative images of birth abounding in the culture around her, caused a woman in labor to tense up the muscles of her uterus. In so doing, she worked against the natural rhythms of labor, in which ideally the three layers of uterine muscles would contract in complementary ways to ease the baby out. Once fear produced the tension that counteracted the natural process of birth, pain set in, and childbirth became an almost unendurable agony.[75]

Instead of assuaging this agony by dulling the pain through drugs, Dick-Read advocated turning to the beginning of the cycle, by calming the fears of childbirth. By teaching women how to relax in labor, and to look on childbirth as an opportunity to achieve "transcendental joy" and the "holy estate of motherhood," he averred that the pains of parturition could be transformed into the work of childbirth.[76] Dick-Read castigated his fellow doctors for their ignorance, arguing that if they understood the potential importance of childbirth to a woman's life they would improve their care—ceasing to leave their patients in hospital rooms alone, unknowing and afraid.[77] With the right care, childbirth was ripe with religious potential, according to Dick-Read:

> Many women have described their experiences of childbirth as being associated with a spiritual uplifting, the power of which they have never previously been aware. . . . Why is this? It is not sentimentality; it is not relief from suffering; it is not simply satisfaction of accomplishment. It is bigger than all those things. Can it be that the Creator intended to draw mothers nearest to Himself at the moment of love's fulfillment?[78]

Natural childbirth was to be a religious experience that confirmed for a woman her God-given role as a mother. Despite its "naturalness," doctors or antenatal instructors needed to train women—at least those 95 percent of women capable of birthing "normally"—about the ways of natural childbirth, and, in so doing, knowledge would replace fear, and pain would be no more.

Voicing a conviction shared by many present-day home-birth advocates, Dick-Read asserted that achieving natural childbirth would not only improve a woman's experience, but also alter society itself. The pain and fear associated with labor, Dick-Read prophesied, "extend their evil influence into the very roots of our social structure. They corrupt the minds and bodies of successive generations and bring distress and calamity where happiness and prosperity are the natural reward of a simple physiological performance."[79] Embedded in Dick-Read's notion of the natural were visions of gender that cast women as spiritual guardians of the generations and portrayed men as inherently aggressive innovators, a dualism that found favor in later instances of alternative-childbirth literature.[80]

By the fifties, birthing women themselves began to question publicly the dominant medical model of an anesthetized birth during which they lay alone and immobilized on their backs, with their pubic hair shaved, their hands strapped to a table, and their legs held high in stirrups.[81] They were in part spurred on by Dick-Read's model of natural childbirth, but were also interested in other issues like breast-feeding. In 1956, a group of Catholic women formed a new voluntary organization, La Leche League, which urged mothers to ignore their doctors' orders about formula feeding and to breast-feed their babies.[82] La Leche League not only threatened the formula industry, but also agitated for changes in hospital policies, advocating unanesthetized birth and rooming-in as important benefits to a mother learning to nurse her baby.[83] Reworking an older maternalist movement that had supported "scientific motherhood," La Leche League emphasized that a mother—not her doctor—knew her baby and her own body best. According to historian Lynn Weiner, La Leche League "arose to defend traditional domesticity against the assaults of modern industrial life and to dignify the physical, biological side of motherhood."[84] As such, theirs was a message that was (and continues to be) a complex mix of valuing the knowledge women could attain in birthing and mothering and of decrying the social and economic conditions that take mothers away from their young children and into the workforce.[85]

More direct criticisms of the medical model of childbirth came from a range of other sources. In 1957, Patricia Cloyd Carter, a mother of nine children, six of whom she bore alone at home without any assistance, wrote and self-published *Come Gently, Sweet Lucina*.[86] Most likely the first how-to text for home birth in a culture of medicalized birth, Carter's book was a quirky assortment of physiology, literary quotations, autobiography, and jeremiads against the medical approach to childbirth.[87] Though its title invoked Lucina, "Goddess of Childbirth," and its body was peppered with several biblical allusions and references to God, Carter's book was driven less by religious motivations than by political ones. She condemned the ignorance that most women lived under with regard to their bodies, and advocated sex education in schools as a means to dispel the fear women had of childbirth.[88] Even more avidly, she called for a universally accessible system of socialized medicine in which doctors and midwives could attend home births, during which they would not intervene unless necessary.[89] With her self-published book, Carter became an early home-birth activist who, like many others, shifted between proclaiming women's equality to men and celebrating the naturalness of a woman's role as birthgiver and mother.[90]

In the late 1950s, articles about home birth and natural childbirth began to surface in popular women's magazines. An exposé in the *Ladies' Home Journal* of the "cruelty in maternity wards" generated a barrage of letters testifying to the profound pain, loneliness, and dissatisfaction hospital birth elicited in many women.[91] Tied to the increasing influence of psychoanalysis, some forms of which considered childbirth to be a necessary fulfillment to a woman's life, and to a postwar celebration of domesticity, several commentators came to portray fully experiencing a "natural childbirth" as a woman's right.

Just as in the formation of La Leche League, religion played an important role in the turn of many Christian women to natural childbirth.[92]

In a religious context that was spawning the Christian Family Movement and other groups that focused on ethics in the family, infusing birth with religious meaning was an attractive concept. Historians Richard W. Wertz and Dorothy C. Wertz claim that in the climate of the 1950s, "before the civil-rights movement made social action a viable choice for Christians, having a natural birth was perhaps the only ethical action, Christian or otherwise, that many women could take."[93] Though this seems a limited view of ethical action, Christian childbirth activists like Helen Wessel, author of *Natural Childbirth and the Christian Family* (1963), might have heartily agreed.[94] Even Dr. Robert Bradley, in his popular *Husband-Coached Childbirth*, first published in 1965, often couched his message in religious terms, as he considered women who gave birth without drugs to be especially open to birthing with God-given "serenity."[95]

By the late 1960s and early 1970s, however, feminism and the women's health movement were bringing a new perspective to the significance of home birth, one with a decidedly less Christian ring.[96] Feminist critics continued the tradition of earlier activists like Patricia Carter in their insistence on women's right to knowledge and autonomy over their bodies and in their calls for a more accessible health-care system, but their critique extended beyond birth to mothering and marriage.[97] Woman-centered, not "family-centered," birth was the concern of many feminists, who felt that a positive childbirth experience did not necessarily have to strengthen a male-female bond, but could foster a woman's autonomy and nurture a diversity of relationships, including those between mothers and daughters, women friends, and lesbians.[98]

Feminist critics of medicalized birth were not only childbearing women, but also certified nurse-midwives and direct-entry midwives who were taking practical steps to assist women to give birth at home. American certified nurse-midwifery grew out of public health nursing, in an effort to provide midwives with nursing training. Organizations like the Frontier Nursing Service, established in 1925, drew on British nurse-midwives to develop a school that could train nurse-midwives who would provide care to women in rural and hard-to-reach areas.[99] Until the 1950s most births attended by certified nurse-midwives were at home, at which point many certified nurse-midwives stopped the practice in an effort to gain hospital privileges and professional legitimacy.[100] Their professional organization, the American College of Nurse-Midwives (ACNM), insisted until 1980 that hospitals or birth centers were the only safe sites for birth.[101] Even before the ACNM ended its censure of home birth, however, some certified nurse-midwives attended home births regardless of the policy against them.[102]

Direct-entry midwifery (also known by the less precise term "lay mid-wifery") grew in the 1960s and 1970s, as women began helping their friends to give birth and then gradually trained themselves with the help of books, doctors, and experience. Many of the early direct-entry mid-wives cited spiritual reasons for turning to midwifery, or did so within a religious (often countercultural) community. For example, Ina May Gas-kin, author of *Spiritual Midwifery*, and the head midwife at the Farm, a countercultural community in Tennessee, is one of the most respected of direct-entry midwives.[103] Currently, direct-entry midwives seek their training primarily through direct experience, either in apprenticeship to another direct-entry midwife or in a midwifery school that is not a nursing program (though some may already be nurses). They work independently of doctors and practice in the home or sometimes in free-standing birth clinics.[104] The legality of direct-entry midwives continues to vary state by state, with some practicing legally as licensed midwives and others forced to work "underground" with ambiguous legal status.[105] The Midwives Alliance of North America (MANA) is the direct-entry midwives' parallel to the ACNM, although MANA welcomes the membership of interested certified nurse-midwives, and there has been increased collaboration between the ACNM and MANA in recent years.[106]

In addition to midwives, a small number of doctors, mostly family practitioners, began to attend home births in the 1970s and 1980s. Some even teamed up with direct-entry or certified nurse-midwives. By the mid-1980s, however, they began to move back to the hospital under mounting pressure from other doctors opposed to home birth, although many continued to provide back-up support for midwives.[107] Those doctors hostile to home birth also tried to pressure home-birth midwives by denying certified nurse-midwives hospital privileges and not allowing direct-entry midwives to accompany their clients to the hospital when necessary.[108]

In taking on childbirth as a political issue, the feminist movement for women's health found itself with some unlikely allies, who would be more aptly called maternalist or traditionalist women—women such as the founders of La Leche League and Patricia Carter, author of *Come Gently, Sweet Lucina*. Feminists and traditionalists have been able to unite over their skepticism of the hegemony of medical approaches to birth and infant feeding and in their assertion that women have valuable knowledge about their own bodies. They have differed, however, over issues of abortion and family structure, with the traditionalists generally being anti-abortion and supportive of heterosexual, husband-headed marriage.[109] By focusing on consumer advocacy and choice and avoiding conflicts around sexuality and abortion, these allies formed a grass-roots, if fragile and loosely organized, "alternative birth movement" that has had significant—

although not always intended—effects both on trends in hospital care and on the visibility of home birth.[110]

Analyzing this loose coalition, several commentators have emphasized the importance of religion to traditionalist women's views of childbirth, but have said little about such motivations on the part of feminists. For example, sociologist Barbara Katz Rothman described traditionalist women as holding a "religious or spiritual commitment to home birth," while characterizing feminist birth activists as those who raised "questions about medical expansion into ethical concerns, [that brought] essentially moral issues under medical control."[111] This division between the ethical as feminist and the religious or spiritual as traditionalist is less clearly evidenced in the language of feminist advocates of home birth and midwifery care. For example, in a guide published by the ACNM, references to the "spiritual connection to midwifery as it has been practiced throughout history" are paired with rooting the turn to midwifery in the heritage of the women's health movement of the 1960s and 1970s.[112]

In the 1990s, the spirituality attributed to home birth ran the spectrum of New Age blends of Christianity, Judaism, and Eastern religions to conservative Christian interpretations.[113] Feminist commentators on birth also turned to religious interpretations in making sense of birth, arguing that identifying with the "supernatural" was a greater source of power than turning to the "natural."[114] The kinds of power embedded within or created by this claiming of the supernatural, however, are many, and are not necessarily controlled by either feminist or traditionalist women. Though they may exercise control over their place of birth and their choice of attendants, home-birthing women cannot control the particular process of childbirth that their body undergoes, nor can they control the readings of their actions made by the wider society.

Just as the twilight-sleep feminists of the 1920s are seen by current home-birth feminists as misguided about their desire for oblivion in birth, the latter's subsequent revaluing of childbirth pain and the fulfillment of childbirth may be read by other feminists as equally amiss.[115] As anthropologist Emily Martin has written, "Many women may agree about the desirability of overcoming the medical control of birth, but within that agreement may be enormous diversity."[116] Religion is one neglected source of diversity that has historically empowered women to question medical control over their bodies. The consequences of that empowerment, however, have been both a reentrenchment of other hierarchical relations of authority, especially those between husband and wife, *and* a challenging of those same hierarchical relations. This study explores these consequences, finding that notions and practices of authority and surrender intersect in ways not always predictable for feminists and traditionalists alike.

Making Meaning out of Birth:
Social and Cultural Perspectives

Intertwined with the history of childbirth in America are cultural scripts about how to birth; both history and methods play a part in shaping women's stories and ways of birth. Anthropologists have been the scholars most dedicated to interpreting the cultural meanings generated by childbirth, and especially in the last two decades the anthropology of childbirth has blossomed. While ethnographic research in the first half of the century collected details of childbirth practices as part of cross-cultural surveys, more recent scholarship has focused on childbirth as an interpretive key to specific cultural contexts.[117] Much of the research on childbirth has come from medical anthropologists concerned with questions of the cultural mediation of birthing practices, most specifically with how biomedical obstetrics and traditional birthing practices have intersected.[118]

A primary motivation for renewed attention to childbirth as a subject of anthropological study came from feminist scholars striving to improve the conditions under which women gave birth. As scholars became part of an increasingly recognizable "alternative childbirth movement" themselves, either personally or as advocates for the women they studied, they started writing books that were a hybrid of popular and scholarly texts.[119] Joined together, a feminist and postcolonial critique of the hegemony of biomedical obstetrics stressed the interrelationships among sexism, poverty, and cultural imperialism in the transformation of twentieth-century birth.

While scholars focusing on North American birthing practices have emphasized the paternalistic, interventionist, and capitalist nature of obstetrics, many of those studying childbirth in nonindustrialized countries have sought culturally appropriate ways to adapt the benefits of modern medicine to traditional birth practices.[120] These latter scholars have grappled most directly with the reality that "in the world as a whole, every minute a woman dies as a result of complications during pregnancy and birth, and every minute eight babies die because of poor care for their mothers in pregnancy and birth."[121] The vast majority of these deaths occur among poor women with little access to health care; that is, not among the middle-class North American women about whom I write here.[122] These very different cultures of birth are related, however. As anthropologist Carol MacCormack has pointed out, the inequities of the worldwide distribution of and access to reproductive health care are "linked in a curious way, with Western women having more Caesarian sections than they want or need, and women in poor countries suffering unto death because none are available."[123]

Set in an international context, where midwifery thrives in several European countries, the struggles of women in the United States who seek less interventionist births at home with experienced midwives appear quite reasonable in the international geography of childbirth.[124] Seen only within the context of birth in the United States, however, home-birthing women represent a minority view considered extreme in both medical and less specialized circles. Condemned by some medical and legal professionals as child abuse, and vaunted by many midwives and childbirth activists as the safest and most satisfying method, home birth takes its place within a constellation of meanings that shape the practice of childbirth in the United States.[125]

Anthropologists who have turned their attention to birth in the United States have argued that home birth is forced into its marginal position because of competing ideologies of birth.[126] Robbie Davis-Floyd described two opposing models of childbirth operative in the late-twentieth-century United States as the "technocratic" and the "wholistic" approach.[127] According to Davis-Floyd, where the technocratic model considers the institution (i.e., the hospital) as the significant social unit, values technology, and considers pregnancy and birth inherently pathological, the holistic model sees the family as the essential social unit, esteems the natural, and views pregnancy and birth as inherently healthy.[128]

The "ideological polarization" between these two models is largely rooted in contrary notions about who holds power over decision making, and who is considered knowledgeable about the body.[129] In the technocratic model, doctors, based on their medical training and their readings of machines such as fetal monitors, make the significant decisions about how a woman's labor should progress. In the holistic model, midwives and birthing women collaborate to decide how best to assist a birth, based on the emotional and bodily experience of the laboring woman and the learned knowledge and (sometimes) intuition of a midwife.[130] However, midwifery care within a hospital complicates this dualism, as do those doctors who are themselves critical of the medical model of childbirth. While some home-birth advocates argue that certified nurse-midwives working in hospitals have been co-opted, some of these same certified nurse-midwives are among those most dedicated to safeguarding home birth, and they work both in the hospital and in homes. And certainly most midwives, including direct-entry midwives, work with the support of at least one doctor.

In general, however, the tensions between doctors and midwives have overshadowed their cooperation. As well, since much health care in the United States is structured as a profit-making venture, ideological competition between the technocratic and holistic models is also about money. American obstetricians and hospitals, fearing for their business if women were to turn in large numbers to lower-cost, lower-technology births in the home, have aggressively sought to convince women that the hospital can be just like home, but better.[131] Commercial billboards sponsored by hospitals picturing tiny newborns in their mothers' arms, or declaring the benefits of the nearby hospital's "birth pavilion," bring this struggle for market share directly to the consumer.

While feminist arguments about the patriarchal, class-bound, and racist character of the technocratic model of obstetrics are persuasive, some of these same feminist authors have complicated their portraits by describing women's own role in shaping this model.[132] Questioning women's agency in shaping the medicalization of birth—arguing that women have both encouraged and resisted it—has led some scholars to caution against a romanticization of birth on the part of childbirth activists. Some women, these scholars remind us, insist that they prefer cesareans and epidurals to the sensations of vaginal birth.[133] Issues of "false consciousness"[134] and socialization complicate the "purity" of agency in any case, but the point is that birthing women make choices and are able (or not) to enact those choices based on a range of interconnecting social contexts, like education, class, race, and ethnicity. Women's subsequent interpretations of their experiences of childbirth also reflect the diversity of their cultural and social identities.

Hoping to address the social and cultural complexity of childbirth, home-birth practitioners have called for studies that go beyond issues of outcome and safety in home birth. They suggest that studies attending to factors of cultural diversity and satisfaction in childbirth would best be explored through a feminist, qualitative approach.[135] Using such an approach here, my goal is to bring attention to one particular source of meaning and diversity—religion—in the range of factors that affect ways of birthing. Cultural anthropologists agree widely about the need to locate "fertility and birth within cosmological, social, psychological and spiritual contexts."[136] Especially in the case of research on Asian and African women, anthropologists have considered the complex relationship between women's bodily experiences of pregnancy and childbirth and their religious experiences, including their negotiation of official theology, androcentric religious and familial authority, and personal beliefs and practices.[137] Despite this insistence on attending to the religious dimensions of birth, the majority of childbirth research on Western women—those women most fully oriented to the biomedical obstetrical model—has neglected or skirted questions of religion in favor of a more conventionally political or sociocultural approach.[138] Research that has considered birth as a "rite of passage" has paid some attention to the role of religion in Western women's experiences of childbirth, but even in this genre the ability and interest of scholars to analyze religion is mixed.[139]

Scholars of religion, in addition to anthropologists, have turned their attention to the meanings of childbirth in ways that reflect the interdisciplinary nature of their field. For example, while Susan Starr Sered posed the question "Childbirth as a Religious Experience?" from an anthropological perspective, Kathryn Allen Rabuzzi and Bonnie J. Miller-McLemore took more prescriptive, theological approaches.[140] From feminist perspectives, all of these authors analyzed the lack of attention given to women's experiences of childbirth in "official" religion, finding too that the hospital model of birth often ignored or obviated the religious dimensions of childbirth.[141] Historians of religion have also drawn attention to the difficulties women had in negotiating space for their religious beliefs and practices in the context of the hospital maternity ward of the past.[142] Other scholars have given health professionals advice on how to respect the intersection between culture, religion, and childbearing for an increasingly diverse society. Much of this literature clearly establishes that religion is often an important part of a woman's experience of childbirth. Furthermore, research has shown that both where a woman gives birth and the kind of care she receives have a significant impact on whether she feels comfortable expressing her religious identity in the process.[143]

All of these overlapping contexts for interpreting the meanings of childbirth—demographic profiles, historical perspective, and anthropological analysis—contribute to my own interpretation of home birth as well as those of many home-birthing women themselves. Readings of scholarly and popular texts joined together with personal experience provide the material for telling procreation stories. For my part, my desire to tell and interpret these stories is tied to a wider project of "rematerializing the human body" in the study of religion.[144] As sociologist Meredith McGuire describes this project, scholars of religion must overcome the problematic legacies of a dualistic epistemological tradition that has assigned the study of "mind" or "spirit" to social scientists or religion scholars, while leaving the "body" to biologists and medical researchers.[145] Reclaiming the "mindful body" as a focus of research will render more visible noninstitutionalized forms of religious practice and the symbolic and political power they convey.[146] Interpreting the religious dimensions of home birth, as women viscerally experience them and then translate them through stories and action into a grass-roots movement, is part of this reclamation.

Turning now to these stories, I begin by jumping into the thick of the debates surrounding home birth: Is it too great a risk, and for whom? Who adjudicates what is risky in childbirth, and what roles do risk, fear, and death play in home-birthing women's assertion of birth as an ethical and religious act? I begin with the question of risk as a way of setting individual women's procreation stories within a wider cultural context in which their childbirth choices, by going against the grain, highlight the ethical responsibility women bear in the act of giving birth. In claiming this responsibility, home-birthing women not only assert their agency, but also confront a cultural and religious legacy in which children are viewed as offspring of the father's seed, via the somewhat incidental mother's body.

3

Risk, Fear, and the Ethics of Home Birth

KATHRYN MORRIS was sure she was dying in childbirth. Despite having planned a home birth, she found herself on an operating table in a hospital, undergoing an emergency cesarean. Kathryn had planned to give birth with the same certified nurse-midwives she had been using for several years for her gynecological or "well-woman" care. In the course of her labor at home, she became preeclamptic; her blood pressure rose to dangerously high levels, and her contractions followed heavily one upon the other.[1] The midwives strongly advised that she move to the hospital, so she left home with her husband driving the car as the midwives followed close behind. As she lay on the operating table, she recalled, she could feel the obstetrician's hands on her belly and reaching through the incision inside her. She had not received enough anesthetic, and her birth became a horrific ordeal in which she confronted the fragility of her own flesh in a most visceral way. The impelling force of her own physiology transformed Kathryn's carefully laid plans for a peaceful birth. Death, instead of hovering at the margins of birth as an unspoken fear, claimed center stage.

Kathryn's experience makes clear that childbirth is at once a cultural event and a physical happening. At times, the unpredictability of the physical process of childbirth can lay waste to religious or cultural expectations surrounding birth, as it did in Kathryn's case. Though the physical and cultural aspects of birth are often closely intertwined—as with women in my study who viewed the physiology of the birthing body as designed by God—they can also be in conflict. This shifting line between the cultural and the physical is what causes many of the debates around home birth to arise. Do a woman's cultural or religious expectations about birth validate her refusal to accept the biomedical approach to birth? Put simply, do women's experiences of childbirth—religious or otherwise—matter enough to hazard what some call the physical risks of home birth?

The dominance of the biomedical approach to childbirth has established a climate in which these questions are often answered with a resounding "no." Seeking a fulfilling experience is considered secondary to or even incompatible with the safety of a woman's baby in the eyes of some critics of home birth.[2] As one scholar put it, "A woman's interest in an aesthetically pleasing or emotionally satisfying birth should not be satisfied at the expense of the child's safety."[3] In the course of presenting my research, I have often been asked the question, "What about the women whose babies die, or who die themselves?" This is a question so loaded with cultural expectations about the dangers of childbirth and, for many questioners, personal experience of difficult or traumatic labors, that I have often approached it gingerly. My usual answer is initially twofold: first, none of the women I interviewed had experienced the death of a baby in childbirth, so I did not directly address it in reflecting on their stories. Second—and this part of the answer enters into more sensitive and sometimes polemical territory—when compared to hospital births, planned, midwife-attended home births result in equal or lower rates of infant and maternal mortality.[4]

But those answers do not get at the heart of the emotions—fear, anger, and confusion to name a few—that lie behind the questions. For most of human history, to give birth has been to approach death. In North America it was not long ago that women frequently died in childbirth, more often from postpartum infections or "childbed fever" than from complications of birth itself. Globally, the maternal mortality rate is still shockingly high, especially in poor countries.[5] The fear of death in childbirth is still something that haunts all childbearing women, and often their partners.

The persistence of this fear can be found most readily in the genre of the "I almost died" or "the baby almost died" story—the kind of birth horror story told to many pregnant women. I have heard many of these stories as a pregnant woman and in the course of telling others of my work, both casually and in more professional settings. One of the most vociferous of these storytellers was a man, who, after he heard me present some of my work at an academic conference, approached me asking if I had children myself. When I said that I did, he asked me, "Did you birth naturally?" After I gave him a qualified yes—without embarking on a discussion of what he meant by "natural"—he launched into a monologue that according to my field notes went something like this:

> Obviously I'm not a woman by nature, but I strongly disagree with home birth. My sister planned a home birth but didn't have one. It's a good thing she didn't, because at the hospital she had complications that could have taken the life of her and her baby. Childbirth is not about an experience. It's about procreating a new life into the world. If you want an experience, ride a roller coaster.

After a long day of sitting in uncomfortable chairs in a dark conference room, I had no desire to respond to this man. I could have asked him whether his sister's midwife advised her to go to the hospital, but instead I quietly said that many women would not agree with him, and excused myself from his presence. But his angry, verging on threatening, words stuck with me.

This man's response highlights the emotionally volatile hub of debates over childbirth: Is a woman the vessel for bringing about new life, or does her experience of birth matter in and of itself? For women who have had difficult births but have emerged with children not scarred by the process, the memories of their own birth experiences might pale with time. For women who feel that their difficult births or their birth-damaged children were a result of iatrogenic causes—that is, induced by a caregiver's treatment—their traumatic experience may be harder to bear. For women who recall their days and nights of childbirth with pleasure and fondness, their experiences are cherished. No matter what the circumstances, the question of the relative importance of a woman's bodily and emotional experience in childbirth and the condition of her baby is an ethical question that strikes at the very heart of North American debates over women's bodily autonomy and human cultural freedom.

In this chapter, I explore this volatility of home birth by considering competing notions of the "risks" of childbirth. In a society increasingly driven by calculations of risk or risk aversion—whether in decisions on the stock market or in decisions about smoking or drinking—thinking about how notions of what is risky are arrived at is an important process.[6] Even more difficult in a society awash in statistics and actuarial calculations is the process of making decisions about what constitutes a "tolerable" level of risk, whether when deciding on the safety rating of the automobile that will transport one's family, or on types of birth care. Many women committed to alternative processes of childbirth have developed a critical assessment of conventional understandings of the risks of childbirth, preferring the monitoring accomplished by a midwife's hands, fetascope, or hand-held heartbeat monitor to that of the constraining and impersonal cords of an electronic fetal monitor. For some, especially home-birthing women, novel approaches to fear and death arise from their critical assessments of risk and their processes of ethical decision making. In what follows, I explore the fear of death engendered by childbirth by comparing two stories, Kathryn's and that of another woman, Tessa, who both felt they came close to death in childbirth, but in very different ways. Finally, I turn to a discussion of how considering birth as an ethical act and rethinking risk has shaped the way home-birthing women are translating this ethics of birth into political and religious action. Before these more specific investigations, however, I lay out some different approaches to the "ethics of birth" and suggest some of their consequences.

Birth as an Ethical Act

The controversy surrounding ways of birthing is rooted in divergent ethical understandings of the risks of birth, both for the baby and the mother. Childbirth is inherently tied to ethical values, since birthing brings about a new human being entirely without her or his own agency and for whom others are responsible. Decisions about how best to bring this new life into being are ethical because they are shaped by understandings of what is of value in a culture, and by ideas about how human relationships should be organized. Childbirth entails two ethical considerations simultaneously, since birthing women not only make choices affecting the well-being of their babies, but also make decisions that will shape their own bodily and emotional experience.

The first consideration, that of the baby's well-being, is more complicated than a simple concern to nourish and bring to life a healthy child. In the culture of North American childbirth, pregnancy and birth, while also considered processes of consumer decision making, are embedded with moral virtues.[7] Pregnancy constructed as consumer decision is framed as a moral question of how to be the best "fetal environment" one can be, causing a woman to ponder carefully everything from what she eats to what prenatal tests she decides to have.[8] The decisions women make vary widely. Similarly, the second consideration, that of the woman's experience, produces widely divergent responses. While some women view an epidural or a cesarean section as a preferred mode of birth, others want to feel every stage of labor. In terms of home birth in particular, some women understand the voluntary suffering of the pain of home birth as at once an ethical and a religious act. It is ethical in that she keeps her body free of drugs that may harm her baby, and religious in that through pain and exertion comes her own transformation. Her birth becomes both a physical act of bringing a child into the world and a source of her identity, replayed often in memory and speech.

The relationship of a birthing woman to her fetus/baby is a complicated relationship of self and other, in which the boundaries between the two are not clearly drawn. The ambiguity of these boundaries in the process of creation provokes what philosopher Sara Ruddick calls "the capacity to wonder."[9] According to Ruddick (and to the women in my study), birthing is an ethical act foundational to any society. As Ruddick states, in birthing women's "efforts of self-(re)presentation, they find themselves invoking the promise of birth: this body counts; each birthgiver's bodily labor, each new body she creates, is a testament of hope."[10] Basing the promise of birth on the bodies of mother and child, however, means that such women contest—implicitly or explicitly—a dominant "theory of procreation" that has denied the significance, ethical or otherwise, of women's carrying and birthing of babies.

This theory of procreation, according to anthropologist Carol Delaney, asserts that "paternity has meant *the primary, creative, engendering* role. In the Bible (and in the popular imagination) it is symbolized by the word 'seed.' . . . The child belongs to the father because it *is* his seed."[11] In this millennia-old theory, the mother merely provides the matter for the fetus to grow within. She is not a "co-creator" of life and as a result she does not carry the same responsibility for, or power over, her child. For Delaney, this procreation theory is not merely the result of flawed understandings of human biology. Instead, the meanings of paternity and maternity "are rooted far deeper and their extent is far wider than the discourse and domain of reproduction; ultimately they are rooted in a cosmological system, in this case the monotheistic world view that is elaborated somewhat differently in Judaism, Christianity, and Islam."[12] The power of this theory remains despite modern understandings of reproduction, Delaney suggests, and it is reinforced by repeated references to the biblical story of Abraham and Isaac, in which "definitions and assumptions about paternity made it possible for Abraham . . . to think that the child was his to sacrifice."[13]

Delaney's articulation of the procreation theory embedded within popular understandings of paternity is convincing, but it is not the only theory at work today (though it may be a dominant one). In contrast to the model Delaney describes, in which the child is viewed as the product of the father's seed and his "property," many feminist theorists and birthing women place more emphasis on the relationships between mother and child engendered by pregnancy and birth. In this alternate "theory of procreation," pregnancy and birth are moral acts that call forth an ethics of responsibility in which differentiating between a birthing woman's experience and her baby's "safety" becomes a very difficult, if not hazardous, endeavor. Home-birthing women in particular do consider themselves cocreators, whether with their partners, a deity, or nature. However, this creative role does not necessarily grant them unlimited power, since, in the words of literary theorist Susan Mizruchi, "Motherhood combines the experience of ultimate power (to create like a god) and utter lack of control."[14] Birthing women are at once acting and being acted upon— theirs is an embodied agency that is necessarily conditioned by the unpredictable (mysterious?) processes of the body. Their assessments of risk and responsibility are therefore made within a worldview that underscores both the strength and the fragility of the human body, as well as the power and chance of maternity.

What I mean by embodied agency under these conditions of unpredictability—what I referred to earlier as agency via other means than rational consent—requires further elaboration. Agency, as anthropologist Talal Asad has recently argued, is a popular theoretical focus in need of some critical attention.[15] Typically viewed as "the individual's capacity to act consciously and voluntarily upon the world,"[16] agency provides a way to construct narratives of resistance in an oppressive world—narratives that too often depend on triumphalist notions of human progress, according to Asad. He writes:

> That the human body has a changing life largely inaccessible to itself, that in various ways its behavior depends on unconscious routine and habit, that emotion, though necessary to every kind of reasoning, may render the ownership of actions a matter of conflicting descriptions—all of this problematizes both the intentionalist claim that the embodied subject is essentially engaged in resisting power or becoming more powerful, as well as the connected claim that the moral agent must always bear individual responsibility for her act. It also problematizes the larger assumption that agency must be defined, in the final analysis, by a historical future of universal emancipation from suffering.[17]

The changing life—or lives—of the pregnant and birthing body are, to borrow from Asad, largely inaccessible, although decreasingly so with the burgeoning of reproductive technologies. Part of what home-birthing women seek in choosing a less medicalized approach to birth is a preservation of this inaccessibility. Ironically, in light of Asad's contention, they must *choose* to retain the unconscious body—they forgo "emancipation" from the suffering of birth for the sake of their babies and themselves. Being neither complete self-determination nor complete submission, embodied agency implies a recognition of limits.

While this kind of embodied agency takes particular shapes in the context of home birth, the assertion that birth is an ethical act shaped by particular theories of procreation applies to all approaches to childbirth. Claims and assignments of responsibility, whether on the part of birthing women, midwives, doctors, or the state, are tied to understandings of who has obligations and knowledge in terms of childbirth. Those with differing approaches do not necessarily understand the physical stages and the pain of childbirth in the same way, and their understandings of the ethics of birth are even more contested.

Operating from within a biomedical model, some argue that the risks of birth demand that a woman give birth in a hospital. While some biomedical advocates urge women to give birth in hospital because it is "safer," others go further and call home birth "child abuse."[18] In the most extreme version of this view a woman relinquishes her role as the arbiter of risk to the medical professional, who decides what is best for the baby and for the woman. The focus in this case is on the relationship between the doctor, backed up by particular forms of birth technology, and the fetus/baby. However, doctors differ in the extent of authority they claim over childbirth, and in response to the increased authority of midwifery they have had to confront directly in the issue of women's autonomy in childbirth.

For example, after midwifery and midwife-attended home birth became legal in Ontario, the Ontario Medical Association rethought its opposition to home birth. Now the organization "does not support physician attendance at births occurring in the home, but acknowledges that an Ontario licenced midwife may attend women who plan home births."[19] However, an obstetrician in another Canadian province made it clear that he thought such qualified support of home birth on the part of the medical establishment to be pure folly. Nova Scotian James W. Goodwin cast his argument in terms of the ethical responsibilities of the midwife:

> With the public expectation of the perfect perinatal outcome, unless one can prove beyond a shadow of a doubt that home birth is absolutely and completely safe, then to advise the client to participate in a home birth is a gamble. Is it ethical or conscionable for the midwife herself to recommend such a course to the client woman if this definition holds true? I think not.[20]

Though no one can guarantee perfect perinatal outcomes, Goodwin seems convinced that midwives are especially accountable to such expectations. At the same time, Goodwin argued that obstetricians needed to adapt some midwifery practices to obstetrical practices. For example, "The woman must feel that she is in control and that she can decide." To this end, after "informing" women of the risks of birth, obstetricians "must allow the woman to choose"—but this tolerance does not extend to allowing her to choose her place of birth.[21]

Biomedical and midwifery approaches to birth share much in common, including agreement on basic human physiology and use of some similar technology, such as hand-held monitors and drugs that counter postpartum hemorrhage. However, they have developed contrary ethical stances to childbirth with varying degrees of explicitness. A midwifery model of birth, drawing from both biomedical and holistic views of the body, attributes the majority of responsibility for decision making about childbirth to the pregnant and birthing woman. Since midwifery considers birth to be a "normal," though not "routine," process for most women that requires care but not usually institutionalization, midwives consider women to have embodied knowledge about their pregnancies and birth processes.[22] When this embodied knowledge is combined with self-education about the demands of pregnancy and the process of childbirth, midwives consider birthing women to be the appropriate decision makers regarding birth, including its location.

Midwifery advocates, including both certified nurse-midwives and direct-entry midwives, stress the right to freedom of choice in the places and approaches of childbirth. Both groups place significant importance on the mother's choices and experience, in addition to their concern for the birthing of healthy babies. Where the American College of Nurse-Midwives stresses the rights of families "to a safe, satisfying childbirth experience, with respect for cultural variations, [and] human dignity,"[23] the Midwives Alliance of North America calls for a more explicitly "woman-centered" approach. In their words, "midwives recognize the empowerment inherent in the childbearing experience and strive to support women to make informed decisions and take responsibility for their own well-being." As well, the MANA "midwifery model of care" emphasizes that a combination of "physical, emotional, psycho-social and spiritual factors . . . affect the childbearing process," and asserts that "the childbearing experience is primarily a personal, social and community event."[24] Though certified nurse-midwives and direct-entry midwives position themselves differently with respect to biomedicine, given their different historical and political situations, both assert an ethical stance that views birthing women as responsible for their own choices in childbirth.

In the midst of these differences of opinion among professional organizations over the adjudication of the risks of birth, many birthing women are critically assessing models of childbirth and acting as ethical decision makers. In particular, home-birthing women reinterpret the medical portrayals of risk in childbirth in two ways. First, they marshal competing statistics that demonstrate the relative safety of home birth, and second, perhaps more radically, they reinterpret the meaning of risk. As direct-entry midwife Judith Dickson Luce asserted:

> Women have the right to choose their own level of risk—to choose what risks they are willing to take in order to live fully. Life is not risk free; birth is not risk free anywhere. Home birth carries a set of risks and rewards; hospitals carry their own set of risks. It is not a question of eliminating, but of weighing them. Taking risks has always been a sign of a full life.[25]

All of the women in my study participated in weighing the risks of childbirth. For example, Alison Lindt-Marliss, who compared the "power of birth" to God in the course of our conversations, also felt that the ways of birth and the ways of God are not always manipulable by human will. Accepting this uncertainty is necessary in home birth, she argued: "You want guarantees that nothing is wrong, and I think that's part of the process; there are no guarantees. It's part of the faith."[26] Alison's notion of God, though nebulously tied to birth itself, was not characterized by an unbridled optimism in the therapeutic possibilities of either one.

In weighing the risks then, these women's considerations included factors not always part of a biomedical approach to childbirth, but most emphatically part of a midwifery model, including religion. As such, birthing women have been developing their own languages of risk and have emerged with decisions not always sanctioned by the dominant culture. For many women, choosing a certified nurse-midwife, legally and professionally accredited to attend home birth, is an acceptable risk. For a small minority of others, unassisted birth without any trained attendant present is a comfortable level of risk. In reconceiving risk, home-birthing women join a wider section of American society, in which for a diversity of reasons, including religious ones, people have countered biomedical definitions of the body, illness, and healing with alternate practices such as homeopathy or faith healing. Home-birthing women themselves represent this religious diversity in their various ways of reconceiving risk. Some make their choices based on a commitment to a particular religious tradition, such as Christian Science or Pentecostalism, while others decide on the basis of less explicitly religious motivations, like a commitment to feminist visions of bodily empowerment or to following "nature."

Languages of risk are culturally shaped, as anthropologists Patricia Kaufert and John O'Neil found in the context of debates over whether Canadian Inuit women could birth in their communities or whether they needed to be airlifted to southern hospitals. Lacking large-scale epidemiological statistics to prove the necessity of hospital birth for these Inuit women, medical professionals turned to a "clinical" language of risk, the professional cousin of what I have called the birth horror story. When challenged at a community meeting by an Inuit woman who questioned medical definitions of risk, a doctor turned to his own personal experience of seeing seven women die in childbirth during his twenty-five years of practice. Though none of these women had lived in Inuit communities, the doctor called on this clinical language of risk to argue against midwifery care in the North and as a way to express, perhaps tacitly, his "sense of vulnerability and responsibility" as a medical practitioner.[27] Questionable use of statistics to back up official policy on the location of childbirth is also motivated by the medical community's strong attachment to newly developed childbirth technology. Given the strength of the "belief in the power of technology to preserve life and, conversely, in lack of technology as a cause of death,"[28] assenting to a community-based (or for southern women, home-based) model of childbirth care is contrary to many medical professionals' understandings of risk.

While the issues surrounding childbirth that confront American home-birthing women and Canadian Inuit women are different, both groups of women do share an understanding of the larger implications of defining the risks of childbirth. For both, the question of "how much risk is acceptable to you?" is necessarily tied to the question "what kind of society do you want?"[29] For their part, by including their own bodily, emotional, and spiritual well-being together with that of their newborn children within this calculation of risk, home-birthing women have placed childbirth within a larger social context of a woman's and a family's life. In the process, they have made explicit the ethical basis of decisions about childbirth—an ethics that the medicalization of birth has obscured. As medical ethicist Paul Komesaroff phrases it, medical modes of thought have transformed life experiences like childbirth and menopause by tacitly introducing an "implicit vision of the good life" under the guise of technical values that highlight rational forms of progress.[30] Childbirth reformers of all sorts have reversed this obscuring of the social and personal meanings of childbirth by insisting that childbirth is not a mere technical process meant to achieve a certain end result, but instead is an experience with profound consequences for many different actors. The birthing women involved in this refocusing on the ethics of childbirth have also challenged deeply rooted assumptions about maternal sacrifice, by insisting that the quality of their own experiences of childbirth is positively linked to the health of their children—a challenge that I explore further in chapter seven.[31] Acknowledging the paradox of ultimate power and utter lack of control in childbirth makes room for an ethics of birth that can encompass the limits and the possibilities of the body—an ethics that understands that one of the risks of birth and of all ways of living is death itself.

Birth and Death

Reconceiving risk entails confronting the possibility of death. To give birth is to bring a new, living creature into existence who will necessarily eventually die. Moreover, it is to experience a sundering of the flesh that itself may, however infrequently, lead to one's own death. This paradoxically intimate relation between birth and death has long been a part of conscious and unconscious religious reflection. As writer Kathleen Norris phrases it, "One of the most astonishing and precious things about motherhood is the brave way in which women consent to give birth to creatures who will one day die." She goes on to suggest the religious implications of such bravery: "That we all begin inside a woman and must emerge from her body is something that the male theologians of the world's religions have yet to forgive us for."[32] Whether for children or for mothers, the stain of birth, at least according to much traditional theology, entraps the spirit in the suffering, polluted, and mortal body.[33]

But for women who are engaging in the ethics of birth from the perspective of practice—that is, through giving birth and reflecting on it—the paradox of birth and death has led to very different conclusions. While most women I interviewed felt that human relationships with family, friends, and the new baby were an important part of the spirituality of birth, several considered childbirth to allow for divine connection in a very particular and palpable way. Spiritual feminist Tessa Welland, age 34, and mother of four, was in many ways a stark opposite to several of the more conservative women I spoke with, who decried the sort of eclectic religious practices Tessa enjoyed. However, she shared these women's conviction that childbirth brought one into direct contact with God.

Tessa's God was immanent and without gender, in that for her "everybody is God," yet God is still otherworldly. In Tessa's experience, she approached this other world in childbirth: "I felt this more intensely each time I gave birth: there's absolutely a point in every labor where it's the line, and I feel like I'm so open physically and spiritually that I could touch the other side." For Tessa, this point was reached when her cervix had fully dilated and her baby had begun to descend: "You absolutely have to be your most open in order to get the baby out." Upon reaching this point, Tessa recalled sensing the spirit of her father, who had died when she was a teenager, encouraging her. The visions of the "other world" opened up by childbirth were tempting, according to Tessa:

> I can see easily how one could die in childbirth. Because it's tempting, you really feel it. You feel it's right there. You touch it. You can taste it. Curiosity makes you want to go there. And so you have to make a decision about whether that's how your evolution is meant to be or not. And I think I always felt more connected to my children as their mother than to a spiritual [realm] that I chose to stay. But I am very clear that there is a very real place in birth that you have to get to that point, you know, just one step from the line.

Tessa looked forward to this life-hanging-in-the-balance point of her labors as a particularly rich spiritual experience. While feeling at once a profoundly physical and spiritual moment beyond her control, Tessa also described pushing out her babies as a time when the mind or will could make a decision about living or dying.

The tendency for childbirth to cause women to contemplate their own mortality and hence their standing with God is a religious theme with deep roots in American culture. Seventeenth-century Puritan minister Cotton Mather felt the risk of death in childbirth was the reason for women's greater religiosity compared to men's.[34] In a different vein, Mother Ann Lee, eighteenth-century founder of the Shakers, considered motherhood and childbirth as a kind of "shamanism" that gave women knowledge of the dead.[35] Contemporary ritual specialists have taken this shamanic element in another direction. Self-described shamanic midwife Jeannine Parvati Baker, in drawing from Native American rituals, advised that performing a celebratory Blessing Way ceremony (a sort of spiritual baby shower) was not enough to prepare a pregnant woman for the experience of birth.[36] Instead, she suggested that a Monster Way ceremony should precede the Blessing Way, as a ritual that acknowledged not just the joys but the fears associated with childbirth:

> There has already been much attention drawn to the Blessing Way but as usual in a culture which fears the unconscious powers, and mortality, little shared about the all important Monster Way which traditionally preceded the Blessing Way. Perhaps it is the attachment on the part of the hired guardian of birth to play "Mistress of Ceremonies" to a pretty ritual [Blessing Way] that this omission has occured [sic]. Perhaps it is more due to our own unconscious need to focus on the more benign and celebratory aspects in birth and avoid the frightening.[37]

In espousing a ritual encounter with the fears around childbirth, Parvati Baker differs from mainstream home-birth advocates, whose ritual suggestions center more around making a woman comfortable in her birthing space, rather than leading her to face her inner "monsters."[38] As an advocate of what she calls "free birth," or birth unattended by doctor or midwife, Parvati Baker is farther away from the medical model of birth than most home-birth advocates, and she chooses correspondingly eclectic language.[39]

Parvati Baker is not alone, however, in wanting to address the fear of death in childbirth in innovative ways. Nancy Wainer Cohen, an author and childbirth instructor, describes how she begins each round of her childbirth classes with a discussion of death, provoked by the small, grey shoeboxes lined up in the corner of the room in imitation of baby-sized coffins in a cemetery. According to Cohen, "Everything that we do around birth in our culture is because we are afraid of death."[40] Inviting frank discussion around fears of death in childbirth often leads to talk of religious beliefs and helps women and their partners in the process of childbirth itself, she contends.

In an era far removed from the high rates of maternal mortality of colonial America, Tessa's intimate confrontation with death accords more with the notion of a shamanic power that evoked not terror, but curiosity. Significantly, in a time when spiritual experience is often constructed as a choice, Tessa considered that it was ultimately within her power to *choose* whether or not to "step over the line." Tessa's and Parvati Baker's linkage of birth, death, and theological reflection is not the preserve of eclectically spiritual folk only, however. Beth Junker, writing in a Christian feminist magazine, described childbirth as a "death and resurrection" in depicting her feeling of imminent death at the point of transition, when the cervix is dilated to its widest circumference. Junker argued from a Christian perspective that "if transition were acknowledged as a deep, spiritual experience in the lives of women, such a reading would mark a most liberating moment."[41] Without disparaging the reflections on birth and death offered by these women, it is important to set their views in context. Tessa's attitude toward death in childbirth takes shape within a climate of improved prenatal and birthing care and lower fertility rates for middle-class North American women.

The relatively low levels of maternal mortality in contemporary North America might suggest that if women do worry significantly about death in childbirth, it is not their own death that they ponder, but the deaths of their children.[42] In 1992 the overall maternal mortality rate in the United States was 7.8 in 100,000, but African-American women were four times as likely to die in childbirth as were Euro-American women. Though these rates are lower than those of earlier times were, in 1994 the United States ranked twenty-fourth in the world in infant mortality, one of the worst rates of the industrialized countries. The 1992 fetal death rate was 7.4 per 1,000 live births, and the neonatal death rate was 5.4 per 1,000.[43] Some studies suggest that home birth has better infant and maternal mortality rates, though the overall infant mortality rates between home and hospital births cannot be compared directly because most women who plan to give birth at home are prescreened for complications. A study of almost 12,000 CNM-attended home births found an overall perinatal (before, during, and after birth) mortality rate of 4.2 per 1,000. When third trimester fetal deaths and known congenital anomalies were excluded, the intrapartum and neonatal mortality rate was 0.9 per 1,000. There were no maternal deaths.[44]

None of the women with whom I spoke had suffered the death of their babies in childbirth, though several had experienced miscarriages. The baby of one woman's sister-in-law died at birth, and since this birth was a midwife-attended home birth, it was a particularly sensitive issue in the extended family when a short time later the woman I interviewed decided to have a home birth as well. A few women had undergone abortions, and all these women, including those who supported freedom of choice, felt some ambivalence about this. One woman in particular tied her initial fear of dying in childbirth to the regret she felt about her abortion. She recalled thinking: "I'm going to die in childbirth. I was going to die in childbirth. That was the fear. That was a big fear, and it came—part of that came through as guilt from the abortion, major guilt, and I had no place to put the guilt." For this woman, talking with a birth instructor helped her to overcome her fears somewhat, as did her subsequent births, but her regret remained, and perhaps even intensified as she became more religiously conservative over the course of her life.

Although no women I spoke with experienced the death of their babies, and obviously none died, Kathryn Morris, whose story began this chapter, did have a particularly traumatic labor during which she not only feared, but also actually felt, she was dying. In contrast to Tessa, she recalled reacting with panic, not curiosity. Considering the role of God and power in Kathryn's birth provides a helpful counterpoint to Tessa's experience. Kathryn, 31, called me after seeing a flyer I had posted at her midwives' office, and said that she wanted to talk with me about her home birth.[45] When I arrived at her small cottage-like home, busy with two barking dogs and a singing bird, Kathryn was aflutter with moving the animals, but welcomed me warmly. A video producer, Kathryn was frank and articulate as she recounted her emergency cesarean birth:

> They gave me all these things—anesthesia, all this stuff, that was in no way in our idea of what we were going to be doing. . . . When she [the doctor] said, "You have to have a cesarean," I was so relieved, because I couldn't take it any

more. I mean, it was really painful, so I was not that disappointed when she said that. And I just couldn't wait for them to put that mask on my face, because I wanted to be relieved of this. And, plus, my blood pressure was really high, so I probably was not feeling on top of all this stuff; probably that was affecting how I was feeling as well, when I think about it now.

So they gave me the anesthesia, and they didn't give me enough, because I could hear them, and could feel her hands on my belly. I didn't feel pain, but I felt her—it felt to me like I could feel her fingers inside, but who knows, I was totally anesthetized, except for that little bit more that I needed to be out. So I was trying to tell them, and I was trying to move my fingers, I was trying to signal to them in any way that I could that they didn't give me enough, but you can't move when you're under anesthesia, and you can't talk when you're under anesthesia.

So I was basically in a total panic, and my blood pressure went up while I was in there, and I think that might have been why, because I was in a panic. I was trying to do this—I couldn't even move my finger, I couldn't talk, and it was horrible. And the thought that went through my mind—the words, I remember the words exactly; they were, "I am going to die on this table." That was the thought—it was horrifying, it was a horrifying experience.

Kathryn's narrative of her birth was the most traumatic story I heard—at several points we were both in tears. This stemmed partly from the vividness of Kathryn's memories, since her baby was only three months old when we spoke. The direness of her narrative, however, also lay in what she called her "unrelenting story": once her baby was born, he was diagnosed with Down's syndrome.

Given the positive cast that spirituality holds in contemporary society, it is not surprising that Kathryn did not characterize her pregnancy and birth as spiritual experiences:

I thought that pregnancy and birth were going to be spiritual experiences. I thought they were going to be experiences that brought me to a higher state of consciousness while I was experiencing them. What I found to be the case is that pregnancy especially, and also birth . . . are very earthbound experiences. They are totally in your body. They are very, very physical. They are the ultimate physical experience. So I kept waiting for this "oohh," to feel this heavenly joy of some kind, and basically what I felt was, you know, uncomfortable—the real connecting to your body more than to the universe. I kept waiting to feel connected to the universe.

Unlike several other women who did speak of such mystical connection, Kathryn never did feel that union while her baby was in the womb or on the way out. Instead, for her, "the child is the religious experience."

Though Kathryn did not instill the bodiliness of pregnancy and birth with spiritual meaning, her pregnancy and birth did become catalysts for religious seeking of a sort. During her pregnancy she was moved to explore her Catholic heritage more deeply. She visited a Catholic bookstore and, once there, found herself in tears as she asked a nun, "Do you have any books for wayward Catholics?" Kathryn described her religious beliefs as being "in flux" as she grappled with valuing Catholic ritual tradition but disputing Catholic social teachings on birth control, abortion, and the male priesthood. In her words, "The thing that I like about religion is that it gives you ritual, and it gives you tradition, and it gives you a way to mark your rites of passage. . . . So I had to struggle between not really believing or not having that faith, and wanting the ritual, and because I was raised Catholic, the Catholic ritual is what has meaning to me." In the course of pregnancy and becoming a mother, Kathryn turned to the religion of her remembered past to build her interpretation of present experiences. Due to a combination of her disposition and physical circumstances, however, she did not find what she needed there.

Kathryn called me because she felt her home-birth story was a significant one to tell. In her words, "It's an important story to know for a couple reasons, like, you can plan a home birth and have everything go wrong, and still survive, and live through it, if you have good caregivers. So, it's like everybody's worst nightmare, practically, but it turned out okay." Kathryn's baby would have had Down's syndrome whether or not he was born at home, so for her that "issue is not related to the home birth at all."[46] Kathryn felt that because of her son's health, she was forced to move past reflecting on her birth experience whether she wanted to or not, and when a social worker visited her to ask about her feelings regarding her hospital birth, Kathryn was clear about her priorities:

> Well, for me, it was like, okay, it was sad, and we didn't have [a home birth], but it was—I mean now we've got bigger things to worry about than that. So I didn't feel much of a grieving process for this perfect birth that we wanted, that we didn't get. Not having it wasn't going to affect me for the rest of my life, or even affect how I felt about the child, or put me into a depression, or anything like that. I had enough other things to do to put me into a depression than that.

When I spoke with her, Kathryn was at the point where she felt "totally in love" with her baby. While she and her husband were still debating whether they would have a home birth if they had another child, she felt certain that she would choose the same midwives, as she was confident in their care, whether at home or in the hospital.

Kathryn's story allows a very different perspective on the religiosity of home birth from that of more "successful" stories. For Kathryn, her birth was not a time of coming to realize her own power or that of God; instead, it was a harrowing bodily experience over which she had virtually no control. While her reflections upon it may change with time, three months after her "nightmare" she felt that the bodily forces of birth were neither empowering nor spiritually enlightening. The lack of power Kathryn felt in giving birth, which was the fault of no one, but caused by a rare condition, may be part of what kept her from her sought-after "heavenly joy." Unlike Tessa, she could not choose how to respond to her encounter with death. Even after her experience, Kathryn believed that birth demanded "faith in nature, which is a spiritual faith as well, but it could also be more of a scientific faith too." In her experience, nature was not always gentle, however; nor was it always on a birthing woman's side. Speaking of the rate at which women "naturally" miscarry in the context of discussing Catholic views on abortion, Kathryn argued, "Nature is not such a life-lover as the church is."[47] Kathryn was aware of "God's" absence in her narrative of birth, even though religious seeking was a significant part of her life at the time. Instead, her birth story told of the brute forces of "nature" and the ways that midwives and doctors manipulated those forces to keep her and her baby alive.[48]

A woman's embodied history and the birthing histories of women in her wider community shape how death appears in her ruminations on birth. Her experiences of birth, her brushes with death, and the more impersonal but nonetheless ever-present statistics on maternal mortality among women like her all play a role in how she makes sense of the unsettling specter of death in birth. While some women find the contiguity between birth and death religiously fruitful, others find it fearsome and wish never to encounter it again. As Rosi Braidotti wrote, "We are all of woman born, and the mother's body as the threshold of existence is both sacred and soiled, holy and hellish."[49] While Braidotti took a perspective from outside the maternal body, Tessa and Kathryn spoke from within it. For them, as for many other women, the conjunction of the holy and hellish in their maternal bodies is a source of contemplation, and for some, a call to action.

The Ethics of Connection: Home Birth as a Social Movement

Despite their very different understandings of death's power in birth, Tessa and Kathryn both answer the question of risk in childbirth in similar ways: women have the right and responsibility to choose their caregivers and their preferred ways of giving birth. In this perspective, a woman's ethical responsibilities in giving birth are not only to bring forth a child to the best of her ability, but also to attend to her own emotional and physical needs in the process. Viewed in its wider context of pregnancy and early care for the child, childbirth is engaged in a web of relationships that constitutes an ethics of connection. Relationships between a birthing woman and her partner, her other family members, her caregiver, her community, and her baby are all reconfigured over the course of pregnancy and birth. For many women, the human connections forged, and sometimes strained, in the course of bearing a child are augmented with a transformed knowledge of self and of powers beyond the human realm. This ethics of connection, both in human and superhuman terms, is at the base of much of the struggle for transforming childbirth in North America. As women, and many men, have questioned notions of risk and danger in childbirth, they have set on a course that employs this ethics of connection to challenge both biomedical practice and state authority. Examining this ethics of connection in the specific context of home birth shows how women and their families conceive of home birth as a political and ethical act and, in some cases, as an assertion of religious liberty in the face of state control.

One woman expressed this ethics of connection, both between humans and with a supernatural power, most emphatically. Elise Gold, a Reform Jewish woman, talked of spirituality as connection with other people in synagogue and in family life. Connection was equally important to her when giving birth with the help of a certified nurse-midwife, and was intimately tied to issues of power and responsibility:

> My body definitely felt powerful. My mind felt powerful. . . . I had taken full responsibility for my life, and the outcome was all in my hands. Yet I had these people [around me]—yet it wasn't the kind of independence, like where you stand alone. I felt like I had that ability to stand alone, but I also could sway a little bit and lean on different people when I needed them, and that they were truly there to support me. Me, what I wanted, not what they would have wanted for me, or how they would do it themselves.
>
> . . . Maybe [I was] the center of my own universe for a time. And . . . [that way] you don't want to live, your whole life—it might sound like I'm talking power, power, power—not power to control other people, just power to control the space around me. And no, that's not something that I want all the time, there are lots of opportunities for sharing. But for that, I think birth belongs to the woman birthing, and not to anybody else.

Unlike the conservative Christian women who gave God most of the credit, Elise felt strongly that the power in birthing should rest with the woman herself, though she also felt the need to nuance her claims for power by acknowledging the value of sharing. Elise later insisted that this power within and between was linked to "spiritual connection." For Elise, the power in birth was tied to "spiritual energy" that did not float untethered, but instead provided, in her words, the "connection" that allowed her to harness her own power.

Elise's commitment to home birth is part of a broader commitment to what she called "home-based living," which included honoring Jewish domestic rituals and homeschooling her children. At the center of this notion of home was Elise's view of God as a pulsing energy, neither male nor female, manifested in each body—a God, however, that she carefully asserted was monotheistic. Elise's sense of the quotidian nature of God's immanence has early-twentieth-century precursors in her foremothers, who advocated " 'true Judaism'—the sense of God's daily presence."[50] Though in practice her life may hearken back to traditional Jewish women's religious practices that one scholar described as "largely private . . . and emotional in nature,"[51] Elise's home-based living is not well described by the reclusive and atomistic sense that "private" evokes. Family and friends infused the "privacy" of Elise's religion, as did a political vision of the significance of her home-based life. She felt nourished by human and spiritual connection at home and at the synagogue, and tied this sense of connection to her place in a wider movement that reclaimed the home as both a religious and a political reservoir of action.

Home Birth and Religious Freedom

Elise's assertion that her home-based living has both religious and political importance is mirrored in the broader home-birth movement. As I show in chapter five, the feminist, or for some postfeminist, home is an important site where political visions are created and nurtured. Home birth in particular is a form of cultural critique rooted in both religious and political motivations. Especially in the case of home births with unlicensed direct-entry midwives, home birth acts as a kind of civil disobedience undertaken by those suspicious of state regulation in the affairs of family life.[52] Most home-birthing families, whether religious conservatives or progressives, would agree that planning to give birth at home is a civil or unspecified right.[53] For example, in their "Declaration of Independence," the National Association of Parents for Safe Alternatives in Childbirth (NAPSAC) declared women's "right to a safe, natural birth assisted by and in the company of those who love them" to be inalienable.[54] However, home-birthing women are not confronting a monolithic state in their assertion of home birth as a civil or religious liberty. As Paula Treichler has maintained, "U. S. policy toward human sex and reproduction . . . remains an inconsistent patchwork of federal and state laws, initiatives, clinical practice acts, programs, lobbying efforts, and ideological pronouncements that involve such concepts as individual rights, free enterprise, market forces, God's will, and the family."[55] Home-birthing women and their families draw their discourses of liberty from the same polyglot sources as those of policymakers, and, depending on where they live in the United States, their choices are affirmed, ignored, or prosecuted.

In my study, women who chose certified nurse-midwives to attend their births were more comfortable with some state sanction of their birthing choices, since their midwives were accredited according to state-approved standards, and were given hospital privileges. Ironically, women from religious groups often presumed to be most at odds with state control of issues of health and lifestyle—namely, Christian Scientists and Amish—were among those who were most concerned to have certified nurse-midwives at their births.[56] Those women who chose unlicensed direct-entry midwives were not guided by institutional mandates of their particular religious traditions, but by their own decisions based in religious, economic, and political contexts.

Unnecessary state intervention into family life in the context of birth takes a variety of forms, according to home-birthing women. In a very specific example, many people who choose home birth do so to avoid interventions that they consider unnecessary or harmful to their baby's well-being, such as the administering of prophylactic eye treatment to the newborn to avoid blindness caused by gonorrhea passed on by the mother. For home-birthing parents, the routine application of this procedure in hospitals (mandated by state law in most cases) shows the state's mistrust of the ability of women and men to know their own sexual histories, and to act responsibly on this knowledge. At home, such procedures can be avoided, or undertaken only if necessary.[57] A more contentious resistance to state intervention is that of women who choose home birth after cesarean delivery. A quarter of the women in my study who chose direct-entry midwives did so in large part because the state deemed it illegal for licensed birth attendants, whether midwives or doctors, to attend a vaginal birth at home of a woman who had previously had a cesarean. These women felt capable of making decisions about their abilities to birth that contradicted the risk assessment of the state, and contradicted the law.

Tessa Welland stated her support of direct-entry midwifery—a support she shares with her husband—most decisively: "I basically, or we both, feel very strongly that citizens of this country need to take the ultimate responsibility for their lives, and we had absolutely no problem doing that. And I would challenge that to the nth degree if I had to." Tessa's willingness to challenge took her to court, as she and her husband were involved in a legal case advocating for the right of direct-entry midwives to practice their livelihood.[58] Another woman, Meg Alexander, extended the notion of the right to home birth to the sphere of religious freedom, arguing that birth was a "religious rite created by God," unlike "humanly" created rituals such as communion. Meg's argument has some legal precedents. In one case in California where a direct-entry midwife was arrested, handcuffed, and jailed for "practicing medicine without a license," the deputy district attorney eventually dismissed the case after deciding she was "a 'sincerely religious person,' entitled to a religious exemption from the law."[59] Writing of this case, Jessica Mitford suggested that the DA had more secular motives; namely, avoiding the bad press of convicting a midwife whose clients stood behind her. Nevertheless, for a midwife to be granted a religious exemption to attend home births was perhaps a step toward Meg's goal.

In addition to valuing a woman's ability to make decisions about her reproductive life, these forms of resistance to state regulation of birth assert that families, and not state-regulated institutions, are the "essential social unit" in which birth should occur.[60] As I will show in chapter five, most women conceived of their homes as safe spaces in which each member of the family was "free" to be him- or herself. Casting the family as a sphere of freedom, home-birthers concur with a portrait in which the family is "seen as representing not only the antithesis of the market relations of capitalism; it is also sacralized in our minds as the last stronghold against The State, as the symbolic refuge from the intrusions of a public domain that constantly threatens our sense of privacy and self-determination."[61] Ironically, however, as many scholars have argued, the nuclear family in its contemporary manifestation arose in conjunction with the state and "their very structures are interdependent."[62] As the power of kinship relations to structure economic and political life outside the household waned, the notion of family was increasingly limited to the domestic sphere. Concurrently, economic transactions were largely removed from that same sphere due to industrialization, and the family came to signify a private, affective realm apart from the rationalized yet competitive world of the state and economy.[63]

Given this historical perspective on the social, political, and economic construction of the family as a supposedly autonomous realm, the family nonetheless remains a social grouping threatened by the state in the eyes of many Americans, including some home-birthing women. Whether it is or not, many of these women want the family home to be a place where values of the wider society, as exemplified by government policies, economic approaches, or competing moral and religious stances, can be filtered out or at least critiqued, and where their parental influences can dominate. To this end, several of the women took the step from home birthing to homeschooling or hoped to once their children were older. Elise Gold considered that her choice of home birth was of a piece with her decision to homeschool: "It's just all tied up with a very strong belief in family and doing so much on our own, away from mainstream, and away from the experts. You know, sort of denying all that expertise-ism out there." Elise considered the experts "out there" a threat to the individuality of children and to the communal network of the family. As in home birth, homeschooling aims to bring siblings into closer contact with one another, and to create a deeply bonded family.

The homeschooling movement is a helpful parallel to the home-birth movement, both in its antiexpert, antistate intervention position, and in how it contains a confluence of diverse religious and political perspectives. Homeschoolers are motivated both by traditional religious reasons and more diffusely by alternative goals that may include spirituality. For example, homeschoolers include conservative Christians (Catholic and Protestant) who do not want their children influenced by secular messages about sexuality and, in some cases, evolution. They also include what are sometimes known as "unschoolers," people like Elise Gold and her friend Alison Lindt-Marliss, who do not want their children educated in what they consider to be an overly structured and standardized environment. In their fight against the state-sanctioned "experts," homeschoolers have effected unlikely alliances. For example, Michael Farris, the conservative Christian president of the organization Home School Legal Defense Association (and past co-chair of Pat Buchanan's presidential campaign), affirmed in a 2 February 1997 article in the *New York Times Magazine* that the "unschoolers' results are really good, and we'll defend them to the hilt. There's not one right way to do it." Based in a common resistance to state structuring of education, homeschooling, like home birth, generates allegiances among those of diverse philosophies.[64]

Even with this attitude of resistance to state intervention in terms of birth, many women who birth at home with direct-entry midwives still fight for state approval; they would rather birth at home with direct-entry midwives legally than illegally. They would rather be able to request medical backup for their home births openly without needing to lie to their doctors.[65] To this end, they join groups like Friends of Midwives and Citizens for Midwifery that do such things as lobby the government to approve certification for direct-entry midwives and educate women about childbirth options, especially home birth. They also launch court challenges based on everything from what might be conservative arguments about religious affiliation to expressly feminist arguments about the right to privacy in procreation, with the assertion that childbirth is a sexual act.[66]

Their collective action situates home-birthing women in a long tradition of female reform efforts in the United States. As anthropologist Faye Ginsburg has shown in her work on the abortion debate in the contemporary United States, despite their suspicions of the state, women activists have worked to "domesticate church and state to serve what they see as women's interests."[67] Where abortion activists on both sides of the issue have considered both the church and the state as worthwhile places to direct some of their reform efforts, home-birthers, despite their insistence on the spirituality of birth, have focused more often on the state as the place to effect change. Perhaps this is partly because of the presumed universality of the spirituality infusing birth—utilizing institutional religion to spread the message of home birth might be considered an inappropriately sectarian venture. Certain activists are religious reformers, like the devoutly Catholic Marilyn Moran, who regularly writes letters to the Vatican about her views on husband-assisted childbirth, or Pentecostal Carol Balizet, who considers her midwifery practice to be a form of ministry. For the most part, however, their voices are marginal both to the home-birth movement and to their religious traditions.

Another reason for the more common overlooking of institutional religion lies in the differences between the contours of the abortion debate and those of the home-birth movement. The terms "debate" and "movement" encapsulate these differences: abortion vividly separates women into opposing views, while home-birth advocates consider women who birth in hospitals—without knowledge of alternatives—not their enemies, but the victims of a profit-driven, woman-degrading, technocratic medical system. The home-birth movement is in some ways the mirror image of the abortion debate. Underlying the acrimony of the abortion debate are similarities in terms of women's views on the value of nurture and family.[68] However, underlying the unity of the home-birth movement (which is rooted in those same values of nurture and family) are subsumed political and religious differences over such issues as abortion and sexual orientation. Addressing religion more specifically than espousing a presumed universal "spirituality"—similar to its nation-building version of "civil religion"—would risk raising differences that might threaten the unity home-birthing women find in their support of choice in the place of birth.

This unity has its tensions, however, that both threaten the movement's cohesion and give it strength. As a Christian midwife who organizes workshops on "Midwifery as a Ministry" contended: "I'm not trying to shove Christianity on anyone, but I really hope to turn the table on new age midwifery."[69] Similarly, while most women I interviewed were comfortable with midwives not of their own religious tradition, others—namely, two Pentecostal women—were very concerned that the midwives who attended their births be Christian. These tensions were felt at the level of choice of midwife, and did not detract, for all women, from the wider commitment to choice in the place of birth.[70]

The collective commitment to home birth across diverse political and religious affiliations is evident at a wider institutional level as well. In Ohio, where direct-entry midwifery was investigated recently by a legislative study council, several hundred people came forth to give their testimonies to the benefits of home birth. These women and men included conservative Christians, mainstream Christians, "secular" folk, and Old Order

Amish, who particularly impressed the legislators, given their usual reluctance to involve themselves in affairs of state. Though the council could not come to consensus (the two doctors dissented), when they released their report in January 1998 the majority decision recommended decriminalizing home birth, developing a registration system for midwives, and offering more public education about childbirth options.[71]

A counterexample, however, shows what happens when differences of opinion overwhelm the consensus. The Midwives Association of North America (MANA) is in the process of trying to establish licensure for direct-entry (nonnurse) midwives across North America.[72] To this end, they established the North American Registry of Midwives (NARM) as an organization that would develop the standards of testing for the certified professional midwives. In the process, NARM initially wanted to adopt the MANA Statement of Core Values and Ethics for all such midwives.[73] MANA, however, includes a range of women, from lesbian feminist midwives to conservative Christian midwives. When a conservative Christian midwife on the board of NARM objected to the Statement of Core Values and Ethics, because it contained a reference to a book with the word "lesbian" in the title, the NARM board was stymied. Attempts to mediate the situation failed, and NARM dropped the code of ethics altogether, deciding that midwives should write their own codes.[74]

The home-birth movement, then, is a collection of women and men at both lay and professional levels who share a fundamental commitment to the choice of birthplace, but not necessarily much else. Home-birthing women feel strongly that a woman has the right to plan to give birth in the place and manner in which she feels most comfortable. She should have autonomy over her birthing body, or be able to transfer that autonomy to God or her husband or whomever she chooses. Within this commonality lie different conceptions of just what sort of bodily autonomy women should have, and what respect for a woman's power to birth entails. Placing children in day care and attitudes toward abortion are two of the most sensitive "motherhood issues" capable of provoking disagreement. Both are issues whose controversial nature revolves around the varieties of power and responsibility attributed to women on the basis of their ability to bear children. In a social context where the politics of motherhood are increasingly complex and contested, "control over the womb—the last unambiguous symbol of an exclusive female arena—is especially meaningful and threatening."[75] How unambiguous that symbol is, however, is increasingly up for question.

As many feminist scholars have shown, the womb is no longer considered a private space. Ultrasounds, court-ordered cesareans, and convictions for "gestational substance abuse" are just three examples of how women's wombs are increasingly open to public display and state control.[76] In a recent example of this "fetal rights" trend, a juvenile court judge in Wisconsin ordered that a woman planning to give birth at home with the help of a midwife be taken to the hospital by police, because a doctor thought she was too small-boned to succeed at home. She was released once she promised to return to the hospital when in labor, but ended up following out her plan and giving birth to a healthy baby at home.[77] In legal theorist Janet Gallagher's view, "the 'fetal rights' phenomenon . . . emerges from a glorification of medical technology resulting in a distorted public view of it, combined with a sharp backlash against the women's movement, especially against the claim to reproductive freedom symbolized by the *Roe v. Wade* abortion decision."[78] Fetal rights arguments extend what sociologist Viviana A. Zelizer called the "sacralization" of the child into the womb, as judges and advocates deny a woman's bodily autonomy in favor of the priceless, and always innocent, fetus.[79] Ironically, in the United States this sacralization of the fetus and newborn baby is not accompanied by concerted and effective efforts to improve the lives of the millions of children who grow up living in poverty.[80]

Arguments against home birth that belittle women's experiences of birth (of the "if you want an experience, ride a roller coaster" variant) and refuse to acknowledge women's right and responsibility to choose their desired place to give birth, fit along a continuum with these fetal rights arguments. They downplay a woman's role and experience in giving birth in place of emphasizing the "outcome" of the baby. However, in a society that proclaims passionate interest in healthy babies, but then fails to find solutions to the problems of child poverty once those babies age, these are not so much positive arguments guarding the baby as they are negative arguments circumscribing the autonomy of the birthing woman.[81] Ironically, even home-birthing women who do not consider themselves prochoice or feminist are hurt by antifeminist moves to curtail women's reproductive freedom.

Body Boundaries

The boundaries of the body have always provoked debate and perplexity over what historian Caroline Walker Bynum called "body puzzles."[82] Home-birthing women are reassembling those puzzles to assert that wombs are not disembodied organs, but the matter of a woman's belly, which, even in pregnancy, she is capable of both understanding and tending. Many home-birthers consider their action a challenge to state regulation of women's bodies and to the medical and insurance lobbies that have profoundly influenced such regulation. At this level, home birth generates a basis of support across political and religious divides, while containing very contentious disagreements over other issues related to the regulation of the body; namely, abortion and gay and lesbian rights.

Advocates of home birth make choice in childbirth a political issue that encompasses physiology, sexuality, religion, and personal history. As such, they argue that "cultural" or "religious" commitments are not mere luxuries meant only for calm times of meditation, or for consolation in times of grief or crisis. In this sense, they are in accord with anthropologist Stacey Pigg, whose study of development training programs for traditional birth attendants in Nepal teased out the ways biomedical approaches to childbirth are seen as "transcendent" and authoritative by the development community. According to Pigg, biomedical approaches to childbirth in Nepal are based on the belief that "the physiological be clearly separated from social, moral, and religious concerns."[83] Ironically, as Western biomedical practice is increasingly exported to "developing" countries, many Western women are critiquing and resisting the assumption that religion and culture can or should be fragmented from physiology when it comes to childbirth.[84] They are insisting that the boundaries separating the religious from the secular and the cultural from the physiological not be enacted on their birthing bodies. In the process, they bring forth an ethics of birth that grapples with questions of responsibility to self and another in what may be one of the most boundary-blurring of human relationships, that of a birthing woman and her baby. In the midst of that blurry relationship, as we will see, they find room for a diverse array of spiritualities embodied in the act of bearing and birthing a child.

4

Procreating Religion: Spirituality, Religion, and the Transformations of Birth

SURROUNDING HERSELF with pictures of voluptuous Goddesses and inviting a sympathetic circle of women friends to the births of her third and fourth children, Valerie Auletta felt she was finally getting birth right. Valerie chose to give birth to her third child at home with direct-entry midwives in part because she wanted to honor and explore her developing fascination with feminist spirituality and empower herself in the process. By contrast, Janet Stein, who lived about an hour away from Valerie, chose to give birth at home without any midwifery or medical care because she wanted to follow the commandments of her Christian God. For Janet, these included submitting to her husband's headship and not letting any figures of authority, be they doctors or midwives, stand in the way of the divinely ordained chain of command from God to husband to wife. Both Valerie and Janet turned to religion to back up their rejection of the medical and legal authorities that would regulate their birthing bodies, but they did so with radically different views of what religion called women to be. My goal in this chapter is to show that despite such marked differences in terms of religious tradition and doctrine, these women developed similar religiously informed approaches to childbirth that depended on seeing birth as not simply a bodily process to undergo, but an experience to be chosen.

Despite the gulf separating Valerie's and Janet's theological visions of women, they shared one thing: a commitment to insisting that birth could and should be a religious experience. Though nineteenth-century doctors and clerics had similar interests in the theological meanings of childbirth (especially regarding the vexing question of pain in the dawning era of anesthesia), in the twentieth century representatives of religions such as Christianity and Judaism left the actual practice of childbirth largely in medical hands. While long fascinated with abstracting metaphors and ideas about birth as fodder for theological rumination or symbolic systems, traditional religious thinkers have ignored the bloodiness and painfulness of birth, and have disregarded what this blood and pain might mean for birthing women. Whether due to repulsion for the messiness of birth, to long-held fears of women's bodies as polluted, or by virtue of a general

inability to see the "sacred" in the stuff of women's lives, "official" religion
has not nurtured the spirituality of birth.

For example, consider the intense hostility many mainstream Christian
denominations showed for the Christian feminist gathering "Re-imagin-
ing," held in Minneapolis in 1993. One of the central images that provoked such hostility was a liturgy recited at the gathering that referred to
the "nectar between our thighs [with which] we invite a lover, we birth a
child."[1] On a more personal level, contemplate Jewish feminist Lori Hope
Lefkowitz's recounting of her baby's birth: "Judaism was not officially
present at the occasion." In Lefkowitz's rueful words: "I was struck by
the irony of Judaism's absence from one of the only occasions that I would
dignify with the language of religious experience: 'Awesome,' 'transformative,' 'at once terrible and wonderful,' and 'miraculous.'"[2]

"Official" Judaism and Christianity may be missing their chance to im-
print the powerful moment of birth with their own particular mark, but
religion is not entirely absent from the drama. What that religion consists
of—and what "languages of religious experience" women use to describe
it—is the subject of this chapter. Valerie and Janet are just two examples
of women who draw from an eclectic range of sources to bring religious
meaning to their births, whether in the home or the hospital. In other
North American settings, women are bringing together the seemingly dis-
parate realms of biomedical and religious understanding to make sense of
a wide range of pregnancy- and birth-related events, including pregnancy
loss and prenatal testing.[3] In terms of childbirth, some of this convergence
of biomedical and religious understandings has taken the form of religiously based birth books, including explicitly Christian and Jewish texts
such as Margaret Hammer's *Spiritual Guide through Pregnancy* and Tikva
Frymer-Kensky's *Motherprayer.* Hammer, a Lutheran minister, and
Frymer-Kensky, a professor at a rabbinical college and the University of
Chicago, represent their respective traditions to at least some degree.[4]
Other examples come from less officially religious contexts—such publications as *Birth Gazette* and *Mothering* magazine—that regularly invoke a
more nebulous kind of spirituality. Perhaps most important, whether they
are more or less comfortable with biomedical approaches to birth, these
women are asserting on the basis of knowledge gained from their bodies
that creating life is a powerful force. To make sense of this power they have
sought a diversity of religious languages and tools that have allowed them
to "procreate religion"—to make religious meaning out of the embodied
memories and human connections forged in the process of childbirth.

Home birth attracts women from a wide range of religious traditions,
some of whom are formally affiliated with churches or synagogues, others
who draw from more eclectic sources. Given this religious diversity, what
can a study of home birth reveal about religion in the contemporary

United States? I contend that considering how home birth attracts religious interpretations—that is, how women turn to religious language and sentiments in telling their stories of birth—shows a particular instance of a discourse of "spirituality" that runs through a broad spectrum of religious diversity in North America.[5] This discourse of spirituality, rooted in venerating nature (in its many guises), affirming "universal truths," and trusting in a power external to the human will (in most cases, God), is found in almost all of the women's narratives I treat here.

Within this spirituality-in-common, however, lie sharp differences in terms of both religious practice and gender politics. Tolerance of other religions, approaches to mothering, relations of authority between men and women, and opinions about abortion and birth control were just some of the issues that evoked divided and often impassioned opinions among these women. In this chapter I explore commonality in the midst of difference through attending to two related themes: how these women spoke of religion, and two, how they understood the process of birth to have transformed their religious lives. I begin with clarifications, by way of scholarly opinions and those of the women themselves, regarding the differences between the terms "religion" and "spirituality" as they are used in contemporary North American society. I then turn to a consideration of what sorts of gods and powers these women implied and invoked in their use of spirituality. In order to clarify the common threads in this discourse of spirituality, I point out both the convergences and divergences in the kinds of religion and spirituality that some of these women discussed in talking of birth. To close, I reflect on the ways childbirth may transform women's religious identities, and set the stage for more focused discussion in the book's final three chapters of how such transformations are realized in the home, the body, and the pain of birth.

Religion and Spirituality

Not all of the women I interviewed considered the choice to give birth at home to stem directly from their religious tradition, but every woman except one considered her baby's birth to be a religious or, more frequently, a spiritual experience. The answer to my question "Was giving birth a religious or spiritual experience for you?" elicited a similar refrain from many women: "Religious, no; spiritual, yes."[6] This refrain reflected definitions I discussed earlier, in which religion comes to mean dead ritual and hierarchy, while spirituality connotes a more personal, immediate, and authentic sacrality. Setting this distinction in the context of how these women spoke of their experiences of birth, however, complicates the neat boundary between the two terms.

In using the term "spiritual," some women, especially those of an eclectic bent, posited a disjunction between institutional and experiential dimensions in which they judged chosen experience as more authentic than the age-old mandates of a religious tradition. However, in keeping with this suspicion of routinization, the intentionality and agency implied by "choice" was often tempered by an assertion that a true spiritual experience must be an organic and serendipitous occurrence. Not all women voiced such disdain for institutional religion. For more institutionally affiliated women, most notably Orthodox Jews, traditional Catholics, and Pentecostals, spiritual serendipity could come only within religious structure, albeit a structure characterized by considerable creativity on their part. Since their religious institutions and leaders were not concerned actively with the process of birth and did not guide their choices specifically, they mined their textual and ritual traditions to make their own versions of orthodoxy and orthopraxy and to provide religious justification for their birth choices.

Despite their differences in approach to the value of institutional religion, all of these women drew from "traditional" religious resources—for example, domestic ritual and devotional traditions or a relationship to God/Goddess—when planning their births or describing them later. In the case of home birth, then, religion and spirituality are difficult to sever, confirming religion scholar Stephanie Walker's broader claim that "analyses of feminist or women's spirituality, often experimental, thrive within conditions of elastic definition."[7] The elasticity of the increasingly ubiquitous term spirituality is found not only among women talking of their lives, but also in scholars' attempts to describe and analyze these lives.

SPIRITUALITY ACCORDING TO SCHOLARS

The term "spirituality" has been a focus of discussion in both popular and scholarly circles in the last several years, and its prevalence continues to grow. Scholars have asserted that over the course of the last half of the twentieth century, the importance of (mostly Christian) religious institutions in the United States faded in the face of a spirituality drawn from wider cultural sources, including diverse religious traditions, political movements, and psychology.[8] According to this view, as people questioned not only religious authorities, but political and educational ones as well, they developed an inward-looking and experientially based spirituality. Sociologist Wade Clark Roof drew the distinction in the following way: "To be religious conveys an institutional connotation: to attend worship services, to say Mass, to light Hanukkah candles. To be spiritual, in contrast, is more personal and empowering and has to do with the deepest motivations of life."[9] Similarly, religion scholar Amanda Porterfield defined spirituality as "personal attitudes towards life . . . that engage an individual's deepest feelings and most fundamental beliefs. . . . [S]pirituality covers a larger domain than that staked out by religion because it does not require belief in God or commitment to institutional forms of worship."[10] "Spirituality" is loosened from institutional constructs and theological norms, and lodged in the "deepest" part of the individual.

What understandings of the "individual self" and the "institution" underlie this view? Roof argued that the baby boom generation—four-fifths of the women in my study belong to this generation—profoundly shaped this shift to spirituality. As baby boomers, they came of age in the 1960s and were young adults in the 1970s, during a time of emphasis on "the pursuit of the self as an ideal: through values such as self-fulfillment, self-acceptance, and the intrinsic benefits of experience itself."[11] In Roof's estimation, "The self is real in a way social institutions are not."[12] The "realness" of the self next to the falsity of institutions, however, needs to be set in context.

The self became increasingly "real" only with the rise of a "therapeutic culture"—a culture focused on exploring the stories, needs, and dysfunctions of individuals. According to historian T. J. Jackson Lears, religion in a therapeutic mode is a twentieth-century development in the United States. He depicted a moral shift from "a Protestant ethos of salvation through self-denial toward a therapeutic ethos stressing self-realization in this world—an ethos characterized by an almost obsessive concern with psychic and physical health defined in sweeping terms."[13] One of the main effects of the turn to a therapeutic ethos was the growing consumer culture in which buying things and services was a path to self-transformation and ultimately helped "create a new and secular basis for capitalist cultural hegemony."[14] Although Lears dubbed the therapeutic ethos "secular," I would argue that it has shaped a later shift to a self-focused spirituality concerned with health and "personal growth." Ironically, unlike Roof's appraisal of the baby boomers, Lears concluded that Americans in the 1920s understood the self in what would now be considered a postmodern way, as "fragmented and socially constructed."[15] The self was not any more real than institutions, according to Lears, but instead was fluid and changing, and shaped not only by "authentic experience," but also by the demands of a consumer market. Accumulating things and services helped to create the self.

Today, practitioners of North American religions are drawn necessarily into a culture in which choice is just as important, if not more important, than tradition. Ironically, even many of those turning to tradition are making a choice to leave more liberal churches or synagogues in favor of "traditional" ones—as many Orthodox Jews and traditional Catholics show. However, this celebration of the self in spirituality—reaching the "deepest" self by "authentically" choosing one's faith—needs to be historically and culturally situated. Paying attention to external influences upon what is considered spiritual or, as I will discuss later, "natural," like gender norms, consumer culture, and the media, does not render individual understandings of the self or the body false. Doing so does, however, grant an important perspective on why people make the choices they do. Such a perspective also questions just how free is choice in North America.

Ways of talking about home birth and spirituality share many parallels— both kinds of discourse presume an authenticity or naturalness, and both claim to strip away misleading institutionally based medical or theological doctrine.[16] Furthermore, religious understandings of home birth could be described as both inward-looking and therapeutic; birth is seen as a particularly intense personal experience that confronts a woman with her deepest fears and strengths, and that, if done right, can lead a woman to new understanding and growth. But in addition to this experiential, therapeutic character, the religion provoked by home birth is also seen as saturated with a kind of power that is not only personal and self-rewarding, but transformative of society and relationships. Thus it is an inner-directed religion often accompanied by a strong political voice and a deep sense of "mission" to let other women know of choices in childbirth. This political, outward focus plays an important role in generating these women's conviction that spirituality, especially when it comes to bringing a new life into the world, is universal.

SPIRITUALITY AS UNIVERSAL

In their different ways all of these women shared a sense that spirituality included a focus on health and personal growth. For an Amish woman, like Mary Rose Erb, growth might be growing into her role as a mother; for New Ager Nina Holly, growth was throwing off marriage and conventional depictions of motherhood. The difference between their explanations and those of scholars, however, was that for most of these women, spirituality was deeply personal but also potentially universally shared and found in community with others; it was not simply a "personal" concern. In this way, the spirituality evoked in home birth disrupts the understandings of spirituality that limit it to an individualistic preoccupation with the self.

Home birth is a therapeutic model of birth in its emphasis on the mother's fulfillment in addition to the baby's well-being, but it is positioned as a critique of biomedical (and cultural) norms of what comprises a healthy pregnancy and birth. Many women viewed their personal choice as embedded within a larger consumer movement against medicalization and for a diversity of health-care options, and part of this view held that simpli-fying birth by reducing its expense and commercialization also allows spir-ituality to surface.[17] The proclaimed universality of birth as a "natural" act with spiritual meanings generated both critique and activism. With the conviction that gentler, safer, and more respectful births were possible for all women, several of these home-birthing women became birth educa-tors, birth assistants, and midwives-in-training after their home births. At least half of the women I spoke with were active in some organized way in promoting home birth. The impulse to activism stemming from home birth puts a different twist on sociologist Robert Wuthnow's assertion that spirituality, as an "interior, entirely individualistic" alternative to reli-gion is "conducive to caring activities only when it occurs within the con-text of [religious] communities."[18] Though not a traditional "charitable" activity, the volunteering that many religiously affiliated and unaffiliated women pour into the home-birth movement (and its close but distinct cousin, La Leche League) as educators and activists could easily be seen as what Wuthnow called "acts of compassion."[19]

The impetus for this activism was tied to the way many women de-scribed spirituality as shaping their particular experiences of birth and as transcending the specificity of religious traditions. In many of the wom-en's descriptions, religion occupied a kind of middle ground between the intensely personal and broadly universal character of spirituality, Some-times they pilloried religion as "ritualistic nonsense" and other times gently discredited it as a "man-made" construct. Even women who saw themselves as part of a religious community and/or who attended church or synagogue often castigated religion in this way. More than half of the women participated in religious institutions to varying degrees, and all the women (save one) had some sense of the "spirituality" of birth.

In describing the spirituality of their births, some women focused on the infant. Tessa Welland, who described her home births as guided not by religion but by spirituality, remembered being "very protective of [her babies'] spiritualness as infants. And in their very early infancy they didn't get handed around, they didn't get subjected to outside stimulus. No bright lights or loud music. So, yes it was definitely rooted in spirituality." Although Tessa did not consider her births to be "religious," she did think that her Catholic background, especially her experiences at youth retreats while an "active Catholic" in high school, shaped her birth choices:

I think that [retreats] afforded me the opportunity to really become in touch with who I was spiritually. And probably to Catholicism's dismay, I realized that I wasn't necessarily a Catholic. But I definitely think that that experience made me attuned to that kind of energy—to have the time to reflect and really think about spiritualism, and to sort of study religion and what it meant in the world, what it meant historically, how it affects people's lives. All of those things were helpful in sorting out who I was spiritually. And helped me to come to those kinds of decisions that were important to me, like birthing my children.

In a common adaptation of the language of physics, Tessa thought of spirituality as "energy."[20] In contrast, she defined religion as a "social construct." In her eyes, "religion is an expression of spirituality. Spirituality is universal. Like you could recognize spirituality manifested in Judaism or Catholicism, born-again Christians, Jehovah's Witnesses." After "church-shopping . . . everywhere but in a synagogue," Tessa said, she and her family found their religious community within domestic rituals shared with their extended family.

Similarly, Christian Scientist Judy Woodman felt that her births were not religious in a "church kind of sense," because to her religion meant "almost human, what's the word, not cultural, social—no—not routine. I can't think of the word, but when there's—ritual! Ritualistic, and that you're going on talking about it all the time." Spirituality, however, was a "very God-centered activity" in her understanding. Judy's fellow Christian Scientist, Heather Monroe, also felt that spirituality transcended particular religions (including her own). She felt that people she knew who had chosen home birth had a "strong spiritual core . . . an understanding of who they are, and a sense of comfort in their own approach to things, rather than someone who expects someone else to tell them what they should be doing." Heather felt that because of the dominance of hospital birth in this country, "You sort of have to have a faith in something, in order to make that choice, only because of what our society dictates." Women like Tessa and Heather considered the spirituality behind home birth to be tied both to self-esteem and to a willingness to challenge the "social constructs" that institutions like religions, medicine, and the state support. For them, understanding one's spirituality was a way to come to self-understanding, but not necessarily self-obsession.

Not all women who shared this approach to spirituality felt that it transpired outside of religious institutions. Alison Lindt-Marliss, who grew up a Catholic and married a Jewish man, appreciated going to synagogue once a week, at the recent suggestion of her adolescent daughter. For Alison, letting a formal religious organization take over the responsibility for "making [one day] in some way sacred" was a welcome relief. She felt that in her family, when it came to bringing attention to religion, "I'm always the one initiating it, and in motherhood that seems to be a big part of life, so I feel like I don't know if I always want to do that. So I'm looking forward to becoming involved with a religious community to take some of that for me, so I don't always have to lead. I can more or less go along." Alison felt that the synagogue as a religious institution could help to elicit expressions of her broad belief that "we're all God's people . . . God's in us." Alison did not consider herself to have a "standard" Jewish or Christian notion of God, and laughingly admitted, "I don't even know what the 'standard' is. I just—everybody has their own belief, that's mine."

Elise Gold, who grew up in a Conservative Jewish home, drew an even more direct connection between spirituality and religion. Elise considered religion to be literally "man-made," with patriarchal roots. Spirituality, for her, was the "ultimate forces of life going in the right direction," and like Tessa, she thought of it as a "positive energy" that was "life-promoting." Though Elise felt that someone of any religion could experience this energy, services at her Reform synagogue were sometimes the occasion when she felt spirituality manifested:

> [T]he whole service is done in a circle of people all singing and dancing and holding hands and . . . you pray to the God within the person beside you and that type of thing. And that to me is very spiritual. Realizing that there is God everywhere, and that energy, you know, however you're going to define God[, is there]. For me it's like sort of an energy, and it's just everywhere. And when we do this, I actually, in holding people's hands, can actually feel [something] . . . almost like an electric charge, like this current? And that, to me, that's a spiritual thing.

Elise felt that this energy was particularly potent during pregnancy and birth: "If you believe that there's God in every person, that's a time when you've got two Gods within you, you know? I don't question that there's only one God, but that same God is just within all of us. I guess two manifestations of the same deity." Elise was very interested in conveying to me her understanding of spirituality, so much so that she called me immediately after our interview to leave a message on my answering machine: "You know when you were asking about spirituality? Well, when I said it was energy, I realized, just thinking about this now, that spirituality is *connecting* to that energy. That's what I meant but just couldn't say before. It's the connection." For Elise, spirituality was a connection to a "god energy" felt most abundantly when bodies were in contact: when people were holding hands in a synagogue, when a woman was sharing her body with her baby in pregnancy, and when she was "bringing this live being from [her] body" in birth.

Though Elise and Alison go to Reform synagogues that are somewhat innovative in their religious practice, other, more traditional women also considered spirituality to be an energy open to a diversity of people, especially in terms of birth. For these women, spirituality was not necessarily antithetical to traditional rituals. Scholars have often ignored instances where adherents of traditional religions experiment with religious innovation in the same vein as more eclectic spiritual seekers. For example, in

drawing what he seems to think is a common sense link, religion scholar
Peter Van Ness offered proof that spirituality in North America has distanced itself from traditional religion. He wrote: "A large number of
Americans apparently believe that the sacred can be experienced without
allegiance to a central tenet of biblical religion; in fact [in a *Newsweek*
survey], 26 percent of the persons polled said that they obtained a 'sense
of the sacred during sex.' "[21] *Why* experiencing the sacred during sex
should be added proof of a lack of allegiance to the tenets of biblical religion is not immediately clear to me.[22] And if we were to transfer the example to self-consciously Jewish and Christian home-birthing women, who
experienced the "sacred" during childbirth (and sometimes experienced
the sexuality of childbirth and used biblical texts to describe their experiences), the link would be equally obscure.[23]

Van Ness's slippage in thinking of embodied or even sensual spirituality
as necessarily "untraditional" points to a difficulty in the ways the term
spirituality is used. Embodied spirituality is not necessarily beyond religious traditions; it may be, but it may also involve a (critical) reinterpreta-
tion of religious tradition within both orthodox and experimental communities. Turning especially to the body as a spiritual resource can result
in both "gender radicalism" (anthropologist Sherry Ortner's term for
breaking gender norms) and the intensification of gender norms within a
religious tradition—rarely does it leave gender, and the power relations
that shape it, untouched.[24]

Home-birthing women interpret the "womanliness" of their childbearing bodies in several different ways, some of which depend on religious
lenses; for example, the idea that God designs women's bodies especially
to give birth. Though they may disagree with the gendered messages that
less traditional women find in the process of birth, even traditional
women, be they Orthodox Jews or conservative Christians, understand
the spirituality of birth as somewhat universal. For example, in Debra
Lensky's present interpretation as an Orthodox Jewish woman, not only
did God design women's bodies in an act of omnipotent creation, but he
also more specifically intervened in her life to lead her to Orthodox Judaism through childbirth activism. Before she became Orthodox, Debra
worked with two other women in her childbirth activism, one a Christian
and the other more eclectically spiritual, with her own "spiritual leader."
Debra felt that her work with these two women did not come about by
coincidence:

> And very honestly it felt very much very designed, very destined that three major
> religions were coming together to work on childbirth and awaken women. And
> the three of us were very much aware, very much aware of what we were doing
> when we worked individually with individual women and as an organization

working for the world. We felt a very strong sense of mission that we needed to bring women back to the realization of who they were and what they were. Not again telling them that you *have* to have children, not again saying to them you *must* birth at home or at a hospital center or anywhere; none of that. But just that they be reconnected to their design, that they honor themselves and that they feel their own strength and their own power in a positive way.

Debra and her friends were not "official" representatives of their respective religions, but nevertheless Debra saw their collaboration as a legitimate and important act of interreligious cooperation. Her perspective begs the question of just how "official" religion is constituted, and how the boundaries of "institutional" religion are drawn. For Debra, partaking in childbirth activism as a Jew made her work *Jewish* work, although no Jewish organization was sponsoring her. The boundaries of what is or is not institutional religion grow fuzzy, as people constitute their actions in the home or in the community as actions fostered by their religious traditions.

Not only did Debra's Judaism support her childbirth activism, but conversely, her experience of childbirth also shaped her Judaism. The childbirth-provoked sense of women's power that Debra described had a profound effect on her Jewish identity. She asserted that her family joined an Orthodox community at her instigation, because of the effects of her experiences of childbirth. Though Debra is still involved in childbirth activism somewhat, the breadth of her ties to that community have lessened as she develops relationships in her Orthodox Jewish community. In some ways her empowering experience of activism, in which she wanted women to "reconnect" to their power without necessarily feeling they had to give birth, is at odds with the very pronatalist environment of Orthodox Judaism.[25] The power Debra felt called to evoke in all women became transmuted in the course of her religious transformation, becoming power less broadly accessible, achieved instead mainly through birth and mothering.

Power rooted in procreation was central to the way many women used the notion of spirituality to describe the significance of childbirth. For most of these women, Christians, Jews, spiritual feminists, New Agers, and even some "nonreligious" women, spirituality was an evocative and useful term to describe their births, generally meaning a personal and embodied connection with a supernatural power that anyone who made the effort could access. Though their religious traditions were markedly different, the relationship they claimed between birth and spirituality was in many ways premised on the proclaimed universality of both. As feminist Alison Lindt-Marliss put it (as she perched at the interstices of memories of a Catholic childhood, a marriage to a Jewish man, and an adolescent daughter seeking her Jewish roots): "Women are born to birth. It's just a faith; that's a matter of faith." This spiritualizing of home birth, however, was rooted in particular models of embodied and spiritual power that were professed to be universal but that were not all shared. For some women, theological models that championed the authority of a husband optimally allowed a woman to find her power; for others, models of mutuality or even independence best nurtured women's strength.

Given these differences, some women were more hesitant to give spirituality such wide applicability. For example, Brenda Matthews, a Pentecostal woman, said she used only selectively a book entitled *Spiritual Midwifery*, one of the long-standing, germinal works in the home-birth movement.[26] In reading this book, Brenda said she wanted "birth fact" and nothing else. She stated: "Spiritually, I am very tuned in to [i.e., suspicious of] things that are not from Jesus, and I am very cautious with something called 'spiritual,' because I'm not sure what spirit they are tuning into. I want God's spirit." However, despite her wry assertion that "I don't open myself up to the cosmos," in the case of birth Brenda did extend the scope of the spiritual, saying, "Every birth is a spiritual experience."[27] For her, childbirth trumps theological differences, if only briefly. Brenda limited that universality again in describing her own first baby's birth: "I had a divine birth, because Jesus actually brought that baby out without me doing anything." Other women, including another Pentecostal and a traditional Catholic were careful to distinguish the spirituality of their births from New Age versions of spirituality, but still happily and liberally made use of the term spiritual to describe their experiences.

This spiritualizing of home birth, however, professed universality rooted in particular models of the body, nature, and God. In the midst of their comfort with the language of spirituality lay different conceptions of what sorts of power spirituality invoked and conveyed. Whence did spirituality come—God, "energy," a woman herself? And what did it allow a woman to do or to feel?

What Kind of Gods, What Kind of Power

Some scholars of twentieth-century North America have suggested a shift in notions of God that mesh with a view of North America's having an increasingly therapeutic culture. Sociologist Marsha Witten argued that secular forces, including the market and psychology, have turned at least Protestant images of God into a "therapeutic" and "anthropomorphized" deity. An immanent, feeling figure has come to overshadow a transcendent, inscrutable God in Protestant discourse; God is now more of a daddy than a judge.[28] Witten's examination of classic theological categories of immanence and transcendence—of a God deeply involved in the world and human lives and a God more removed from the earthly realm—helps a consideration of the kinds of gods and kinds of power that home-birthing women's narratives elicited and constructed. However, such a consideration tends to blur rather than sharpen the line between immanence and transcendence.

The images of God arrayed by these women included a judgmental Father God, who would not allow heathen influences in the birthing room, and a compassionate God, who would not give a birthing woman "more than she could handle." God's gender was a live issue for many of the women, who understood God to be both male and female. Some preferred to conflate God with a "higher power" of twelve-step language or, like Elise, with a mutable, positive energy. In the midst of this diversity, God was both apart from the world—a great and mysterious designer—and an empathic, therapeutic, and active player in women's births. The God present in pregnancy and birth was transcendent, inscrutable, and capable of creating life in the most mysterious ways, as well as immanent and involved, sharing a woman's pain and making sure she could withstand it.

Brenda Matthews felt that God was at once judge and lover, transcendent and immanent. For example, she asserted that God set very specific limits on who was spiritually appropriate to touch the bodies of newborn babies, sent "from the throne room of God to us." When I asked her what would happen if the wrong person touched a newborn, she responded:

> People that are not living under the blood of Jesus—and this sounds very judgmental, Pamela, and I don't mean it in a condemning or judgmental way, but it's the only way I know how to describe it to you. You asked me, so I've got to say it, okay? They have spirits, attitudes—I'll just say those two words—that are noncomplementary to God's spirit. . . . And I believe that people can—and I'm not going to go so far as to say [put] curses on people—that can happen, I believe, but that's not what I'm dealing with, but subtleties, that they can make things difficult for that child's life. They can pray a prayer or make a statement, a proclamation over this tender new spirit—and not that God's spirit is not stronger—but you want it surrounded so it's nurtured in God's spirit, rather than having seeds of something other than God's spirit being planted.

Brenda's understanding of the particular spiritual vulnerability of a baby newly emerged from a mother's womb was not a view limited to her Pentecostal perspective. From obstetricians like Frederick Leboyer to midwives such as Agneta Bergenheim, who contended that some infants enter the world in a "state of spiritual emergency," alternative-birth advocates from a range of perspectives consider the first words spoken to a newborn to be an act with spiritual consequence.[29] Similarly, from a Jewish perspective, Debra Lensky felt the need to whisper the biblical words of the Shema, the Jewish confession of faith, to her infant son immediately upon his birth.[30]

Brenda's God was a transcendent (and male) God whose ways she could not always fathom, but he was also a "loving God who will not stop at anything to protect me and love me." Brenda felt that God did not force her to believe, but that belief necessitated that she take an active role in relinquishing, or "letting go" of, her will: "I have never shirked back from explaining how God delivered me through childbirth. . . . I refuse to take credit for me. Mine was a relinquishing of my will and allowing God's will to take over." Relinquishing will, however, was a complex process of interpreting God's plan for her birth—how much of herself to control and how much to let rest in "God's hand." Though she felt that God was ultimately in "control," she also knew that she had to "train" herself for birth, through avidly reading books about birth and altering her language: "They call when we are in labor 'pains.' I never said that. . . . I changed my vocabulary. I changed every aspect that I could have control over of my environment so that my head was straight, and it was!" Brenda's God was both transcendent and immanent; inexplicably, he designed her body to give birth, but also he acted as a sort of divine midwife, pulling her first baby out into the world. But she had to act as well, both empowering herself and drawing on God's power, mixing approaches and metaphors in recounting her birth narrative.

Similarly, for self-described "born-again Lutheran" Stefanie Harter, God was both an intimate ally and an unfathomable deity. Before giving birth, she said, "I was never really that close to God, but after [my son was] born, I've become a lot closer to him." Perhaps paradoxically, Stefanie felt she grew closer to God through the "amazing" process of creating "a person inside of [me]." That she was capable of such creation made her realize that "we are just small players in a big puzzle. And . . . we can plan a lot of our lives, but we're not the major decision maker. I think there's somebody else that really has a lot of plans, a lot more part in that decision making." Intimacy and incomprehensibility merged in Stefanie's experience of God and childbirth, chastening her sense of holding ultimate power over her life.

Immanence could also describe Christina Upton's encounter with God during her last birth. Though she now attends a Reconstructionist synagogue with her formerly Orthodox Jewish husband, and feels she has drifted from her Lutheran roots, Christina turned to Jesus when her body was in pain:

> I kept crying out, "Jesus, give me strength. Jesus, help me get this baby out." I used Jesus a lot. I grew up in it. I would say I am a Christian and do talk about Jesus a lot, even though I am not sure where I stand in terms of my relationship with Jesus right now. It was so much ingrained in me and so much a part of me, I think, that Jesus was there with me, and he was helping me give birth.

And that was the only sense of religion, I guess, concrete religion. Just the other things that I've talked about, being empowering, it's very spiritual. It just makes you feel so good about your own person, and it's just what God meant for us to do.

Christina's childhood relationship with Jesus was embedded in her body and memory—her habitus—and was summoned by the pains of childbirth. Her "concrete religion" both confirmed Jesus' immanence for Christina and reinforced her wider view of God's wise—perhaps omnipotent—plan for the human life cycle.

The gods of home-birthing women took many different forms—God, Jesus, the Holy Spirit, the Goddess—but they were usually considered both the creator and the enabler of the "natural" processes of birth.[31] He or she was both a transcendent deity, capable of creating the "miracle" of life, and an immanent one, willing to help a woman through the difficulties of birth. In addition to the many women who marveled at God's wondrous design of a woman's body, Janice Pulaski asserted that one thing God did *not* design was hospitals: "When he created us, he didn't create hospitals. [He] kind of created just us, and the ability to give birth." Though this argument is a logical slippery slope, it evokes how some women felt they could *know* what kinds of practices God intended for birthing women. The women who used the language of spirituality to describe their births generally conceived their version of a deity to be an empowering partner with women who had faith in themselves and in birth. What does this commonality amid women of very different religious and political identities suggest about religion in contemporary North America? I now address this question by considering the confluence and divergence in the ways women spoke of spirituality.

PROCREATIVE TENSIONS: BRINGING TOGETHER
BODIES AND SPIRITS

Home birth, as a countercultural movement, has attracted passionate proponents from a diversity of religious and political identities. This includes women like Debra, who have become more orthodox in the process, and other women, like Tessa, who have taken the reverse path and left traditional religion to find more experimental women-centered spiritualities. The cultures these women are countering are not necessarily the same. Yet, in the context of childbirth, their diversity is managed in the service of what is perceived as the greater good: working for alternatives to the medical model of childbirth.

Broadly speaking, these women's common ways of speaking of spirituality tied the body and spirit together in many similar ways. For all of these women, bodily health and wellness were physiological, emotional, and spiritual matters that required recourse to more than just biomedical approaches to the body. Specifically in terms of birth, they felt that each woman's comfort with her choice of childbirth practices allowed her to be more open to spiritual concerns, both in her own birthing experience and in her relationship with her newborn baby. As I will show in my discussion of the meanings of pain, they also considered (but did not always experience) families and friendships to be particularly potent channels for spirituality.

In line with these similarities, two assertions act as currents carrying along the broader home-birth movement and mediating its diversity: (1) given a healthy pregnancy, most women share a common ability to give birth with little interference; and (2), birth is imbued with spirituality, in that it connects a woman to powerful forces both within and without herself. As I have argued, both of these currents are constructed as having something of the "universal" about them. But, as Brenda's concern to distinguish herself from those "not living under the blood of Jesus" showed, universality has its limits. In the face of this difference, the currents of birth as a spiritual event and women as natural birthers do not always flow together harmoniously.

Mediating the procreative tensions in the home-birth movement becomes an exercise in what one might call, after literary critic Gayatri Spivak, a sort of double "strategic essentialism."[32] That is, in coming together through a conviction that women are essentially capable of giving birth with little interference, home birthers also strive to draw upon an essential spirituality that crosses boundaries of place, politics, and religious tradition. The commonality is strained, however, once the strategy dissolves, leaving only essentialism. The procreative tensions bubbling underneath the home-birth movement are exacerbated when certain specific issues come to the fore, such as regulating sexuality and upholding specific religious doctrines. These tensions were demonstrated by the case of the Midwives Alliance of North America, when it faced challenges from its conservative Christian members over its feminist model of midwifery supportive of lesbian midwives. These same tensions—rooted in antagonistic understandings of sexuality, religious truth, and gender—are alleviated when the focus becomes the threat of the biomedical model to women's power to give birth and when spirituality is used as a relatively vague term capable of encompassing a diversity of childbirth experiences.

The flexibility of the spirituality shared by a diversity of home-birthing women is not surprising, perhaps, given religion scholar Catherine Albanese's argument that the left and right ends of the contemporary "American religious spectrum"—what she calls "New Agers" and "fundamentalists"—are characterized by a particular convergence of "mystical/metaphysical" qualities.[33] In her analysis, a focus on healing, a "non-elite, do-it-yourself . . . spiritual democracy," "ongoing revelation," and personal transformation that leads to the transformation of society are commonly held goals for both fundamentalists and New Agers.[34] Home birth is another environment in which these goals converge. Women stress "holistic" views of the body that allow for both self-sufficiency and supernatural influence in birthing, and consider birth to be a time of personal revelation that holds within it the possibility to change the world by birthing a new generation in a gentler way. As Olivia, a "secular" Jew with New Age interests, put it: "If more people give birth naturally, then the whole of humanity can elevate themselves." Women's choice to do so—whether they are traditionally religious or experimentally so—is often a theological action in the face of both ignorance and the trivializing of women's experiences.

More specific examples of confluence in views of spirituality lie in some common practices among home-birthing women. For example, Pentecostal, New Age, and Presbyterian women shared the ritual of burying the placenta and marking the spot with a rosebush or a tree. Debra Lensky, however, once she became an Orthodox Jew, no longer buried her placentas because she felt the practice gave religious connotations to an organ, and was tantamount to "showing appreciation in the wrong place." She admitted that part of her still desired to ritualize the disposal of the placenta, but she finally stated, "It's a small, little miracle that the Creator has given us as part of our bodies, and it comes and goes away with the baby."

Similarly, methods for coping with pain, including prayer, meditative breathing, relying on others, and visualizations, were also common across religious traditions. Many women employed the traditional practice of prayer throughout their pregnancies and births, praying most often to God, but also to the Goddess, Jesus, and, in at least one case, the Virgin Mary. Beyond this, several women, including an Orthodox Jew, a United Methodist, a Unity Church member, and a New Age Jew, partook of more alternative spiritual practices. For example, they repeated affirmations, or positive statements, that they hoped would beneficially affect their bodies. Some women drew these affirmations from biblical passages, while others practiced less scripted affirmations, like Suzanne who repeated the "negative affirmation" that she would not give birth on her back. Similarly, women practiced visualizations in which they imagined their baby in the womb, or their cervix opening, or their baby emerging. Several women, including Debra, an Orthodox Jew, and Nell, a United Methodist, engaged in various forms of "rebirthing," in which they would restage a previous child's birth or relive their own emergence from their mother's womb (as in the more "orthodox" version of rebirthing). Finally, several women across religious traditions spoke of the significance of past lives to their births and their ability to communicate with both fetuses and dead relatives.

A number of women from different traditions had read the same spiritually oriented literature. Many women read the classics of alternative-childbirth literature, such as Ina May Gaskin's *Spiritual Midwifery* and La Leche League's *Womanly Art of Breastfeeding*, which has its own subtly religious perspective. However, women read these books using very different lenses, as shown by Brenda Matthews, the Pentecostal, who was suspicious of "things not from Jesus," and Eva Hechtel, a 27-year-old, who thought *Spiritual Midwifery* was too "seventies" and "hippie-ish." Tina Hostetler, an Amish Mennonite woman (from a group positioned between the more culturally insular Amish and the more worldly Mennonites), and Stefanie Harter, a born-again Lutheran, both read a book of affirmations by Christian author Kenneth Copeland, which focused on the body working as God intended it.[35] A number of Christian Scientists and one Pentecostal woman, Janet Stein, endorsed a baby-rearing book, Gladys West Hendrick's *My First 300 Babies*, written by a Christian Science nurse.[36] The wide availability of childbirth books from a variety of perspectives has contributed greatly to the confluence of spiritualized understandings of birth, especially among highly educated middle-class home birthers.

But there is another important factor—the role of midwives—that explains the flexibility of home birth in terms of its ability to nurture a variety of spiritual discourses. Both scholars and midwives have described midwifery as a "spiritual vocation."[37] However, the certified nurse-midwives and direct-entry midwives with whom I spoke shied away from this designation. Instead, they felt largely that their role was not to impose a spiritual perspective on birth, but to be there to help with the birth, and to let a woman practice and interpret her spirituality as she saw fit.[38]

These midwives assented to an "explanatory model" of birth that did not see birth as an illness, but as a simultaneously physical, emotional, and spiritual event. In anthropologist Arthur Kleinman's terms, explanatory models of healing establish the degree of power a healer has over his or her patient. This power could be virtually total, meaning that the healer has absolute control over diagnosis and treatment, as well as privileged access to the knowledge and tools necessary to the healing process. Alternatively, the power of the healer could be more diffuse, involving the patient in both diagnosis and treatment.[39] To differing degrees, certified nurse-midwives and direct-entry midwives who attend home births assent to a more diffused model of power in which they act as knowledgeable consultants to a birthing woman. For the most part, they see themselves as purveyors of a holistic model of birth in which they have access to deep knowledge of childbirth from both alternative and biomedical perspectives. In such a model, a birthing woman ideally chooses how to use her decision-making power as she travels through pregnancy and childbirth, whether she gives power over to her midwives, contains it within herself, shares it with her partner, or assigns it to God. As such, midwives see the medical model, utilized to different degrees by different women, as only one part of the whole needed to achieve a successful pregnancy and birth.[40] A woman's emotional well-being, her personal relationships, and her connection to supernatural forces, however she designates them, are also considered key to establishing the best conditions in which to give birth to a baby.

In her work on religions dominated by women, anthropologist Susan Starr Sered has shown that healing in women's religions usually is based communally. The authority granted to the healer is not absolute, as "women are allowed space to negotiate explanations and cures that correspond to their own perceptions," and the medical model is turned to as one option among many.[41] The range of women turning to home birth (including and beyond the spiritual feminists Sered noted) suggests that approaches to questions of suffering that grant women agency, at least in childbirth, are employed by women who are part of male-dominated religions as well.[42]

Given the fluidity of power and interpretation within the explanatory model of the midwifery approach to birth, a midwife, though accepting of spiritual practices at birth, is not necessarily a competent interpreter of that spirituality. For example, at Marianne Martin's last home birth, she found herself leaning on her bureau in her bedroom as she tried to breathe through her difficult contractions. On her bureau were some small statues of her favorite saints. As the direct-entry midwives, who did not share Marianne's commitment to traditional Catholicism, watched her clutching her bureau and breathing, they thought she was praying to her saints. But, said Marianne, "I wasn't looking at them [the saints]. . . . I just needed something to hold onto." Marianne recalled that the midwife commented later that "it was a very spiritual labor, that I had broken through it spiritually. So that way they were very tolerant of it, even though I could sense that they were not into the religious vein. I was happy to have them. I was very happy to have them." Even though her actions had not been particularly religious at that point, Marianne did not feel the need to contradict their perspective but instead was simply grateful for her midwives' openness to the possibility that hers might have been a particularly spiritual birth. Marianne's story shows how the word "spiritual" can act as a bridge between people of very different religious perspectives, allowing each to respect and tolerate the other's actions, even if they did not understand them.

Though theological differences characterized this group of home-birthing women, their religious practices in relation to birth shared a kind of flexibility that rendered theological boundaries porous. Open to similar methods of preparing for birth, coping with pain, and welcoming a newborn baby, these women almost all agreed in their insistence that birth could be an empowering spiritual process, and that home birth was the best way to allow such spirituality to be manifested. Though their notions of what sort of power birth brings were not always in accord, they also all agreed that it was a woman's responsibility—not that of doctors, midwives, or politicians—to make her own educated choice about where to birth.

RETHINKING SPIRITUALITY

Given the flexibility of spirituality, and its close tie to personal choice, it is a term that requires further scrutiny. Accepting that contemporary North American spirituality is protean does not entail thinking of it as unconstructed—as somehow just "in the air." Instead, I share and reformulate anthropologist Talal Asad's question in his critique of the scholarly construction of religion as a category: "How does power create religion?"[43] For Asad, the concept of religion is the product of scholars who were part of a very particular colonial history. As they claimed to find texts and practices around the world that could be universally labeled "religious," they simultaneously defined and constructed religion in opposition to other spheres such as the state, law, and science.[44] The scholar of religion, then, needs to be self-aware of the baggage carried within the term itself, and to unpack the many different elements it conveys. Those elements, Asad suggested, can be found by paying specific attention to "the occurrence of events (utterances, practices, dispositions) and the authorizing processes that give those events meaning and embody that meaning in concrete institutions."[45] That is, to show what ways of speaking, acting, and feeling are considered religious, and what sorts of power, whether stemming from individuals or institutions, shape that consideration.

That many of the women in my study preferred the term spirituality to religion in the case of childbirth, and in many cases derided religion as superficial (even when they claimed religious affiliations themselves), does not mean that I simply accept their definition. As I showed earlier, the notion of spirituality in North America has its own history, as does that of religion. Remembering that "religion" is a constructed category used to value some kinds of activity and devalue others, I often use the term religion when describing these women's actions in my own voice, because I want to emphasize that home birth fits within what scholars have studied as religious practice. Repeatedly, in describing my research, I have had to answer the question posed by layperson and scholar alike, "What is religious about birth?" To some extent, in both academic and theological settings, the women's preferences of terms are inverted: religion is more "real" than spirituality, perhaps because it has a longer and more distinguished—though increasingly compromised—pedigree.[46] I often answer that persistent question by pointing to how women make birth religious by recourse both to traditional religious practices like prayer and Bible reading and to innovative religious practices like burying the placenta and visualizing the cervix as a flower. Women's own interpretations of their births as times when they came into contact with God, the Goddess, or a "power beyond" the human realm combine to make the practices of birth religious.[47]

My choosing to continue using the category of religion does not mean I abandon the use of spirituality. The category of spirituality, however, needs to be subject to the same question as that of religion: How does power create the complex of relations and dispositions that these women call spirituality? Though in many instances an explicitly extrainstitutional phenomenon, spirituality is no less "created" than religion. Spirituality may shape itself in reaction to institutions other than religious ones, including those of biomedicine, alternative therapies, and publishing. People interpret their spirituality within a social context shaped by religious and ethnic traditions, their life history, their experiences (or lack thereof) of sexism, racism, or economic oppression, and their fortune or misfortune in life. Choices rooted in "spirituality" then, while often understood as grounding themselves in the depths of one's being or in the mystery of the cosmos, are also grounded in much more material concerns.[48]

One reason I see for these women's preference for the definition of spirituality, beyond a wider cultural language in which spirituality reigns as more authentic than reified religion, is that Christian and Jewish traditions, in different ways, have not valued childbirth as a religious experience. Historically, these religions have even considered childbirth to be polluting. When traditional religions do attend to birth, they quickly move from the messy experience, or supplant the physical altogether with a metaphorical, theological, purified "new" birth of some kind.[49] The choice of spirituality in this context is a rejection of the authorizing powers that have deemed religion the realm in which one truly meets God, but have abandoned childbirth to superstition or, more recently, medicine.[50]

Since religious traditions, contemporary clergy, and medical professionals, generally speaking, have not been concerned with the transformative possibilities of birth for a woman, women have turned elsewhere to find ways to make religious sense of childbirth.[51] They draw from a range of sources—not all of which are explicitly religious—to create spirituality in the context of their births. As Susan Sered suggested in the context of her research on childbirth in Israeli hospitals, however, a deeply rooted conceptual conflict keeps women from naming what they consider to be a spiritual experience as "really" religious. Sered wrote: "Women whose religious lives are constructed within the context of a male-oriented culture that neither celebrates nor sacralizes women's bodies and concerns may lack the language (both verbal and ritual) to express that feeling."[52] In Sered's study, when the foreign territory of the hospital was added to the silences of religious tradition regarding female experience, even women who *wanted* birth to be a religious experience were stymied.[53]

These women create spirituality, then, in reference to religious traditions that they perceive to be ignorant of the diversity of ways in which the body can be the site for revelation or sacralization. Valued by devout Jews and Christians, as well as by those seeking more eclectic sources of the sacred, a North American sense of spirituality is formed in a society that esteems individual conviction of the divine and is fearful of "dead ritual," but also desires communal expression. In the case of home birth, women use declarations of the spirituality of childbirth to support their challenge to the medicalization of childbirth, and in some cases, their challenge to the state sanction of that medicalization. In so doing, they assert that naming a bodily act spiritual creates its power, not only for a woman's relationship to her community and the state but also for its potential transformation of her identity.

Passages into Motherhood

Birth is a passage that brings into being two new identities: a baby and a mother. These new identities are not simply "born" but are arrived at through social and cultural negotiations. As Nancy Scheper-Hughes has shown most movingly in her research on infant death in Brazil, neither the "miracle" of a baby's birth nor "mother love" are universally shared experiences, but are shaped by a "particular social world and historical reality."[54] Middle-class women who choose home birth in North America are making choices about their passage into motherhood under significantly different economic and social conditions than those of poor Brazilian women, but their understandings of the transformative power of birth are also culturally and religiously constructed. Giving birth to a baby does not necessarily make one a mother, but home-birthing women argue that childbirth can be a positive transformation that has a wide range of effects on a woman's self-understanding, as well as on her relationships with her children, her husband, and her wider society.[55] To bring together this sense of transformation with my discussion of birth as religious practice,

I now turn to two questions: how did women use the notion of ritual to understand their experiences of birth, and what sort of transformations do the rituals of birth invite?

Ritualizing Birth

Several women used the term "rite of passage" when describing the significance of childbirth to their lives. Like spirituality, the phrase rite of passage has gained currency in popular parlance to describe a sometimes vaguely religious but nevertheless important change in someone's life. The classic formulation of rites of passage comes from French folklorist Arnold Van Gennep. In 1908, he designated "rites of passage" as those rituals that help a person cross from one social category to another—for example, from young woman to mother—while also trying to reduce the harmful effects to both individual and society of such change.[56] According to Van Gennep, pregnancy and childbirth are two significant rites of passage that widely exemplify the cross-cultural pattern of ritual stages he called "separation," "transition," and "incorporation."[57] For him, "separation" denotes being set apart in some way from the community, "transition" suggests a state of "liminality" or being in between two social categories, and "incorporation" refers to the act of rejoining the community in one's new identity.

Feminist scholars have forcefully critiqued the universality and androcentrism of Van Gennep's tripartite division, especially as anthropologist Victor Turner adapted it. In particular, Carolyn Walker Bynum has suggested that in the case of medieval Christian women, *continuity*, not separation or reversal, was the central image of women's life stories.[58] Similarly, as my discussion of pain and relationship will show, for many women home birth was a ritual of *intensification*, not reversal, of their social position as mothers and lovers. For many women, giving birth simultaneously transformed and underscored those positions. Enacted within the space where most of their mothering happened, home birth was not separation from these women's social worlds, but a move deeper into the center of both the home and the body.[59] Despite these significant critiques, Van Gennep's recognition that rites of passage point to social, not physiological, changes remains an important contribution. Specifically in terms of childbirth, he stated that "social parenthood" is different from "physical parenthood"; with each child she bears a woman becomes a mother in a new and socially constructed way.[60]

In addition to Van Gennep's category "rite of passage" and his insights into how such rites make our social worlds, I also want to borrow his notion of the "pivoting sacred." The sacred was not a stable category for Van Gennep. Instead, he claimed that people are sacred or profane relative to their situation; for example, a woman is differentially sacred depending on whether she is pregnant, menstruating, or in the company of older men or women relatives.[61] Van Gennep's understanding that the sacred is not absolute but relational is a powerful tool in understanding the shifting of categories that can occur in rites of passage. Employing the term sacred, however, can lead to just as many problems as when using the terms religion and spirituality. For my purposes, the sacred means those things, people, or events that are considered to be set apart and infused with either positive or negative symbolic power. This set apartness can occur in the midst of everyday life, or in more rarefied settings like a synagogue or church, or even a hospital. By emphasizing the pivoting sacred, I am underscoring the power relations inherent in classifying something as sacred, as well as the shifting nature of such classifications.

Anthropologist Robbie Davis-Floyd, in a book focused on hospital birth, utilized theories of rites of passage to analyze the transformation of birth in the United States in the twentieth century. Davis-Floyd argued that childbirth has become a "male-dominated initiatory rite of passage through which birthing women are taught about the superiority, the necessity, and the 'essential' nature of the relationship between science, technology, patriarchy, and institutions."[62] In her analysis, medicine has claimed the traditional role of religion in its ritualizing of birth, while trying to avoid "*looking* ritualistic at all."[63] But through a detailed description and analysis of the procedures of hospital birth, Davis-Floyd convincingly showed its highly ritualized character. Furthermore, she established that the "birth messages" of technocratic birth perpetuate "our profound cultural belief in the innate inferiority of women to the men who more perfectly mirror our cultural image of the properly functioning machine."[64] In technocratic models of birth, according to Davis-Floyd, the sacred lies in the doctor and his or her ability to manipulate technology; that is, to achieve "our shared cultural dream of transcendence through technology."[65]

The usurpation of women's childbearing powers by men (for the most part) in technocratic birth has a discomfiting parallel in Nancy Jay's convincing analysis of blood sacrifice in preindustrialized societies. Jay argued that in these societies, "sacrifice remedies having-been-born-of-woman, establishing bonds of intergenerational continuity between males that transcend their absolute dependence on childbearing women."[66] The practitioners of the rituals of technocratic birth, however, do not merely transcend the childbearing woman in making her baby "society's product."[67] They also make her body the very grounds of their transcendence. The birthing woman is not literally sacrificed (generally speaking), but her power to give birth is obfuscated if not appropriated, and is transferred to the doctor to become his or her salvific expertise.

Where, then, does the sacred pivot in the rite of passage that is home birth? As the variety of women's attitudes to their bodies and to their gods showed, some women housed the sacred in an external agency, that of God, Jesus, Mind, or Goddess, while others assumed a more interior sacralization of their own bodies. This latter sacralization was not so much self-focused as it was body-focused in its valuing of the bodily processes of birth thought to be common to all women. The temporary separation of self and body that many women said they effected in the "surrender" of birth is not the same as the often criticized Western dualism between mind and body. For one thing, the body is valued, not denigrated, in this separation. In addition, these women felt they had achieved something great with their bodies: their bodies at once symbolized their own power and that of a wider, perhaps universal force, be it of a deity or of "nature."

To illustrate the relationships among power, the sacred, and ritual, I turn to a woman who felt that ritual and religion were not particularly important to her birth. Eva Hechtel, 27, was particularly clear that her first birth, in a birth center, was not a religious experience, but was spiritual, because she was "in tune to myself and how my body was working." For Eva, a "disillusioned" Catholic who considered religion a "nonissue" in her life, spirituality surfaced when she felt the power to allow her body to do the work of birth. In her words, "I was so successful at birthing because I believed that I had all the power. So I was in tune with what my body was doing; I just could go with the flow." I spoke with Eva before and after her second birth, which took place at home with a certified nurse-midwife. Her home birth confirmed even more intensely her sense that her body could be the site of a spiritual event.

In a written narrative of her home birth, Eva described the moment of birth, when her midwife suggested to her that she catch her own baby: "[T]he next thing I know I'm pushing the little one out into my *own* hands; what utter exhilaration! I lifted him up onto my chest and felt his warm little body curl up in his mamma's arms. . . . The next few moments after the birth were full of exhilaration on my part for this wonderful birth to have produced such a beautiful healthy baby and excitement for [my older son and sister] to have shared in such a miraculous experience. . . ." In using the language of miracle, Eva extended the power in her birth not only to her midwife and her self, but to a broader agency that somewhat mysteriously allowed all these forces to come together.[68]

Eva's disinterest in religion, and her parallel disinterest in ritual, at least in terms of her birth, did not keep her from instilling her births with spiritual and miraculous meanings. In this way, she was in accord with Wiccan feminist Starhawk, who asserted that "birth itself is such a powerful experience that it doesn't seem to require a lot of ritual . . . when it's happening—it just takes over, creating its own ritual."[69] Speaking of birth as spiritual and miraculous while professing to be nonreligious, Eva grappled for a language of difference capable of showing that birth is more than an everyday occurrence, even if it is not quite a religious one. Suzanne Donato, though more overtly religious than Eva in that she is still a practicing Catholic, also spoke of the miracle of birth: "You could say that [it] was spiritual because I was just—it was miraculous. It was like a miracle; it still is. I think about the first moment that I saw each of [my babies] and I'm overwhelmed. . . . My body made this human being. And like, you know, I could do it, obviously God made my body so that I could do that." For both women, speaking of miracles allowed them to convey the enduring incomprehensibilities of the process of birth. They granted agency both to a broader power and to themselves, or more accurately, their bodies. In Talal Asad's terms, the power that created religion in the context of their births was both within them and without.

Despite Starhawk's evocation of a "naturally occurring" version of ritual, Robbie Davis-Floyd's analysis of hospital birth showed that birth is ritualized no matter where it takes place, partly because certain kinds of relationships, be they with a doctor, a midwife, or a husband, value certain kinds of actions and knowledge. Though the rituals of Eva's home birth may have been less formalized than those of the hospital or of other home-birthing women, her midwife's actions (including bringing a large bunch of daffodils to the birth) were already rooted in a pattern of relationship that Eva had formed with her. This pattern was partly based on Eva's ideal belief that "you need to love the woman" who helps you give birth to your child.[70]

Birth is an uncertain process that more often than not prompts people to surround it with rituals, be they medical, religious, or folkloric. Those who choose to give birth at home believe that the rituals encompassing birth can be less technical and time-bound than they are in hospitals; or with Starhawk, they believe that there is no ritual to home birth except that which birth creates on its own. While the word they turn to in describing this looser form of ritual is most often "natural," their births are still ritualized, if only in opposition to the rituals of the hospital.[71]

The difference between birth as a rite of passage at home and at the hospital lies predominantly in where the power flows—where the sacred pivots. Women who had experienced both kinds of births felt the answer was clear: at the hospital the power flowed through the doctor; at home the power flowed through the birthing woman. Where the power originates—God, nature, the woman herself—was often less clear. During Joanna Katz's first two hospital births, she "felt just like a little girl being told what to do. . . . And I hated that feeling. That's not a feminist feeling.

That is a horrible feeling of being just nothing, like this useless nothing."
The lack of power she felt spurred her to investigate midwifery care, and
transformed her last birth experience: "That was one of the things that
was so wonderful about going to the midwife to begin with. I felt like a
human being, I felt like a person. I didn't feel like a nothing." In large
part, Joanna described the power she felt as stemming from different styles
of relationship in her birth care, both with her midwife and with family,
and from claiming her home as a safe space in which to give birth. Joanna
asserted that birthing at home brought power back to her that she rightly
deserved and allowed her to infuse her home and family relationships with
new kinds of religious meaning.[72]

For Joanna, home birth set her on a path of conscious ritual innovation
that led her to call a mohel (one who usually performs circumcisions for
Jewish boy babies) to her home to name her newest daughter—an innovation I discuss further in the next chapter. For Eva, the ritual in birth was
more spontaneous and informal.[73] Even for women like Eva, for whom
ritual is not usually a central part of their interpretation of birth, some
common features of what religion scholar Catherine Bell calls "ritualization" help a woman to understand the activity—the performance—of
home birth. For Bell, ritualization is characterized by "strategies of differentiation through formalization and periodicity, the centrality of the body,
the orchestration of schemes by which the body defines an environment
and is defined in turn by it, ritual mastery, and the negotiation of power
to define and appropriate the hegemonic order." In offering ritualization
as a family of activities, Bell sought to show that ritual was not simply
"natural."[74]

Though Bell's notion of ritualization may be so broad that everything
(and nothing) could be considered ritual, the characteristics she isolates
are helpful for considering how such a malleable experience as home birth
becomes ritualized. For example, home-birth advocates reject the formalization and periodicity—the rules and timing—of hospital birth and assert
that there are diverse ways and paces of birth.[75] The centrality of the body
in home birth is (almost unavoidably) apparent in the faith women and
their midwives have that the body was designed to be capable of birth.
Through birthing at home, a woman defines her environment as a place
of safety and well-being, which in turn designates and shapes her body as
such.[76] Ritual mastery, though for most contemporary birthing women
not achieved through repetition (i.e., birthing frequently), is part of their
experience as a form of "embodied knowing"; that is, they are good at
birth because they listen to their bodies.[77] Finally, home birth is a negotiation of power in quite explicit ways, as women seek to subvert the "hegemonic order" of birthing customs in the United States and to claim for
themselves a power stemming from birth.

In outlining her notion of ritualization, Bell also stressed that ritual is a "flexible strategy" that calls forth both "consent and resistance" as a socially performed act of differentiation—in the case of home birth, an act performed in contrast to another, dominant way of giving birth.[78] The lines between consent and resistance are not always clear, however, and often remain unarticulated or "misrecognized"—lodged in the body.[79] Any act of ritualization carries within it the potential to transform relations of power and to re-embed them in new ways. The ritualization of home birth reclaims a variety of forms of power for birthing women, some that allow women to claim their births were feminist acts, others that allow them to assert they were thwarting the power of "secular medicine" but submitting to the headship of their husbands. Home birth affords flexibility in its ritualization, while leaving "echoes in the body" of pain, power, and creation.[80]

Passages and Transformations

If home birth is a rite of passage, what sorts of social transformations does it entail? The kinds of mothers that home birth brings forth are many. Obviously, where and how a woman gives birth is not the only thing that shapes how she will mother her children, but many women made a distinct connection between their birthing and their mothering. Many women also made a link between birth and shifts in their religious identity. While some scholars of the life cycle would argue that such shifts are rooted in a pervasive pattern of parents turning to religion when confronted with educating their children, others might see this shift as part of a generational turn based in particular historical conditions of the baby-boom generation.[81] In the case of these home-birthing women, both the historical generation of which they are a part—a generation permeated by feminist perspectives and consumer activism—and the challenges that the parenting of children raises across generations have merged to make birth a significant event in many of these women's religious lives.

While about a quarter of the women concurred with the opinion that the prospect of raising children spurred them to reconsider their religious lives and sometimes prompted them to join a church or a synagogue, many of them saw birth itself, not just parenting, as a catalyst to religious inquiry. Furthermore, it was not birth in general, but often their different experiences of second or third (or more) births that prompted their religious transformation. In this way, since home birth is often a second or third birth, it complicates life-cycle theories that consider lives to be led in straight lines and in discrete stages. Within a particular life-cycle stage there is considerable diversity of women's experiences.[82] Some women have very different experiences during different births, and some women never experience childbirth at all.

Several women felt that the decisions and physical processes entailed in home birth transformed them from passivity to assertiveness, and that such a transition was tied to a new religious awareness. As Janice Pulaski phrased it, "I definitely believe that you get in touch with a higher power [when] giving birth. You go to . . . a higher place in your mind. I also feel like there's a whole new thinking that emerges once you've given birth." Janice continued in an animated voice, "You feel like, don't mess with me now, I'm a mother. I used to always be more of a kind of let-people-walk-all-over-me type—'Okay, if it makes you happy go ahead'—because I'm not a fighter-type person. Now [I think], don't mess with me! There's just a difference there. I'm more apt to say, 'No, I don't go with that idea, and I don't like it.'" Though Janice was disappointed that she ended up in the hospital after a long first labor, this outcome did not take away her new-found assertiveness.

Alison Lindt-Marliss felt that giving birth granted her a new spiritual connection "to other women, a connection to what was within me, and what is beyond." She continued by warning that if in the hospital "you take that away, that's a woman's power, that's where she gets her strength. I've gained a lot of self-confidence from that—wow, I did this—it's not an egotistical feeling either, it's just a very powerful feeling, and I think women are being robbed of it." Meg Alexander, 37, and mother of two, concurred with Alison's opinion that obstetrician-attended hospital births are less likely than home births to be empowering experiences, having experienced both. Describing her home birth, Meg described her sense of empowerment with the language of spirituality:

> I saw it, I felt it, I experienced a spirit-type thing moving through me, changing my perceptions of things with seeing the purple, hearing the noises [in a] funny [way]. I know it's probably physical . . . your body going through physical changes, but something was making that happen. My body was being altered so that it could work with something that was greater than it. That's why, I think, that if women [are medicated] . . . most women who have births that are really medicated . . . I'd be interested to find out how many of them do find it something spiritual. The women that don't want to go through labor and don't want to experience the pain . . . they don't have a spiritual experience.

Although Meg's assertion is no doubt exaggerated, as some women I spoke with did find their previous medicated hospital births to be "spiritual," Susan Sered's research on childbirth in an Israeli hospital lends some credence to Meg's view. Sered found that even self-consciously religious women who "intended to draw upon religious rituals and symbols during the birth . . . felt the hospital atmosphere was a deterrent."[83] Sered attributed this in part to the fact that the hospital is not a woman's own territory, contrary to the home, where "women feel far more empowered to care for their babies, both in the physical and the spiritual realms."[84] Without the eyes of "experts" watching their mothering, the women felt much more competent. Women's disempowerment in the hospital setting is doubled when considered together with Sered's analysis of the conceptual conflict that keeps women in male-dominated religious traditions from seeing their lives and actions as "religious." That is, both religious institutions and medical institutions can belittle women's abilities as mothers and meaning-makers.

In the United States, the "natural childbirth" movement has permeated women's consciousness about childbirth more fully than in other countries, whether or not American women practice it.[85] Alternative philosophies of childbirth found in both home and hospital offer a discourse that values women's bodies and sees birth as a potentially empowering act, and these philosophies have infiltrated biomedical discourse to varying levels of effectiveness. Women of all varieties of religions, both male- and female-dominated, have drawn on this discourse to assert their own worth and power. Combining the celebration of women's abilities with moving birth into the home has led women to become ritual innovators and theological contemplatives who are very tangibly "creat[ing] religion."[86]

The celebration of the body does not always result in empowerment, however. Olivia Eldrich, 37, felt that her experiences of birth, though largely positive, did not significantly change her disposition. Olivia was the only woman who felt that home birth could have transformed her submissive character, but did not, because she refused the opportunity.

> Any time a woman gives birth, she can realize what the truth is about being a woman, being a human being, being a part of the life cycle. But, no, I chose time and time again to shut the door to my abilities, and my talents, and I chose to remain submissive, and to take a lot of stuff that was thrown at me. Home birth gave me inner strength, but not enough at the time. I wasn't ready anyway. I hadn't had enough experiences I suppose, outside of doing that. But for now, choosing to do that, I realize it was a great choice. If I had ended up in a hospital, I wouldn't have had that experience, for my own self-esteem, number one, and also just the experience alone, was wonderful.

Home birth, then, is not an unfailing tool for consciousness-raising. Just to start, the social and emotional contexts of a woman's giving birth may or may not encourage her to set her experience of birth in a wider frame of empowerment. Though the "truth about being a woman" does not comprise only one version, Olivia's phrase evoked a common perception among many home-birthing women that the process of birth can tap into deeper meanings within the body, be they religious, political, or both.

One woman who most dramatically showed the transformation that giving birth can effect in a woman's religious life was Debra Lensky. Debra's narrative of her "life cycle" began with her terrifying discovery of her first menstrual period and her equally frightening difficulties in learning how to insert tampons: "I was just crying and crying and crying. I ran out of the bathroom saying, 'I'm not a woman. This is not right. There's something wrong with me!'" Debra repeatedly grappled with what she called the "woman issue," especially since from her childhood she had a strong sense that boys were more valued than girls. When she decided to forgo her career as an accountant after her first child was born, she found herself asking, "Who am I? What am I? Do I have to be home in order to take care of babies? And that's my value? That's my *whole* value? Nobody cares about me doing this kind of thing."

She recounted that only when she had her first home birth, after a cesarean and a vaginal birth after cesarean (VBAC) in the hospital, did her anguish begin to abate. With her third birth, Debra feared she was carrying a girl, when she wanted another boy. Given her very conflicted attitude to being a woman, Debra said, "The thought of carrying a girl inside of me was very, very strange. I couldn't eat, I just could not take care of myself." She did end up giving birth to a daughter and feeling shocked, with a "sense that something major was going to happen in my life, you know, an awareness of something. . . . That was like the finishing touches of really coming to grips with being a woman." As Debra became involved as a childbirth educator, she felt a religious shift in her life. What first was trust in "nature," learned in her birth classes, became trust in God: "As you start to live in trust and you start to live with truths, you begin to— you start to seek for a greater meaning in the world. So the three of them add up together, and you come to God basically."

Giving birth to a girl at home, and becoming aware of the power of childbirth, were catalysts in Debra's and her husband's transition to Orthodox Judaism, in Debra's view:

> The transition had to do with . . . coming to an understanding of who I am and what I am, and that first part of it was recognizing the woman inside of me. And I remember one day saying to myself, "Hah! Now you understand that you're a woman and you're delighted and you appreciate what it is to be a woman. Now you need to find out what it's like to be a Jew, that you're truly a Jew and that you need to understand that and start living that also." And so it's really, for me; it was through childbirth that I was able to take those steps and become myself first as a woman, and then [to find] my connection to God. And my connection to God, as I was given it in this world at this time in this life, was

that I was born a Jew, so I had to find my connection through Judaism. . . . That's how it was, so it was a road, it was a real road, but the basis of that road was trust in the design. And the basis came from childbirth, and the basis is childbirth.

The design Debra trusted in was that of God. She came to terms with being a woman by finding divine justification for the differential treatment of women; not by challenging it, but by reinterpreting and embracing it.[87]

Not all women, however, thought the power unleashed in childbirth needed to be channeled through a woman's role as wife and mother. For Christian Scientist Heather Monroe, now a single mother, giving birth at home allowed her to feel a type of power that had broader significance: "I feel like I went through that experience [of birth] with a sense of dominion, and expressing dominion in any part of one's life is, I think, a spiritual activity." The "dominion" she felt in her birth then remained with her as a particular insight to draw on in other situations. The significance of birth to her life lay both in its difference from any other experience and its parallels to wider religious concepts:

> The experience itself is so different from anything you ever experience except when you're having birth, so in that respect, I think, it's a spiritual experience, just as any other rites of passage. . . . Which isn't something that I generally think about in a religious context, in the religion that I am [part of]. But, I think it is, because it has so many—the whole concept of birth has so many spiritual parallels—the birth of an idea, the whole sense of bringing forth that which was already present. And so, I guess experiencing it in one's life is a way of having something to relate those concepts to. So in that way, it's an experience that you never forget. . . . [It's] spiritual and significant . . . because of the feelings that you have, the lessons that you learn, the insights in relation to the experience.

The power that lies within the passage from pregnant woman to birth giver can be limned and incarnated in a myriad of ways. Above all else, birth can make a woman into a mother, help her find her "don't-mess-with-me" voice, or give her insights that she can take into other realms of work and life. A woman's sense of embodiment, religious identity, marital relationship, and work are all part of shaping what sorts of traditions she draws from and reinterprets in birth, and what sorts of lessons she learns in the process.

Religion and Home Birth

Home birth is not a private act, although it occurs in a "private" place. It is an act shaped by legal regulation and medical procedures as well as by a woman's choices, be they religiously, politically, or personally motivated.

Given the activism it often provokes, it is an intimate event with public consequences. Even without instigating direct activism, many women considered home birth a communal act, in that it shapes the world by bringing human beings into the world "without violence." Historian Nancy Cott has argued that in the nineteenth century, women and clergy rested their belief in women's transformative powers as mothers in a "faith in the malleability of the infant character."[88] Present-day home-birth advocates consider that malleability to begin in birth itself, if not pregnancy.[89]

Contemporary clergy, however, generally have not been concerned with such transformative possibilities, most likely because of their acceptance of birth as a medical procedure. Though these homebirthing womens's religious traditions often do not value the rites of passage that are central to their lives as they become mothers, they still find religious and spiritual meaning to instill within these rites.[90] The spirituality that these women evoked should not be disdained as narcissistic "sheilaism" that begins and ends with the woman as individual.[91] Though the actions prompted by the religiosity of birth may not be social in the same way as going to church or working in a soup kitchen, women see the birthing, mothering, and activism emerging from their childbirth choices as directly improving the lives of women, babies, and families. Home birth often creates new social networks, as women consider others who have given birth at home to be sympathetic and like-minded people.

Interpreting these women's religious lives with equanimity, however, should not lead to a romanticization of birth, spirituality, or women. All parts of this trio are socially located in particular histories—none come to us in a "natural" form—and lying beneath layers of artifice, be they medical, religious, or gendered. Instead, in choosing to birth at home and interpret their actions with religious lenses, these women are creating religion in ways that are transforming their personal identities, the birth process in the contemporary United States, and, in some cases, their religious traditions. That they are doing so from radically different political and religious perspectives is paralleled by examples of women's religious inclinations in other areas. For example, religion scholar Marie Griffith, in her study of the evangelical women's prayer group Women's Aglow, argued that despite the vitriolic rhetoric that passes between feminists and conservative Christian women, these two female cultures are "overlapping" in some important respects. Most importantly for my consideration of home birth, she writes: "One shared premise is that the social and cultural tasks, traits, and affinities traditionally coded as 'female' or 'feminine' ought to be accorded greater respect and value than they have been."[92] That a revaluing of women's ability to give birth has come from both traditionalist and feminist women should perhaps give us pause in the way we use those altogether inadequate and polarizing labels of conservative/liberal or traditionalist/feminist. What may seem like a strange confluence of divergent religious values and political dispositions is in fact a characteristic of women's spirituality as an observed phenomenon, which the starkly gendered character of birth brings into sharp relief.

Women's religious lives in a diversity of settings seem consistently woven through with the concerns of generativity, relationship, and healing, with maternity as a very common symbolic resource.[93] Perhaps these strange confluences, or what in the home-birth movement become strange alliances, only seem odd when viewed from the symbolic and material terrain of androcentric institutions. What is strange is itself constructed within a particular grid of power. Representatives of Christianity, Judaism, and the American Medical Association have all, in their own ways, downplayed or subverted the potential symbolic power within maternity. Home-birthing women, along with many other North American women, are building new frames for understanding the meanings of childbirth—reinterpreting home, the body, and the pain of birth—using the materials at hand, be they religious, spiritual, or otherwise symbolic. I turn now to more particular analyses of how these home-birthing women are accomplishing such meaning-making, beginning with an inquiry into the significance of "home" in the practice of home birth.

5

A Sense of Place: Meanings of Home

DESCRIBING THE BIRTH of her fourth child, Joanna Katz affirmed: "She was a home baby. She was born in our midst, in a loving way, in a very caring way, with people that we love." Joanna, like other women who have given birth at home, insisted that place matters. Her insistence runs counter to the portrayal of a world shrunken by electronic media such as television and the Internet, which substitute social and spatial boundaries with homogenous, "placeless" spaces.[1] Home-birthing women are acutely aware of how place shapes a woman's experience of birth. Squeezing into a car in the midst of labor to rush to a hospital, a foreign environment peopled with strangers (some of whom are very ill), is not their picture of an ideal way to give birth. Instead, they assert that place has the power to shape a woman's bodily, emotional, and even religious responses to childbirth. For them, home space best nurtures an indispensable, keenly felt, sense of place.

Home is an overwhelmingly rich symbol especially interlaced with re-membered and imagined mothers, as scholars ranging from Robert Orsi to Gaston Bachelard have noted.[2] For actual mothers, the simultaneous denigration and celebration of domesticity common in Western societies has meant that the symbolism of home has been a source of both strength and constraint.[3] The women I spoke with embedded the home with mean-ing, both as a physical space and as a metaphorical concept. For these actual mothers, the physical and metaphorical meanings of home intertwined to make the home a place to encounter sacredness in its many forms. Cultivat-ing the home as a sacred space is an activity common to many religiously inclined women, as they transform "profane" domestic spaces by making use of "commonplace" concerns, experiences, and things.[4] For many home-birthing women, the intimate and messy bodily experience of birth at least temporarily transformed their home space into a charged, even sacred realm.

In the midst of positive declarations of the importance of home, its meanings often emerged in converse relation to that which was "not home." Viewing their homes as places of safety, women positioned their domestic spaces in contrast to the outside world, or more specifically in the case of birth, the hospital. In this chapter I discuss how home-birthing women construct these many-faceted meanings of home in distinction and relation to two institutions: one, the hospital, and two, the church or synagogue. While women most commonly referred to the hospital in negative terms, they spoke of religious institutions, as places and traditions, in both rejecting and accepting ways. In different ways, both the hospital and the religious institution acted as foils for asserting these women's preference for the home as the site of birth.

The "discourses of domesticity" involved in this construction of the home inevitably arise from or respond to feminist concerns in some way, given the strength and ubiquity of feminist critiques of the home in North America. From questioning who does the housework to naming and decrying domestic assault, feminists have ensured that the home is now widely acknowledged as a political site—a site of power. Just how home-birthing women have worked with this insight is what I interrogate here. I do this by asking what meanings they impute to the hospital and holy places, and by asking how they relate to discourses of domesticity—both feminist and not—that have shaped North American home life over the past century. First, I devote some attention to drawing a broad picture of the physical spaces of home that I visited in the course of meeting these women.

Pictures of Home

As physical spaces, the homes I visited in the course of my interviews were spread out over two states. I drove along highways flanked by legions of slate-gray houses arranged in neat suburban rows and turned onto back roads that carried me past white clapboard churches, llama farms, and flea markets. As I drove, the reality of a midwife's life became clear to me: attending home births means a lot of driving. Some of the women I visited lived in rural settings, in old farmhouses with wood stoves, or in newer custom-built homes (often also with wood stoves). Most of them lived in small towns or in suburbs, in single-family homes; a few lived in apartments.

When I asked women what their homes meant to them, I was struck by how so many quickly exclaimed, "Everything!" Most women felt their family was their home—the relationships contained within the physical building were more important than the walls themselves. While this understanding of home is no doubt sincere, the downplaying of the importance of physical setting is probably easier when one has a comfortable space in which to live. This said, the range of "comfort" that these women spanned was great. At one end, Brenda Matthews, a Pentecostal woman who administered her husband's home chiropractic clinic, lived in a palatial, newly built home set back from the road along a winding drive, hidden behind trees. At the other end, Wendy Pearson, a stay-at-home mother married to an electrician, lived with her family in a narrow, rented semidetached house on a wide, busy street. She curtained off the kitchen and back room in the winter to keep these rooms unheated, in an effort to save money.

The stuff of middle-class family life when young children are around— lots of toys, some pets, and scattered books—usually filled the living rooms, dens, and kitchens I visited. The few women who now had only older children, like Brenda, seemed to live in more orderly spaces adorned with white rugs, dried flower arrangements, and little clutter. Especially when my young daughter came along, I had been keenly aware of our surroundings, watching for what havoc a crawling baby could cause in each setting. The women I spoke to most often suggested the living room as a comfortable place to settle, where children could play while we talked.

Being in these women's homes while asking them about their home births lent a particular tangibility to our conversations. Not only would they describe their birthing labors to me, but they would also point to the chair that they had leaned on during a contraction, or the place on the floor where they had birthed their babies. A few women even took me on tours of the house to show me the place of birth, which most often was the bedroom. That so many of the women gave birth in the bedroom holds meaning in itself. The bedroom, in its idealized role as a place of rest, lovemaking, and intimacy, is cast in a cycle of continuity: where the baby was conceived, so shall she or he be born (though some women chose to give birth in the living room for this same reason).

For some women the bed itself held meaning. As one woman who birthed on her grandmother's bed mused, "I think it's really beautiful that we can continue the cycle, and maybe [my daughter] can take that bed with her and have her babies in it." The artifacts of home birth— beds, clothing, rugs, and chairs—recalled memories of particular births, and sometimes even prompted remembrances of ancestors. Objects not only provoked recollections, but also became an extension of embodied memory, housing particular moments in their texture or shape. Many women spoke of how, as they go about their daily lives, their surroundings remind them of their birthing experiences, prompting them to tell their birth stories to their children. In addition to delighting their children (who seem always to love hearing about their beginnings), these stories lend a sense of "set-apartness," or sacrality, to the artifacts of birth. But this sacrality is simultaneously deeply quotidian, as often the same rug on which a child was born is the rug on which he lies while he draws a picture. Having the artifacts of birth occupy the space of daily life prompts stories and memories that bring birth into the flow of the everyday world, making birth at once "normal" and "sacred" in the family's life. These artifacts, while steeped in the everyday sacred, were therefore not likely to be open to profanation. Spilling milk on the rug, while messy, was not a cause for spiritual distress.

Despite the importance of their material surroundings, home, as several women described it, was not necessarily restricted to the physical environment in which they lived. Half of the women had moved several times, whether due to job losses, transfers, or growing families. A few women's earlier home births had been at the homes of their parents or parents-in-law. Others had birthed in interim apartments or in housing affiliated with an institution, such as a Christian Science nursing home. For most of the women, home meant a place where they felt at ease to be themselves. In the case of birth, for all of these women being herself—whatever shape that took—required being at home, not the hospital.

The Home versus the Hospital

While the home gains significance in distinction to the general "outside world," perhaps its most salient meaning in regard to home birth arises from a contrast with the hospital. The majority of women agreed that the hospital was a place for sick people, not for pregnant women with uncomplicated births. A smaller number felt that the hospital was a place enmeshed in a system of economic inequality and corporate greed, unlike the home where different ethics, based on love and mutual support, ideally reigned. A very few, from surprisingly diverse perspectives, saw the hospital as a place where Satan prevails; but while some of these women referred to a somewhat metaphorical devil, for others his evil presence was much more real.

Childbirth Is Not an Illness

Women commonly asserted that the hospital is not the place for birth because childbirth is not an illness. Most of the women were careful not to seem like "hospital bashers" or "technophobes."[5] They aimed their critique primarily at maternity wards and the practices of obstetricians, leaving the work of the rest of the hospital without comment. About one-third of the women had given birth in a hospital prior to their home birth, and they said that it was this often negative experience that had led them to seek an alternative.[6] Two of the women had worked as labor and delivery nurses, and they commented that what they had witnessed in their jobs prompted them to choose midwifery care.

Other types of hospital experiences, whether due to their own illnesses or that of family members, were the triggers that led some women to question whether the hospital was the best place for birth. For Tessa Welland, 34, having her baby in a hospital never seemed a possibility, since while growing up she had spent long hours in hospital rooms with her terminally ill father. Tessa's house sat on a large lot, tucked away in a quiet, wooded, hilly corner of the state. She welcomed my daughter and me into her spacious bungalow by quickly vacuuming the dog hairs off her toy-strewn rug. We sat on the floor between the wood stove and the birdcage, while my daughter played and the dog and Tessa's 4-year-old daughter came in and out. Once settled, Tessa told me of her belief that the home is the "optimal place" for birth, not just for the sake of the baby but for the whole family. Consequently, although her first baby had been born in a birthing center with certified nurse-midwives, her last three had been born at home with direct-entry midwives.

Perhaps Tessa's memories of her mother's hospitalizations during child-birth had more influence over her choice than even her memories of her father's death in the hospital. Tessa was the fifth of seven children, the last two of whom had died at birth or soon after. Tessa recalled loving her mother's pregnancies, and being distressed when the babies died. She re-membered her visits to her mother in the hospital: "They wouldn't allow children into the hospital at that point, so we'd walk around the hospital and wave up to her on the third floor. So it was sort of very alienated, which is probably another reason that when I became pregnant myself there was no way I wanted to associate [with that]." For 5-year-old Tessa, the message of her mother's births was: "Babies born in the hospital died."

Tessa knew that the majority of birthing women and their doctors have not shared her conviction that home is the optimal place for birth. In the wider society, the hospital is seen as the safe place for birth, and people who choose home birth are often characterized as dangerous and irresponsible parents. For example, in an official publication, a former executive director of the American College of Obstetricians and Gynecologists went so far as to call home birth a form of "child abuse."[7] A 1995 *New York Times* article quotes Stanley K. Peck, director of medical quality assurance in Connecticut's Department of Public Health, who used similarly alarming language in asserting that women had no right to a home birth with a direct-entry midwife "any more than they have a right to have brain sur-gery at home."[8] Equating the process of birth with brain surgery, Peck endorsed the medical view of birth as a surgical intervention into a wom-an's pathological body, a view much criticized by home-birth activists.[9]

The contrary view of home-birth advocates considers the vast majority of births to be "natural" physiological processes, requiring support but little intervention. These advocates offer multiple arguments to demon-strate the safety of the home as a place of birth, including tacitly religious arguments about purity and pollution.[10] For example, they argue that being born into the home where one's family eats, sleeps, and bathes is actually safer than making one's entry into the world in a hospital, where the illnesses and germs can overcome the "sterile field" of the actual delivery. Kathy Martinelli, 34, and Euro-American, used this argument in convincing her "very clean" mother of the merits of home birth. Kathy, a tall, unpretentious, special-education teacher, gave birth at home to her first baby at 33. When her mother (who herself had been born at home) objected to home birth on the grounds that it was not sanitary, Kathy told her: "What it comes down to is you live in your own germs, your body gets used to them, and so will your baby." She went on to say: "And where you pick up most of your germs and viruses, and all this, is around sick people in the hospital!" Her mother was not entirely convinced, Kathy felt, until she witnessed Kathy's own home birth, and saw her healthy new grandson. Purity, in the view Kathy represents, is found not in the sanitary procedures of the hospital, but in the familiarity of the home.

Much of the discussion of purity and pollution from within home-birth circles responds to medical portrayals of the home as a source of contagion. Since the rise of obstetrics, doctors have used the language of purity and pollution in trying to establish the dangers of midwives and the risks of home birth. One Mississippi doctor argued in 1926, in a statement liberally laced with sexism, racism, and antireligious rhetoric, that African-American midwives were "filthy and ignorant and not far removed from the jungles of Africa, with its atmosphere of weird superstition and voodooism."[11] More recently, some obstetricians have drawn stereotypical portraits of the unhygienic, untrained midwife working in the dangerous conditions of the home.[12]

In contrast to the depictions of the home as a place of pollution and danger, Robbie Davis-Floyd cites many studies that have indicated "that there is no case to be made for the greater safety of hospital birth over planned, midwife-attended home birth."[13] Davis-Floyd goes on to suggest that "the real issue in the home versus hospital debate is not safety but the conflict between radically opposed systems of value and belief"—in her terms, the contrasting models of technocratic versus holistic birth.[14] For many of the women in my study, the opposition between these belief systems goes beyond concerns with appropriate technology to include more specifically economic and religious critiques of the medical model.

The Business of Birth

Just as the view that pregnancy and childbirth are not pathological was a dominant influence in shaping women's perceptions of hospitals, a critique of the economic structure within which hospitals operate was another frequently elaborated theme. For Tessa, choosing to birth at home was not simply a rejection of a medical model of birth, but an assertion of a different value system:

What do we value in our culture? We value technology and science, and we value money. And I don't want to live in a culture and be a member in a culture where that's . . . the major value. I think that the values should be much more . . . holistic . . . and that technology is necessary and good when it's used appropriately, but the value of the society should be on the family, and it should be on the spirituality of the infant.

Childbirth technology should not overshadow the techniques of family relations, which for Tessa meant that her family should be involved intimately in welcoming her new babies. Her older children were present at their siblings' births, and her mother, brothers, and sister were all present at one or more of the births. Asserting the importance of her family to the process of birth subverted the authority of the hospital as the proper socializer of the newborn child.[15]

Larisa Marquez had an even more pointed economic critique. Larisa was a young woman who lived with her husband in a second-story apartment on a busy urban street. In her living room, adorned with Guatemalan fabrics and posters celebrating revolution, Larisa told me about her life after coming to the United States from Venezuela at the age of 10. She had attended Episcopalian youth groups all through high school, but was no longer affiliated with any religious institution. Her primary source of community was now an alternative-food co-op, where most of the members were vegetarian. In this environment, her questioning of the institutions of her society grew. Accordingly, when she became pregnant at 23, she knew the hospital was not the place for her:

I don't believe in the "system.". . . I'm not into banks, hospitals, anything that's basically the norm. I don't really agree with it because I see a lot of flaws, a lot of things wrong with it. Like medicine and stuff like that, that's not even my thing. I don't believe in even taking a Tylenol, even if I have a headache. I'd rather take the headache, and not work. I think that American society is too quick to jump and say they want a quick out.

Larisa's criticisms went beyond an alternative view of health and illness to include harsh words for the economics of the medical system:

When I found that I was pregnant, I wouldn't have it any other way but a home birth, because I don't really believe in the hospital. I see the hospital view as . . . a business. The amount of money that a lot of doctors and nurses get paid, not nurses but mostly doctors, get paid to [do] what they do, it's ridiculous. And the use of drugs in this country is crazy. . . . A very sterile setting is just not preferable in my life, so I just didn't do it.

After a three-day labor, Larisa did end up going to the hospital to have her baby—vaginally and with an epidural—but she still maintains that the hospital is not the place for normal birth. Larisa chose direct-entry midwives in part because a woman she knew from her co-op recommended them, but also because they were less expensive than the certified nurse-midwives in the area. Money was an issue for Larisa and her husband, a craftsperson, since they did not have medical insurance. Even after her difficult labor, she said she would plan to have any subsequent births at home, and if she was still in the area, she would probably use the same midwives.

While cost was a factor for many women, home birth being much less expensive than hospital birth, many had to pay out-of-pocket expenses for their births because of the strictures of medical insurance. Those who opted for care from a certified nurse-midwife were often covered by insurance, at least partially, but the fees of direct-entry midwives were never covered. Hence, while home birth may often be understood as a challenge to the dominant economic system, just as frequently it requires a substantial outlay of money, approximately $750 to $3000. Even though many direct-entry midwives use a sliding scale to set their fees, home birth is generally not an option for those who cannot afford this expense. Not all certified nurse-midwives who attend home births choose to or are able to accept Medicaid reimbursement, and many direct-entry midwives, due to their unlicensed status, cannot interact with state or private health insurance even if they choose to.[16] The economics of birth in the United States—like the economics of all kinds of health care—are affected by the structure of the insurance system, no matter what mode of birth is chosen.[17]

No Room for God

According to some women, the hospital in its need for sterility endeavors to exterminate not only germs, but also the spirit. Using religiously motivated criticisms of the hospital, some women argued that the religious aspects of birth were best respected in the home. Tessa advanced such a critique when she argued that the spirituality of the mother, baby, and family could flourish better in the home. But the kinds of "spirituality" that can be fostered in a home as opposed to the hospital are many. For women like Tessa, who grew up in Christian traditions but have turned to nature-focused and women-centered religions, the hospital's technological face stands in the way of a woman's ability to have a powerful encounter with the divine. For a woman like Janet Stein, however, whom I described in the introduction as a charismatic Christian with strong beliefs, the hospital occludes the religiosity of birth for very different reasons.

Janet, a tall, curly-haired, animated Euro-American woman, greeted me at the door of her town house wearing a tie-dye T-shirt. She had given birth a few months earlier to her first child, at the age of 44. In the two years before giving birth, Janet had experienced her share of change and stress. After being single all her life, she married her husband David (who had converted from Judaism to charismatic Christianity five years before they met), became pregnant, and suffered a miscarriage. She seemed to take pressure in her stride, however, confident of her Lord's guidance. With what amounted to a literal demonization of the hospital, Janet also displayed confidence in her view that birth in the hospital is spiritually dangerous, for two reasons. First, she believed that the medical system has shut God out of hospitals by practicing abortion, and second, that a husband's headship of his wife is questioned when he must defer to the wishes of an obstetrician. The first problem was very serious in Janet's opinion:

> I think that medicine has taken a wrong turn. Our generation, and maybe the generations before . . . just like with education and politics and a whole lot of things—as they get God out of it, and they push him to the side, they start making some real wrong decisions, one of the worst being killing children in the womb. And I think that has brought a curse on the whole industry, if you want to call it [that], or the whole practice. When you're shedding innocent blood, there's a curse from God, and I think that that's one of the biggest mistakes they've made.

Janet contended that medicine was not always so dismissive of God: "Back in the old days—I don't know how far back you have to go—medicine and God just went hand in hand." As God was increasingly "pushed out," hospitals became ridden with demons, Janet asserted, since "whenever you are doing Satan's work, you're inviting demons into the premises." She felt the hands of an obstetrician who had performed abortions were particularly dangerous. "To have people [whose] . . . hands . . . have caused abortions and taken the lives of innocent bodies, and whatever, disposed of them, to have those same hands touching my baby—I don't think so." Janet felt she needed to turn to midwives, and to birth at home, to avoid any contact with a medical system that performed abortions.

Janet's choice effected an ironic inversion of the history of relations between midwives and obstetricians. In the early decades of the century, obstetricians (both male and female) formed alliances with middle-class women reformers, and set out to discourage the use of midwives by painting them as abortionists. In the process, they ignored the obstetricians who were performing abortions, mostly on middle-class white women, to concentrate their attempts at defamation on immigrant midwives who cared mainly for working-class immigrant women.[18] Eighty years later, Janet's view turns the tables through her religiously based critique of obstetricians who perform abortions and her support of midwives.

Janet's critique was influenced by Christian midwife Carol Balizet's book, *Born in Zion*.[19] Janet recommended the book as one she and her husband had found particularly helpful in preparing for home birth. Similarly to Janet, Balizet argued that Christians opposed to abortion should not make use of the medical system for their own purposes, for any reason:

> God gave Adam dominion over the world, and Adam relinquished it to Satan through his disobedience. Likewise Jesus Christ gave healing to the Church, and we have pretty much turned it over to the world system. The result is the perversion of an institution which had as its original goal the saving of human life. Now it produces death. The ones who are killing all those babies are doctors of medicine. They do it in and through the system of medicine.[20]

For Balizet, as for Janet, Satan is a real force in the world and must be contained, especially at the vulnerable rite of passage that is birth.

Janet also drew her second concern, that of destabilizing a husband's authority by investing power in doctors, from some of Carol Balizet's writings. In a paraphrase assenting to Balizet's interpretation, Janet said:

> The way God has set it up in the Scripture it says that the man, the husband, is the head of the household spiritually before God, not that he's smarter than anybody or anything, just that God has given him authority to make decisions, including medical decisions. And that if you abdicate that authority, if you hand it over to someone who is not supposed to have it, like going against what you really believe is right . . . you are really opening the door to danger to your family.

Despite Janet's strong feelings that her husband should have authority as she gave birth to their child, she also worried about what she called his "controlling" ways. She frequently alluded to conflicts she felt with her husband over her relatively newly assumed role as mother and homemaker, since she had been single and active as a spiritual counselor and church worker for almost twenty years before marrying her husband. Marrying and giving birth to a child placed her in her "proper" role as wife and mother. Her new marital status, however, did not take away her experience of twenty years of living as a single, autonomous, and, from the stories she told, rather adventurous woman, who had (with God's help) driven demons from a number of people and places.

Simply being at home and with her husband did not ensure a godly birth for Janet; care had to be taken to invite only spiritually appropriate attendants. Like many other women, a major reason Janet gave for choosing to give birth at home was to have some control over the people who took part in the experience. In addition to not wanting strangers at her baby's birth, a woman might want to keep strained relationships, such as those with a mother-in-law or even a husband, from adversely affecting the birth. For Janet, this control was necessary to keep spiritually inappropriate people from threatening the holiness and success of the birth.

Janet took care to keep her home under Christian influences. She decorated her walls with prints of Jesus and plaques inscribed with biblical verses, stacked religious literature on the coffee table, and adorned her refrigerator with biblically inspired magnets. Especially at the time of birth, Janet was concerned to keep "evil" forces out of her home. She interviewed a number of midwives, one of whom she declared too "New Age," before she settled on two certified nurse-midwives. Janet dismissed these midwives as well, a few weeks before her birth, because they wanted her to take some final tests. She and her husband agreed that the pregnancy and the birth were in God's hands, and that taking those last-minute tests was a sign of fear:

> So we didn't want to do any unnecessary [tests]—and we had said that from the beginning. So all of a sudden they were not only insisting but they were giving us ultimatums. David and I did a lot of talking and praying about it, and he talked to [the midwife] a lot. David felt this way, and I really agreed with him, that if they're just responding in fear now, what's going to happen during the birth? Again, we wanted it peaceful. We wanted to have people that had faith and that would believe in God, and also we didn't want to jeopardize [the baby's] health by unnecessary testing. So we really prayed a lot about it, analyzing different possibilities. So we started looking for another midwife. We kind of felt abandoned there at the last minute.

Janet found a direct-entry midwife at a Christian birth center an hour and a half away from her home, but this midwife could not commit herself to driving so far to a home birth. In the end, Janet gave birth to a healthy baby girl with just her husband, her mother, and her friend Brenda in attendance, while the Christian midwife talked her husband through the birth over the phone.

Brenda Matthews, Janet's friend, was also very concerned about having spiritually appropriate birth attendants. Brenda, who administers her husband's chiropractic clinic, is a 44-year-old, very lively Euro-American woman with intense brown eyes and a meticulously ordered home. She has three children aged 12 to 20, who were all born at home with the help of direct-entry midwives. As we sat in the formal living room of her large home, Brenda told me of being a "spirit-filled born-again Christian, with a chiropractic philosophy." While in some quarters such a combination could raise eyebrows, Brenda seemed totally at ease with her combination of alternative healing and charismatic Christianity. When they were expecting their first baby, Brenda's husband was in chiropractic school. Distressed by their negative interactions with an obstetrician, and generally antimedical in orientation, Brenda and her husband were put in touch with an underground network of home-birth midwives through their friends at the school. Perhaps it was the blend of Christianity and chiropractic that led to an eventually problematic mix of people at Brenda's first birth, which was only resolved, in Brenda's understanding, by divine intervention.

I first heard Brenda's story from Janet, who recounted this tale with almost the same amount of detail as Brenda. Prefacing her story, Brenda said, "My first birth was very different. It was really something. We were so out there with Jesus, and I don't mean to sound bizarre, but our dependence was totally on him, because we were entering a realm that I knew nothing about. I mean I had read all these books, I had all this intellect, but experience-wise I did not know where I was walking." With that, she launched into her tale of divine intervention:

> A woman came in—I'm going to jump around a little bit—a woman came that was uninvited. And she was part of a cultish church, and it was very interesting, because she started talking to me in these like . . . I don't know what she was trying to do, but spiritually I knew that I had to repel her. And I just told her to stop: "I'm fine. Please stop doing that."
>
> Well, we got down to where I was pushing, and I pushed . . . for two and a half hours. It was really a long time, but the reason I pushed is because she was there. . . . Then she got a call that there was an emergency at home. She left. Within ten minutes, my son was born. The irony was that when she [the woman] got home, there was no one home and no one had made the call. So I know that I had divine intervention to get her out of there, because my baby was starting to [be in] distress, and I was exhausted, and he was actually born without me pushing at all. I had lost all my energy . . . and I just said, "Jesus . . ." I said it right out loud. I said, "Jesus, if this baby is going to be born, you have got to birth him."
>
> And with that, he came out like a corkscrew. I don't even know if I had a contraction. I don't know anything. I know that I had reached my exhaustion point, and he came out. He came out! . . . And they were like, "Did you push?" And I [said], "No!" It was so cool. I mean, every birth is a spiritual experience, but it was truly [one]. . . . I had a divine birth, because Jesus actually brought that baby out without me doing anything, because I couldn't.

Brenda went on to explain how God had worked his power on another woman, a closer friend whom she had also invited to the birth. This woman was physically unable to enter the birthing room, in Brenda's recollection, because of her problematic, "cultish" spiritual state. Brenda said that she had been "witnessing" to this woman, and that inviting her to the birth was part of her witness:

> And she came to our bedroom door, and the energy—and I know it was God's energy—was so strong she could not penetrate it. She said that my husband and I were totally encompassed in this brilliant light, and that it was such an energy

field—in her explanation—that she could not penetrate the door. She could not. She watched from the door of him being born. She couldn't even come in the room after he was born. It wasn't until I got up to go the bathroom that I was actually able to hug her. It was just really, I mean Jesus really had that birth.

Using childbirth as a way to witness—to show people the power of Jesus— was also something that Pentecostal midwife and author Carol Balizet endorsed, although in her case the invited guests became large crowds, each person undergoing his or her own spiritual crisis while the birthing woman labored in another room.[21] Brenda's witnessing was on a smaller scale, and while it was not always successful (given the example of the "cultish" woman who left), she was confident in the "birthing energy" that emanated from her Christian God. Janet was more successful than Brenda had been at keeping spiritually suspect people from her baby's birth, but it did not matter in the end. According to Brenda, Jesus was stronger than any force of evil, especially when she was safely in her home where the power of Jesus was acknowledged.

A link between the devil and the hospital was not made only within charismatic circles. Meg Alexander, a petite woman with long brown hair and a quick smile, had attended a Presbyterian church but was now think-ing of moving to a Unitarian fellowship. Her home was a spacious old colonial farmhouse, painted white, within a hamlet surrounded by horse farms. As we sat around her kitchen table drinking tea, she described her first birth using language as evocative as Brenda's. Her first baby's birth had taken place in a hospital, and had ended up as a cesarean:

> I thought about God with [my first baby's] birth, because I was lying there thinking, "God, how can you do this to me?" And when they put the pitocin in the IV, they didn't tell me. And I remember lying there in bed and the con-tractions were getting horrendous because I was on pitocin, unknowingly, and I thought to myself, "This has nothing to do with God; this is the devil doing this." I was sure it was the devil. Nothing could be that terrible. It's like evil!

Meg's view of the devil was not as theologically elaborated as that of Bren-da's and Janet's. While Meg's critique of the medical system paralleled Janet's in seeing the devil at work in delivery rooms, she did not tie it to wider issues of abortion; nor did she share a belief in the headship of men. She proudly wears a T-shirt proclaiming "Women of Earth, Take Back Your Birth!" and chooses to conceive of God as nebulously gendered.

For Meg, the wires and tubes of hospital technology and the loss of decision-making power that women encounter in the hospital are what render the delivery room an unspiritual site, not the fact of whether or not the obstetrician performs abortions. Her view is more akin to a romantic perception of the world, in which mechanistic technology enters in as a force of disenchantment.[22] The bustle of bodies and machines drives spiritual concerns from the scene:

> You know, I was thinking the other day about hospital births. When you go to the hospital and there's all these doctors and nurses, there's a lot going on. And there's a lot of intellectual thought, and there's technology and machines and the drugs and things. It's almost like there's no room for God there. And that would be the thing that would help the labor go well. But they're so busy bringing these other things in, they push him out! Or it out, or her. I don't think God's a he. I think [God is] more female than male, but both. And I think I didn't want to go to the hospital because I knew that the kind of experience that I needed wouldn't be allowed there.

Meg had her next baby at home, in the hope of having a more spiritually aware birth, one that would be less traumatic for both herself and her baby. She achieved what she desired, and her critique of the hospital grew more explicit as a result.

These three prongs of critique—namely, a view of the birthing body as essentially healthy, a challenge to the wider economics of the medical system, and an assertion of the irreligious nature of the medical system—often work together. Women of various religious sensibilities plumb the meanings of home by contrasting it to the hospital in different ways. Common to all of them, however, is a conviction that by seeing the hospital as the only appropriate site for birth, their society is impoverishing family relationships, spiritual growth, and community. By actively reclaiming the home as a site of birth they insist on the power of childbirth to call people back to awareness of what is fundamental in their lives—whatever that may be. The diverse and innovative effects of this reclamation of home become increasingly apparent in looking at the ways these women have developed their sense of place through interaction with their religious traditions, both historically and in the present.

Places of Worship: Religious Practice in the Home

If the opposition between the home and the hospital is one way that meaning is instilled in the home, another less pronounced opposition—or perhaps more appropriately, distinction—for some women, was that drawn between the home and the church or synagogue. For many women, home birth gave a new sort of sacrality to their domestic spaces and the relationships contained within them. Being on their own turf allowed a certain freedom in the practices of birth, and some of those practices were religious.[23]

That women have made their homes into places of worship is not new. In the last two hundred years, religious influences have shaped the North American home both as overt home improvement techniques and in more tacit ways. From Nancy Cott's analysis of the "bonds of womanhood," to Colleen McDannell's study of the Victorian home, scholars have viewed the nineteenth century as a defining period that shaped both the ideology and the experience of the North American home, at least for middle-class Euro-Americans.[24] Put briefly, much of the scholarship on domesticity in the nineteenth century argues that with the decline of agriculturally based households and the rise of industrialization, economic production moved out of the home and into the factory, rendering the home solely a site of *re*production. With this decline in the home economy, women lost their previous importance as economic producers in the home, and their roles became separated from the market economy, focusing instead solely on childbearing, child tending, and housekeeping.[25] Interpretations of the significance of this change varied, as some historians argued that the rise of a "separate sphere" trapped women into greater subordination to men; others claimed that separate spheres allowed women to cultivate domestic networks among themselves that enhanced their self-esteem and power.[26]

Religion played an important and paradoxical role in shaping the form of domesticity in the nineteenth century, at once theologically underwriting the "natural" role of woman as mother in the home, while also allowing communities of women to develop in the form of maternal and missionary associations. The latter gave women a chance to learn organizational skills and to form an identity outside of the family.[27] While much of the literature on religion and domesticity drew its conclusions from Protestant women, mainly those from New England, Ann Taves and Colleen McDannell argued that Catholic women also lived within an ideology of domesticity.[28] Domestic religion, in McDannell's view, formed a bridge between Protestants and Catholics to the extent that "when Protestants and Catholics agreed on a set of home virtues, rituals, and symbols, this overarching domestic religion gave them a common language to speak to one another."[29] Like the idea of civil religion advanced by scholars of public religion in America, domestic religion succeeded in linking Americans through a common morality. The alliances between traditionalists and feminists in the home-birth movement are an echo of this earlier common language.

In the nineteenth century, much of the discussion of the virtues of motherhood focused on a woman's role as her child's greatest moral influence. Writing about motherhood, clerical and popular authors did not focus on a woman's experience of pregnancy and birth, but on her role as guardian of the home. Whether for reasons of modesty or concern, as historian Sylvia Hoffert phrased it, "They were more interested in what it meant to be a

mother than in what it meant to become one."[30] So, while the practice of
separate spheres may have cultivated a network of women supportive of
each other in childbirth, ideological commentators on the virtues of motherhood were largely silent on the significance of giving birth.[31]

Later feminist historians and anthropologists have challenged the metaphor of "separate spheres" for drawing an overly simplistic dichotomy between the lives of women and men, and for ignoring differences based on
race and class.[32] Despite these criticisms, the metaphor still resonates with
scholars and the people they study, as Linda K. Kerber asserted: "For all
our vaunted modernity, for all that men's 'spheres' and women's 'spheres'
now overlap, vast areas of our experience and our consciousness do not
overlap. The boundaries may be fuzzier, but our private spaces and our
public spaces are still in many important senses gendered."[33] The gendering of space applies to birth as well. Along with a decline in the home
economy, one could argue, came a decline in home birth. As work moved
from the home and its environs to centralized buildings in the name of
efficiency, so too did birth travel from the home where women did the
attending to the hospital where men were in charge. In the process, however, the purity of the home—so celebrated by advocates of domesticity—
was inverted. In the case of home birth attended by a midwife, the home
was no longer considered pure, but instead was a host of contagion, ama-
teurism, and danger.[34] Home-birthing families, since the 1970s, have been
working to invert the purity/pollution opposition one more time.

One of the foremost ways in which the notion of separate spheres has
been useful in providing a nuanced account of women's lives is through
the study of domesticity as it is enacted and constructed in physical spaces,
as opposed to simply through ideology.[35] I am concerned to develop a
similar sense of the importance of how homes, as physical spaces, are lived
in and thought of. Many of the women I interviewed could be seen largely
as occupying a "separate sphere." Though I hesitate to use this term for
fear of seeming to be an advocate of an essentialized division of labor based
on gender (which I am not), it was true that most of the women I spoke
with lived primarily domestic lives. While eight of the women worked
full-time (or almost full-time) outside the home, the other four-fifths
concentrated their energies on the labor of child-rearing and housekeeping while their husbands worked outside the home, much like their nineteenth-century counterparts.

The separateness of the spheres of home and work is not clear-cut, however, as most of the women who said they were "stay-at-home moms"
continued to work part-time in their pre-children occupations; for example, as veterinarians or counselors, or in newer careers as labor assistants
or vitamin salespeople. Those without paid work were often volunteers,
like the many La Leche League leaders. The blurring of boundaries of
work and home was even more apparent in several cases in which the

women did work at home on their own or with their husbands, running home-based businesses, such as desktop publishing, chiropractic clinics, or kitchen-equipment sales. Three of the women homeschooled their children, a job in itself. One of these women shared the work of homeschooling with her husband, and they both worked outside the home as well. Several other women said they planned to homeschool once their children were older.[36]

Despite the range of ways women arranged their patterns of work with their spouses, most of these women, across religious and political divides of traditionalism and feminism, felt that women held a special, home-based power that men could not wield. Based on what the women considered to be their natural capacities for nurturing and their abilities for domestic organization, most of them (even some who worked outside the home) considered women to be the hub of the family, ensuring that the life of all the family members ran smoothly.

Much as Colleen McDannell suggested of nineteenth-century women, the women in my study shared a common language of domesticity, which granted an important place to the process of birth in the life of the family. Across religious traditions, for example among Orthodox Judaism, Methodism, Catholicism, Seventh Day Adventism, feminist spirituality, and Old Order Amish, these women held common views of the meaning of home and motherhood. This commonality is more remarkable than a simple unity between Protestants and Catholics, not only because of the great diversity within Protestantism and Catholicism, but also because Jewish women of various levels of orthodoxy also shared this vision of home.[37]

The unity of women in approaches to birth, in particular, does not necessarily stem from a common moral or religious vision, but draws from the feminist health movement, a consumer approach to health care, and a turn to the "natural" in food and alternative medicine.[38] As I showed in the previous chapter, this unity contains contrary views as well, since some of the women take contrasting positions on politicized and religiously shaped issues such as abortion and homosexuality, while still maintaining a common view of motherhood. Home-birthing women draw from sources outside their religious traditions and outside the dominant medical model to come to their beliefs about home birth, but even some of these sources, such as advice books, are layered with religious meanings. The religion practiced in home birth is a combination of a woman's religious tradition, her reception of alternative-birth philosophies, her notions of what and who babies are, and her relationships with family and friends. With a long history of domestic religion behind them, women selectively draw from and reinterpret their religious traditions in the act and aftermath of childbirth. Crafting their homes as places where the sacred can surprise them, or simply come when entreated, they make space for domestic epiphanies.

Domestic Epiphanies

As I described in the last chapter, while many women said that they did not explicitly choose home birth for doctrinally based religious reasons, most of them recounted what they considered to be religious or spiritual moments in the course of their giving birth. Some women planned their babies' births to incorporate religious practices, while for others such religious moments apparently arose organically as unexpected epiphanies that emerged from the work of giving birth. Considering how women spoke of these expected and unanticipated religious moments illumines how these women continue, revitalize, and reinvent their religious traditions through the practices of home birth. The women's giving birth made their homes sacred spaces, sometimes just for a few hours and sometimes for much longer.

Continuity of Tradition

Perhaps the clearest illustration of the continuity of tradition effected by home birth came from Amish women. For these women, their homes were central to their daily lives. They spent most of their time in their homes, looking after children, cooking, sewing, or running home-based businesses, such as selling household-cleaning products or kitchen utensils. Quick outings such as a trip to the store were unlikely diversions from the home, since to get anywhere, be it a friend's home or the small town several miles away, a woman had to take her horse and buggy. For these Amish women, seeing the home as a place of religious practice was not a foreign notion, since Amish Sunday church services are regularly rotated among the homes of various church members.[39] Though the women did not use the term "sacred space" to characterize their homes, it is within their domestic spaces that religion—on individual, family, and community levels—is manifested.

While all the Amish women I spoke with claimed to prefer home birth for its "natural," not "religious," qualities,[40] their communal identity as world-avoiding, pious people of the land contributed to how they understood their choices. Annie Stoltzfus, a 27-year-old Old Order Amish woman with five children under 6 years of age, lived on a prosperous farm with a relatively new house and barn. Thinking about why she chose home birth, she mused about the differences between Amish and "English" women (women outside the Amish community): "Maybe English women would rather prefer the hospital; you get real good care there." In other words, the English woman, with her acceptance of the ways of the world, might want to be pampered, but Annie "prefer[s] the natural."[41]

Despite her sense of the good care one received in the hospital, Annie held a negative vision of the hospital, stating: "I was never in the hospital for anything. They say the first thing, you get in there and they inject you." For Annie, the care of a certified nurse-midwife in her own home allowed her births to join the flow of her daily life. Her births fit into her daily routine even to the point where her labor began at nine o'clock in the evening, after she had sat down to relax after her day's work, and ended before the morning milking. Annie gave birth in the calm of the night, with just her husband and the midwives in attendance, and with some silent supplications to God to assist with the pain: "I like to ask the Lord to help me. That's a comfort."

As continuous as home birth may be with Amish women's sensibilities, Amish women share with other American women the disruption in birthing practices that hospital birth introduced. All five of the Amish women I interviewed were born in hospitals, though their mothers had been born at home. These women's birthing histories are typical. Hospital births gained popularity among the Amish in the 1950s and 1960s, only to be reversed by a rise in home births beginning in the 1970s.[42] A 1978 study of the Lancaster County, Pennsylvania, Amish found a further similarity to a wider trend of home birth, in that women are more likely to choose it for a second or subsequent pregnancy. In 1978, of 472 pregnancies, 90 percent of Amish women having their first baby went to the hospital, but 59 percent of women having their last baby stayed at home.[43] So, while Amish women interpret their choice to give birth at home as a practice in continuity with their daily lives (and hence their religion), it is also made in response to the North American medicalization of birth.[44]

Another example of the practices of home birth sharing a continuity with religious tradition is the experience of Elaine Thatcher, a Christian Scientist, whose home births took place a decade ago, in a Western state. Now she lives with her husband and two children near a Christian Science community, in a two-story coach house on the grounds of a large estate. Elaine, too, was in search of the "natural" when she chose to give birth at home. Though a desire to avoid "medical intrusion" was an important reason for her home birth, Elaine reflected that she was motivated "even more than that [by] a desire for the quietness, and to see it as a very holy experience, and a very natural experience. And somehow, having a baby in the hospital makes it unnatural. It makes it an illness." Describing the birth of her second child, Elaine illustrated what she experienced as the quiet holiness of her birth:

[The midwife] and her assistant, who came with her, just sat on the floor over in a corner. John and I were singing hymns together and listening to some hymns on a tape. And just being quiet. And [the midwives] were so, just so wonderfully supportive of that.

When I asked Elaine if she had sung through the contractions and the breaking of her waters, she responded,

> Yes. And hymns—to me hymns are very, very important. Simply acknowledging the presence of God and my relationship to God. And so to keep—it was just wonderful to keep that in thought the whole time. Because pain is simply fear. Just fear. So if you're not afraid, then there is no pain.

Echoing Grantly Dick-Read's notion of the fear-tension-pain syndrome, but with particular Christian Science inflections, Elaine stressed the importance of mental and emotional preparation for birth. For Elaine, however, singing hymns was not a way to invest the birth with a special meaning beyond her daily life, since for her, "birth itself wasn't the point." She wanted to get through the experience as fast as possible and with little fuss. Singing hymns was a way to focus her energies and allow the natural process to proceed as it would.

Elaine's disinclination to attribute meaning to the physical process of birth itself is not surprising, given the focus in Christian Science on "mind" or "spirit" to the exclusion of the material. The mind, when properly attuned to God, is in total control of the physical body, which in the Christian Science view does not really exist. As such, pain becomes an emotional state of fear, as Elaine suggested, banished with an effort of will. Finding the holiness of birth in singing and emotional connections, not in the physical labors of her body, made sense in Elaine's theology.

For some women then, being at home allows them to give birth in a way they consider in continuity with their religious lives. They do not cast birth as a "peak experience." Instead, they choose to interpret birth as a process following nature, one that demands quiet and little interruption, and, one that—like the rest of their lives—benefits from calling on God for comfort and aid.

Revitalizing Tradition

Giving birth at home can also be the impetus to revitalize and reinterpret one's religious heritage. In some instances, reshaping practice and space in the context of home birth brings about new interactions between family relationships and religious traditions. For example, Joanna Katz, who called her baby a "home baby" at the beginning of this chapter, is a 40-year-old Jewish woman who has gradually shifted from Conservative to Reform Judaism over the course of her married life. Concurrently, she has also shifted from hospitals to home as the place to give birth, having had her last baby at home when she was 39. Jacqueline, the fourth of four girls, was born at home with certified nurse-midwives attending.

Joanna's story of her "inspired" decision to have a home naming shows the "do-it-yourself" quality of many home-based rituals. Reflecting on her experiences of taking her other daughters to the synagogue for naming ceremonies in the midst of "strangers," Joanna felt that these rituals were not "warm" enough. Especially given the contested role of women on the *bimah* (the raised platform at at the front of a synagogue) in Jewish history, Joanna felt that naming ceremonies in the synagogue did not give full honor to women.[45] In the end, her decision to have her baby daughter named at home was personally choreographed, coming out of her positive experience of home birth. She recalled telling her husband:

> I don't want all these strangers around [at the synagogue]. I really don't. I really . . . I want to have an experience like her birth was to us. I mean her birth was family and close friends and . . . I don't want her sitting, I don't want to sit up there and make a show. This isn't a spectacle—I don't want to sit up [on the bimah] and everybody have to get dressed up, and we all have to look cute up there, and everybody's going to say, "Look at the family with the four girls!"

Laughing, Joanna continued by telling me of her inspiration to have a home naming, which her husband agreed to right away: "I said, 'We had a home birth, how about having a home naming?' So he said, 'You know, that's a great idea.'" Choreographing her home naming, Joanna turned to Jewish tradition by asking her family doctor to lead the ritual because he was also a *mohel*, the expert qualified to conduct the more official ritual of welcome for boy children, the *bris*, or circumcision:

> And he did a different kind of ceremony, which we had never had before. It was right here in the living room, with our kids involved, just like they were with the birth. That's exactly what we wanted. . . . The kids did everything, and then he did a foot ceremony with her . . . almost like when you're baptized and you put the holy water on the baby. He had this prayer with the water, and washing the baby's feet with the water, and having everybody involved in that. And our kids, too. And we had our kids say prayers over the wine and the challah and stuff. And it was great. To me, that brought me closer to my religion and closer to my baby all in one act. It was wonderful. It was just this real—it was a great finale for a home birth. That's the way I looked at it. I'd say, "We had a home birth, we had a home naming, this is what it should be like."

Turning effortlessly to Christian examples, such as baptizing, to describe her ritual innovation to me, Joanna was visibly thrilled with how she had woven her religion and her childbearing together in her home. She saw the naming as the "culmination" of her experience of birth: "It was like the end and the beginning all combined. . . . It was like officially, here she is. . . . So that's why I say, to us the religion, the religious aspect of it and the home birth, they went together." For Joanna, consciously ritualizing her daughter's birth in home space also brought her family and her Judaism together in new ways. Joanna's choice to have a home naming for her last daughter was a statement about the intimacy her family shared in the birth of Jacqueline, and a commitment to continue that intimacy. As well, living on the border between Conservative and Reform Judaism, Joanna felt that welcoming her daughter into the world and the Jewish community with a *mohel* as the ritual expert would adhere to tradition while conveying the idea that girl children were just as welcome and just as Jewish as boys were.

The ritual innovation, or "inspiration," as Joanna phrased it, of a home naming was also an enactment of Joanna and Andrew's choice to switch to Reform Judaism. They had made this choice recently because they wanted their girls "to grow up in a manner of good self-worth, and feeling that they're a really important part of their religion." Joanna added, "And the fact that because we do things our own way, as opposed to the way of the Scriptures and the Laws, it's still okay." Though Joanna asserted her authority to make ritual choices in her domestic space that were not in accordance with a more Orthodox approach to Judaism, she also appealed to tradition to legitimate her actions. With the mohel's help, she affirmed the historical roots of her home-naming ceremony, and she also suggested that domestic rituals surrounding birth are in keeping with the domestic emphasis in Jewish women's religiosity in general.[46]

Joanna's story of how having a home birth led her to hold a home naming for her baby daughter exemplifies how the act of giving birth in the home can lead to a revisioning of religious practice and domestic space, and how the two intersect. Similarly, Elise, Joanna's friend, also began to develop domestic rituals drawn from her Jewish tradition after giving birth at home. For example, when I went to speak with Elise, a Reform Jew, she had just held a hair-cutting ritual for her 3-year-old son in which all the guests who gathered at her home cut small snippets of hair from her son's head to mark his passage from infancy into boyhood. Home birth is not a necessary precursor to interest in reviving traditional domestic rituals, but at the very least, it may contribute to a revaluing of the home as a site where rites of passage can be celebrated.

Whereas Joanna's experience of the intimacy of home birth drew her family together both emotionally and ritually, from Debra's Orthodox Jewish perspective the rituals of home birth demanded a form of gendered separation in the family. Wearing a wig in the tradition of Orthodox Jewish women, Debra spoke to me with enthusiasm in the living room of her older, spacious and sparsely furnished house on a tree-lined street, as she sat on the couch nursing her six-month-old baby. Though her husband was present at her first home birth (and almost caught the baby because Debra's labor was so quick), at her second home birth he had taken their three older children out for a short while when Debra unexpectedly gave birth, with the midwives' assistance. By the time of her last home birth (and her first one as an Orthodox Jew), Debra no longer wanted her husband present, especially at the moment of birth, because of halachic codes (those of Jewish law) limiting what a husband can see of his wife's body.[47] Perhaps given the emphasis within the home-birth movement on fathers' participation in birth, Debra was noticeably uncomfortable with discussing her reasons for not wanting her husband at the birth. She worried that "without all the understanding that goes with [halacha], it could sound—it could come across [as] cruel" that the law denied her husband a direct role in the birth. To show the benefit of such gendered restrictions, Debra described the supportive women who surrounded her during labor. Debra called on several women friends in her Orthodox community to be with her during birth. For "spiritual reasons, I wanted their energy, I wanted their trust." She also turned to her ten-year-old daughter for support.

The birth of her son *was* accompanied by trust, in Debra's recollection, despite some initial difficulties in his breathing. By giving birth at home with people she trusted, Debra felt that she had achieved the right atmosphere for her son's first moments in the world, in which she could welcome him into his religion and into life, with both spiritual and midwifery support:

> It only took a couple of contractions, and I was holding onto my friend, and the baby was born. The baby came out, and I sat down, and they lifted up the baby to me. [My daughter] had caught the baby along with the other two [midwives]. She was *thrilled*. She was flying! And it was total silence. It was just so sweet, so quiet. And the only thing for the baby to hear first was the *Shema*, that he knew that he was in good company, that he wasn't so detached from where he came, and that it would be okay, he shouldn't worry, right. And so I whispered into his ear the *Shema*, and I was holding him.

Debra reacted quietly and prayerfully to her son's birth by reciting from Deuteronomy 6:4–9, which begins, "Hear O Israel: The Lord is our God, the Lord alone." Meanwhile, the midwives observed the meconium (the baby's first bowel movements that can be a sign of distress), and saw that the baby was not breathing immediately. Debra described the scene as the midwives started counting the seconds until he breathed:

> There was no fear. I can't tell you. There was not one ounce of worry in that room, not one ounce. It was very quiet, very, very peaceful, very sweet. The baby was there—I was holding the baby, I was stroking the baby and talking to him and saying, "I know this is not—you know, you'd rather be where you were. It's very sweet there, but you know all these people have been waiting for you for so long. I have been waiting for you for *so* long." I'm trying to remember

exactly what I said, because it was just so, so, so sweet. I said, "You don't have to worry. There's plenty of Torah to learn . . . and it's really, really a very nice place to be."

And [the midwife] came over with some oxygen, and they were still counting very, very carefully and quietly. She suctioned him, and she gave him a little bit of oxygen, and then he came around. It took a little bit, a few minutes, what was it? Two minutes, I think, two to three minutes maybe, maybe about three. And finally he took his breath, and he came around. His color wasn't *great*, but it was okay. It was within range, and he was a little scrawny. The heavy meconium was kind of making them a little bit nervous, whatever, but when he started crying, he started crying! It was nice and strong and it was just so very sweet, it was just so very, very sweet.

Debra felt no conflict between her religious ways of welcoming the baby and the midwives' more technical approach. The picture she drew was one of mutual respect, where both religious and midwifery techniques participated in ensuring the baby's safe arrival into the world.

Watching Debra give birth to her baby with the help of the midwives profoundly moved the two friends Debra had invited to the birth. As Debra recounted, one of the women, a teacher in a local religious school, commented that she would never teach the story from the Book of Exodus of the Hebrew midwives Shiphrah and Puah the same way again.[48] To this, Debra replied: "Good. That was the purpose!" Debra considered that asking these women to be at her birth was a way of honoring their friendship and of giving them a gift. Like Brenda, Debra felt that inviting others to her birth was a powerful way to witness to her faith. While these friends concurred, especially after participating in the birth of Debra's son, another woman did not understand her invitation this way and chose not to attend the birth, even after Debra called her while in labor to invite her one last time. Debra felt this friend was "disconnected from the energy of birthing, [and] so disconnected from the honor of being there." She was disappointed that her friend chose not to share in the birth.

The difference in understanding between Debra and her friend stems in part from Debra's unusual position between two worlds, that of an alternative-childbirth educator and that of an Orthodox Jew. Debra retained her passion for noninterventionist childbirth after becoming Orthodox. For example, she offered childbirth classes for the women in her Orthodox community. She also maintained her ties with her non-Jewish direct-entry midwives during her later births, despite the fact that there was a Jewish midwife in a neighboring area who attended the births of Orthodox women. Debra's passion for and exposure to the alternative-birth movement outside of the Orthodox community also meant her perspective on birth was just as shaped by women-led resistance as by the

Torah. This combination made her somewhat of an oddity among her new friends, who for the most part favored hospital birth.[49]

Many of the women whom I considered to be revitalizing aspects of their traditions in conjunction with having home births were Jews, perhaps because Jewish women have a richer heritage of religious childbirth lore and domestic ritual upon which to draw.[50] I encountered some instances, however, of Christian women drawing specifically from their religious tradition to ritualize birth in the home. Elizabeth was a soft-spoken woman living in a rented house with her daughter and her husband, Mark. They were in the process of deciding whether to move to a nearby intentional community rooted in anthroposophy (a twentieth-century religious movement based in the writings of Rudolf Steiner, who effected a blend of Christianity, Eastern mysticism, and various nineteenth-century health and education reform movements).[51] She had grown up Episcopalian, but had converted to her husband's faith, Roman Catholicism, when pregnant with her first child. Together, they introduced a number of religious rituals into their baby's home birth. One ritual resembled the older Christian tradition of churching, in which the birthing mother could not enter a church for a set number of days after giving birth, after which she was required to go to church to undergo a ritual of purification and thanksgiving. Even though Elizabeth did not tie her decision to stay home until after her baby's christening to the ritual of churching, her choice evoked the older ritual.[52] Elizabeth's version focused more on the baby than on the mother:

> I stayed in the house for three weeks, because in the Roman Catholic religion, which a lot of people don't recognize any more, you're not supposed to take the baby out of the house until it's been christened. So I didn't even go for the christening. Mark and my daughter went to the church. So it was three weeks I stayed in the house. Even though Mark had baptized her as soon as she was born, we [had] decided we wanted an official wammy-jammy before we did that.

With a sense of ritual autonomy that seemingly echoed Joanna's, Elizabeth was clear that though her husband brought the baby to be baptized in the church, the baby had been already sufficiently christened at home. By baptizing their baby at birth, Mark had assumed the role of "domestic priest."[53] According to Elizabeth, he used "regular tapwater, and he baptized in [the name of]the Father, the Son, and the Holy Spirit, which is the perfectly acceptable way to baptize a baby."

Elizabeth and Mark had started going to a traditional Catholic church in recent years, where the Mass was said in Latin and there was a greater focus on pre–Vatican II liturgy. Mark was the driving force behind this shift in religious practice; he was especially concerned that Elizabeth be baptized while pregnant so that she could take communion, thus blessing the fetus. Elizabeth, while not in conflict with Mark's desires for Catholic ritual in their home birth, was somewhat ambivalent about the importance of such ritual to herself. Elizabeth admitted that she was "like a lot of people, not really consistent" about prayer. She recalled praying a bit more during her pregnancy, but then added, with a smile: "It was during my pregnancy that I converted to Catholicism, so it was at that time I was most enamored with the church. And the Latin rite is so mystical. I guess I was really taken by it, as most people are in the beginning of a relationship when it's easy. As things get . . . as you get more used to it, you get married, the honeymoon's over." Elizabeth's frank evaluation of the consistency of her religiosity seemed to suggest that Mark was the impetus behind the revitalization of Catholic traditions of childbirth. For Elizabeth, the formally religious aspect of her birth rituals was less important than the emotional and psychological safety she felt home birth offered.

The main reason for giving birth at home, according to Elizabeth (though perhaps not to Mark), seemed to be an echoing of a theme I discussed earlier, that of a mistrust of hospitals. Elizabeth's mistrust, however, was fed by a fear of strangers and a longing for the safety of the home she had created after moving out of her childhood home, where she had been sexually abused:

> When I was younger, I was always afraid to be home because of the things that were happening at home. And then when I moved out, and had my own home, it really became a place of safety for me, and a place of refuge. And I really feel that. . . . And I feel very safe and secure when I'm at home, whereas the rest of the world is a little frightening to me.
>
> But I really . . . I would have had to have a home birth because it would have been so terrible for me to be in a hospital. To be in some place strange, with strange people, it would have been beyond uncomfortable, it would have been— psychologically, it would have been terrible for me.

For Elizabeth, being at home for her baby's birth made room for a number of practices, the most important of which was probably not explicitly religious in nature, but instead, was the act of giving birth in what she had constructed as a place of safety.

Suzanne Donato, an Italian-American Catholic woman, felt that the process of becoming a mother also brought her into contact with a wider, and more domestic, set of Catholic rituals. I met Suzanne, a dark-haired, friendly woman, at a postpartum group, where she invited me to talk with her, even though she did not think there was anything particularly religious about her two births. Once at her house, however, we began talking while her young children played, and she told me of her prayer group that was centered around issues of motherhood. Made up of her mother-in-law, sisters-in-law, and some friends, the group meets in one woman's home each week to share coffee, snacks, prayer, and conversation. Started by a woman who had made a pilgrimage to Medjugorje, in Yugoslavia, to visit the site where several local people had claimed to witness Marian apparitions, the group calls itself "Mary's Children," and their activities consist of prayers to the Virgin, rosaries, novenas, and chaplets. The prayers focus on appealing for the well-being of the women's families, including petitions for safe and easy pregnancies and births, when appropriate. The group closes with a Bible reading, sometimes chosen at random, other times selected with a specific purpose in mind.

Mary's Children has roots in a long tradition of popular Mariology. Historian Robert Orsi described Italian-American women's devotion to Mary as "quite different from official versions but consistent with a long European popular tradition: the women in the community believed that Mary had suffered the pains of childbirth, that she had menstruated, and that she worried constantly about her child."[54] Suzanne joined the group when she was pregnant with her first child, and found that it changed her prayer life significantly:

> I think [my relationship with Mary] probably changed when I became pregnant and I started going to these prayer meetings, because it all kind of coincided and that was when I started . . . to me prayer was always to God or to Jesus. I never really prayed to Mary before. So once I started with these meetings, she became more of somebody that I pray to more. And I ask her for a lot of help. Like, please help me, please help me be a better mother. Please help me be like you. So it's like asking your sister instead of asking your father. You know, your father's the head figure in the family. It's like going to your sister or your mom. . . . It's like someone a little bit closer to you, more like you.

For Suzanne, as for many stay-at-home mothers (and not just those who give birth at home), having children meant her life began to center on her home. In the process, her religious life developed domestic dimensions alongside her church attendance.

The religious rituals associated with her home birth took place within the prayer group, amid two generations of women who themselves were praying for Suzanne and her babies. For Suzanne, special candles, music, or prayers were not part of the actual experience of birth, but prayer did have an effect on her birth experience, as she recalled, somewhat ironically:

> I am not a real unconscious pray-er. If I do [pray] it's like, "Oh my God, please help me." So that was the extent of my prayer during birth. At our prayer meetings we would ask for help and ask for safe delivery. And it was funny, we have this big box that we put special intentions in, and I was being really sarcastic one day and I said, "Does anybody have any special intentions?" And I said,

"Yeah." I said, "I want a boy, and I want a twenty-minute labor!" Or something like that, being really sarcastic. And that was basically what I got, so it's just like, oh my God, you've got to be careful what you pray for!

Unlike Elizabeth's drawing from Catholic tradition, which seemed largely out of her hands and at the instigation of her husband, Suzanne surrounded herself with a domestic Catholicism that was woman-centered in both constitution and focus. Suzanne's husband, a Catholic, but largely uninterested in matters of faith, played no role in his wife's domestic rituals of pregnancy and birth. The people who introduced Suzanne to an active prayer life centered on Mary were instead the women in her husband's family, his mother and sisters.

Revitalizing tradition, then, can take the form of critically domesticating otherwise institutional rituals, such as Joanna's naming ceremony. Or it can result in reviving older traditions of domestic religion that centered around pregnancy and birth, such as Debra's decision not to have her husband view the birth, and Suzanne's prayer group. Traditions revitalized in the process of home birth can be family-centered, women-centered, or both. Whether revitalization means ritual innovation or ritual reconstruction, in the context of home birth it always means a revaluing and remaking of the sacred in the home.

Inventing Tradition

A third group of ritual practices that I loosely group as those "inventing tradition" are undertaken by women who invent new rituals to infuse their births with meaning. Some of these invented rituals are consciously chosen, while others are more aptly described as coming upon a woman as she tries to make sense of birth. An example of the latter type of invented ritual comes from Meg, the woman on the road to Unitarianism, who earlier had had a cesarean in the birth of her son David, and who had stated that there was "no room for God" in the delivery room. After the birth of her daughter at home, Meg and her son David buried the placenta:

I guess a couple of weeks later David and I went out to the backyard to bury the placenta. That was a moving experience. I didn't expect that. I wasn't quite sure what to do with the placenta once I knew that's what it was in the refrigerator. And I didn't want to do anything for a while. . . . David and I went out and dug a hole, and I was telling him about what the placenta was, and why I was burying it; it was good for the ground. And then as I dumped it out of the bag and onto the ground I just kind of looked at it, and I thought, "That's the end of my pregnancy."

That was symbolic of the pregnancy, and to bury the placenta myself, it was kind of like a funeral. It is! I just thought of that. It's like a funeral. And we stood there looking at the placenta, and I thought, "Well, I guess we should say something."

We said something symbolic; I don't know what. And I said, "David, do you want to throw the dirt on it?" And it was just like a funeral. And it's kind of like saying that pregnancy is over, and saying good-bye to it, putting it where it belongs.

For Meg, the feeling of closure brought on unexpectedly by burying the placenta was unlike her earlier experience of David's birth in the hospital. Though she recalled fully enjoying both her pregnancies, she could not say the same for both her births:

I didn't feel like I gave birth to [David] at all. So there was no end, no finalization. And with her [her daughter], I knew during my pregnancy that I didn't want to stop being pregnant. I loved being pregnant. I didn't want to end it. I felt very spiritual when I was pregnant, because I felt I was like God's helper; I was helping to create this life. And it was like I was working hand in hand with God. God was giving me the spirit, growing the spirit of life in my body, and I was trying to nurture it, giving it a good home to grow in. So I loved pregnancy. I felt honored, I felt like a priest or something. You know, I was walking around creating life. Heck, that's about as spiritual as you can get. And with [David] it was just abruptly stopped. And with her I didn't want it to stop, but I made it stop; I gave birth to her. And then when I buried the placenta, that was really saying good-bye to the pregnancy.

Finding herself in the backyard with David, making up their good-byes to the placenta as they went along, Meg's actions took on ritual significance; the significance may have increased with her telling of the story. Her ability to birth her baby under her own powers and in her own home had given her the sense of a fitting resolution to the heightened spirituality she had felt while pregnant, in a way that had never emerged after her cesarean section.

While Meg's placenta ritual was a seemingly "organic" development, the act of burying a placenta is common to many home-birthing women. Even Janet, the charismatic Christian, buried her placenta and planted a rose bush over it. Some bury the placenta for "environmental" reasons, asserting that a buried placenta makes good garden fertilizer for a suitably symbolic plant.[55] Others consider burying the placenta to be a ritual drawn from ancient or nonindustrialized societies.[56] Yet other women fry up their placentas and eat them, convinced of their nutritive value for the postpartum mother.

The invention of rituals, then, is not necessarily a making up from scratch, but it is often a conscious cobbling together of practices from multiple traditions. Women draw from the authority of traditions they consider authentic or woman-friendly, and in some ways deny the inventiveness of their actions by invoking the specter of authenticity. In this way, Debra's reshaping of Orthodox Jewish tradition for her home birth is quite similar to the efforts that followers of Goddess spirituality make in developing rituals based on ancient or Celtic Goddess traditions.

For example, for the women who considered themselves followers of the Goddess, or followers of more explicitly woman-based forms of spirituality, the conscious construction of rituals often meant an adoption and adaptation of what they considered to be Native American birthing practices. Tessa, who works as a birthing instructor, a doula, and as a midwife-in-training, has created Blessing Way ceremonies for some of the women she has worked with. For one of Tessa's own births, her women friends organized such a ceremony in her honor:

> I had a Blessing Way for [my daughter], which is a religious ritual, and that was really special. It's a takeoff on the Native American ritual where you celebrate the birthing mother, and there's a number of ways you can do it. You light special candles, the East and the South and the West and the North, and the earth and the sky and the universe. And you make a crown for the mother, and everybody brings a flower, and you use the flower in the middle for the wish and prayer for the mother. And there can be other rituals that involve a weaving; you do ritual songs that go with the weaving; and the flow and the ebb. And you weave a string or something in between every person, and then they tie it off and connect them in . . . with the mother. There can be washing with blue cornmeal—which is sort of a significant symbol in the Native American culture—of the mother's feet. And you know, the ritual of washing feet you can see that historically [in Christianity]. . . . And that was really neat.

Tessa regretted that a Blessing Way ceremony marked only one of her births. No friends had initiated the process for her before, and "It wasn't something that you put on for yourself." Now she does about one Blessing Way ceremony a month for certain clients and friends.

The ceremonies do not fit every client, though, and she offers them based on her "inclinations" of a client's receptivity. The ceremony, she said, is not connected with "personality, but with what I perceive as spiritual development. Some people [think], 'She's losing it this time! We know she's had four kids and three of them at home, but she's definitely losing it now. If she starts talking about homeschooling and doing these rituals, it's a little too much!'" For Tessa, seeing beyond specific traditions by being open to a wider form of spirituality and creating new syncretic rituals within home-based communities was a sign of spiritual development. She did not seem concerned about appropriating the Blessing Way ceremony from Native American cultures.[57] Instead, she had a somewhat pragmatic approach to ritual borrowing—if the symbolism fits, wear it.

Tessa's approach to ritualization agrees with much of the philosophy of Jeannine Parvati Baker, a self-described "shamanic midwife" from Utah. Parvati Baker also draws liberally from Native American culture, seemingly without qualms.[58] Tessa's and Parvati Baker's Blessing Way services are a reinvention of traditions; while espousing a countercultural model of birth, the two women operate within a market system. They both offer their services for a fee, so their rituals, while home-based, are not reproductions of an earlier time when women aided each other freely in community, in expectation of similar aid when they would need it.[59] While this view of an earlier era of midwifery may be idealized, Tessa and Parvati Baker do not attend women's births as "friends," as was the case with Debra's Orthodox Jewish birth; nor do they offer their prayers without a fee, as did the women in Suzanne's prayer group. The commodification of religion and birth is not new or "bad." Joanna's *mohel* undoubtedly charged a fee, as did the midwives attending all the other women's births.[60] But even when women's rituals of birth honor women, family, and home in a new and radical way, they often remain tied to the very cultural and social structures they mean to disrupt.

The plethora of paid services that have grown up around home birth— from magazines to doulas to ritual specialists—are evidence that even alternative visions of health and spirituality are tied into the consumption-oriented society that is North America. In some cases, choosing home birth is partly a process of what sociologist Pierre Bourdieu called "distinction," setting oneself apart from others, whether in terms of class or lifestyle.[61] The home is one of the prime places in which the "social capital" of distinction is displayed, in the tangible form of decor, furniture, or books. Tessa drew her distinction in terms of spirituality: only women of a certain spiritual development were ready for Blessing Way ceremonies, and were capable of fully understanding the countercultural choices of home birth and homeschooling. Not all women drew the same kind of distinctions or social capital from home birth, however. For Janet, a home filled with Christian people and Christian markers of identity helped her to make her home a safe place for birth. For Tessa, wind chimes, wood stoves, family members, and pets contributed to her sense of place. Contesting medical models of childbirth did not necessarily result in a complete lifestyle shift. But especially for women who consciously invented rituals for their births, their choice to give birth at home was often a sign that they embraced a holistic lifestyle in other dimensions of their lives as well.

The invention of tradition as I have characterized it includes personal acts imparting value to the process and spaces of home birth. Though these personal rituals often had diverse cultural roots and sometimes deceiving cultural pedigrees, some women felt that they arose organically from experience, and imbued them with a sense of authenticity as a result. The rituals evoked a sense of individualized spirituality, in that women felt free to pick and choose their practices. However, such rituals are also premised on a sense of belonging to a community, whether it is a woman's family, her midwives, or a wider community of birthing women. The invention of tradition also includes a conscious borrowing of religious practices from many cultures. The rituals, while individually "customized," consciously intend to draw from deeper cultural pools that value birthing mothers as sources of wisdom and view women's birthing bodies as founts of power.

All of these women, whether continuing, revitalizing, or inventing their religious rituals, valued the home in a specific way. When they spoke of home as a place of safety, they meant that quite literally: the home, they feel, is the safest place for most women to give birth to their babies. Harnessing arguments drawn from antimedical, economic, and religious critiques of the hospital, all these women valued the home as the place for a woman to experience one of the strongest forces her body will ever feel: the pangs of birth. Because the home-birthing woman can surround herself there with as much or as little religious ritual as she desires, the home can be the place for both intense and casual religious practice. For these women, the home is a space where freedom of the body and freedom of religion can coexist, in contrast to the bureaucratic space of the hospital, which is necessarily constrained by the limits of communal space. The home, while perhaps being a place of safety for these women, is also a highly contested cultural space, given the influence of feminist discourse on family relations—whether these families are feminist or not. To bring a different lens to the meanings of home, then, I close with a discussion of domesticity that draws from feminist analyses.

Domesticity and Its Discontents

The picture I have drawn of home as a place of safety and self-esteem is at odds with much of the literature on women and domesticity. For example, the struggles of being a stay-at-home mother, confined to the domestic sphere, and the dangers posed to women from domestic violence, are two of the themes commonly treated in scholarly literature on domesticity, whether historical or contemporary situations are being addressed.[62] While these two themes deserve consideration, many other questions are posed by domesticity. The fulfillment and meaning that some women find in being at home is real, but such experiences are also influenced by a burgeoning consumer culture, shifting notions of gender, and changing family arrangements. The comparative danger of other domestic spaces, whether childhood homes, those of other women, or perhaps at times her own, also shapes a woman's view of what constitutes a "safe" home for birth. The two women in my study who spoke of being sexually abused as children were nevertheless especially explicit about believing their own homes now to be "safe," even though their childhood homes had been unsafe.

Historian Bonnie Smith described the modern home as an institution "bearing an intense rhetorical and experiential burden."[63] Arguing for the importance of paying attention to "discourses of domesticity," Smith contended that the home has been not only the site of the reproduction of the human species, but also the literal and metaphorical source of political systems and their discourses. Furthermore, Smith asserted, "the conditions of gender difference grew in this atmosphere, separating clearly the destinies of men from those of women. Using the culture of those separate destinies as sources of power ever since, the social and political order has lived in the discourse of domesticity and family."[64] The confluence of discourses of reproduction and domesticity in home birth offers a particularly compelling opportunity to understand how gender differences have been used as sources of power, and how the practices of domesticity have enabled social, political, and, I would add, religious orders to be manifested.

Borrowing the term "discourses of domesticity" from Smith, I mean to indicate not only ways of speaking about women in the home, but also to show how such ways have shaped women's practices in the home. As Michel Foucault succinctly phrased it, discourses are "practices that systematically form the objects of which they speak."[65] Academic analyses of women's domestic activity, especially those of feminist scholars, have been both interpretations of and interventions into discourses of domesticity. This was demonstrated most clearly to me by the women who considered themselves feminists, but who felt frustrated or betrayed by what they saw as a feminist rejection of their choice to stay at home with their children. As Alison Lindt-Marliss, a mother of three who homeschools her children, phrased it: "I feel like I've been neglected by the feminist movement, and put down, and degraded. So, even though I consider myself a feminist, I wouldn't align myself with them, because I feel that they don't recognize, or value, what I do."[66]

Other women did align themselves with feminism, with fewer qualifications. Simone Taylor, 32, and mother of two, whose birth story began this book, considers herself a feminist. She was in the middle of her ministerial training at a Presbyterian seminary when we spoke, and feminist theology was of great interest to her. Simone found African-American womanist theology more compelling than Euro-American feminism, because "it so specifically seeks to uphold and promote family values, and obviously not Dan Quayle's family values, but they try to enter into a discourse whose basis is the community." On the contrary, Simone said, "a lot of feminist theologians don't start out with a sense of that importance, but rather of the importance of their own individual identities as women."

Many of the women had knowledge of and experience with feminism in their lives; some still considered themselves feminists, and others did not. Overall, however, all of the women felt *something* about feminism, and related their lives to the feminist movement in some way.[67] Feminist scholarship and advocacy then, a discourse that ideally tries to be self-conscious about the way it "forms its objects," both constructs and critiques the rhetoric and experience of domesticity. Some of the women I studied found support for their home-birth practices within feminist discourse, and others found their choices about their family lives reproached by feminism. That many of these women felt alienated from feminism, but yet could condemn male control over birth—even in some cases using the word "patriarchy"—shows the multiplicity of ways that feminism emerges in North American culture. Their ambivalent use of feminist terms also shows the complex ability of feminist discourse to seem both empowering and antagonizing to particular women.

One example of a feminist analysis of "home" that a stay-at-home feminist might find antagonistic is an essay jointly authored by Biddy Martin and Chandra Talpade Mohanty, "Feminist Politics: What's Home Got to Do with It?" Martin and Mohanty argued that Euro-American middle-class feminists cannot fight sexism and racism without a cost to themselves; they cannot just "add on difference without leaving the comfort of home."[68] Through a reading of Minnie Bruce Pratt's 1984 essay, "Identity: Skin Blood Heart," Martin and Mohanty pushed for a politicized understanding of "home" that acknowledged how the varied privileges bestowed by race, class, sexuality, and religion form both the physical spaces and personal relationships of home. More specifically, they identified Euro-American middle-class, heterosexual, Christian women as those who most need to temper their notions of home as a safe space by becoming aware "of the price at which secure places are bought, the awareness of the exclusions, the denials, the blindnesses on which they are predicated."[69] Disrupting the stability of home also disrupts the stability of the self, according to Martin and Mohanty, laying bare how our identities shift according to our social and physical contexts.[70] Such a shaking up of self and home would render impossible a middle-class Euro-American's propensity to be "unconstrained by labels, by identities, by consignment to a group, and . . . to ignore the fact that their existence and social place are anything other than self-evident, natural, human."[71]

Martin and Mohanty's challenge to middle-class Euro-American women to recognize how varieties of privilege shape their experience of home provocatively shows that notions of home can be just as diverse as notions of mothering.[72] But how does such a challenge actually work in a family's life? What would it look like for a woman with small children to disrupt the "secure place" of her home? Are "constantly shifting" relationships a model for home life? Establishing their homes as safe spaces was a goal of all of the women I interviewed—Euro-American, African-American, middle-class, and working-class. Having a home birth was one of their most symbolic and strategic ways of accomplishing this goal—giving birth at home demonstrated their conviction that home is safe, while it also drew together their families, and at times established community, in an act that was a tangible way of making a family.

Feminist theorist bell hooks called for a revaluation of the home and the work women do therein by addressing the question of the politics of domesticity in helpful ways. Home has the potential to have a "radical political dimension," in hooks's analysis, in that it can provide a place where resistance to domination can grow as people nurture and care for each other. Hooks was specifically concerned with African-American traditions of "homeplace," in which women nurtured their families in the face of racist and sexist oppression while doing double duty by taking care of Euro-American homes and families as domestic workers. In this context, argued hooks, "creat[ing] a homeplace that affirmed our beings, our blackness, our love for one another was necessary resistance."[73] In the contemporary situation, hooks asserted, women's domestic resistance work has been degraded as African-American men have taken on sexist, bourgeois norms belittling "women's work," and women themselves have been distracted from the project of "teaching critical consciousness in domestic space" by the lures of "compulsive consumerism."[74] In hooks's opinion, the "primacy of domesticity as a site for subversion and resistance" needs to be reasserted across differences in class and education so that African-American solidarity can be renewed.[75] Although maintaining home as a safe space has often meant struggle in the African-American experience, hooks demonstrated that safe spaces are goals for African-Americans as well as for Euro-Americans.

Hooks declared that home is a political site worthy of struggle. This assertion, especially her comment that the devaluing of homeplace came with an adoption of "white bourgeois norms where home is conceptualized as politically neutral space,"[76] provides a helpful perspective on home-birthing women's expectations for home. Whether they acknowledge it or not, women who give birth at home know that home is not a politically neutral space. Bringing their children into the world in their living rooms (as some home-birthers do) can draw censure from family, neighbors, and even the state. Homes are policed in a variety of ways, and are not spaces of immunity from outside powers.

Home-birthing women also know that the work they do in the home, whether in birthing, mothering, or homemaking, can profoundly influence not only their own lives, but also the wider society. Home birth is in part a response to what Nancy Hewitt called the "cultural roots of contemporary denigrations of domesticity." Namely, a culture rooted in experts, including doctors and home economists, who tried to professionalize child care within the home because women were considered insufficiently educated for the task of producing future generations.[77] Ironically, in Hewitt's view, it was from "this heritage of reductionist theory and embattled professionalism that Betty Friedan and later feminists inherited their fundamental critiques of the family."[78] Home birth, as a revaluing and deprofessionalizing of at least one aspect of domesticity, runs counter to some of these deeply ingrained feminist rejections of home life.

From a feminist perspective that values the possibilities of domesticity, the issue becomes what sort of homes these home-birthing women are creating, what sort of girls and boys these women are mothering into adults, and the roles their partners (usually men) play in the process. Certainly, not all of these women assented to feminist principles even when they shared child care with their husbands and worked outside the home, though most did support certain feminist causes, with a desire for pay equity being mentioned often. While most women adamantly stated that they wanted their daughters to grow up with as much self-esteem as their sons, many felt that their own role in the home was a special one, naturally given to them as women and mothers, that could not be replicated by their husbands.

Asserting the naturalness of their role, many women also affirmed that they achieved personal fulfillment and self-esteem through being at home to raise their children. As such, their choice is not necessarily self-abnegating surrender to patriarchal norms of women's domestic roles, but it might be an assertion of self in opposition to sexist and capitalist notions of success.[79] As Elise Gold, a former pension actuary, contended:

> I believe that feminism is that women should have the right to choose the way they want to live their lives. I think that where the feminist movement went wrong was making women, helping make women, feel that their place was in the work world. And minimizing the role of motherhood, minimizing or almost

making it a shameful thing, you know: "I'm a housewife at home, just a housewife, and all that." But I think that feminism and motherhood do go very much together, as well as home birth and that type of thing. If you really believe in women and the power of women, then it's not too hard to see that women's bodies can make life and birth these babies and nourish them as well. So it's not "Oh, I can be a truckdriver because a man can be a truckdriver." You know, well, maybe I could [be], but I don't choose that role. And I also don't like to judge and say that no one should—if a woman wants to do that.

Elise, who homeschools her three sons, realized that choosing not to work outside the home had financial costs. Not all women or all families can bear such costs. In order to have the choice to reject a "successful" career that would provide good financial rewards and intellectual stimulation, a woman must be in the position to imagine herself both with or without a career. She must be sufficiently educated and connected to be able to embark on a career, and she must have the financial wherewithal (usually in the form of a working, wage-earning partner or extended family support) to choose to stay at home. The majority of working women do not make their choices about employment from such a vantage point of privilege.

Elise's version of feminism—one that sees birth and mothering as expressions of women's power—has been called alternately maternalist, gynocentric, difference, or even conservative pro-family feminism.[80] Critics of gynocentric feminism, even sympathetic ones like philosopher Iris Marion Young, worry that celebration of the body and mothering will do little to change inequalities rooted in sexism. As Young contended, a feminist claim that women "have a right to the positions and benefits that have hitherto been reserved for men, and that male-dominated institutions should serve women's needs, is a direct threat to male privilege." On the other hand, she worried that a gynocentric exposition of "masculinist values as body-denying and selfish" is not such a threat.[81] Young's division between an effective "equality feminism" and a symbolic "difference feminism," however, is blurred in the case of home birth, as gynocentric women like Elise and Tessa subvert one of those same male-dominated institutions in their refusal to give birth in a hospital.

Mothering in a feminist age (or at least in a feminist-influenced age) is a contentious activity for all women, feminist or not. When women make a countercultural, and hence a cultured, decision to give birth at home—an act they see as a way of constructing a good home—many also feel that the mothering that follows birth must be accepted as "natural." This tension between the cultural and the natural mother materializes most tangibly in women's understanding of their bodies. At the same time that women consider their homes safe places for birth, so too do they imagine their bodies as safe (not pathological) spaces for birth. I turn now from the home to the body, keeping alive the question of how notions of the "natural" shape the discourses of home birth. As many feminists have ably pointed out, arguments based on an assertion of what is natural for women often submerge a woman's sense of place under an urge to put a woman in her place.

6

Natural Women: Bodies and the Work of Birth

THOUGH SHE no longer believes in the God of her childhood, Olivia Eldrich does believe in nature, and that the body is its most powerful oracle. According to her, this belief led to the success of her first birth at home: "I am so grateful I did it at home. So glad. Because my first birth would have ended in a cesarean, if I did not believe strongly in nature. I know that the body tells the truth. You ask it a question, it will tell the truth." Olivia's faith in nature and her body has been especially influenced by New Age thinking, but her use of the notion of nature to make sense of her birthing body is not entirely new. For example, characterizing the nineteenth-century debate over the use of anesthesia in childbirth, historian Mary Poovey asked the following: "Does the woman in labor properly belong to the realm of nature, which is governed by God, or to culture, where nature submits to man?"[1] While the dichotomy between nature and culture is no longer considered quite so distinct, and scholars are widely agreed that childbirth is a cultural act, this question has more contemporary relevance than might first appear.[2]

In their everyday talk, home-birthing women in North America seem to opt for the first "natural" choice, albeit with varying restraints on God's control. They also participate however, in a culture of birth that challenges the control they see wielded by a biomedically dominated obstetrical establishment over women's reproductive lives. Without entirely relinquishing the techniques and knowledge base of biomedical obstetrics, they insist that birth is a natural process that can be infused with, and understood through, religious perspectives. As such, they inhabit "post-biomedical" bodies—bodies that do not entirely deny the usefulness of biomedicine but challenge its hegemony via alternative systems of knowledge, such as religion.

Amid diverse religious and political identities, and with both forthrightness and subtlety, home-birthing women root their challenge in the wisdom and "truth" found in their bodies. They maneuver between essentialism and agency in their search for the natural, refusing to let the maternal body be either entirely biologically determined or entirely independent of any kind of biological necessity. Sustaining this refusal is a belief in nature that is often a refraction of a belief in a god or goddess. In this chapter, I continue my focus on the feminist tensions and notions of agency embedded in the discourses of home birth by asking what these women mean by this use of the word "natural," and how their understandings of nature and their experiences of their bodies shape each other.

Just as women's understandings of their homes were developed in distinction to other spheres, like the hospital, the church, or the synagogue, so too were their notions of nature shaped through a process of distinction, in this case opposing nature to "technology." The opposition between nature and technology can be overly polarized, however, since believing in nature does not necessarily mean that women forgo the ability to intervene in natural processes. Whether they acknowledge them as such or not, home-birthing women utilize technologies of the body—skills that manipulate or work with the body to read its messages or ease its pain. Using technology in childbirth means applying one's base of knowledge to shape the experience of birth, whether that knowledge comprises symbolic rituals like a Blessing Way ceremony, manual skills like perineal massage, or hospital techniques like cesareans and episiotomies.

The intertwining of nature and technology—in the broad sense that I use it—runs through the stories that I tell here. "Labor," the most common metaphor the English language provides for childbirth, crystallizes this intersection of technology and nature: birth requires work—cultural and physical labor. Women choosing home birth are making a choice to do much of that work themselves. They are opting for simpler technologies to assist with the physical work of birth, forgoing electronic fetal monitors and epidurals in favor of hand-held dopplers or fetoscopes, warm baths, and the human touch of massage. In tackling the cultural work of birth, however, they are engaging in complex cultural and religious labor that helps them to find ways of carrying their bodies through birth and to find the language to interpret their experiences.

Drawing, perhaps unconsciously, from notions of the religious life that consider authentic spirituality to require discipline and work, many of these women see childbirth as part of a lifelong process of seeking and learning. They see their approaches to childbirth evolving over the course of their procreative lives, as they read birth books, practice birthing postures, explore their bodies, and learn from their own and others' birthing experiences. A certain pragmatism shapes their labors, as they draw selectively from medicine, midwifery, and religion in working with technologies of birth as "natural women."

My main entrée into this cultural and religious work of birth is through attending to the metaphors that women use to describe what they think is natural about birth and their bodies. The intimate interrelation of language and bodily experience—the reciprocity between what one says and one's feelings of embodiment—is a powerful basis for making meaning out of a life.[3] While this whole book is about how birth is a particularly profound source for such creative conceptualization, this chapter focuses specifically on how women talked about and worked with their birthing bodies in making sense of childbirth. Before turning to these words, I lay out some of the parameters of my own understanding of the word natural, and point to some of the potential pitfalls of its use.

What Is Natural?

Home birth does not come naturally in North American society. Struggling to find ways to birth their babies in accordance with their views of the natural, home-birthing women act counter to the dominant habitus of their culture. For sociologist Pierre Bourdieu, habitus is "society written into the body, into the biological individual," and works to structure actions and beliefs while making them appear natural.[4] While the hospital has come to seem like the "natural" place to give birth in North America (even effectively adopting the phrase "natural childbirth"), home-birthing women argue that it is not. Their rejection of the hospital as the natural place to give birth is itself, however, premised on varying assertions about what is natural about women and childbirth.

The interpretations of the natural that home-birthing women achieve are not simple victories of women against misogynist or demonic structures of oppression, which reach a "true" version of nature. Instead, they are multiple interpretations of nature that draw on and are structured by women's experiences in a diversity of what Bourdieu terms "fields," arenas of activity "with their specific institutions and their own laws of functioning" in which people hold "specific stakes and interests."[5] Such fields include science, religion, economics, education, and specific professions. Women draw from their experience in a range of fields, including in some cases medicine, to assert the naturalness of birth. For example, notions of gender—of what it means to be a woman, man, or mother—profoundly influence what is construed as natural in home birth.[6] But this gendering of birth is also embedded in the particular combinations of religion, class, race, sexuality, and political conviction that each woman brings to the practices and interpretations of birth. For example, Liza Rossiter, an African-American woman married to a Euro-American man, felt that her earlier flouting of societal convention in marrying "interracially" set her on the path to challenge conventions of childbirth as well. Resisting racist presumptions of what was "natural" in love helped Liza find a countercultural version of the natural in birth.

Liza's example furthers the question "How are the natural bodies of home-birthing women gendered?" to ask what combinations of religion, politics, race, sexuality, and class lie within the gendered habitus of a home-birthing woman? Judith Butler's notion of the "performing" of gender may provide some clues. The difficult question that Butler tried to address, and which is of key importance to any analysis of birth, is how the material reality of the body—of flesh and blood—and the social and cultural construction of the body interrelate. She reflected: "Surely bodies live and die; eat and sleep; feel pain, pleasure, endure illness and violence; and these 'facts,' one might skeptically proclaim, cannot be dismissed as mere construction. Surely there must be some kind of necessity that accompanies these primary and irrefutable experiences." Butler's answer is to say that yes, there is something "unconstructed" about our bodies, but in understanding and expressing such forms of material being, we necessarily make use of cultured discourse.[7]

When women say—as they did again and again—that their body is speaking to them or "telling the truth," the body's voice is not somehow pure, or before culture.[8] The language that it speaks, whether in pain, pleasure, or merely discomfort, is always a translation through a woman's layers of personal and psychic history and cultural values. This translation or construction is not necessarily fake or dispensable, as Butler asks, "What are we to make of constructions without which we would not be able to think, to live, to make sense at all, those which have acquired for us a kind of necessity?"[9] That women give birth is, at least so far, a material necessity for human procreation—where and how birth takes place and what it means in a woman's life is less of a given, but is undoubtedly related to the material process of birth.

The materiality of birth, then, is absorbed and refracted through constructions—for instance, those of gender, race, religion, class, and sexuality. For a counterexample to Liza's, consider how race is sometimes used as a proof of the naturalness of nonmedicalized birth. A common trope both among some women I interviewed and in home-birth literature is an assertion of the naturalness of birth that relies on examples of the "tribal" woman who gives birth easily without intervention and recovers in hours. In relying on this trope, Euro-American women do not find an *Ur*-birther (or a "purebirther") even if they are seeking one.[10] They are constructing a vision of birth (which they hold as positive) that is sedimented by layers of religious, political, and economic imperialism, and by racist myths and desires for the simplicity of the "primitive."[11] For example, as one Euro-American woman phrased it:

> When you read about all the women in other countries, the "non-Western, non-industrialized countries," they all give birth, go out, and do their job the next day, or the same day, and it's like, not a big deal. And none of them tear. None of them have to get stitches, so I knew there had to be a way that that would be possible. And to me, I feel God would not create something, and put it inside a body that's not capable of coming out without any problems, and so, that's why I didn't want an episiotomy.

This woman's perspective on childbirth in non-Western countries, encouraged by some classic childbirth books like Suzanne Arms's *Immaculate Deception*, comes out of a sense of solidarity with all women—but a solidarity that is perhaps more often imaginary than real. While the non-Western woman may act as a source of hope in a North American context, in her own life childbirth is not so easy; the lifetime risk that an African woman will die from pregnancy- or birth-related causes is one in fifteen.[12]

Maternal mortality in the Third World has a number of causes, most notably lack of food and debilitating disease.[13] Certainly, introducing hospital birth in poor countries is not necessarily the best route for solving the problem of maternal or infant mortality.[14] When home-birthing women in North America claim the "simplicity" of non-Western women as an inspiration, they not only romanticize the difficult realities of many women's lives but also perpetuate a mystifying form of racism for the empowerment of the "civilized."[15] As feminist theorist Donna Haraway has asserted, there is no place of innocence from which to create or assume the natural.[16] Euro-American home-birthing women in the United States, then, are implicated in a diverse range of oppositional discourses, some of which place them in the position of the dominated seeking justice, and others of which find them lodged with the dominating, reworking racialized stereotypes for their own ends. This paradox takes its place with many others in a world in which women who are staunchly against the use of birth technology live with computers, cell phones, and microwave ovens, but are basing their struggle to birth at home on the grounds of what is natural.

Remembering that these women told me their particular stories of childbirth knowing that I too was a home-birthing woman and a mother, and trusting that I would be a sympathetic listener, I now turn to their accounts of birth. Their stories are a "performance" of gender and religious identity told for my benefit at a particular time, and in retelling these partial accounts I have tried to be mindful of the responsibility of re-presenting their words within the frame of my own.

Metaphors of the Birthing Body

Exploring the diversity of ways women use the idea of the natural in terms of their bodies calls for close attention to their language. One of the earliest and most lucid calls for attention to the relationship between language and the body came from a linguist, George Lakoff, and a philosopher, Mark Johnson. Lakoff and Johnson argued that metaphor is a means for "imaginative rationality." In their words, "metaphor is one of our most important tools for trying to comprehend partially what cannot be comprehended totally: our feelings, aesthetic experiences, moral practices, and spiritual awareness."[17] Metaphor hovers between direct bodily experience and its categorization, mutually interacting with social and bodily experience both to express those experiences and to structure them.[18] For example, in one of Lakoff and Johnson's illustrations, the idea that one is "up" when happy is tied to human upright posture. In terms of birth, women draw on metaphors of nature to describe their birthing bodies as a way of translating the bodily experience of birth into language. These metaphors are excursions into imaginative rationality. They categorize birth—make sense of it—in a way that depends on imagining it as like something else. Thus, birth is neither entirely free of necessity or the natural body nor entirely formed by language or categories, whether they be biomedical categories or those of midwifery. In this slippery gap between language and bodily experience lies the potential to change the way words structure bodily life and what bodies are heard to say.

The language women use to talk about their births not only describes the process of birthing, but also ties birth into wider webs of signification that shape notions of what it is to be a woman. Numerous scholars have demonstrated that the dominant metaphors describing birth in contemporary America are characterized by mechanical images, in which a woman's body is fragmented into working parts over which she has little control. As Emily Martin phrased it, "Medically, birth is seen as the control of laborers (women) and their machines (their uteruses) by managers (doctors), often using other machines to help."[19] The mechanicity of the dominant medical view is perhaps best encapsulated by the canonical obstetrics textbook, *Williams Obstetrics*, which defines birth as "the complete expulsion or extraction from the mother of a fetus."[20] Feminist scholars and birth activists have criticized mechanical metaphors for the process of birth because of their negative implications for women's agency as birth givers and their limited view of the significance of childbirth in a woman's life. As well, birthing women have developed contrary metaphors that describe birth as more than a mechanical process in which the woman is alienated from her labor. Discussing these alternative-birth activists who have searched for new imagery, Emily Martin argued for the power of language to shape the body: "There is a compelling need for new key metaphors, core symbols of birth that capture what we do not want to lose about birth."[21] She went on to note, however, that any attempt to conceive new languages for birth would be fraught with the contradictions arising from living within an androcentric society shaped by mechanical images of birth and bodies that obscure a woman's personhood in casting her as a machine.[22]

Home-birthing women in particular are working toward creating new visions of birth that center women and babies as the prime actors in the picture. As Martin predicted, however, their visions are not seamless utopias. Unpacking what women mean by the word natural when speaking of bodies is a powerful way to see the tensions within women's imagery of birth. These tensions include, for example, paradoxes of agency and submission that arise when home birth is posited both as a conduit for women's power and as a confirmation of women's "necessary" tie to domesticity, which, for some, means subordination to men's authority. To explore these tensions, I now turn to the variety of metaphors women used in speaking of their bodies, which ranged from the body as animal to the body as machine. I consider most carefully the stories of eleven women, whose use of metaphor reflects that of many of the other women I spoke with. Throughout, I ask how these languages of the body take for granted what it is to be a woman and how they contest that taken-for-granted quality of "womanhood," as well as how religion factors into these negotiations.

I found several overlapping narratives of the natural in women's home-birth stories. First, some women described birth as an "animal act," and used other mammals as examples of the natural way to birth. In this view, giving birth like an animal is not simply innate to women's bodies, but is a socially developed "instinct" that must be uncovered, given our society's surrender to complex technological manipulation. Second, in a related vein, some women saw their bodies as sources of powerful and particularly feminine instincts and wisdom, which childbirth activated in a new way. This perspective encompassed women who practiced Goddess spirituality, channeling, and "New Age Judaism." These women wanted to retain control of where and how they gave birth, but maintained that the power and physicality of the act of birth itself was beyond human control. A third mode of the natural was widespread across a range of Jewish and Christian identities—God has designed women's birthing bodies and if women recognize this state of "divine nature" they can ease the process of birth. While some women made only cursory reference to the God-designed body in the context of childbirth, for other women this was a notion that guided their lives in intimate and tangible ways.

Birth as an Animal Act

The equation of childbirth with animality is a potentially dangerous alliance—one that can denigrate women as much as celebrate them. As feminist theorist Mary O'Brien pointed out, seeing birth as an animal act can place the process of birth wholly within the sphere of biological necessity, and outside the realms of the social and cultural. In such a view, the treacherous possibilities of tying women to nature as childbearers become clear: women, due to their "natural" roles, are less fully human (or cultured) than men.[23]

Within the alternative-birth movement, however, the language of animality has been given a positive cast, acting as proof of the "naturalness" of birth in the face of increasingly high-tech manipulation. Likening birthing women to cats and sheep, "husband-coached" childbirth doctor Robert Bradley praised the woman capable of reaching a state of animality in which she let go of her inhibitions and fears of birth. Home-birth-friendly obstetrician Michel Odent echoed, or perhaps intensified, Bradley's praise for animality in developing the "*salle sauvage*," the birthing room in the French hospital where he worked.[24] For these writers, animality in birthing, while "instinctual," is still an achievement, demanding training and the proper surroundings. Giving birth like an animal, then, is not simply innate to women's bodies, but is a socially developed "instinct."

How do home-birthing women use the language of animality to describe their experiences? Not surprisingly, the two veterinarians in my study made the most recourse to such metaphors. In what follows, I juxtapose and interpret the stories of these two home-birthing veterinarians, paying particular attention to how they spoke of animality, and how their professional and religious identities shaped their attitudes to the body.

Marianne Martin, 38, a Euro-American veterinarian, is a mother of three who lives on a quiet suburban street. She is a self-described "traditional" Roman Catholic who attends a church that has returned to the pre–Vatican II Latin Mass.[25] Her husband, Tom, is a police officer, and he shares Marianne's commitment to traditional Catholicism. Since her children were born, Marianne has scaled back her veterinary work to part-time, and together with Tom she homeschools their children. Marianne's first birth was planned as a home birth but became a hospital cesarean due to placenta praevia.[26] Her subsequent two births took place at home, with the help of direct-entry midwives. Ironically, she was first drawn to home birth by a commencement address extolling its benefits given by a nurse-midwife at a joint graduation for doctors and certified nurse-midwives (CNMs), at which Marianne's sister was graduating as a doctor. Remembering that her veterinary training also advised that pets should give birth at home, Marianne and her husband chose a home birth.

Describing her second labor at home, Marianne, a petite and energetic woman, found the image of dogs and cats most helpful: "I didn't want [Tom] to touch me or anything. I didn't want anybody to touch me. It was like I felt like an animal, like the dogs and cats. I just wanted to be left alone and work through it myself." Marianne enjoyed the comfort of knowing the midwives were there, but she wanted very little intervention: "I wanted the midwives there just in case I needed them for something that went wrong, and just to help me to know that it was progressing the way it was supposed to. Because I still didn't feel like I knew exactly; you know, it was only my second time. I didn't want anybody's help really." Marianne's desire for solitude extended even beyond touch, as she became annoyed when her husband tried to vocalize with her as she moaned through her pains.

Marianne's choice to have a home birth after having had a cesarean was a difficult decision to enact, especially since it was illegal in her state for certified nurse-midwives to attend vaginal births at home after the mother had undergone a cesarean. As a result, her only choice—and not a bad one in her view—was to have a team of direct-entry midwives. Despite her medical training as a veterinarian—or perhaps because of it—Marianne chose not to heed medical warnings about vaginal births after cesareans. Instead, she trusted her body's ability to give birth, and the abilities of the midwives to help her give birth at home. Marianne drew on her medical knowledge and clinical experience with animals to support her trust in what she considered to be her body's natural processes. Also, when seeing a doctor for prenatal checkups, Marianne reminded the doctor of her medical background as a way of supporting her refusal to have prenatal testing. Citing insufficient study of the safety and long-term effects of dopplers (which read the fetal heartbeat through sound waves) and ultrasounds, Marianne used her medical training to avoid certain technological interventions.

Marianne went for prenatal care to this doctor in order to have medical backup in case she had to go to the hospital, but she did not tell her that she was planning a home birth. While this duplicity was a vexing ethical problem for Marianne, she felt the benefits of home birth for her and her baby superseded the medical protocol. After she had her second home birth, she debated whether to tell her doctor (a colleague and friend of her sister's) that she had planned to give birth at home. Marianne recalled that her husband urged her to tell the truth, saying, "Our faith teaches us to tell the truth. If you think you're not lying, you're really not telling the truth. So it will help her, if you tell her." On the basis of relieving her conscience, as well as providing a different perspective on birth to the obstetrician, Marianne elected to tell her doctor that the home birth was planned. Although the doctor was surprised, she did not chastise Marianne or take any action against the midwives. Marianne both used and feared medical authority as she sought a more natural, animal-like birth.

She turned to her own scientific knowledge to buttress her nonbiomedical approach, while worrying about how not to close off hospital technology should she need it; she made her decisions within a postbiomedical body.

Christina Upton, another veterinarian, effected a similar blend of borrowing from and critiquing medical approaches to birth. Christina lives in a large restored farmhouse in the country, with paddocks for horses in the back. Like Marianne, she has chosen to work part-time since becoming a mother of three. Her first birth took place in a hospital with a certified nurse-midwife, and her last two were at home with a different certified nurse-midwife. Christina, 41 when she gave birth to her last baby, comes from a Lutheran background, and her husband, also a veterinarian, was raised in an Orthodox Jewish family. Together, they now go to a Reconstructionist synagogue.

Christina, a tall and inquisitive woman, met many of my questions with her own. Similarly to Marianne, she also took animals as birthing examples based on her veterinary experience. As we sat on her living-room floor while our two daughters played, she commented, "I have witnessed many animal births. We just had a baby foal born last week. She [the mare] had it out in the field, and fortunately everything went well. We had intended to be there as her 'midwife,' and she said, 'NO!' And she did it on her own! She had a field birth in the lovely, soft earth, which is the way Mother Nature intended it." Christina felt that watching animals give birth, combined with her scientific learning as a veterinarian, has shaped her own feelings and decisions about birth. She also feels that her scientific knowledge has not alienated her from her body: "I have a degree in biology, and I feel very close to my body and just all the biological processes. And also . . . well, being a veterinarian and watching animals across the species [give] birth, they do it with such finesse and ease. And I said to myself, 'Well, isn't that the way humans were supposed to birth too?'" While speaking of being close to her body as if it were an intimate and trusted friend may sound like one degree of alienation, it may be more a sign of the difficulty of speaking of "one's" body in English in any other way than as removed from the self.

Unlike Marianne, however, whose veterinary education provided some of the rationale for her refusal to obey medically sanctioned laws, Christina's education as a veterinarian had led her to see birth as a natural process in need of little medical intervention, but one that should accord with laws requiring state-sanctioned medical supervision. For Christina, it was very important that she give birth with the help of a certified nurse-midwife, although she was quick to say she thought some direct-entry midwives could be very competent. (Christina, unlike Marianne, had never undergone a cesarean, so she could choose between a state-sanctioned CNM and a direct-entry midwife.) Christina considered her midwife to have medical knowledge on a par with that of a doctor, and thought her own medical training was an asset to having a home birth, since she had a "knowledge of the basic physiology of the body." Christina was critical of the "meddling" of the medical system in the ways of birth, in that doctors made decisions for a woman, "rather than allowing a woman's body to tell her what needs to be done." While Christina demanded non-medicalized space in which to listen to her body, she was grateful to have a basement full of medical supplies from her husband's veterinary practice, to use if she needed them.

Though they share a view of birth that considers animals' ways of birthing to be models for humans, Christina and Marianne have fundamentally different perspectives on women's bodily autonomy. Home-birthing women who ground their birthing decisions in "nature" situate themselves in a variety of positions regarding the social significance of the biological processes of birth. Some women see themselves working in tandem with natural forces in a way that grants them freedom to intervene in their bodies' biological state. Other women consider that their biological status as women is something with which they cannot toy, since nature, guided by God, has made them a particular way for a particular purpose. Abortion is the most obvious of issues that bring these different approaches to bodily autonomy to light. Where Christina and Marianne might be placed near one another on a continuum of attitudes to the medicalization of birth, they would be at opposite ends of a continuum in their attitudes to abortion. While their similarity of approach to the naturalness of birth as an animal act is partly explained by their common education as veterinarians, the disjuncture of their opinions on the subject of abortion stems from differing religious identities and differing physical experiences.

Christina bases her views of the significance of procreation for a woman's life on a philosophy that is a melding of God's will with evolutionary imperatives:

> It's the cycle of life that's meant to be, and it's completed [in birth]. . . . This is what God meant, this is one of our intended focuses on this earth, to recreate our species. It's a completion of life—fulfilling that biological, the biological species preservation. It just feels so good. I mean, just having the baby and loving that baby and nurturing and being able to breast-feed. That's so important to me, too; the completion of your maternal life cycle. It feels so good to be able to provide my babies with their total sustenance for those first months. It makes me feel so good about myself.

Christina fits together her view of God with her scientific training with very little difficulty. For her, God is responsible for the "miraculous nature of birth itself," and this view is perfectly compatible with the biological process of reproduction.

Participating in the "cycle of life" has given a great deal of joy and self-esteem to Christina, but it has also brought its sorrows. Christina and her husband chose to terminate their third pregnancy, because prenatal tests revealed that the baby had serious genetic abnormalities:

> I had lost a baby in between Jake and Susie. I was five months pregnant, and the baby—I'll be very honest with you, because I don't tell many people, but—I was twenty-three weeks, and we elected to terminate the pregnancy because the baby had trisomy 18, which is a severe genetic anomaly. He had multiple anomalies, cardiac, genitals. Developmentally, we were told—and we did a lot of research—that this baby probably would not live very long if he was born.

Christina found that her midwife supported her during the abortion process, just as she had supported her during her earlier home birth:

> I went through that with my [midwife], and she was right there for me. And when I went into the hospital to terminate the pregnancy, she was there for me, and so I have a little special part of me [for her]. But that was rough. That was real rough. . . . So that was a special relationship, and something of a growing experience, I'll tell you. It makes you really appreciate your children. We were just so—we were praying for Susie that she would be, there would be no problem. I feel very lucky. . . . I never thought I would do that, never in my wildest dreams, but given the circumstances and what the baby would have gone through, all these things taken together, this is what our choice was.

Christina could accommodate her difficult decision within her physiological and religious view of the natural cycle of life.[27]

Her decision fit within what Margarete Sandelowski and Linda Carson Jones called a story of "nature's choice," in their study of parents grappling with detected fetal anomalies. These authors found that women who terminated pregnancies, in which prenatal tests predicted the baby would have died either in the womb or shortly after birth, felt that "nature had already determined the outcome and, by terminating pregnancy, they were simply acting in line with what nature intended."[28] Christina's perspective on the animal world, her medical training, and her belief in God all shaped her sense of what was natural for her body. Within her perspective of God's intentions for nature, she retained a notion of personal agency that allowed her to intervene in the cycle of life when she deemed it necessary, or when nature seemed to call for it.[29]

Marianne, on the other hand, is strictly opposed to abortion and prenatal testing. She has not had personal crises in which she contemplated abortion, but she did recall having some doubts as a young woman. Now she is certain of her view—a position that she has come to from her experiences both as a Catholic and a veterinarian, and that she shares with her husband:

We're very antiabortion, we're very pro-life in general, antieuthanasia. I would never have an amniocentesis done. I am very vocal about [it]. . . . Many people don't realize what an abortion entails, what it is. Most people think it's just a blob of tissue, and what's the big deal if she doesn't want to be pregnant. I thought that too at one point, a very short period. . . . Most Catholics—well, I shouldn't say that because the church has changed so much—but the Catholic teaching was always against abortion, even when I was younger. Even when I was going to the New Mass churches, the priests usually were antiabortion. But there was a point where I was reviewing things in my own mind. I thought well, what's the big deal, what's the big deal? But when you investigate and find out exactly what's involved, and especially when you have children—I have found so many people have become more conservative in their values [once they have children], not necessarily real conservative, but more conservative than they were.

A turning point in Marianne's views of abortion came when as a young and "unassertive" veterinarian she spayed a pregnant cat despite her own unease with the process. The cat later died, and the owners of the cat (a mother and daughter who were also Catholic) were distraught. As Marianne recalled: "They were yelling at me, and I was crying. She said, 'Well, why do you do it then?' And then it hit me: 'Why do I do it?'" After that experience, Marianne decided she would never spay a pregnant animal again. She has since become an active and "very vocal" antiabortion activist: "I hand out brochures and pamphlets; not necessarily graphic things, but just from my medical experience." Marianne's resolute stance on abortion is part of her wider, religiously inspired view that the body must be guided by God's will, as it is interpreted by her Catholic faith. For birth control, she has practiced only natural family planning and opposes homosexuality and birth control to the extent that she homeschools her children to keep them from exposure to sex education and views of sexuality different from her own.[30]

Sharing a perception of birth as natural and a view that likens human bodies to those of animals does not necessarily mean that people will share other practices of the body. Bodily autonomy, practices of sexuality, and reproductive choices are forged in the midst of religious beliefs, secular education, and personal experience. Marianne and Christina have negotiated their bodily perspectives in such a way that they share similar attitudes and practices when it comes to the process of birth. The wider nets supporting their birthing choices, however, are made up of different configurations of religion, politics, and experience. Conversing over their births, they would probably have much to discuss. Were their talk to move to wider questions of sexuality and reproductive choice, the conversation would probably become strained, if not acrimonious.

Intuition and Instinct

Other women drew on the metaphor of animality in a slightly different way. They held that giving birth has the potential to deepen and confirm a woman's natural intuitive powers and her ability to be in touch with her instincts. The language of instinct drew most often on a metaphor of the body as a speaking voice within a woman's self—a sort of anthropomorphism of the body. This silent voice, experienced somatically, was a voice of resistance that was not always easy to hear or follow. These women's views of instinct were akin to those of Michel Odent, and many had read his book *Birth Reborn*. In a direct critique of certain kinds of childbirth education, like the Lamaze method, Odent contended that birth is a time for women to find their instincts, not a time for them to be "taught." Odent was "convinced that there was some universal component in the behaviour of mother and newborn, and that—given the right kind of environment, where she could feel free and uninhibited—a woman could naturally reach a level of response deeper within her than individuality, upbringing or culture."[31] Odent realized that such statements risked eliciting charges of essentialism. He combined his advocacy of home birth with physiological proofs, asserting that "there is nothing shameful or sexist in recognizing that instinct plays a part in our behaviours, especially those that exist at the intersection of nature and culture, such as lovemaking, labor, or the newborn's search for the mother's nipple."[32] Women need to prepare themselves to attend to instinct, according to Odent; but once ready, birth can take them "naturally" to a place in their bodies beyond culture.

Poised between nature and culture, instinct was a powerful cue for some women. Instinct, however, seemed to leave more room than the more biologically based metaphor of animality for a combination of beliefs about birth and the religious responses it evoked. Three women, all of whom professed some form of "experimental" or alternative spirituality, made most explicit use of the language of instinct. Valerie Auletta, a mother of four children, aged 1 to 13, gave birth to two of her children in the hospital (one by cesarean) and gave birth to the last two at home with lay midwives. Valerie is Euro-American and grew up as a Lutheran. She married a Catholic and now considers herself "more paganish than anything else." She and her family attend holiday celebrations at a Unitarian church and practice a number of domestic religious rituals centered around goddesses and the seasonal rhythms of the year. They live in a large rented house in a suburban neighborhood.

After giving birth at 22 to her first child in a hospital, with epidural, episiotomy, and forceps, Valerie grew depressed and began to inquire into alternative methods of childbirth in an effort to address what she felt were the roots of her malaise. She eventually planned to have her second child with midwives in a birthing center. While visiting her mother in another state, however, she grew concerned about her baby's movements in the womb, and upon going to the hospital was told that her 29-week-old baby needed to be delivered prematurely by cesarean section. After his birth, Valerie's son needed supplemental oxygen until he was 4 years old. Looking back over her medical records, Valerie felt this cesarean had been unnecessary and resented the trauma it had caused to her son, and to herself.

When Valerie became pregnant again, almost four years later, she decided to have a home birth. Like Marianne, she had difficulty finding a midwife who would attend a vaginal birth after cesarean (VBAC) at home, but she was eventually successful. Valerie recalled that her first home birth was somewhat disrupted against her wishes when a certified nurse-midwife, whom the lay midwives had called for backup, contacted the emergency paramedics to tell them Valerie was a VBAC. She gave birth in her bedroom surrounded by twelve paramedics and police officers who, she recalled, were eager to catch the baby and receive their "stork pin."[33] Instead her husband and the midwife caught the baby. Five minutes after the birth, one of the police officers smelled the scent of burning sage, which Valerie's friends had lit in a celebratory ritual gesture, and asked that Valerie's husband produce the package from which it came, to ensure that it was not an illegal or toxic substance.

For her second home birth, Valerie achieved what she desired. Ideally, Valerie would have liked to give birth outside in a grove of trees, but she realized the difficulties of this in suburban America. Instead she painted her walls with a mural of trees, and felt that this interior decorating successfully transformed her bedroom into a "natural" environment. With her last birth, Valerie found the freedom to enjoy a birth that was "peaceful, basically peaceful and unrestricted. If I felt like walking or being in the shower, I wouldn't have anybody questioning me." In this peaceful environment, Valerie felt her instincts come to the fore: "Natural is overused, but with his birth, I was really able to just be very instinctive, and it was great, it was wonderful. I was able, I was very—almost animistic. I wasn't thinking at all. It was great. It was wonderful." For Valerie, being instinctive meant she could give birth without analyzing what was going on, or worrying about negotiating over unwanted interventions.

Valerie's comment on the ubiquity of the word natural evidenced the discomfort many home-birth advocates feel with the phrase "natural childbirth." Episiotomy, anesthesia, and even forceps can fall within the phrase as it is used in the hospital, they argue, making natural childbirth a "slippery concept."[34] For the baby to emerge from the vagina in whatever way possible does not constitute a natural birth, in this view. Instead, a natural birth should be drugless, with very minimal intervention.

For Valerie, part of what spurred her to have a home birth after two highly interventionist births was her exploration of Goddess spirituality. Whereas she felt that her obstetricians had "major doubt as far as a woman's ability to actually give birth," her Goddess-based worship gave her trust in that ability. In her words, she used to be a "New Agey type, transcending everything," but women's spirituality brought her in touch with the corporeal. "The thing about women's spirituality is, you have a body, and you're on this earth in that body. . . . The spiritual side is a part of you, [but] it's not everything." At her last birth, Valerie surrounded herself with like-minded women friends (one of whom is an artist who makes Goddess sculptures), and she felt herself to be in the middle of a "supportive circle" that allowed her to birth in the manner she desired.[35]

For their last home births, two women considered women's intuition and instinct to be enough of a guide that they chose to give birth unassisted, without any birth attendants present save for their husbands. Nina Holly, an Italian-American woman with three children, is a writer, musician, office worker, and former birth instructor. I called her after reading an article on home birth that she had written for a local holistic health magazine. Nina grew up as a Catholic but now considers herself a spiritual person open to all religions. A tall, thin, dark-haired woman who seemed comfortable talking about her life, Nina practices channeling and homeopathy, and is a vegan. When we talked, Nina was in the process of separating from her husband, so she came to my house for the interview.

Nina's first birth, when she was 25, took place in the hospital with a midwife despite "instincts" telling her to give birth at home. As she recounted her narrative, her husband was not supportive of a home birth, nor was her wider family, and she felt pressured to go to the hospital. For the most part she enjoyed her birth there, but felt that there was "too much commotion." She also felt that her pushing stage was prolonged by not being able to move about as freely as she wished and by being in a hospital environment surrounded by her husband and a labor assistant dressed in scrubs. For her second birth, she chose to have a home birth with direct-entry midwives. As in her hospital birth, Nina felt the need to labor alone for much of the birth, and found herself reaching a "meditative state":

> I was in this white void, and I was just lying in its lap or arms or something. And it was like this religious kind of thing. It was like it was God, you know, whatever that means. And I was getting messages, like "Don't concentrate on anything, don't tighten up any part of your body, because any part of your body you put energy in is going to take away energy from your uterus. Let all the energy go to your uterus, and let it do its work." I was just kind of thinking it;

I don't know if it was just me thinking it, or kind of a higher power thinking. I was kind of getting guided to do these things. But not from something specifically outside of myself, but not necessarily from me either, you know.

For Nina the work of birth was to cease trying to control her body with her conscious mind. Following her instincts while guided by a god within and without, Nina felt little need for human guidance except for some fine-tuning of her visualizations, and deciding when to push:

I was visualizing my cervix soft and open . . . and I wanted to know if I should be visualizing it at seven centimeters or at five or at nine. I wanted to know what to work with. One of the things I think orthodox medical things are good for is just telling you what's wrong. Once I know what's wrong, I can better use psychic things or homeopath or herbs to heal it. I don't necessarily have to use the medicine they tell me, but I like to know.

For Nina, appropriate use of technology applied even to the relatively low-tech intervention of manually checking the dilation of the cervix. In her understanding, a dilation check counted as an "orthodox medical thing," but was something that she found helpful. She appreciated, however, that the midwife, after checking her and finding that she was fully dilated but had a small cervical lip, chose to leave Nina to finish "working with" her dilation on her own:

So, she left me. You know, every other midwife in the world probably would have stayed, and she knew not to. And I thought that was amazing. . . . By that time, I think the other midwife was here. My husband was still sleeping. And I'm in there visualizing the lip. Me and this other white power thing were pulling on it. And I moaned; I moaned really loudly. And it woke my husband up. And then I moaned loudly again, and he came in and sat with me for like twenty minutes. . . . When he got in the room, everything shifted, the energy shifted. And, again, I should have just done it alone. I could have done it a lot more smoothly and easily if I had just one hundred percent [gone with my instincts] and nothing else. But I got a little nervous. I was like, "What if I start pushing too early, and my cervix tears, or it swells up. Oh my God." I just completely lost my confidence. And I [said], "Just get the midwife, I think I'm ready to push. I don't know, and I want her to tell me if its OK. I don't know what to do."

After successfully pushing out her second child at home, Nina decided that for her third birth she did not need any midwives at all. She labored alone and with her husband. When she reached the pushing stage, she applied her own warm compresses to ease the baby's head through her perineum, and pulled the baby out herself. As she phrased it, "I was my own midwife."

Like Tessa, the woman who performs Blessing Way ceremonies, Nina felt that arriving at a point where she was confident enough to give birth unassisted was tied to reaching spiritual and bodily maturity in other areas of her life. She no longer felt the need to set aside specific times and places to meditate or to listen to and identify her spirit guides; and following her vegan diet had become a normal part of her day, no longer requiring strict discipline. Similarly, her earlier experiences of childbirth integrated birth into her life so that it was "a natural part of [her]." Birthing, spiritual direction, and a vegan diet were all ways that Nina sought not only to follow, but to find her instincts on intersecting spiritual and bodily planes. Finding her instincts required work that blended discipline with an eventual releasing of control over her physical and psychic self. Nina asserted, however, that she is still working toward her goal: "I'm not this self-actualized master or anything. So I'm still at some point between integrating everything that's me into me, and finding out what I should do." If there is a next time, Nina said, she wants to give birth in total solitude, with no other human beings present.

Miriam Shonovsky, like Nina, also chose to give birth to her last baby alone. Miriam grew up in a Jewish home and is married to a university professor in the sciences. She lives in an older three-story home in a small university city. Miriam has been pregnant six times. Her first baby died in the womb at five months and was removed by a hysterotomy, her second child was born by cesarean section, and her subsequent four babies were born at home, three with the help of direct-entry midwives and the last with no attendants present.[36] Despite coming from a highly medical family (her father, sister, and brother-in-law are all doctors), the traumatic experience of her first two experiences of birth led her not to a more medicalized perspective on birth, but to an alternative approach. She became increasingly radicalized in her later births, until she chose to have her last baby at home without attendants, on the basis of "instinct."

Miriam, a wiry, intense woman with a halo of frizzy gray hair and a forthright manner, holds a religious outlook that is a liberal mingling of a variety of traditions: Judaism, Zen, paganism, Native and Goddess spirituality, and Christianity. She said that her births are what led her on a New Age spiritual path. Birthing, in her words, showed her that "magic was real" and opened her up to new ways of thinking and encountering other faiths, leading her to talk to Christ and to give her daughter Native American names. Home birthing gave her confidence to explore spirituality in many different directions, she claimed, while still feeling grounded in her own experience.

Miriam's last baby was unplanned, and she was ambivalent about having a baby in her early forties. She felt that following her instinct was necessary to overcoming her ambivalence, and that instinct was inextricably tied to taking total responsibility for the birth of her baby: "Somehow I thought

to make sure the bonding was okay, for this birth I had to take charge. . . .
I didn't want to answer to anybody. This was going to be my thing."
Miriam felt her earlier home births, however, were the preparation she
needed to be able to follow her instincts to the point of birthing without
the help of midwives. When she first chose home birth, she knew very
little about her body, but she felt that it was unlikely she could progress
in her labor according to the specifications of the hospital: "And I just
thought, maybe I should have this baby at home. And it was totally instinctive. I didn't even know what dilation meant! I knew nothing about my
body. I was totally ignorant and stupid. My mother's idea was that anything below the waist down is disgusting." With each home birth, Miriam
felt she learned more about her body and the process of birth, from both
an intellectual and an embodied perspective.

Miriam felt that her midwives were instrumental in helping her come to
greater knowledge of her body, in part due to their very "hands-off" approach to birthing. For example, during her third home birth, "The only
thing [my midwife] did for me was when I asked her how dilated I was,
she told me to put my hand up my vagina, and I'd feel my baby's head.
And I thought, 'Oh! I can do that?' So then she went downstairs, and [my
husband] caught [our baby]." With the midwife's encouragement, Miriam
became familiar enough with her birthing body that she felt confident in
her abilities to birth on her own. For Miriam, her last home birth was an
"incredible" experience, in which a "love for the whole universe" washed
over her. She considered her unassisted birth to be a uniquely empowering
experience that transformed her life, and sent her on a search for a woman-
based spirituality that would honor the power in birth.

These women draw on instinct, then, to establish the naturalness of
giving birth at home without medication or monitoring devices. But in
these women's experiences, instinct is also a learned capacity to listen to
one's self and one's body. The "truth" that their bodies speak to them
changes over the course of their bodily history of birth in which they
learn and develop techniques of childbirth. Provoking both animality and
spirituality, the language of instinct acted as a powerful legitimator of
birthing decisions that were often in opposition to the preferred ways of
family members, medical experts, and even the law itself.

The God-designed Body

Unlike those women whose eclectic spirituality nourished "instinct,"
women from more traditional religions drew more heavily from a metaphor of a body designed by God. Language about birth and the body
often carries within it references, offhand if not deliberate, to God's perfect design of women's bodies for the purposes of birth.[37] "God talk" in

terms of birth sometimes seems to operate almost at a subconscious level or, perhaps, at the level of a cliché or stereotype. For some women, such as Suzanne, the Italian-American woman who meets with a prayer group, the references to God's design of women's bodies were briefly stated. As Suzanne phrased it when comparing her perspective on God to that of her husband: "He's a chiropractor [who] has a lot of faith in innate intelligence, which in my definition is God-given intelligence. You know, it's creative—you're created with intelligence that makes your body work properly." Women who speak in this matter-of-fact way about how God shapes the human body are part of a larger group whose discourse celebrates women's procreative powers. In the words of the La Leche League classic *The Womanly Art of Breastfeeding*, "Having a baby is a natural, normal function for which a woman's body is superbly designed."[38] While some of this wider discourse is not explicitly religious, the discourse as a whole operates out of a conviction that some larger force, be it evolution or God, tailors women's bodies for the process of birth.[39]

Yet for many of the women I interviewed, God's design of women's bodies is more than a useful metaphor—it is a tangible reality. Not a deist-derived notion of a God who designs and then withdraws from the world, the God-designed body is imaginative categorization embodied, as women think of their bodies as crafted by God and as continuing sites of revelation. Some women's beliefs in God's design of the flesh were intricately woven into how they made sense not only of their births, but of their entire lives as well. Usually being women with strong, though not necessarily conservative, religious identifications, these women included Natalie, a Christian Scientist; Debra, an Orthodox Jew; and Carrie and Janet, Pentecostal Christians. Comparing their understandings will allow me to explore some of the tensions that emerge when feminist and traditionally religious notions of embodiment are conjoined.

Natalie Ruppolo is a Euro-American woman in her mid-thirties who grew up in a Christian Science home, and who is now a Christian Science practitioner.[40] She gave birth to her only child at home, while she was in her mid-twenties. Her husband, a nominally Catholic Italian-American, was much older than she, and had thought all his life (and throughout a previous marriage) that he was infertile. After two months of marriage, and Natalie's incessant prayers to achieve pregnancy, she became pregnant much to everyone's surprise. Natalie attributed her pregnancy to God's will. When she felt worried that her prayers were ineffective, she reassured herself by saying, "God's will is going to be done and that supersedes any health laws, that supersedes any laws of medicine or laws of physics that say that it is impossible, and I don't need to finagle anything. I don't need to manipulate anything, and I certainly don't need to influence God to know what's best for our family." Though she needed to be attentive to her spiritual state and devote herself to the communicative work of prayer, she did not think herself capable of "manipulating" God.

Natalie, blonde and professionally dressed, spoke with me in her orderly home office on a quiet suburban street. For Natalie, her body is an "embodiment of her thought." When she is connected to God and sees herself as "a transparency . . . the spot where God's love shines through," her body is in harmony and good health. When she loses that sense of attunement with God, she feels her body becoming "clogged," and she needs to refocus her attentions on her relationship with God, through prayer. Natalie's view of the body is a rather "disembodied" one, in that she does not dwell on the material specifics of the bodies God created, but sees them as mere vessels for "Spirit."

Other Christian Scientists told me of their strategies for dealing with labor, in which they repeated sentences from Mary Baker Eddy's *Science and Health*, such as "There is no life, truth, nor substance in matter." While women found comfort in these mantra-like repetitions, they were not always easy, because, as Judy, another Christian Scientist, put it: "Sometimes the body's screaming so loudly" that it cannot be ignored. Even for women who deny the existence of the material, the body has a voice. Like Judy, Natalie placed herself in the difficult position of denying her physicality while being caught up in the throes of labor. But for her, as for the other Christian Scientists I spoke with, understanding matter as error while in the process of birthing was not perceived as a contradiction or dilemma.[41]

Natalie drew heavily on *Science and Health* as a guide for living, and gave me a copy as a way of explaining her faith to me in more detail. Mary Baker Eddy's text is filled with denials of the flesh and her denunciations of medicine's acceptance of the materiality of bodies: "No more sympathy exists between the flesh and Spirit than between Belial and God."[42] For Eddy, Christian Science was "natural, but not physical," and was premised on the belief that "Mind," or God, controlled the body totally.[43] This separation of the natural and the physical was unique to the Christian Scientists among the women in my study. While other women nuanced the natural in diverse ways, it was always a category that encompassed the physicality of birth.

Natalie found the resources in her faith in God to resist was she saw as an incompatible belief system; namely, medicine. Following Eddy's emphasis on the power of Mind or God over the flesh, Natalie felt God was in control during her pregnancy. Though she hired a certified nurse-midwife, her first way to deal with difficulties such as anemia was to turn to Christian Science modes of healing (namely, prayer) instead of taking iron supplements as her midwife suggested. Natalie drew a parallel between her choice to put her faith in a Christian Science view of the body and other women's choices to put their faith in the medical view of the body.

I felt that at home, having this home birth, that God was my primary caregiver. I was fulfilling the laws of the land by having the midwife. I felt supported by having someone who was experienced at this there, but I didn't feel that she was in charge of the case. I felt that God was in charge of the case, and I think that would apply if someone were in the hospital. On one hand, they're trusting the physician who is delivering, but ultimately they are trusting the system that's governing the physician. So you've got to have faith in what you're doing. And one way or the other there's got to be some higher power, if it's medicine or if it's God. You've got to have trust in the system that you've turned to, trust enough to then leave the individual responsible for taking the human footsteps [to] do what they have to do, because they're governed by that higher system. The doctor is governed by medicine, and that midwife was under God's authority in our home.

Whether or not the midwife saw herself as under God's authority, Natalie felt that by virtue of entering her home, the midwife had entered a realm of authority that was not medical, but was not entirely distinct from the state. As part of a religious group that has often come into conflict with the medical and legal system because of its views of the body, however, Natalie made sure to emphasize that practicing a minority form of child-birth was legal, while also faithful to her vision.[44]

Throughout her experience of pregnancy and birth, as in the rest of her life, Natalie constantly sought out God's will, in part by using her body as a barometer. Despite the "disembodied" stance of many Christian Science texts, and the denial of matter espoused by many Christian Scientists, their faith is characterized by a fascination with the body as the means through which to read the intentions of God.[45] The Christian Science emphasis on Mind consistently returns to the body in order to evaluate spiritual concerns surrounding health and "harmony."[46] But this absorbed fascination with the God-designed body does not cause Natalie to celebrate her body; though she may use it to measure the state of her relationship with God, it is not the means by which she glorifies her God, or fulfills a God-given role as mother. Now that she travels extensively for her work, Natalie and her husband, a retired police officer and now a taxi driver, share child care and household tasks. Natalie remarked that this sharing of conventionally gendered responsibilities has allowed her to "stop . . . drawing lines of distinction between male and female," so that she considers both herself and her husband to "represent the male and female attributes of God." Natalie feels that there is balance in her family, which allows her to leave for her work without upsetting the equilibrium: "There is no void when I'm gone. The mothering and fathering is still going on."

Natalie's vision that belief tangibly affects the body and that God is the optimal caregiver prompted her to oppose the dominant method of childbirth in her society. The close connection between God and her body, however, did not cause her to revel in her body. For women who came from more conservative Jewish and Christian traditions, however, pregnancy and birthing were means both to glorify their God, and to enact bodily one of the most important of their religion's roles for women, that of mother and nurturer.

For Debra Lensky, experiencing childbirth and teaching childbirth classes taught her the power of God's design of a woman's body and eventually prompted her to become an Orthodox Jew, as I discussed in the last chapter. Describing her process of learning about childbirth and about God, Debra commented:

> What I learned, *really* learned about, [was] what birth was about and how safe it really is. And how we're really designed to give birth as women. There's really a lot of untrust out there in the [birth] education and in our system of medical care. I started to take more responsibility and started to really believe in my own ability to give birth. It's not *my* ability to give birth; it's really a God-given ability to give birth. And when you start trusting the design of the Creator, then you have the guts to go against a society at large.

Key to the interplay between God and the body that Debra evoked was her belief—her willingness to trust and believe in the Creator's design of her body. Though this belief helped her to "go against society" both by joining a religious minority and by giving birth at home, she remained pragmatic about when to enact it.[47] Her belief in design did not keep her from having a toxemia-induced cesarean after two successful home births (and then another home birth after that). Like Nina, the vegan who exercised a discerning use of "orthodox medical things," Debra continued to draw selectively from medical culture when she deemed it necessary. She was ready to admit when her God-designed body needed medical intervention, but considered herself a fit and responsible judge of her body's needs.

Debra felt that her understanding of God's design and her sense of her own power that she had gained in childbirth were significant catalysts in her and her family's conversion to Orthodoxy. As she asserted, her family followed her lead in becoming Orthodox because of the "strength that I gained through childbirth." Part of this strength lay in realizing her "true nature" as a woman, which was to bear children and raise them, freeing her husband to work and study Torah. For Debra, strength was at the root of her adoption of a traditionally female role, one that to other eyes might appear constraining or submissive. In a metaphor I have heard repeated by Mennonite women and Jewish women alike, Debra reflected: "They say that the man is the head of the household, and that's true; he is. He should be the head. He's the king. He makes the ultimate decisions, right? But the woman's the neck, and the way she turns the head, that's how he goes." The power behind the throne, in Debra's opinion, is rooted in awareness and insight that women have based on the capabilities embedded in their bodies.

Debra's sense of God-designed embodiment was most noticeably shared with two Pentecostal Christian women, Carrie Ryan and Janet Stein. Carrie, now in her mid-thirties, grew up as a Catholic but for about the last seven years has attended a charismatic church that is home to many people like her, who have left more traditional denominations in the process of becoming "born again." Along with their four children, Carrie and her husband, both Euro-American, attend church together. In her words, Carrie was saved five months after the birth of her second child, and after many long years of grappling with the trauma of sexual abuse, alcoholic parents, and drug addictions. She initially sought help from secular counselors to deal with her troubles, but it was never enough. Her life turned around, she asserted, once she handed her life over to God. She forgave her abuser and overcame her addiction.

Prayer (in which she talks to God and God responds), speaking in tongues, and visions are all part of Carrie's everyday religious life. Friendly and reflective, Carrie spoke to me with a calm conviction about her religious life without approaching me as a potential convert, as Janet had done. We chatted over tuna sandwiches in the kitchen of her rented house (her husband, a contractor, was building them a new one), while her six-month-old, her four-year-old, and my daughter played. Carrie said she had chosen home birth long before she had been saved, on the recommendation of a friend and on the basis of reading. In her telling, however, her two births after she had been saved were remarkably different from the first two.

Comparing her "saved" births to her "unsaved" ones, Carrie felt that she initially chose home birth out of fear of going to the hospital. Her first two births were generally successful, but she bled quite a lot afterwards, and experienced the crowning of the baby's head as excruciatingly painful. Once she was saved, however, Carrie experienced pregnancy differently, committing her babies to God and scouring the Bible for passages she could relate to her births. She no longer prayed in a "fearful" way to God about the health and safety of her babies, but drew confidence from the "word of the Lord" and from the visions he bestowed upon her, which guaranteed successful births. In Carrie's words, prayer had the effect of "having my body submit and line up to how the Word of God said my body should perform." When it came time to birth, Carrie felt that God did not let her down.

> So the birth came and it went and it was wonderful, except for the quickness. I had been praying for the fast delivery, that I'd be delivered speedily, and I was quoting the Word in Isaiah [where] God says that he's the one that brings us to

the point of delivery, and he's the one that will deliver us.[48] And I was thanking the Lord for that—that it was going to be a good speedy delivery, and that his plans were good for me, and there was no evil involved, as he was a good God.

And I also committed to him the crowning of the head. I said, "Lord, I can't stand this part. Please help me, somehow, some way." Pam, it was wonderful. Her head came down, and I knew it was there, and I said, "Father, here it comes. I can't stand this part." I said, "Lord, please help me, and [snaps fingers] the head was out!" And I said, "Wow, Lord!"

Not only did Carrie consider that God had saved her from the pain of crowning, but she also felt he kept her from bleeding in the same copious amounts she had at her first two births. The midwives, the same women who had been present at her earlier births, expressed surprise at Carrie's small amount of blood, and asked her to what she attributed the change. Carrie replied, "A relationship with Jesus Christ. . . . He promised me in his Word that these things would be different." For Carrie, Jesus was actively involved in her births, helping her body conform to God's design.

Unlike Natalie, who assented to the Christian Science opposition between the natural and the physical, Carrie considered the natural and the physical synonymous. The natural was the realm in which the midwives operated, but it was also a plane on which God connected with her in profound ways: "I just saw [birth] as a natural process, that God had created so unbelievably, so phenomenally, that it was just a wonderful process that he created. You know, I didn't see it as a miracle, because I saw it as just the hand of our Creator knowing exactly what he was doing. And maybe to a human it might be a miracle, but it wasn't a miraculous event as far as miracles go." The intimacy of God's natural, not miraculous, participation in her last birth enlivened Carrie's spiritual imagination, as God had showed her the profound significance of birth:

Something that the Lord showed me in the birth was [that] Christ was birthed onto this earth. And he had eternally been with his Father, and God willingly sacrificed him to take my place for what I had earned and what I deserved . . . so that I could be united with him. God showed me that the same thing I experience in the natural and the physical realm [in birth] was what he experienced in releasing his Son. [It was the same as] the separation that he had with his son at the cross when Jesus took upon himself the sin of mankind, and he was for the first time in his life separated from God.

For Carrie, viewing her body as designed by God was not a notion that rested lightly at the back of her mind, but was an ever-present way of interpreting her bodily experience. Her body was a site to encounter and experience God and Jesus. "As Scripture says, I'm in him and he's in me, and he came forth from God." Her dramatic comparison of her birthing experience with what she called God's "birthing" of his son Jesus on the cross not only reinterpreted what many feminists have considered a metaphor of violence (if not child abuse),[49] but also prompted her to consider the amorphousness of God's gender:

> I can remember just kneeling on the floor next to my bed after I had [my last baby], thinking about the intensity of the birthing experience and saying to the Lord, "Why did you create my body, Father, to do this? . . . Couldn't you have just put a zipper in my abdomen, and just [said], 'Okay it's time.'" And it was at that time that the Lord showed me as a woman the privilege—for me to be able to experience that. How he, too, is a Father, the birthing that he went through. It was just neat because Elohim, the Hebrew word for God, is a neuter; it's a neutral term, not signifying maleness or femaleness, but that in the Spirit, there's neither male nor female, and God is described as Father a number of times, but also is the breasty one—many-breasted. As far as the two sides, they're both there.[50]

Kneeling by her bedside, the intimate internal dialogue she carried on was not with her "instinct," but with God. For Carrie, the "pain and joy" of birth brought her to a renewed understanding of her belief in God's love and Jesus' atonement. In her words: "the love that God had, the love that he could have for the world, that he sent his only Son, it was a reality and a revelation, it was fresh to me."

Though Carrie drew on her understanding of God's separation from his Son to make sense of her own experience of birth, she did not transpose her fluid sense of God's gender onto her own life. Carrie considered that clearly delineated gender roles, in which the husband was the head of the household, were important to a smoothly running Christian family. She felt it necessary and God-ordained to submit to her husband and to rein in her willfulness when it ran counter to his wishes. Carrie, like Debra and Natalie, felt God working in her body through birth. Though these three women shared understandings of God's power to affect the body, they did not all share views of what was "natural" about the body, or about a woman's social role.

Another Pentecostal woman, Janet Stein, had yet one more way of understanding the natural in terms of God's design, in which she contrasted not simply the natural and the physical, but the natural, the spiritual, and the medical. Whereas most women used the word "natural" in a positive, affirming way, for Janet, natural was on the verge of meaning "worldly"—poised between the spiritual and the medical. Her usage of the term echoes that of her Pentecostal foremother, Agnes Ozman LaBerge, who wrote early in the twentieth century: "Women in the natural look for and only expect sorrow and travail in childbirth. But Christ Jesus has suffered and purchased redemption, giving us this supernatural life in the Holy

Ghost. . . . I am so rejoiced and so thankful after proving this promise at childbirth."[51] Testifying to have given birth without pain, LaBerge felt she had "proved the promise" of God's gift of supernatural life.

Janet gave me several testimonies of "supernatural" healing. When she wants to achieve a change in her body, she turns first to God: "There [are] situations in our family where it's like, 'Okay, God, I really think there's a spiritual and a natural way to bring healing to this situation,' instead of going the medical route, because sometimes the medical route will kill you." The spiritual is her first approach to healing, followed by the natural, and then, as a last resort, the medical. During her baby's birth, for example, Janet's foremost concern was not that she had good midwifery care, but that the proper people were praying for her, ensuring God would care for her throughout the process. According to Janet, even her husband's Jewish parents were beginning to see the virtues of trusting the body to Jesus and God: "I think that they just keep on seeing that there's more to this than just natural. It's something supernatural going on."[52]

Like Carrie and Debra, Janet too felt that her husband was invested with spiritually sanctioned authority in the home, and she considered this authority to extend into decisions about bodily health. Though she followed through on this belief in the end by having no midwife at her birth who would contest her husband's role, she did have some doubts about how her husband's "authority" would work in practice:

> I was concerned about how we were going to interact, and I told him, I said, "That's my biggest concern. It's not the pain; it's how we're going to flow together." Because he can tend to be controlling and [think he knows] exactly what to do. I said, "If you do that when I'm in labor, I'm going to say, 'Get out of this room!'" You know, it's like the last thing you want is a man telling you how you're supposed to feel when you're in labor!

For Janet, there are limits to a husband's authority, based on the body. Though he may tell her how to act, he cannot tell his wife what to feel.

In explaining to me her perspectives on the pregnant and birthing body, Janet gave me a copy of a booklet on morning sickness that she had consulted herself, and that she had recommended to clients she met in her role as a spiritual counselor. Compiled by a Christian organization called the Institute for Basic Life Principles (IBLP), the booklet emphasized that a woman's body was designed by God, and offered its Christian interpretation and treatment of morning sickness, drawn from both scriptural and medical references.

The booklet argued that Christian women were more likely to suffer from morning sickness than others, because of Satan's insidious attempts to "destroy the Godly seed."[53] If the treatments suggested in the booklet (improved nutrition, less stress, fasting) failed, the authors advocated that a woman look on her suffering from morning sickness as "spiritual warfare" and suffer willingly for God.[54] After all, the authors noted that in 1 Timothy 2:15, "God does not state that a woman will be saved *from* difficulty in childbearing, but she will be saved *in* difficulties that are connected with childbearing."[55]

Janet's enthusiasm for this booklet, and the wider organization it represented, allowed me another perspective on the postbiomedical implications of understanding the body as divinely designed. A chart within the text offered "prayer targets against Satan's kingdom," intended to protect the developing fetus in the womb. Every step of fetal development, including fertilization, the division and multiplication of the cells, and development of the reproductive organs and facial features was committed to God. For example, for day four of development, when the cells multiplied, the woman and her husband were to "acknowledge that in the DNA are the sins of the forefathers. Claim the blood of Christ for them."[56] On day eighteen, when the spinal cord forms, the couple was to think about how the spinal cord relays messages to the brain, and "pray that each member will be controlled by God's spirit."[57] Though Janet did not manage to use all the prayers in the chart, she did heartily endorse their overall message that bodies are terrain on which God and Satan do battle, and that even such a scientific concept as DNA can be neatly woven into this cosmic duel.

For all of the women who conceived of and experienced the body as a divinely designed and mediated site, giving birth at home was the logical outcome of such a perspective. At home they felt most free to express their religious identities and to do the work (mostly prayer) that they felt needed to be done. While some gave only passing reference to God's role in shaping a woman's body, other women considered their bodies the prime means through which they read their relationships to God. But as the range of stories I have told here shows, this embodied spirituality can take a diversity of forms, and have a diversity of consequences.

Embodiment, recently much celebrated by some feminist authors, does not necessarily imply empowerment in terms of male-female relationships, but it can result instead in an underscoring of difference that bolsters male dominance.[58] Adapting how some scholars have posed questions of embodiment and empowerment in women's religious lives to the context of home birth might result in a question: Does the religious significance attributed to home birth sacralize women's "natural" roles or emancipate them from biologically determined social roles?[59] The dualism inherent in setting sacralization against emancipation, however, ignores ways in which sacralization—giving religious value to a bodily process like birth—can work toward forms of emancipation that may be either overtly feminist or submerged within various kinds of coding.[60] For example, Janet's warning to her husband that she would scream "Get out of this room!" if he tried to control her birth was a window to how Janet, though she assents to the headship of her husband, is pragmatic about its execution. This pragmatism—espousing subordination but declaring its limits—is paralleled by women's pragmatism in preferring the natural but also drawing from various technologies of birth. [61] From one perspective, such accommodations could resemble problematic contradictions; from another, this pragmatism looks like a creative paradox. Focusing on how women use metaphors of the "body as machine" provides another lens on such creative paradoxes, as mechanical language, much despised by some feminist critics and home-birth advocates, becomes empowering in some women's usage.[62]

God and the Cyborg Body

The language of the natural is not the only reservoir of metaphors from which women drew in making sense of their birthing bodies. Despite what might be seen as a contradiction, some women used the metaphor of the body as machine to depict their births as natural. Ironically, instead of alienating women from their bodies, the metaphor of the machine seemed to help some of them focus on their power. In exploring this seeming contradiction between the natural and the mechanical body, I turn to the work of feminist theorist and biologist Donna Haraway, an advocate of the benefits of hybridity between machine, animal, and human.

In her iconoclastic "Cyborg Manifesto," Donna Haraway challenged feminists to abandon their longing for "organic holism" in order to embrace the possibilities offered by a politics of cyborgs—"creatures simultaneously animal and machine, who populate worlds ambiguously natural and crafted."[63] Haraway argued that women must not shy away from technology, but should take pleasure and responsibility in the midst of the diffusion of the boundaries between machine and organism effected in the postmodern climate of North America.[64] Women must adapt to this increasingly "globalized" world, in which technology continues to collapse the boundaries formerly maintained by the intractability of physical distance. Advocating the cyborg as a model for the postmodern feminist to emulate, Haraway felt she was "blaspheming" against "organic feminism," which draws on ecological and pagan metaphors to provide models for women to resist capitalist and patriarchal domination.[65] Instead of endorsing an "earth mother" approach, Haraway insisted that women must critically befriend technology, and not root themselves in a primeval Edenic innocence: "The machine is us, our processes, an aspect of our embodiment."[66] Haraway's message of the cyborg resounds like a sermon delivered by the most fiery of preachers. She used the language of religion not to invoke it but to debunk it, as her closing phrase revealed: "I would rather be a cyborg than a goddess."[67]

Embracing the cyborg, for Haraway, is accompanied by tension over viewing mothering as a source for political action.[68] She objected to what she called a dependence on metaphors of rebirth and reproduction within "holistic" feminism and suggested that "cyborgs have more to do with regeneration [than reproduction] and are suspicious of the reproductive matrix and of most birthing."[69] While she frames her manifesto within a rubric of "ironic blasphemy"—a critique within the community of feminism that aims to hold incompatible things together, in tension and in humor—her attack on a maternal politics that considers birthing a central point of oppression and liberation seems offered seriously.[70] For Haraway, it seems, sacralizing birth would not lead to emancipation.

Many feminist theorists of the medicalized body would not share Haraway's evangelistic championing of the subversive potential of technology. For example, in an antithetical argument to Haraway's, Ynestra King asserted that "women should seek to hold on to reproductive and procreative powers as a political strategy and a recognition of the biological fact that women bear children out of our own bodies and therefore have a particular claim to control how this process is carried out."[71] Similarly, from a stance of feminist spirituality, Carol Christ wrote, "Women must positively name the power that resides in their bodies and their sense of closeness to nature and use this new naming to transform the pervasive cultural and religious devaluation of nature and the body."[72] For these feminists, control over the process of birth allows women to abandon control over their bodies in the midst of birth. In this view, surrendering to "nature" and not to mechanical views or manipulations of the body ensures that a woman will be a cocreator instead of an automaton.[73]

Haraway's embrace of the cyborg, however, does find its parallels among some home-birthing women. At the level of language at least, perhaps the machine really is "us," as resolutely antitechnology home-birthers found the metaphor of the machine a helpful way to express their birthing experiences. Their versions of the cyborg added a twist to Haraway's creature, since these women enlisted metaphors of the machine to further glorify God's role in designing their bodies. Theirs was not a celebration of the genderless and god(dess)less possibilities of the cyborg, but a reveling in the ability to birth with, as the bumper sticker says, "God as my pilot."

The women who referred to their birthing bodies as machines were also women who considered God to be in control of their births. God's control did not mean that they had no power in giving birth to their babies; instead, they used mechanical metaphors to place their minds outside of their bodies and to let God fill up the void. Brenda Matthews, the charismatic Christian who exclaimed "Jesus really had that birth!" described her birthing body this way:

I was actually watching the labor from the side. I was watching this magnificent machine of a body bring a child into the world, and as long as I didn't interfere with it, it would be doing what it needed to do. . . . I almost removed myself and watched my body go through labor. It was fantastic! I could feel the next stages. I told them [that] when I got to my next stage, I could say: "Okay, now *this* is happening.". . .

You know, I have to say something here. I never talk like this about myself, so this is really weird. I'm feeling like I'm excited to share this because it's been inside of me, but I don't—because I feel like I'm bragging—and I don't mean it that way. But, all my midwives said that they'd never been with a mother [who] was so in tune with her body. But it was a conscious effort, do you know what I mean? Like I worked hard to remove myself, to understand and allow my body to do the job God created it to do—inherently, innately, my body knows how to give birth. Yes, I wanted my mind to understand it, but mainly it was to dispel any fear, which was why I was devouring so many books to make sure that I understood the mechanics of it, so I wouldn't be fearful.

Brenda, a very articulate woman, struggled to find the right language to describe her bodily experience of birth. She felt circumscribed both by her desire not to seem to be bragging about being a good birther and by the paucity of language capable of depicting her experience:

Instead of my mind being in the forefront, I put my mind—I don't know what you would call it. I have never tried to say this, Pamela, before. Like I said, in a spiritual sense I could say I just allowed the Holy Spirit in me to do it, but the best way for most people to understand it would be to say that I removed myself, not consciously. I don't know how to say it! I don't know how to say it. I was not making my body do anything. I was becoming. . . . I went along for the ride. I wasn't a mindless wonder. I was totally aware, but I was watching. My conscious mind was watching and going with what innately my body knew to do.

While she could refer to the Holy Spirit to provide a quick description, she knew that to my noncharismatic ears, and those of most of the people who would be reading her words, the Holy Spirit would not provide enough explanation. The tension between portraying herself as a willful, conscious actor and as a woman who submits herself to the will of God appeared often in Brenda's storytelling. She clearly did not want me to think that her dependence on God for direction in her life made her a "mindless wonder" (a phrase she used often), but she also wanted to convey the importance and the reality of God's working in her life. Turning to the metaphor of a machine in depicting her body allowed her to describe her body as a finely tuned instrument, designed by God, that for the most part she controlled. In special circumstances, however, God stepped in to take the controls.[74]

Marianne Martin, the veterinarian who was a traditional Catholic, also made recourse to mechanical images of the body (in addition to animal metaphors) in describing how God worked with her body to help her give birth to her children. Marianne's hybridity of animal, body, and machine was similar to Haraway's in that she distanced herself from a "pagan" holism, but had different goals:

> I felt very in tune with God and nature—not the New Age nature stuff—I just felt like this is what our bodies were meant to do. And I let my body . . . I went on cruise control, or whatever it is, automatic pilot. And it worked, because God [was] working with my body to make it work, and I was just really proud of myself. And I felt like, "Wow! This is great that you could do it." Because alone you could never do it, but there's something in us. In that one pregnancy [book] where they talk about the century-old woman that's in you, that everyone's afraid to give birth, and that you have this century-old woman in you that has been giving birth for centuries. That's part—because you know God made your body to work—so that's the part that makes you work. But I didn't realize how automatic it would be, that you would just really get so focused that I would be able to do it so well. You know what I mean?

For Marianne, an adoption of technological motifs to explain her body did not signify that, as Haraway put it, " 'God' is dead; [and] so is the 'goddess,' "[75] but instead that God was in control. Distinguishing herself from a believer in New Age naturalism, Marianne effected a blend of the natural and the mechanical that considered her body to house within it both a "century-old woman" with vast birthing knowledge and an instrument panel setting her on cruise control. Organizing all of these diverse motifs was a God flexible enough to accommodate a wide range of postmodern metaphor mixing, including a reassuring nostalgia for the women-who-birthed-before, an instrumental focus provided by the mechanized body, and an embodied version of spiritual discipline.[76]

Diffusing the boundaries between animal, human, and machine does not necessarily translate into a cyborg politics that strives for a genderless, godless utopia. Instead, the examples of Brenda and Marianne show that metaphors of the body as machine are just as pliable with respect to religion and gender as metaphors of nature. That an embrace of (at least metaphorical) hybridity between machine and body may take place even within an antitechnological ideology of birth shows that boundaries between nature and technology are rather porous when it comes to metaphor making. As Brenda's confidence in the protective power of God's energy, and Nina's concern to channel correctly a more ambiguous energy, showed, Pentecostal and New Age women alike draw on the scientific notion of "energy" to describe the "vibes" generated by the work of birth.[77] While for some women this birthing energy is directly tied to the Christian God, for others its origins are more enigmatic, seeming to come from within and without the self. Haraway herself was aware of the powerful and creative nexus where religion meets the body, as she pointed to the "continued relevance of spirituality, intertwined with sex and health, in political struggle."[78] The aims of such political struggle, however, are myriad, and can include goals that are both progressive and conservative, as shown in the microcosm of political struggle that is home birth, which encompasses women from a wide range of political perspectives.

Loving and Hating the Body

So far, the metaphors that I have highlighted, whether rooted in traditional religious understandings or more eclectic religious sources, have all affirmed the body as a powerful if not sacred site. (Even the complex Christian Science understanding of the body sees it as a place where God's work is done.) However, that women value their bodies in birthing does not necessarily mean they cherish them in the rest of their lives. For some women, pregnancy and birth are the only times they love their bodies; in their everyday lives they ignore, insult, or deny their flesh. For others, birth is an empowering bodily act that transforms their sense of self, both socially and sexually. Taking time to consider stories women tell of their birthing bodies alongside the language they use to describe their everyday bodies opens up a discussion of the relationships among birth, sexuality, and religious conceptions of embodiment.

Viewing a woman's body as "naturally" good at birthing does not necessarily translate into a wider respect for the body in general. The attitudes of home-birthing women toward their bodies, apart from the act of birth, range from delighted empowerment to disgusted faultfinding. Perhaps it is not surprising that women who have so much confidence in their bodies' abilities to give birth are not immune to cultural castigations of the female body. As feminist theorist Sandra Bartky notes, "Normative femininity is coming more and more to be centered on [a] woman's body—not its duties and obligations or even its capacity to bear children, but its sexuality, more precisely, its presumed heterosexuality and its appearance."[79] A focus on femininity that values an athletically supple and firm body, perhaps supplemented by breast implants, is at odds with a body transformed by childbirth, with breasts that leak and sag with milk and a belly striped with stretch marks. The breast-feeding mother is not the paragon of femininity in North American society, but instead must fight for her rights to nurse her baby.[80] To revision the nursing and mothering body as beautiful and sensual demands an oppositional stance to dominant norms of femininity, which some home-birthing women have and others do not.[81]

Valerie Auletta, who finds sustenance in Goddess-based spirituality, loved her body best when she was pregnant. She felt that she took better care of herself then, and could ignore her own troubled image of her non-pregnant body. Surrounding herself with lithographs and sculptures of Goddesses with generous bellies and breasts was one way Valerie tried to stave off the wider society's negative messages regarding the maternal body. After each pregnancy, Valerie confronted anew the realization that her ample body was not the desired shape in a culture of thinness, but each time it was somewhat easier. For Valerie, that she is now comfortable with sharing the video of her last home birth with anybody "says a lot about the changes in me. I mean, I wouldn't have been able to do that, I don't think, with any of the others." Partly, she is happy for others to view her home birth as a way of showing a positive birth experience and of spreading the message that home birth is safe, but also she feels she has become "a lot more self-accepting." In her words, "Maybe it has to do with getting older. There are only certain things you can change."

Other women also felt that birth allowed them to settle comfortably into their bodies in a new way. As Liza Rossiter put it, "My body and I have come to terms. We've accepted each other, warts and all." Liza, an African-American woman in her mid-thirties, found that going through birth without drugs, and with a commitment that her body could birth at home, was empowering. Especially after her second birth (her first home birth), Liza found "a strength that I didn't know—I wasn't sure—that I had. I'm glad to know that I do have it. I'm sure there will be things in the future where I'm going to need to draw on that strength." The embodied memory of birth became a tangible strength she stored up for use in future situations; for example, in what she expected would be an increasingly complicated relationship with her parents as they aged.

The empowerment that birth offered extended into Liza's sense of embodiment: "There was a time when I wasn't happy with my body. I felt like my hips were too big, and my complexion wasn't what I would have liked, and my hair was something that I struggled with, and as you can see, I now wear it short and natural. . . . This is the happiest I've been with myself ever." Liza felt that having children—both the process of pregnancy and birth and the work of mothering—has transformed her attitude toward her body for the better: "Having kids makes you focus more on the essentials which can help you get through the day." Birthing and mothering have given her new confidence, which in turn has allowed her to feel comfortable without going through the rigors of straightening and then curling her hair, but instead, wearing it naturally.

Not all home-birthing women are so comfortable in their birthing bodies, however. Charlene Roth, for example, likened her postbirth body to a "chick gone to pot" and a "little dumpling." A Beachy Amish woman,[82]

who now attends a nondenominational Christian fellowship with her formerly Old Order Amish husband, Charlene was unhappy with the transformations childbirth made in her body, but she felt that "as long as [my
husband] loves me just the way I am, it's the most important thing."
Despite coming from a religious minority that holds norms of femininity
that strive to be countercultural, based in modesty and valuing maternity,
Charlene was critical of her body, wishing for the return of her "coke-
bottle figure."

Charlene was uncomfortable with her body immediately upon giving
birth to her babies:

> I don't know what is wrong with me. I love my kids once I get to know them,
> and once we're bonded, but, right at first, it's, I don't know. . . . [I always
> thought I'd] be the loving kind of mother that would just take him into my
> arms, and breast-feed him, but I'm not. I'm the kind that, I would get cleaned
> up first, and then I can sit down and enjoy my baby. Because where you're sit-
> ting, you're sitting in all this mess, and so usually I want to—as soon as my baby
> comes out, I want to go and take a shower. . . . When [my son] was born I just
> went and said, "Can I take a shower?" And my husband was over there, and he
> said, "Don't you want to say hi to your son?" I'm like, "Just let me take a shower
> first.". . .
>
> And I came out, after I had my bath. I came out and I got a drink, and then
> I sat back. [My midwife] asked me right at first, would I like to nurse. I told her
> not here on the couch. She said, "Why don't you go to bed then." So she nested
> me out here, and she was sitting here in the chair, and she said, "You know, this
> isn't normal." And I didn't realize that it wasn't normal to act that way.

Charlene's worry about what was "wrong" with her shows the disciplinary
power of "natural" maternal reactions, even in the context of a midwife-
attended home birth. Though Charlene felt birth was a natural process
perfectly suited to the home, she did not want to encounter the bodiliness
of birth after the fact, in the form of blood-soaked cloths or blood-stained
legs. She did not want to look in a mirror while giving birth, claiming
that would "gross [her] out," and she did not want to hold her baby until
she and the baby had been washed.

Charlene's notions of cleanliness were contrary to those of most home-
birthing women, and in that sense her midwife's assessment of her reaction as not "normal" was apt. Judging from conversations with midwives
and birthing women, most home-birthing women's first reactions upon
giving birth are not to want to shower, but to want to hold their babies,
oblivious to blood, vernix, sweat, and any other bodily effluvia. Charlene's
reaction, however, accorded with her wider understanding of the body.
She felt that public breast-feeding was "disgusting," to the point that she
switched to bottle feeding once she was able to go out regularly after her

babies' births. Charlene's differences from the "norm" show that despite the claim that home birth allows a woman freedom to act as she likes, expectations of what is natural can curtail that freedom. In Charlene's case, a body-affirming stance that led her to home birth also brought her to worry about the legitimacy of her maternal response—a worry compounded by her midwife's comments.

Given the variety of women's reactions to the bodiliness of birth, in terms of both the immediacy of producing a new body from their own, and the long-term effects of pregnancy and childbirth, it is hazardous to attribute a common sense of embodiment to home-birthing women. They are not all "earth mothers" rejoicing in the powers of their bodies to nourish their babies inside and outside the womb. While some women discover a strength rooted in their bodies upon giving birth, others want to avoid the "messiness" of birth, and seek to ignore embodiment instead of cultivate it as a terrain of identity. Attitudes to the body are shaped by a range of sources, including images in popular culture, birth books, religious traditions, education, proximity to feminist influences, experiences of racism, and even one's own personal metabolism. Framing the question of the significance of embodiment to home-birthing women by asking questions about the meaning of the natural, however, can open up a larger perspective on how gender and religion shape identities born from reproduction.

Making the Natural Body

What does considering the natural body reveal? First, understanding the diversity of ways that the word "natural" is used to manifest a birthing ideal shows the power that a desire to be natural holds in guiding women's birthing choices. Whether the natural represents an evolutionary world where humans take their place alongside animals, or a divinely designed world where God orchestrates wombs and perineums, being natural is conceived of as an unquestionable good. This approach to birth parallels a wider trend in consumer culture, where the natural is bestowed with salvific powers, as witnessed by the ubiquity of the term on food labels and clothing advertisements.[83]

Some cultural critics like Donna Haraway, however, characterize this love for the natural as a misguided reaction to the technologized world of late capitalism. Certainly, for some women, a commitment to the natural can backfire if a woman needs to turn to technology that exceeds her boundaries of the natural in order to birth her baby. Women who choose home birth run the risk of feeling like failures if they end up giving birth in the hospital, whether vaginally or by cesarean. Kathryn Morris, who did end up with a cesarean, complained of the videos and books in her home-birth-friendly Bradley prenatal class (a class based on the idea of "husband-coached" childbirth advanced by Dr. Robert Bradley):

> Because they're so much trying to show you that you can have a natural birth, they show the most perfect births. And the women don't make any noise; they're like, "Oooh!" You know they're moaning, but no one's screaming, no one's doing anything. The baby pushes out, and everything's perfect and wonderful. And they're real births that happened that way, but they're like—they set you up a little bit for feeling like, well, "What if I can't do it like that?"

The language of nature and superb design can be disheartening if a woman's body does not fit the mold.[84] However, the women I interviewed who experienced traumatic births or went the hospital, including Kathryn, interpreted their "failure" in a way that bolstered their commitment to home birth.

Most women's understandings of the natural, whether religiously or scientifically inspired, were flexible enough to accommodate plans gone awry. They needed an oppositional discourse rooted in nature and opposed to technology to give them the strength to choose a method of childbirth scorned (or unknown) by many. Again and again, women talked about the responsibility and extra effort that choosing a home birth demanded of them, as they researched their options and spent several hours attending prenatal appointments, often at a considerable distance. They chose to birth at home to retain responsibility for their births, and to control the access other people had to their bodies and to the bodies of their babies.

Constructing the natural is a political act. Home-birthing women enact strategies of resistance that reinterpret history, the body, and the process of birth itself as they transform the culture of birth in which they live. As part of a wider, mostly feminist-led critique of contemporary birthing practices, home-birthing women point out the historical disjuncture of hospital birth within the span of women's birthing history. They reclaim what Marianne called the "century-old woman" within their own bodies, as an embodied birthing guide.[85] They reinterpret the pathologized female body as having specifically feminine power and ability—a power and ability that are deemed "natural," but with a critical dimension.[86] And they construct birth as a bodily process that, in addition to bringing a baby, can bring revelation, healing, and strength.

As many feminist anthropologists have found, however, with resistance can also come accommodation.[87] In the case of the conservative Christian and Jewish women I spoke with, embracing the power of God in their lives gave them the strength to resist what they viewed as a dehumanizing biomedical system that was physically and spiritually dangerous. Embracing God's power also brought with it an acceptance of gender subordination; while God glorified and honored their bodies in designing them for birth, he also compelled them to submit, by nature, to their husbands. But just as Debra was pragmatic in her interaction with the medical system—having a cesarean when she realized her toxemia made a home birth impossible—so were these women pragmatic about their subordination. Acknowledging her husband's authority did not always mean that a woman was in his thrall, as shown by Janet's warning to her husband about his "controlling ways."[88]

The story of resisting the medicalization of birth is not a wholly feminist tale. Though originally led primarily by feminist activists seeking bodily autonomy for women, the home-birth movement has now diffused, with many versions of empowerment and embodiment at play. Some of these versions use the physical process of birth to, in Judith Butler's language of gender performativity, "re-materialize" women into roles as domestic, heterosexual child rearers.[89] But others figure childbirth within a feminist vision, as a display of women's power to bring forth life, but not necessarily as an indication that she must be the sole caregiver of her children. This diffusion of alternatives has led some feminists, such as Adrienne Rich, to lament of the alternative childbirth movement: "Its feminist origins have been dimmed along with its potential challenge to the economics and practices of medicalized childbirth and to the separation of motherhood and sexuality."[90] Though in some cases the feminist origins of the home-birth movement may have dimmed, the economic, religious, and embodied challenge that conservative Christian and Jewish home-birthing women pose to the medical model of childbirth remains strong. (And conservative religious women are some of the most vocal women about nurturing the connection between motherhood and sexuality.)

The strength of these women may be most potent as part of a larger group of home-birthing women who, by their very presence, demonstrate that there are alternatives to birth in the hospital.[91] Their strength also lies in the connections, both implicit and explicit, that their birth choices effect with less conservative women, such as Natalie, or the many more overtly feminist home-birthers, like Valerie and Miriam. This coalition of women is divided along other axes, but is united by their efforts to "go against society" in challenging the legal, medical, and insurance systems that structure birth in North America. The network that is emerging from this diversity of women choosing a similar practice, for example in terms of the use of the same midwives and the development of activist groups, insists that birth is not a mere physiological extraction of a fetus. Instead, these women claim that birth is a profound personal, spiritual, communal, and, for some, sexual experience.[92]

As Judith Butler notes, any political struggle, and any performativity, carries with it the risks of "political unknowingness," and, in some cases, "the incalculable effects of action are as much a part of their subversive promise as those that we plan in advance."[93] Though a growth in versions of conservative Christian and Jewish home birth that espouse male headship and female domesticity may be signs of the depoliticized movement Adrienne Rich described, I would argue that they are signs of the fecundity of birth as a site for appreciating the performativity of gender. Sometimes this performativity results in a reiteration of gendered norms at odds with feminist goals, but it also has the capacity to lead a variety of women to a sense of bodily empowerment that pushes them to political action in opposition to medicalization.[94] Ironically, perhaps, their resistance is rooted in diverse notions of what it is to be natural. They make use of nature in an oppositional discourse that refutes the Western "biomedical habitus"[95] through a combination of religious and physical "proofs."

Home-birthing women, despite some of their own claims to the contrary, cannot construct their resistance to medicalized childbirth from a basis of purity. There is no "pure body" or place of innocence from which to make use of nature in this work of home birth.[96] Around the world, forces of colonialism, biomedicine, capitalism, and poverty (with malnutrition as one of its most insidious forms for childbearing women) have shaped the process of childbirth in historically specific ways.[97] Women seeking a more natural way to give birth in North America do so, generally speaking, with access to more and better food, running water, electricity, and emergency medical services should they need them.[98] Acknowledging these ways in which technology supports middle-class North American women's choices to renaturalize birth does not lessen the critical power of their actions. It does, however, support Donna Haraway's insistence that women must both critique and make use of technology.[99] For North American childbearing women, this means their childbirth choices are always made against a backdrop of biomedical support. Home-birthing women, opting for a nonmedicalized birth, do so as postbiomedical bodies—they have foresworn biomedical approaches, but still rely on them to some extent, either implicitly or overtly.

Home-birthing women's pragmatic renaturalizing of birth accommodates various forms of technology, while emphasizing that birth is a "spiritual" or "sacred" event. Why does it matter that so many of the women I interviewed felt that God, or another sacred being, had a hand in designing their bodies or helping them give birth? The word God, like the word nature, has a multiplicity of meanings. In the study of North American birthing practices, scholars have tended to be less attuned to religious identity and have largely marginalized religion, especially conservative varieties. And those who study North American religion have generally ignored childbirth. By contrast, anthropologists studying childbirth in Third World settings have often watched for the interplay between religious, medical, and "pragmatic" practices.[100]

The persistent assertion of the sacred in postbiomedical bodies in North America is something that crosses boundaries of feminist and nonfeminist, Jew, Christian, spiritual feminist, and more. Insisting on the existence of an active deity who has designed nature and who acts upon their birthing bodies, or who provokes their bodies and their instincts to speak, these women are recapturing not only discourse but also their physical bodies, which long have been assumed to be the terrain of biomedicine. Asserting themselves as natural women who co-create with their God or some other sacred being, they reclaim nature as a sphere in which gods and goddesses, not men, have the ultimate control. The potential effects of this renaturalizing of both God and childbirth may provoke apprehension in feminists, but to ignore the varieties of the natural would be to neglect some women's reclamation—by way of religion and nature—of a complex and ambivalent bodily power. Drawing on the power of a god/dess in order to find and voice their own convictions, these women follow in a long tradition of religious women who, by valuing their bodies as sites of revelation, carve out cultural space in a society that has often ignored women's knowledge and experience.

Natural Women

Home-birthing women assert that they are constructing a space for birth that allows their varying commitments to come to bear on their birthing bodies. They assert they are trying to make a place where they can experience birth through the many prisms of their identities, not simply as patients needing to be delivered. Their religious beliefs and practices, their varying convictions about gender equality, their views about the boundaries of their bodies and how to protect them, and their concerns about the safety and comfort of their babies are all enacted in the process of giving birth at home. The awesome power of their bodies to squeeze, sweat, and open up until their babies emerged provoked sheer admiration in most women. Their births proceeded according to a pattern whose beginning or end they could not determine, nor could anyone else. The awesomeness of this experience also provoked a struggle to find the right words to describe this feat of birth—words that through much of Western history have remained unspoken.[101] This struggle for the proper language often seemed most intense when women tried to describe the pain of childbirth. Along with the creation of a new human being, pain is what makes birth seem so awesome to observers and birthing women alike. The embodied agency of birth is in large part rooted in the surrender of rationality and control to the sensations and rhythms of labor. I turn now from metaphors of the body to languages of pain, further exploring the ironies of finding agency in surrender while embracing the agony of creation.

7

Sliding between Pain and Pleasure: Home Birth and Visionary Pain

Power is only Pain
Give Balm
to Giants
And they'll wilt, like Men
                              Emily Dickinson, 1861[1]

CREATING NEW VISIONS of childbirth involves creating new meanings for the pain of childbirth. From their own particular perspectives, doctors and clergy have debated the meaning of childbirth pain for at least the past one hundred and fifty years. In the late nineteenth century, some argued that God ordained women's pain in childbirth, while others claimed to the contrary that God granted anesthesia as a gift of forgiveness to women in labor.[2] Over the course of the twentieth century, proponents of both anesthetised and drugless childbirth largely circumvented questions of meaning in their focus on eliminating—not interpreting—labor pains. Women involved in the revival of home childbirth in North America and elsewhere, however, are again pondering the significance of pain in childbirth. Their commitment to experience the now avoidable pain of birth in a culture that is generally averse to pain generates a combination of condemnation and awe from several quarters. This is perhaps not surprising in a world where, in the words of Talal Asad, "The infliction of physical pain [has] now become scandalous."[3] According to Asad, even the religiously motivated pain of the ascetic or martyr is now seen as a premodern oddity that evokes moral condemnation. In this view, pain is destructive to the human subject, and when it can be done away with, it should be.

Simone Taylor has a rather different view of pain and its effects, at least in terms of childbirth. A labor and delivery nurse before she was a Presbyterian seminary student, Simone gave birth twice with the help of midwives—the first time in a hospital, and the second time at home. Describing birth as a process of "sliding around between pain and pleasure," Simone gave the pangs of childbirth an explicitly theological meaning:

I remember, in labor with [my first daughter]: I'm standing in the face of God. I mean, I am creating, in a way that was more immediate and intense than anything I've ever experienced. And it was wonderful, and it was awful also. And I think that when you read Scripture that talks about [it], in such traditional language, the fear of God was among them, and you know, they trembled at his awesome terribleness, and all of these words . . . are actually negative and frightening, and it's because they don't have other language to explain what they feel in the face of the divine. And so to me, that's sort of the pain . . . is the coming up against something so much more divine than anything—any other experience.

As part of a larger alternative childbirth movement that has worked toward decreasing drug use in both the home and the hospital, Simone and other home-birthing women have tried to reclaim childbirth pain as a source of meaning, instead of viewing it as something to be avoided. In the process, they often make recourse to religiously inflected language that describes newfound knowledge of self, and sometimes tells of renewed or novel intimacy with deities and loved ones. Their experiences and interpretations of pain bring forth important questions about the relationship between agency and pain, especially regarding how to evaluate the pain of childbirth, which is so intensely infused with a long history of gendered meanings.

Unlike the more general descriptions of pain offered by some scholars, for these women the pain of childbirth is not a sensation that obliterates pleasure or severs connection to other human beings.[4] Instead, many of these women understand the pain of childbirth to have opened them to connection with others, and even in some cases to have brought multiple forms of pleasure. For some, childbirth pain sparked visionary experiences. Considering these women's interpretations of the pleasure and connection in pain pointedly illuminates their varied convictions, both religious and political, and shows the intimate connection they posit between pain and power. Much of my aim in this chapter is to present women's own interpretations of their childbirth pain to show how embracing the pain of childbirth fosters some particular kinds of agency. Entertaining this notion means I must also grapple with the complexities of making power from pain. Is suffering the pain of birth without drugs a trial that turns a woman into a martyr unnecessarily? Does finding pleasure and connection in childbirth pain spiritualize suffering in ways that have traditionally been oppressive to women? To answer these questions, I first situate home-birthing women's approaches to pain within a larger historical and social context, and then present some women's stories of the pain, pleasure, and connection in childbirth. After considering these stories of pain and intimacy, I close with a reflection on the relationship between pain and power and on the resources and dangers of such an alliance.

Approaching Pain

The pain of childbirth is different from most other kinds of pain. It is of limited duration, can be expected nine months in advance, and thus can be prepared for, and has an outcome that is often accompanied by such elation and/or distraction that the previous hours of pain are soon distilled into a less intense memory. As other scholars have suggested, pain and time are inseparable—pain has a rhythm. When spaces of ease interrupt its throes, the sufferer has time in which to reflect on his or her pain, put it in perspective, and gain some autonomy.[5]

The pains of birthing allow this space for reflection in two ways. First, during the first stage of (a noninduced) labor, the contractions are predictably wavelike, growing in intensity as they peak at transition, but usually granting ebb times in which the woman has freedom from the pain. Second, the pain of birth generally ends once the baby is born, or soon thereafter, and the birth becomes an event open to reflection without the dread of it recurring immediately. Especially for middle-class women in North America, the pain of childbirth is not a regularly recurring event, since for the most part North American women regulate their own fertility and have an average of two children.[6] For many women, birth pain is so intimately linked with the joy of meeting one's long-awaited child that in remembering their pain they encompass it in a purpose and achievement so great that the pain itself is dulled if not dispersed. They gain a degree of control over their suffering through remembering and retelling the stories of their births. The stories women tell are shaped not only by their own social location—whether they are well-off or poor, healthy or "high risk"—but also by the layers of history that undergird North American approaches to the pain of childbirth.

A Brief History of Childbirth Pain

At least as early as 1871, doctors were advocating "natural" methods (besides the newly introduced method of anesthesia), which they claimed could abolish pain in childbirth. Martin Luther Holbrook, an American doctor, laid out a regimen of healthy, outdoor exercise, comfortable clothing, and most important, a fruit diet, in his book *Parturition without Pain: A Code of Directions for Escaping from the Primal Curse* (which came with a recommendation from women's rights activist Elizabeth Cady Stanton).[7] Though Holbrook saw childbearing as a woman's divinely ordained purpose in life, "as if the Almighty, in creating the female sex, had taken the uterus and built up a woman around it," he did not feel her pain was divinely sanctioned.[8] He invited those who disagreed with this on theological grounds—all men, he pointed out—to undergo themselves the pains of labor, arguing that "there has been enough suffering in childbirth to satisfy not only a God, but a devil."[9] Holbrook's method, though with its twentieth-century counterparts as we will see, was less than persuasive next to the attractive possibilities of pain-free childbirth promised by the new techniques of anesthesia.

As more and more nineteenth-century doctors began using anesthesia for a range of medical purposes, a debate grew over the use of obstetric anesthesia in particular—a debate that contained a variety of religiously informed arguments. One of the most prominent arguments against the use of anesthesia in childbirth was that of biblical literalists, who based their opposition on Genesis 3:16, where God punished Eve for her part in the Fall: "I will greatly increase your pangs in childbearing, in pain you shall bring forth children."[10] In a less literal mode, some medical practitioners, most notably hydropaths and homeopaths, rallied a perfectionist argument in their opposition to anesthesia. Namely, they asserted that women could be free of the pain of childbirth if they followed the "laws of Nature," but if they sinned against such laws, for example, by not exercising, or leading intemperate and slovenly lives, labor pain would be their due.[11] Hydropaths felt that if one followed divinely intended laws of nature, all of life could be lived without suffering, and that pain was thus proof of an individual's sins against nature. In both the literalist and perfectionist arguments then, to use anesthesia to thwart pain would be to contravene divinely sanctioned punishment.[12]

Physicians who supported the use of anesthesia in childbirth also drew on religious arguments, though to a different end. For example, two nineteenth-century physicians, Dr. Mary Seelye and Dr. Eliza L. S. Thomas, felt that there was no conflict between considering pain to be a result of the Fall and using anesthesia to overcome pain. Thomas went so far as to suggest that anesthesia was "One of Heaven's best gifts bestowed on erring mortals as if in relenting forgiveness of their disobeyance of Nature's laws."[13] In their search for painless childbirth, these women doctors presaged their later feminist counterparts of the 1910s.

Doctors from both wings of the anesthesia debate could agree on one point: whether or not anesthesia was employed, obstetricians, not midwives, were the proper attendants at birth. This assertion needed to counter one main objection. Critics of the rising profession of obstetrics argued that doctors (who were mostly male) "stole the affections" of their female clients away from their husbands both by using chloroform, which produced "sexual excitation" in women, and by their intimate examinations of women's bodies. To counter such unseemly associations of doctors with women's sexuality, obstetricians debated the principles, not the practices of birth—they focused on the mechanics of childbirth, not the intimate exploration of a woman's body by a man other than her husband. Obstetricians strove to make childbirth into a science that was the preserve of doctors, not midwives, "by moving the entire discussion of obstetrical practice onto spiritual, philosophical, and scientific terrain—terrain that women, equipped only with practical experience, could not enter."[14] Ironically, today the discussion has shifted once more, as doctors have largely abandoned the "spiritual and philosophical" terrain of birth and midwives have laid claim to it.

Whether or not these nineteenth-century practitioners advocated or opposed anesthesia, their arguments drew on the notion that pain (and its overcoming) held profound meanings that could not be explained by merely documenting a physical process of muscles and nerves. This view of the inherent meaning in pain gradually became viewed as outmoded, so that by the early part of the twentieth century, North American women themselves were active in combating the notion, whether rooted in religion or natural law, that birth pain enhanced a woman's character. The struggle of these American upper-middle-class women focused on a childbirth method called "twilight sleep," in which a combination of narcotic and amnesic drugs caused a woman to forget her labor entirely, although her body still felt the pain.[15] Feminist activists took the lead in bringing twilight sleep from Germany to America in the 1910s, and in the process "helped change the definition of birthing from a natural home event, as it was in the nineteenth century, to an illness requiring hospitalization and physician attendance."[16]

In terms of shifting approaches to childbirth pain, however, the most important effects of twilight sleep and other forms of drugged birth were that they made experiencing birth pains seem downright uncivilized. Charlotte Tell, a supporter of twilight sleep, wrote in a 1915 issue of *Good Housekeeping*,

> [In the past], when women felt the religious significance of giving birth—just as men felt the religious significance of going into battle—they so frequently regarded the act as a great, mystical freeing of the life from the womb—not merely a birth but a resurrection—that they completely lost consciousness of pain. . . . Today, on the other hand, and particularly in this country, we are all, men and women alike, inclined to think of our bodies not as instruments of cosmic forces, but as personal possessions of ourselves, tools of our own desires— very exalted desires in many cases, but still merely personal. . . . [T]o inflict upon the modern woman many burdens and sufferings which a cruder type of woman took as a matter of course is unnatural.[17]

For the woman who possessed a demystified body, shorn of its cosmic significance, the only "natural" way to birth was to be fully drugged and

restrained so that her birthing body did its animal act without the knowledge of her modern mind.

In the aftermath of World War II, however, an era dawned that saw "a
surge in family life and a reaffirmation of domesticity that rested on distinct roles for women and men."[18] In a climate in which the ideal woman
assumed her "natural" role as a wife and mother, "natural childbirth"
emerged as a competitor to drugged birth. The method of natural childbirth avowed that a woman could prepare herself to experience unmedicated birth without undue pain, or even, in some cases, with pleasure.
Part of the goal of proponents of natural childbirth was that by rendering
childbirth more pleasurable they might make women happier about having babies and about staying home and raising them.[19] As such, like most
other movements in alternative childbirth, natural childbirth was largely
a middle-class movement—a movement for women who had the time and
money to attend childbirth classes and seek out pathbreaking doctors.

The confluence of pleasure and pain in childbirth has provoked great
suspicions in critics of unmedicated birth. Echoing nineteenth-century
worries about "sexual excitation," some critics have worried that pleasure
in childbirth was inappropriately erotic.[20] In the fifties and sixties, when
natural childbirth was making headway into American birthing practices,
its often psychoanalytically minded critics queried: Does natural childbirth grant license to women's masochistic tendencies? Is natural childbirth a pathological outlet for women's narcissism? The pathologizing
of maternity added to the branding of women's reproductive organs as
physically abnormal the notion that the state of pregnancy rendered a
woman psychically deviant, as pregnant women were thought to be
"overly identified with their fetuses, their mothers, their fathers, and even
their doctors."[21] Concerns about the fusion of pain and pleasure remain
issues today, as critics of home birth cast it as a means for a woman to
enhance her pleasure or satisfaction at the expense of her safety and that
of the baby.[22] According to such understandings, pain and pleasure do
not mix.

Tensions over the meanings of pain within the alternative-birth movement are rooted in some long-standing ironies. On the one hand, a femi-
nist-inspired twilight-sleep movement sent women from the home to the
hospital to give birth and thereby gave physicians almost total control over
childbirth. On the other hand, a domesticity-affirming natural-childbirth
movement tried to wrest some (but not all) of that control back from the
doctor. Despite their differing motivations and methods, supporters of
both twilight sleep and natural childbirth shared the goals of reducing
the fear and pain in childbirth. Contemporary home-birthing women
also share those goals, although they insist that various forms of power
shape the definition and experience of pain. With a sometimes hazy con-

fluence of feminist convictions and maternal yearnings, many home-birthing women consider that to feel their own pain is to reclaim their own power.

Stories of Pain and Pleasure

What sorts of power do women feel they reclaim by giving birth at home? What kind of agency—what kind of self—do women seek through giving birth without drugs coursing through their bodies? At a very basic level, the primary reason many women gave for choosing an unmedicated birth was a desire to keep the baby free from the influence of drugs. As such, they made their choices because of their concern for their newborn babies—they acted as agents responsible for the care of another. Their decisions reflected their assertion that all drugs cross the placenta, and can have a variety of effects, including reducing oxygen to the baby, interfering with the establishment of breast-feeding, and potentially causing brain damage.[23] Ironically, for the mother, labor-inducing drugs such as oxytocin and the pain-relieving drugs used in epidurals often increase her pain in the midst of birth and afterwards. Oxytocin often stimulates quick and very intense back-to-back contractions, and epidurals often leave women with lingering headaches and backaches after birth.[24]

Most women considered the rationale of keeping a baby from the influence of drugs to be a straightforward, physiologically indicated reason to insulate oneself from drugged birth by staying at home. When it came to discussing their own experiences of birthing pain, however, the meanings they gave to their pain were diverse. They often tied their physical pain to a struggle or realization that illuminated their personal history or current relationships. The meanings invested in pain ranged from considering it an arduous ordeal that brought empowerment, to more explicitly theological understandings linking the pangs of birth to Christ's suffering on the cross. A second, and sometimes equally important reason for forgoing drugs during birth rested in the desire of some women to experience fully the sensations of birthing. For some, this meant feeling intense pain, greater than they had ever known. For others, birthing ran currents of pleasure through their entire body, a sensation that a few compared to orgasm. Yet others occupied a sort of middle ground in this continuum of sensation, experiencing drugless birth as neither intensely painful nor profoundly pleasurable. As I show in what follows, in these home-birthing women's accounts, childbirth pain is often invested with the power to grant women understanding of their gods, their intimate relationships, and themselves.

Enduring the Pain

A number of women approached pain as an unavoidable fact of birth that just had to be endured gamely. A few of these women assented to a version of the nineteenth-century biblical literalism that considered birth pain to be God's punishment for fallen humanity, but for the most part pain was seen to be a natural, and not entirely negative, aspect of giving birth to a healthy baby. Amish women especially, at least in their conversations with me, did not reflect very much on the significance of pain. For example, Mary Rose Erb's response, when I asked her about the portrayal of birth pain in Genesis 3:16, was typical: "I guess that's the way he made it." All five of the Amish women said their favorite part of birth was when it was over. In the midst of her labor, Tina Hostetler, an Amish Mennonite woman, said her prayers consisted of "begging the Lord to get it over with."[25] These Amish women's disinterest in exploring the meanings of pain corresponded with a frank and unromanticized description of the rigors of birth. As Charlene Roth phrased it, childbirth was

> like having a horse. I don't know. The pain. It's a wicked pain. Oh, I don't know how you describe that pain. It's like trying to push a football or a basketball through a hole that's too small. I don't know. It's crampy, achy. I don't know. It's—you're so overwhelmed with everything. I know that even all the pain that you feel you can't express it. Achy. Dull, achy. I just don't know how to express it.

Charlene, like other women, struggled to find an adequate language for the pain of birth. Despite her assertion of the inexpressibility of pain, however, she emerged with quite graphic metaphors and similes for the sensations of birth. Though she may not have liked the "wicked" pain of birth, and not have seen anything redeeming in it, Charlene felt that it was something to endure for the sake of her baby.

Similarly, Annie Stoltzfus, an Old Order Amish woman, felt that giving birth was "her duty." In the midst of her labor, she did not want to be distracted by such things as watching in a mirror as the baby's head emerged, but wanted to focus on maintaining composure: "You kind of have to keep control of yourself if you have so much pain." Annie controlled her vocalizations during the pains of labor by two means: breathing and prayer. In so doing, she blended strategies for dealing with pain, which she had learned from her midwife, with those that she had developed within her religious tradition. In her words though, what she liked best about childbirth was, "the minute it was all done and [having] a healthy baby. That's a blessing. It's such a great relief when it's over."

Other women who considered that childbirth pain simply needed to be endured for the sake of the baby were less controlled in their reactions.

Stefanie Harter, 34, came to the United States from Scandinavia at the age of 19, and has a two-year-old son whom she cares for at home. A small, energetic, talkative woman, Stefanie is married to another Scandinavian émigré, and they attend a Lutheran church. Stefanie considers herself more a "born again Christian" than a Lutheran, however, and regularly watches an early morning Bible study program on television.

Stefanie described the stage of transition[26] during her labor in language as evocative as Charlene's: "I thought it was something from a horror movie; it felt like somebody was just taking a shredder and ribboning my insides out." Though she had been worried about disturbing her neighbors in the adjoining town house, Stefanie's response to transition was to scream and curse:

> [A]t that point, I just—I swore at God, I swore at my mother. I hated her and my father. I mean, I cursed everybody I could think of, you know. And [my husband] was like, "I did this to Stefanie, oh my God!" And that helped, just getting it out. I guess, in one way, that was a lot of pain or whatever from my childhood that just had to get out. . . . They all pretty much knew I was having a home birth, the neighbors. . . . And that was more my concern, that I was going to be quiet, and not bother anybody. But I had to learn to just let go.[27]

For Stefanie, childbirth pain was not only something that needed to be endured for her baby, but was also deeply connected to her past. In her interpretation, the pain she experienced in labor set Stefanie on a path to "letting go" of memories of more embedded physical and emotional pain:

> My father sexually and physically abused me when I was a kid. And my mother, I think I never really forgave my mother, because she kind of did not take my side. She was like, "Well, he promised he wouldn't do it again, so let's start from new." They'd done it, you know. There is no turning back; they do it once, they do it again. So I think I've always had a little—and probably still do—that, you're supposed to look out for your kid. I know with my son—if anybody hurt him—once—you know, they're dead meat. And I think that's a mother's responsibility to protect her children, whether they're one, five, ten, fifteen, until they move out of the house. And they knew that; we had talked about my childhood.

> PK: The midwives?
> SH: Yeah. They knew that, so that's why they also knew that, you know, you got to get this out of your system.

Stefanie felt that her physical pain was so acute because her past emotional pain had been so devastating.[28] Nevertheless, in retrospect, she would not have chosen to give birth any other way. Her reason for enduring the pain linked her determination to protect her baby from the horrors she had experienced as a child with her desire to bring him into the world without drugs:

> And again, I feel I would rather have the pain. I mean at twelve o'clock I screamed, "I want drugs now! I don't care what it is, just take this thing out of me!" And [my husband] ran downstairs, and he's like [whispering] "She wants drugs." And the midwife said, "Great! We've got another hour and a half, two hours left, that's it!" They knew that was, you know, [near the end]. We started pushing. . . . No matter how bad the pain would have been, I would never have wanted drugs, because I wanted him to be born free of anything. Because I don't care what they say, if you put something in your body—I don't care if it's five hours or two hours—it's in your system, and it goes right into [the baby].

In a way, Stefanie's cry for drugs in the middle of her labor shows that home-birthing women value the "modern mind" in the same way as the twilight-sleep advocates who went before them. Having made the decision not to alleviate her pain with drugs on the basis of scientific knowledge and personal commitment, Stefanie did not want her mid-birth bodily desperation to change her plans. In the end, Stefanie was happy that she had chosen to give birth at home, because there she felt comfortable enough to "let go" in the ways she needed—by cursing at those people (and God) whom she felt had betrayed her in other critical moments in her life. Being able to talk about her past with her midwives had helped Stefanie establish a supportive environment for birth in which the layers of pain held within her body could be addressed, expressed, and let go.

Letting go in the midst of enduring was also a prominent theme for Alison Lindt-Marliss. Alison emphasized that childbirth pain was real, but that it was limited. She was convinced that those limits, and her sense of connection to all women who had given birth before her, helped her to endure the pain that she described as "very intense."

> It hurt more than anything that I had ever experienced. Your whole body, I didn't feel like it was [bearable], you know. It was a lot in my back, but it seemed to be everywhere. Just this power of pain. But I also kept in mind that my mother did this, my sister did this, every woman [did this], that I can do this, that I had an athletic body. I've felt cramps—nothing like that sort—but I knew that I could do it, that my body could do it, and that there was an ending, and it was for a reason. And all these other women have done it.
>
> So those thoughts [were] in mind, that this is going to end, I can do it, everyone else has done it, and, you know, my body's strong. That helped me endure it. I get . . . annoyed with the philosophy that . . . if you just think about the flower, or the pretty picture on the wall, then you won't feel the pain. That

didn't work for me. That's false, and I feel that you're trying to buy into that, and if you don't do it, you feel like you're a failure. . . . I like [to think] that this is the pain, and this is what we're going to do with it, but I can get through it. This is going to end.

Accepting the pain, but asserting that she could "do" something with it, led Alison to endurance through "letting go" in a number of ways, from loosing herself from inhibitions about her bodily urges, to reaching back into her childhood to find comfort. As her husband rubbed her back, Alison found herself crying out "Mommy!" and being embarrassed that she had to have a bowel movement. She eventually felt able to release herself, bodily and emotionally, into her earliest embodied memories, within an atmosphere she felt was supportive and nonjudgmental. For Alison, distractions from the pain, whether in the form of "pretty pictures" or drugs, would have been counterproductive to the work she needed to do to birth a healthy baby and to keep the "power of pain" she needed to feel to endure the rigors of childbirth.

Sara Flaherty, 36, had a similar approach to Alison's realism. A nurse who has worked in labor and delivery, and who has had four home births herself, Sara and her second husband, Peter (the father of her third and fourth children), both grew up as Irish Catholics. Sara is highly critical of hospitals in terms of birth, and of the Catholic Church in terms of its stance on annulment and abortion. She still sends her daughters to catechism classes, but rarely attends church herself. I spoke with Sara about four weeks after she had given birth to her fourth child, her son, who was born so quickly that he arrived before the midwives did. Her husband ended up catching the baby, while the midwife talked him through it on the phone, an event that she and Peter both seemed to have taken in stride.

When I asked Sara to describe the pain of birth, her first response was "toe-curling," and then she elaborated on how she would explain it to a pregnant woman. "I would tell [her], 'Be ready.' It's total. It's a whole, total body thing. I don't think it's just your uterus. It's hard." Sara thought that part of the reason why her last baby had been born so quickly was that she had exercised regularly during her pregnancy, and her body was in peak condition to give birth. Even so, she averred that the pains of birth taught her something:

I learned how tough I was. How much I can [endure]. Like my husband said, "I can't believe women who don't get anything for the pain." And he even says to his friends, "You think"—I forget how he puts it, but . . . they'll say, "Oh, you're the man," and he'll say, "No, Sara's the man.". . . I wonder how it is for the husband to watch, because how can [anyone] know what you're going through really, unless you do it yourself.

> [I learned about] my endurance, I guess. . . . You know what I learned? I
> think the best thing that I learned is that you have no control. That's the thing.
> I'm a control freak. . . . Yeah, you have no control, your body's controlling you,
> and there's nothing you can do about it. You have to go with it. There's no way
> out. Not at home, anyway. At the hospital, you can always say shoot me up.

Despite her endurance and acceptance of the pain, it was still the least
favorite part of Sara's labors. But she would not want to birth any other
way. In her words,

> It's a whole experience, I think that's part of it . . . not to have that [pain] is
> not to have a big part of the experience. That's . . . where you see what you're
> made out of really. I mean, it's hard work. I have a lot of respect for women who
> give birth without drugs. It's a whole different ball game.

The respect Sara accords to women on the basis of giving birth without
drugs is rooted in an idea that one can test oneself in birth in a way
uniquely open to women. Though she did turn to sports analogies, she did
not draw a parallel to men's experience in wartime, something a number of
others have done, from Homer, to Mussolini, to Simone de Beauvoir.[29]
Sara, and other women like her, are trying to invest the pain of birth with
meanings distinct from militaristic notions of suffering for one's country.
The suffering of birth, for these women at least, brings not death but life,
both in terms of the baby brought into the world and in their understanding of their own capacities for strength and generativity.[30]

Surmounting the Pain with Spiritual Poise

Another approach to the pains of birth was that of women who sought to
surmount the pain through either mental or physical means. Though some
of the women admitted that their goal of surmounting the pain was not
always realized, they still felt that this approach was the most appropriate
way to deal with the labor of childbirth. Not surprisingly, many of the
followers of Christian Science described their approach to birth pain based
on an assertion that pain could be surmounted if one realized its illusory
nature. Heather Muncie, 32, gave birth to her daughter at home when
she was 22. Heather is somewhat unusual among home-birthing women
in that it was her mother's example that had led her to plan a home birth,
since her mother had given birth at home to Heather's sister sixteen years
after having had Heather. Christian Science, however, was passed down to
Heather through her grandmother—her mother dabbled with it, but it
was her grandmother's faith.

Heather had already been working as a Christian Science nurse when
she gave birth to her first and only child, and thus was very familiar with

the religion's tenets. In describing her experience of the pain of birth, Heather used the evocative phrase "spiritual poise" to name her approach to labor:

> [The pain] was an intensity, and that was the complete focus, that this was hap-
> pening. And I think the most significant thing for me in reference to the pain
> was [that] during that time when I was having contractions, I was completely
> at peace. . . . I don't know how to describe it. Would it be a poise? A spiritual
> poise, and a complete trust in the experience.

Though spiritual poise was her goal, for Heather the physical experience of birth at times exceeded her mental control. As she laughingly phrased it, during the last hour and a half of her labor she was "more 'not poised.' " The contractions would cause her to scream, but then in between she worked at "quieting my thought, and recognizing that this was a right experience, and it was a normal thing to be doing . . . just sort of mentally preparing myself." Though these moments of spiritual poise in between the intensity of the contractions kept her focused, they were not enough to keep her physical experience from erupting in anger, as she remembered "that feeling of how dare you do this to me, to my husband, like, it was his fault. Sort of narrowing in." In retrospect, Heather remembered her ex-husband (they are now divorced) as being very supportive during the birth and during their early period of parenting.

Other Christian Scientists, like Elaine Thatcher and Judy Woodman, recited biblical passages and selections from Mary Baker Eddy's writings to explain their approach to surmounting childbirth pain.[31] Judy Wood-man, who had actually recited from Eddy's writings while in labor, had a very succinct description of the Christian Science approach to pain. She asserted that pain was not denied or ignored in Christian Science, but that

> we try to stay in the absolute in thought, so that the human reflects that. It's
> like your body's subordinate to the thought, and so, I can stay with that absolute
> really easily, because I know that's the absolute truth. And the more I stick with
> that, then my body responds to that. So instead of, "Oh my gosh, this really
> hurts; I have to pray so the hurt will go away," I think, "Okay, God made me
> in his image and likeness, and therefore, I'm idea, I'm not really matter." And
> so as I'm thinking about that, then the body just has to respond to that.

Although Judy admitted that it was difficult to stay in the "absolute" in the midst of labor, she stood by her resolve to deal with pain, in childbirth and more generally, by subordinating her body to her thought.[32]

In addition to a Christian Science approach to pain, there are other Christian perspectives that consider pain to be surmountable. Many of these perspectives root their understanding in an interpretation of Genesis 3:16 that considers the curse condemning women to give birth in pain to have been nullified by the coming of Jesus. For example, women living in the Padanaram Settlement in Indiana, a utopian, (seemingly) Christian village with "back-to-nature ways," turned to a "birth code" revealed by God in their quest to give birth without pain.[33] The birth code required that during pregnancy a woman meditatively recite such sayings as "Be still and know that I am God," drawn from Psalm 46:10, and other mantra-like sayings such as "In Him there is no pain." As well they were to sing songs with titles such as "He Gave Me a New Life" and "Shut In with God."[34] The testimonies of women from Padanaram, at least as published in the community's promotional booklet *Faith Babies*, attested to the efficacy of the birth code to alleviate pain. As one woman declared:

> It was truly a miracle—me of all people, who would scratch my finger and cry, had a baby without a single pain. By putting myself in God's hands and letting Him run the show, I experienced a rebirth of myself. I felt fresh and clean as if I were starting a new life right along with the new life that was in my arms.[35]

The Padanaram method of painless childbirth echoed the Christian Science approach in its call for learning a "separation of the mental plane from the physical." Its emphasis on a Father God "running the show," however, ran quite contrary to Christian Science notions of a Mother-Father God who less actively controls her or his believer.[36]

While the testimonies of the Padanaram women all asserted that the birth code worked to render birth painless, women who spoke with me were less triumphant about their abilities to birth "above the curse," even when they felt that painless childbirth could happen. Charismatic Christian Carrie Ryan was convinced that painless childbirth is possible, even though she had not experienced it herself. Part of her confidence stemmed from her reading of the Bible, specifically the text of Isaiah 53:4, 5, which, according to some Christian readings, refers to Jesus as the Messiah: "Surely he has borne our infirmities and carried our diseases."[37] As well, Carrie understood Galatians 3:13, which reads, "Christ redeemed us from the curse of the law by becoming a curse for us," to be further evidence of the possibility of painless childbirth.

For Carrie, more tangible evidence of a religiously inspired painless childbirth was the birth story of her friend, who had given birth to her first child under hypnosis, but then was born again and realized that hypnosis "was no longer an option for her [because] she knew it clearly violated her understanding of the Word of God." As Carrie told me, her friend "started daily speaking the Word over her body"; namely, the passages from Isaiah and Galatians. "Every single day, many times during the day, she would speak [those words], and then she birthed without pain." While she was convinced that these daily recitations worked for her friend, and she had tried them herself, Carrie felt that the pain she experienced during her "unsaved" births kept her from having sufficient faith to give birth without pain.[38] Despite the fact that her births turned out differently, Carrie hopefully affirmed, "I believe that as somebody renews their mind, that as they grow in the things of God, that [painless childbirth] is absolutely a possibility."

In those approaches, surmounting the pain demanded an almost meditative state of preparation in the nine months prior to birth. In Carrie's charismatic approach, reading the word of God over her body was one more attempt to make her body "line up" according to her beliefs and one more way to connect to God or Jesus through asking him to bear her pain. By comparison, in the Christian Science perspective, the woman herself could overcome pain, not through denying it, but through focusing on an absolute realm that encompassed a truer reality in which matter was error. Though the exemplary testimonies of the women at Padanaram assured the reader of the possibilities of painless childbirth, the women I met were less convinced of the efficacy of this technique in their experiences.

The self-recrimination that Carrie verged on in describing her lack of faith shows one of the potential dangers in attributing potent meanings to pain: If one's body does not "line up" with one's faith (as Carrie put it), then is one to feel failure? When such deeply held beliefs are tied to surmounting pain, is a woman shamed if she screams out in pain or, as Judy Woodman put it earlier, "the body's screaming so loudly" that the mind just cannot control it? These vexing questions are always on the shadow side of finding meaning in pain or in the absence of pain. As Carrie showed in her honest appraisal of childbirth pain, spiritual poise and the ability to redefine pain were severely tested in childbirth.

Exulting in Sensation: Pain and Pleasure

Marianne Martin, the Catholic veterinarian I discussed earlier, was one woman who sought to endure the pain of childbirth, but who also felt some pleasure in the process. Both her endurance and her pleasure were tied into a sense of childbirth as a particularly spiritually charged time. Marianne connected her endurance to explicitly religious resources, when describing the birth of her daughter:

> At the beginning of my labor, I remember I was starting to feel pain with contractions. I had never had a vaginal birth, so I was afraid. Kind of like, "I hope it works out." But I remember [the midwife], once I started feeling pain, [was] in the kitchen, and I said, "I'm starting to feel pain. Is there something I should be doing? Like should I do some positions?" She says, "No, that's part of it. . . .

The more pain you feel, the more effective your contractions are becoming, and the more your labor is progressing. So that's normal." So I said, "Okay, that's cool. I'll do it. I'll deal with it then."

So then I just prayed. I just pictured Jesus on the cross, and I said, "You put up with a lot of pain on the cross and let me offer my pain up with yours and help me to endure it." So it wasn't really an official prayer; it was just like a little prayer.

Marianne further extended her understanding of what she called the "good meaning of suffering" by saying that in her second home birth she was "offering up my pain to make it useful [for] . . . the souls in purgatory, people that I know have died, and other people in the world that need help." In Marianne's interpretation, the "good sacrifice" of birth makes a woman a companion to the suffering Jesus in bringing compromised souls everlasting life—not an insignificant task for someone who believes in a theology of redemptive suffering. Echoing the birth imagery of earlier women mystics in her Catholic tradition, but with a twist, Marianne transformed her real birthing body into a metaphorical site of passion.[39]

Just as a medieval woman mystic found unparalleled pleasure in the midst of her suffering, so too did Marianne find that with her embrace of pain came sensations she considered pleasurable. She described her second baby's birth this way:

With her, she never went through the thing where they crown, and they tip their heads, their head comes out, and their body comes out. She came out in a swoosh of water. It was so neat. I felt her little fingers and her little toes coming right through my birth canal. I could feel everything because it was so—I guess because it wasn't slow, you know, move-stop, move-stop, move-stop. It was like a smooth, sudden motion, and it just felt like blup-blup-blup, like I felt the whole thing come out.

Though she had to endure pain before her daughter finally was born, for Marianne, simultaneously feeling her own body and her daughter's in that last moment before the baby left her womb was a delight that she continued to hold clear in her memory. As such, Marianne crossed the (blurry) line between women who endure and those who exult in the pains of birth.

The notion that within pain can be pleasure is a difficult and pervasive problem in human experience generally, and within feminist theory more specifically. Though not all home-birthing women may share Marianne's understanding of the value and even pleasure in pain, many do assert that in enduring the pain of birth, a woman can bring forth a healthier baby, learn about herself in the process, and be readier to engage in the pleasures of meeting her baby face to face. As Marianne showed when she spoke of feeling her daughter's "tiny fingers" leaving her birth canal, women who sought to endure pain were sometimes the same ones who found giving birth to be pleasurable. Though none of the women I interviewed experienced childbirth as solely a pleasurable sensation, many, in struggling to find language to describe the bodily experience of birth, tried to infuse the word "pain" with positive connotations, or with pleasure itself.

Nell Reid, 37, and mother of two, attends a United Methodist church, as well as "spiritual growth" workshops, together with her husband. Nell acknowledged that the contractions during her two births had hurt at times, but that "pain" was not the word she preferred to describe her experience: "Pain to me is like you got your finger cut off, something that's uncontrollable or didn't have a meaning to it." Instead, she described the sensations of birth as "intense, challenging, and hard." In addition to shaping her experience by changing the language she used to describe labor, Nell tried to deal with the "intensity" of birth by layering on top of the contractions an affirmation suggested to her by her sister-in-law: "God doesn't give you what you can't handle. You'll only get as much as you can handle, and it's just one contraction." Even though the God of her affirmation gave Nell so much pain to endure that she decided to go to the hospital near the end of her first birth, she stayed at home for her second birth and felt that her births were best encapsulated not by pain, but by "exhilaration."

Alison Lindt-Marliss, the "realist" with an aversion to the "pretty pictures" approach to childbirth pain, spoke most ardently about the pleasure of childbirth. She described the birth of her second child (her first home birth) with recourse to Michel Odent's *Birth Reborn*:

> Basically, once I was dilated, there was just a pause, and then he was born. I pushed twice, and it was a sensation that was so powerful, my whole body was tingling, and it was a very sensual experience to me. Michel Odent describes that, it's almost like an orgasm, but not sexual. I don't know how you do it, but it's just like, "Waah!" And right after he was born, I said, "I've got to do that again." I didn't want another child or anything at that time, but I just went, "I have to do this again." It was so powerful.

While turning to the language of orgasm to describe her sensation, Alison differentiated the sensuality of the experience from sexuality. That a woman's vagina and breasts are both maternal and sexual can be an uncomfortable overlap for some women. Alison was not overly concerned with distinguishing between her maternity and sexuality more generally, but neither did she seem interested in exploring their confluence, at least with me. Discomfort with viewing birth as an aspect of women's sexuality is a societal reality, according to legal theorist Brenda Waugh, who argued that there are legal consequences to this uneasiness with maternal sexuality.

She offered the example of women who have argued in court, without success, that their right to privacy in procreation should grant them choice about place of birth and birth attendant, since they see birth as part of the procreative, sexual process. They lose their cases, wrote Waugh, because "the legal definition of procreation construes the privacy right to procreate only to the heterosexual masculine right to intercourse."[40] In Waugh's interpretation, birthing women who resist deeply engrained representations of childbirth as simply painful are a threat not only to medical models of birth, but to androcentric norms of sexuality that place a premium on penetration. Even, or especially, sex, another intimate bodily act that attracts notions of the "natural," is embedded in habitus with its socially legitimated, but not monolithic, expressions.

Several women writers, however, echo Alison's allusion to the complex relationships between sexuality and childbirth. For example, in her poem about childbirth, "The Moment When Two Worlds Meet," Sharon Olds writes:

> . . . that is the center of life, that moment when the
> juiced bluish sphere of the baby is
> sliding between the two worlds,
> wet, like sex, it *is* sex,
> it is my life opening back and back . . .[41]

The meeting of two worlds in childbirth, in the form of the baby who is both of the mother and of the world, can be a powerfully transformative time for a woman, and one filled with mingled and sometimes contradictory sensations: pleasure, pain, sexuality, and relief.[42]

Sharon Olds's poetic words find a remarkable parallel in Simone Taylor's description of "sliding" between pain and pleasure. In thinking of pain, Simone merged her nursing and seminary training with her experience as the daughter of a scientist father. A self-described feminist, Simone turned partly to biology to understand the significance of birth pain, but relied ultimately on her mother's more theological explanation to make sense of the pain:

> [My mother's] feeling is, we were made to do this work, and it's not easy, and it's inherently painful, and it's part of the . . . Pain and pleasure are a continuum, and without the pain, there would not be the pleasure. We wouldn't have a place to slide around, and that this is just an intense experience of pain. It's also an intense experience of pleasure, and joy and hope. And so theologically, I think I would look at the pain—if I was being really pressed to look at it—positively, which is a good thing to do. I would say that the pain is part of the glory, or the tremendous mystery of life. And that if anything, it's kind of a privilege to stand so close to such an incredible miracle. And that there's pain

involved because it's such a tremendous event, that it's like, it's like living in a
different dimension briefly. And that it's a painful process, because it's like two
worlds colliding.

Simone turned to biblical sources to meld the agony of pain with the
ecstasy of creation, making birth a visionary—perhaps mystical—experience for her.

Though Simone recalled feeling such visionary highs during her midwife-attended hospital birth four years ago, this time, a few weeks after
her second birth at home, she recalled feeling somewhat more "earthbound." Meg Alexander, the woman who felt God was "pushed out" of
the hospital delivery room, had the reverse experience. Meg, however, had
three years of distance from her last birth, which took place at home. Meg
compared her two births, the first one by cesarean:

> [My home birth] was the most rewarding hard work. It was so satisfying. The
> pain—people judge things on the amount of pain; they're totally disregarding
> a lot of other things that are going on at the same time. I experienced tremen-
> dous pain after the cesarean. But it was a hundred times worse because there
> was no one there to share it with me, no one. I was alone in recovery. No one
> was telling me what was happening. I had no idea what was happening, or why.
> I thought for sure I was dying. And it was pain caused because somebody had
> cut me open. And because somebody had ripped my baby away from me. And
> there was just nothing good about that kind of pain. And no support, no expla-
> nation, nothing. It was just pain by itself, pain.
>
> But this pain [of the second birth at home], it was like, Oh! Poets. I read
> poetry describing that feeling at that moment. I can remember how [the poet]
> put it, something like, "the universe giving its whole to you." And you feel like
> the universe is moving through you . . . if you just let it, and trust it. And you're
> only a human being, so if it breaks you, it breaks you. But what's more important
> is if you let that move through you.

Meg, whose vehement opposition to hospital birth technology I discussed
earlier, turned to the television series *Star Trek* for an analogy to describe
her pain more fully:

> You know *Deep Space Nine*? My son likes to watch that. It's awesome watching
> that spaceship travel through space. You like to imagine that's like the speed of
> light. Well, that's pretty awesome, but it's just as awesome to feel labor passing
> through your body. And it's the same thing. You know, it's the universe. You
> may not see [it]—it's not outer space with all the stars, but it's human beings
> creating life. It's a different thing, but it's the same thing. It's the universe right
> through your body. And at that moment, that's what I felt like. I felt like, and I
> knew, that this is a really miraculous thing that is happening to me, and I don't
> care how much it hurts, because this is a once-in-a-lifetime thing. And I just
> felt so honored to be able to feel that.

According to Meg, being surrounded by supportive women was part of what transformed the pain of birth and allowed her to "trust" it. The quality of her relationships with her midwives was markedly different from her previous experience with health-care providers in the hospital. Many women shared the notion that giving birth while supported by trusted family, friends, and midwives changed the quality and meaning of pain. Exploring further the significance of pain and relationship will show the transformative possibilities in the experience of pain itself.

Pain and Relationship

Scholarly treatises on pain often seem to share a fundamental position: pain is a private and lonely experience of the individual.[43] In her work on "the body in pain," Elaine Scarry suggested that pain was inherently unsharable, because of its inexpressibility. According to Scarry, "Physical pain does not simply resist language but actively destroys it, bringing about an immediate reversion to a state anterior to language, to the sounds and cries a human being makes before language is learned."[44] One of the quandaries arising from the unsharability of pain, in Scarry's interpretation, is that for the sufferer pain produces certainty—one is sure of one's pain—but for the observer, pain produces doubt. Is that person really in such pain?

The ambiguity of pain, for Scarry, makes it a force in the world of both destruction and creativity, as human beings relate to each other with greater and lesser degrees of compassion, as sensible, sensing, others.[45] It is the vulnerability of our bodies, in Scarry's analysis, that leads us to creation: we make coats to keep us warm, chairs to relieve us of our weight. In her words, "The act of human creating includes both the creating of the object and the object's recreating of the human being."[46] Belief also becomes a form of material making, accomplished with the body. Discussing representations of childbirth in Genesis, Scarry argued that the maternal body is one of the richest sites for the intersection of belief and making. In her words, "Belief in the Scriptures is literally the act of turning one's own body inside-out—imagining, creating, the capacity for symbolic and religious thought begin with the capacity to endow interior physical events with an external, nonphysical referent."[47] In Genesis, symbolically transforming wombs into wells and altars draws on the "capacity of substantiation" within women's bodies, to make broader meaning in the world.[48]

Though Scarry did not discuss childbirth pain in her declaration of pain's unsharable nature, her recourse to childbirth to describe the creativity of the body is instructive. The pain of childbirth as interpreted by women in labor, however, does not necessarily fit Scarry's description of pain, in that it is not always considered unsharable or provoking of skepticism. These home-birthing women did share her understanding of childbirth as a meaning-making activity that transforms the maker in the process. A reading of Scarry thus provokes the question, What, if anything, makes the pain of childbirth different from other kinds of pain? Some of the difference lies in the rhythm of childbirth pain—wavelike and with a determined end. Childbirth pain is not necessarily the obliterating pain that Scarry describes both because of its purpose and because it can evoke communication that is wordless—whether between a woman and another person, or a woman and her god.

The ways that these women stretch language (or find it inadequate) in describing the sensations of childbirth, however, show that their experience of pain is different from, but still linked to, Scarry's notion of pain as being anterior to language. Marianne's description of feeling "blup-blup-blup" as her baby emerged, and Alison's resort to "waah" to describe the feeling of pushing out her baby, show that the intense sensations of childbirth can also be resistant to language. Perhaps neither pain nor pleasure can encapsulate what childbirth may feel like. Attending to the linguistic and metaphorical innovations women employ to describe their bodily memories of birth shows the difficulty of conveying such sensations in words. Perhaps many feelings, in addition to pain, are resistant to language.

What seemed clear for the majority of these home-birthing women, however, was that the pain or pleasure of childbirth did not feel like a solitary experience. Instead, the bodily rigors of childbirth opened them up to connection, be it with children, friends, midwives, spiritual powers, or husbands. Certainly, for some women, the suffering of birth did seem solitary at times. During her second home birth, Tina Hostetler found herself looking around at her midwives and her husband as they sat in living room glancing at photo albums while she was in the midst of labor. On seeing the "normalcy" in the room, she recalled thinking, "This is so weird. It doesn't seem like long ago I went through this before—when I was in pain and it was *just up to me to have this baby.* [I thought], Why am I doing this? I couldn't believe I was doing it again, knowing what I was going to go through. But now I'd do it again." Tina's sense of solitude in the midst of supportive people was not unique, but it can be compared with several narratives in which women felt that their childbirth pain was sharable, and that in such sharing their pain was transformed.

Jesus with Skin On: Husbands and Home Birth

The majority of women considered their husbands to be their greatest supporters in the midst of labor—their husbands were not considered skeptics, and in some cases even were considered participants in the pain.

For some women, being in constant physical touch with their husbands—often to the exclusion of verbal contact—was necessary to endure the pain of contractions. Often a woman told of how prearranged plans for the husband to catch the baby had been waylaid, since she could not bear to have her husband move from the position in which he was supporting her—as she reclined into his lap, hung her arms around his shoulders as they stood, or even, in one case, as he held her aloft from under the arms. The pain of labor was literally shared through their bodies, as men emerged from their roles as supporters with sore muscles and aching backs.[49]

Alison Lindt-Marliss, who earlier compared the sensations of birth to the sensations of orgasm, asserted that the people who surrounded her as she gave birth precluded the need for drugs. Alison felt that drugs took away from the sharability of pain—drugs were a poor substitute for love:

> I realized that when . . . people are saying, "Oh, here, have an episiotomy, or here, have this drug," they're saying that instead of saying, "Here, I'll rub your back through this contraction; here, I'll do this for you." So they're giving you a substitute of the care, of the nurturing. They're giving you a machine, or a drug, instead of their love. And the women that I had with me, and my husband, and some friends, I knew would just give me the love. And that's what you need: somebody [saying] "You're doing a great job Alison." That's what they [my husband and friends] did. [They said], "You're doing a great job. One more contraction; you can do it. Anyone can do one more contraction." As opposed to the nurses going, "She's not getting anywhere, doctor." [Laughs.] Who can birth under those circumstances? Sure, give me the drug. Obviously, I can't do it. But, the midwife's going, "You're doing great. You're going to see that baby soon. You're opening up." It's a whole different atmosphere.

For Alison, childbirth pain could be endured, if not alleviated, because she had others around her supporting her with tactile and verbal expressions of love. These were not skeptical observers doubting her pain, but a gathering of midwives, family, and friends who had committed themselves to being with her throughout her labor, because they believed that it was difficult and that they could help her through it.

Alison felt that of all the people at her birth, her husband especially was capable of sharing her pain. During her third birth (in which she regretfully said she had not recovered that sensation of intense pleasure she had experienced during her second birth), Alison described her relationship with her husband this way:

> I felt so connected to him. We were so much in love. I remember, because [this baby] was the last, I felt like [we were] one. I felt we were united. We were birthing this baby together. He was holding me up; he was like a tree . . . that image of him as the tree, and I was just holding on to him and bringing this

new life. It enhanced our relationship, very much. We have a good relationship anyway, but it was just such a bond. It's one of those overused words today, but the connection was so intense and deep—very powerful—that he was just there with me the whole time.

Alison believed strongly that a powerful connection develops between a man, a woman, and their child when they work together to give birth. She asked, "If your husband's so involved in the birth process like that, how can he leave your child later, or divorce you? Even if he does divorce you, how can he abandon that child? What a start they have, what a connection." For Alison, going through the arduous process of childbirth together brings families into relationship in lasting and profound ways.[50]

Carrie Ryan voiced a particularly evocative image of the support she felt she had received from her husband during childbirth:

> [My husband] was wonderful. He was so supportive; he was there to encourage me, to speak life to me, to hold me when I wanted to be held, to just be there. To pray for me, when I got to the point where I could just literally no longer pray myself. He was just praying, and putting his lips right to my ear and just speaking the Word of God to me to keep me encouraged. I said to him afterwards—I get teary-eyed when I think about it—but one time he came into the shower, and it was literally Jesus with skin on. He just stood there, and it was Christ. I know He dwells in me, and I know He's omnipresent. I know He's there. I know that the presence of God was there. I knew that, but it was literally like having Him in bodily form, standing right next to me, and it was just strengthening at that time when you really need it.

When her own words and prayers waned in the midst of exhaustion, Carrie depended on her husband to "speak the Word over my body." Not only did she hear the words, she also envisioned him as the embodiment of Christ—she turned metaphor into presence. Given Carrie's earlier paralleling of her experience of birthing to God's experience of separation from his Son on the cross, her conflation of her husband with Christ is that much more powerful. Seeing her husband as Jesus with skin on, Carrie drew her husband into an expiatory drama in which he shared her pain in what for her were real and tangible ways.

The notion that her husband could tangibly affect her bodily experience of pain was also shared by Carrie's fellow charismatic Christian, Janet Stein. In Janet's experience, her husband's prayers took away her pain. She described her experience of being healed of pain by his prayer in both her pregnancies:

> One thing that was so amazing through this pregnancy, and also the one before, even through the miscarriage: when David prays for me physically, there's an immediate change. I'll be praying for healing—and see, before I was married I

had to pray—I had good friends pray for me if I was struggling with some physical thing—but I tell you what: when David prays for me, there's an immediate change. Like one day during the miscarriage, it was just one day of real, real pain and discomfort, and I kept thinking I should call him at work or I should call him and ask him to pray, but then *he* called. I told him I was miserable. He prayed, and I don't know how fast, whether it was minutes or it was within the hour, no more pain. I had no more pain throughout the miscarriage.

According to Janet, the power her husband has to alleviate her pain stems in part from love, as Alison also asserted in the context of her birth. For Janet, however, her husband's power also emerges from his position as the "head" of his wife. Whereas Janet's and Carrie's experiences of their husbands' ability to share in, if not remove, their pain were tied into models of marital hierarchy, Alison's experience was based in a model of mutuality. For all three women, the presence of their husbands, whether in the flesh or through prayer, evoked a change in their bodies, transforming their pain into connection.

Not all women, however, felt such deep alliances with their husbands in the process or aftermath of birth. Some women felt that giving birth in the intimacy of their homes underscored, painfully or sometimes just prosaically, the lack of connection between themselves and their husbands and showed them how they needed to depend more on themselves and less on others. For example, Olivia, a "New Age Jew," felt that her husband did not participate in her births by sharing her pain, but instead remained emotionally removed from the process. Her desires for her births to be the bonding experiences—not only between her and the baby, but also between her and her husband—that are idealized in home-birth literature did not come to pass. "I expected more love surrounding my husband and me. I always did. And I was ready to give it, and put it out. . . . So the whole thing, the whole triangle—my husband, me, and the baby—were never connected the way I wanted them to be. And I've done a lot of crying about this, and I guess I could cry again, but I'm too angry right now." Olivia fit her disappointment within a worldview that understood some people to be less spiritually and emotionally evolved than others. According to her, her husband had a fair bit of evolving to do.

Another woman had experiences similar to Olivia's, but since the woman's birth was not preceded by the same expectations of closeness with her spouse, she did not feel a similar sense of disappointment. Wendy Pearson, 25, said that she was accustomed to avoiding dependence on others, including her husband, and not counting on help in her day-to-day life. Wendy is Euro-American and was one of the few working-class women with whom I spoke. A small woman with reddish hair, Wendy had worked part-time in a pet-supply store before her second baby was born. When we spoke, she was staying at home looking after her two children, aged 1 and 4. She rarely saw her husband, who when not working as an electrician, spent much of his free time as a volunteer firefighter. Wendy attends a United Methodist church with her children (her husband does not attend), where she runs the nursery and is active in a Bible study group. She expressed some frustration at the small amount of time she spends with her husband and was even more frustrated with the limited time her son had with his father.

In remembering her early attitudes toward birth, Wendy recalled that she always wanted to "get married and have kids," but she was scared of birth "because people always tell you, 'Oh, it hurts so much, you'll never feel pain like that again in your life.'" But, she added, "I was more scared of being in the hospital, and the place, than I was of the pain." Wendy's first birth took place in the hospital, because her husband was not comfortable with a home birth, and she remembers it as a terrifying experience:

> Once I got there, they put me in bed, put the monitor on me, and I was not allowed out of bed again. They put an IV in me, which there was no reason for. They said I had to have it. And I'm telling them, no, and I'm fighting them, so they had somebody else come in and hold me down, so they could put an IV in my arm. They broke my water and didn't tell me. They had induced my labor the day before and didn't tell me. [The doctor] stripped the membrane, and didn't tell me before he did it. . . . I didn't know why it hurt so much. And he left the room, and I was screaming. I didn't know what [had] happened. And then the nurse told me that he [had] stripped the membrane so I would be in labor the next day.[51]

The next time, her husband agreed to Wendy's demand to give birth at home because he saw, in her words, how "terrified" she had been during her hospital birth and how "determined" she was never to go back.

Wendy's sense of her need to be independent extended into how she dealt with the pain when giving birth at home. She recalled hardly noticing the midwives, and said that the only aid she called for was from herself and from God: "I remember when I was screaming. . . . I remember, I was asking for help, but I was doing it outside and inside, I was praying at the same time, that you [God] had to help me deliver this baby because I was determined to stay home." According to Wendy, she prayed because "I knew I was the only one who could do it, and he [God] was the only one who could help me, really." With her prayer came help, in her view: "That was when it changed from really hurting, to only hurting some. And that was when I didn't scream quite so loud, and I don't know. . . . I don't know if it was just coincidence, or what you'd want to call it." Where Janet called on God through her husband, Wendy did so directly, partly, no doubt, because her husband was not particularly religious, but also because she tried "to do a lot of stuff on [my] own."

Part of Wendy's birth plan was that she would catch her baby herself. She felt that since she had carried the baby inside her for nine months, she wanted to be the first to touch it. She had told her husband that he could catch if he wanted to, but he demurred. In the end, she recalled, she did not catch the baby because she was too busy concentrating on what she was doing. Despite not being able to catch the baby, Wendy felt her home birth was in keeping with how she lived her life more generally:

> I try not to depend on other people to help me with things. I think that I have to do most of it myself. And really to deliver a baby, you have to depend on yourself. So I think the fact that—I mean, it's not always good, you sometimes need to depend on other people. But for certain things, you can't, and I think the fact that I've done it for a long time has helped.

Wendy included her husband among those people she tried not to turn to for help. Wendy's husband was by her side for the birth, holding her hand, and stayed home from work for two days afterwards taking care of her as she took care of the new baby. She had no quarrel with how he supported her during her birth, but neither did she feel that the experience affected their relationship in any significant way. Instead, she said, "Things are still about the same." Where Olivia cried about her lack of connection with her husband, Wendy simply stated it.

So, while for some women going through the pain of giving birth at home strengthened their connections to their husbands (and for some, gave their husbands new respect for them), for others giving birth underscored their individuality, whether in the form of aloneness or independence. For women with male partners, men are always a part of birth, whether by their absence or their presence.[52]

Midwives: Friends and Professionals

In addition to relationships with husbands, several women drew support from their midwives. Though contemporary home birth implies a relationship with a midwife that is a hazy cross between professional and friend, most women found that the care they received from their midwives was of an intimacy that shaded into friendship. The women who chose direct-entry midwives more often felt their relationships were based in friendship rather than in professional commitments, partly because they were seeking a more intimate form of care, and partly because the midwives were more informal. For example, the women's prenatal visits took place in the homes of their midwives and were less governed by regulations. Most of the women, however, felt some of the postpartum disjuncture of midwifery care. Once the baby was born, the midwives they had visited regularly for the last eight months were no longer a routine part of their lives.

All but one of the women spoke very highly of their midwives and found that the care they received in labor was supportive and helpful, as did Raina Lennox, a 26-year-old, African-American Seventh Day Adventist. Raina, whose husband was a quality-control technician in an electronics company, gave birth to her first child in the hospital when she was 22. Though she had discussed with her obstetrician her desire to have a natural childbirth, she felt that in her brief ten-minute prenatal appointments he did not spend a great deal of time listening to her. In the end, she recalled that while in labor she had to fight with her obstetrician to avoid procedures like internal monitors and IVs. In Raina's words, "Natural childbirth for him was a vaginal childbirth."

For her second birth, three years later, Raina chose certified nurse-midwives to attend her birth at home. She enjoyed the longer prenatal visits she had with these women, and she trusted them. In the midst of her labor, Raina appreciated the strategies the midwives suggested to deal with the pain:

> I think the midwives helped me, because they were like, "Okay, put your chin toward your chest." The midwives—actually I really leaned on them at that time. They told me to touch the baby's head, and when I did that, my sense came back, like, "Okay, now I know why I'm doing this. I've got to keep pushing to get the baby out." But I actually was more comfortable with the baby staying in at that point because it hurt so bad. "Well, just stay there; I don't care any more!" It was very scary, but once I put my hands on the baby's head, a sense of calm came over me a little, and then I started working, and then I knew I had to push, so then I started pushing.

Raina did not want drugs to take away the pain, both to keep her baby from their influence and because drugs effect a changed "state of mind. You detach from the birth, you forget what's going on. And it's already so emotional. I didn't want anything interfering with that." Raina felt that by helping her to connect with her almost-born child, her midwives led her to experience the pain more positively.

Raina was pregnant with her third child when we spoke, and she had chosen to work with direct-entry midwives for this birth. She had developed a friendship with a direct-entry midwife at a childbirth study group she had started to attend because of her interest in becoming a certified birth attendant. She was looking forward to having a midwife at her birth who would remain a friend long after the birth of her baby.

For another woman, Sondra Tanner-Gordon, 31, touching her baby's head as it crowned was less helpful as a way of dealing with the pain. Sondra, a Reconstructionist Jew and a lawyer, who now works part-time from her home, gave birth to both her children at home, each time with the same certified nurse-midwives. Sondra had a more problematic relationship with her midwives than Raina, which she attributed partly to her sense that her midwife stereotyped her as a "corporate conservative" as opposed to a more "holistic progressive." Sondra characterized her births as "just pain"—there was nothing spiritual about birthing itself. In this state, she found little respite through relationship with either her midwives or her baby:

> [At] one point, [the midwife] was saying something like, "Oh, you can reach down and touch your baby. It's right there. Feel her head." I was like, "I don't want to feel her head, just get her out. I don't, I don't care." I was just in too much pain, and I felt bad about that afterwards, but I really didn't care. Touching her head was not "it" for me. I think she was trying to be encouraging to let me know that the baby was right there.

In Sondra's recounting, her birth pain was actually increased by her midwives, as they applied fundal pressure (pushing down on the abdomen) to help the baby emerge. Though she acknowledged that she thought this was a necessary procedure, she was surprised at even this level of "low-tech" intervention applied by the midwives.[53]

Despite regretting her response when the midwife asked if she wanted to touch her baby's head, Sondra had little good to say about her relationships with her midwives. She did not feel that they wanted feedback about their work or wanted to continue a relationship after the birth: "I felt very unsupported in the aftermath of the birth. I felt what they do is birth. You know, now I've got this newborn baby, and the person that I've been talking to more than anybody the last nine months, I wouldn't say isn't interested, but doesn't make me feel that they're the ones I should call." However, she did have the same midwives attend her next birth, and while the birth went well, Sondra felt they were distinctly "unhelpful." Though she trusted their skills, Sondra emerged from her two births feeling a clash of personalities between her and her midwives that had resulted in less than harmonious births.

The majority of women, however, felt an intimacy with their midwives that was at once bodily and emotional. For example, a number of women spoke about how touched they were by the gentleness with which their midwives treated them after they had endured the rigors of labor. Meg Alexander described feeling like a "goddess" after her birth and "the Queen of the Nile," in part because she felt so "connected with the universe" but also because of the care her direct-entry midwife took with her. As she stepped out of the shower, the midwife was holding a towel ready to dry her off and make sure she did not slip. Meg remembered the midwife's gesture as "practical, not mushy," comparing the midwife to her paternal grandmother. But she also felt this small gesture of intimacy was representative of the caring that midwives provided: "That's just how these women are. They just take for granted that they do things like this for each other."

Liza Rossiter, who had experience with both a birth center and home birth, also remarked on the intimacy she felt with the midwives after giving birth. Liza was moved to tears as she remembered the care her direct-entry midwife gave her just after the birth, by drying her off after her shower, and wiping her feet. She mused that her home midwifery care was "on a different plane" from what she had received in the birth center—especially given what she called the "spiritual moments" the midwives evoked. For Liza, spiritual moments occurred in the midst of their caring for her body: "I know feet-washing is something in the Bible that is considered special. And after I got out of the shower, I guess this sticks in my mind, for some reason, that [the midwife] was drying my feet, and I wasn't expecting to get that kind of attention, so that touched me. And even when I talk about [it]—you can see my eyes are watering—it affects me; it really does. And they fixed us breakfast. The labor assistant fixed breakfast for us." Stories of the gentleness and practicality of midwives abounded in women's recounting of their births. In addition to holding, massaging, oiling, and drying these birthing women's bodies, midwives did the dishes and the laundry, made breakfast, and even, in one case (in order to get the labor moving of a woman who was worried about her unwashed stairs), washed the stairs.

The bodily intimacy engendered in helping a woman give birth can be experienced as movingly gentle or painfully harsh, depending upon the exigencies of a woman's birth and her personal relationship with her midwives. Since many of the women I interviewed shared the same midwives, it was clear to me that the relationships between a midwife and a birthing woman differed according to personality. Precisely because the line between professional and friend is blurred in complicated ways, relationships between midwives and birthing women can provoke intense, if short-lived, intimacy, as well as disappointment. In the regular, hour-long conversations during which midwives and their clients learn to know each other over the course of nine months, trust that affirms a woman's ability to birth often develops. At times, however, that trust does not solidify, whether because of personality differences or personal circumstances on the part of both the midwife and the birthing woman, and such women do not experience the quality of care they seek. Most women, however, found that their midwives provided them with as little or as much attention as they desired, so that they could focus on relationships with their family members, including their children.

Children at the Birth

One of the benefits of home birth, for many women, was the potential for older children to be present at the birth of their younger sibling. Children (as well as the baby being born) were another source of support for women in labor, and some women felt that the bonds they developed with their children while in labor transformed their relationships. Several women sent their children to relatives or neighbors while in labor, because they did not want their children to be upset by seeing them in pain. Others, however, who wanted their children to see birth as a "natural" part of family life, allowed their children to stay in the house and be part of the birth if they desired. These women usually arranged for a friend or relative to stay with the child in the house, in case she or he did not want to participate in the birth. Many women were particularly hopeful that their girl children would be present for the birth, so that they would have (hopefully) positive images of a woman giving birth if they ever did so themselves in the future.

Joanna Katz, the woman who had a home naming for her fourth daughter, told a particularly moving story of how Adrienne, her oldest daughter, acted at her home birth:

> When I was really in pain and I was trying to hang on to my bed, and get up and get down, and squat, and just try to get through the contractions, my oldest daughter got really upset. And she went out of the room, [but] she kept coming up to check on me, and ask if I needed anything. And I kept saying, "No, I don't need anything. I'm just really not feeling well, and I'm really in pain." And she went and she sat down on our stairs, on the top of our stairs, and she started to cry. And she was really upset. And I didn't know any of this until afterwards. And the midwife and Elise told me. And Elise went over and checked her. Elise was our birth coach—birth assistant—she helped with our kids.
>
> And she sat down with Adrienne, and she said, "You know, Mommy's going to be OK. This will pass. It takes a while, but . . . this is the end, this is the beginning of the end. And I know you're really upset. Do you want to talk about it?" And Adrienne said, No. Because Adrienne's not a very verbal child. She's a very quiet, sedate child. And she's fairly mature for her age. And she just sat down, and she said, "I just need to be here right now. And I'm upset but I'll be OK." And they said, "You know you can be strong for yourself as well as for Mom. And I know you're upset, but you also know, trust me, if you need to cry, its OK." And Elise said, "With that, she got up; she pulled herself together." She said, "I'll be fine." She got up and came in and held my hand through the rest of my labor. She sat there and did not let go of it. And I squeezed her hand so tight. I kept joking, "Oh, Adrienne, I'm going to break your fingers!" Because I mean I was squeezing her hand so tight, it was really incredible. And she just got this inner strength; that to me was amazing, just amazing.
>
> And she did not leave my bedside. And she was brushing my hair. Like a mother would do to a child. She was just stroking my head, and just holding my hand, and saying, "It's OK, Mom, it's almost over. The midwife's here, we're all here with you. And it's going to be over soon." And even when the other

kids were getting excited when I started to push out, and they started to see the head crown and stuff, she just sat there and she just held onto me, so tight. And it was just an incredible bonding between me and Adrienne.

Several women echoed Joanna's story of the bonding that developed between her and Adrienne as a result of her baby's birth. Debra Lensky described her nine-year-old daughter, who helped the midwives catch the baby, as the "best natural support person. . . . Every once in a while she would ask if there's anything that she could do, in such a sweet, kind, loving way. You felt the love just pour [out]." As with women's descriptions of their husbands as trees or Christ, in talking of their children women described their emotions as tangible entities, "pouring" forth in the intensely physical context of birth.

Other women spoke of their younger children who eagerly held mirrors for their mothers or held flashlights for the midwives as their mothers pushed out their siblings, and who snuggled up to the new baby as the family cuddled on the bed with their newborn. Liza Rossiter joked that her three-year-old daughter must have been "a midwife in another life," since she was so unfazed and delighted by her mother's birth. Older children, then, transformed their mothers' pain into relationship, as for Joanna when her daughter wiped her brow as a "mother would a child." Children helped their mother feel that not only was she fostering new relationships between herself and her children and the newborn baby, but that she was also affecting the relationships her children would have to their babies in the future. Though a mother cannot control how her child will be affected by witnessing her give birth, those who chose to invite their children to their births ultimately felt that the experience was a beneficial one for their families as a whole.

Pain and Power

The generally positive interpretation these women gave to their pain suggests some difficult questions. Does suffering childbirth pain in the age of anesthesia suggest unnecessary martyrdom or a spiritualizing of suffering? Do problematically essentialized views of women's childbearing role lie beneath the view of pain as empowering? Tikva Frymer-Kensky, a Reconstructionist Jew and Hebrew Bible scholar, asserted that contrary to spiritualizing suffering, experiencing the pain of birth "prevents people from totally spiritualizing the birth and the baby."[54] She continued: "The pain brings women more fully into their bodies, ready to feel both the effort and the ecstasy with all their being."[55] Jeannine Parvati Baker, the "shamanic midwife" I described earlier, endorsed the ecstasy of childbirth even more heartily, declaring that "all those years of orgasms" were good practice for birthing her baby. For Parvati Baker, the kind of ecstasy childbirth engenders has religious parallels, or is religious itself, as she asserted when describing the act of pushing her baby "down into that space just before orgasm when we women know how God must have felt creating this planet."[56]

Other authors are less convinced. A more guarded voice is that of pain specialist Dr. Ronald Melzack, who concluded that labor pain was one of the most severe types of pain, but that the severity differed among individuals.[57] Taking her cue from Melzack, and probably oblivious to Parvati Baker, scholar Mary S. Sheridan claimed that "totally unmedicated or pain-free parturition, a vogue now generally over, is unrealistic." She added: "'Natural childbirth' fits well into a culture that prizes stoicism and is ambivalent about the reality and meaning of women's pain."[58] For Sheridan, the problem with labor pain in contemporary America is that there is *not enough* provision of anesthesia for birthing women because of gendered dismissals of women's pain, quite the opposite of a home-birth view of medicated birth.

A similar response to the "vogue" of unmedicated birth in the popular birth-advice book, *What to Expect When You're Expecting*, advised women that childbirth was "not supposed to be a trial by ordeal or a test of bravery, strength, or endurance." The "enlightened" view, according to these authors, would recognize that "wanting relief from excruciating pain is natural."[59] In another vein, feminist author Marina Warner argued that unmedicated birth is a sexist construct that acts as "a means of underpinning women's subjection to their biology, and of denying them freedom to reject it or overcome it through the medical means available."[60] Similarly, in *Gyn/ecology*, author and feminist theologian Mary Daly affirmed Kathleen Barry's statement: "Natural childbirth, as we know it now, is nothing more than a romanticized means of helping women to better adjust to the abnormal and intensely painful delivery process mandated by men."[61] In these views, women who embrace the pain of childbirth are embracing subjection—to fully exercise agency they would need to forgo pain through anesthesia.

On a parallel plane to those who see birth pain as unnecessary, some feminist theorists have criticized what they see more generally as a spiritualization of women's suffering. Two Christian feminist theologians, Beverly Wildung Harrison and Carter Heyward, argued that "*pain—the deprivation of sensual pleasure*" has deep roots as a "foundation of Christian faith," so much so that "to be Christian was to accept or even to seek pain."[62] Furthermore, they argued, the confluence between pain and pleasure found in Christianity's "patriarchal heterosexism," and especially in erotic relations, has meant that "women have no body rights, no moral claim to our bodies as self-possessed. . . . *Women in Christianity are meant to live for others.*"[63] According to this view, a woman fusing her labor pains with the suffering of Christ on the cross could be read as one more example of female submission to Christian sadomasochism. But is it?

Within interpretations of pain lie notions of gender—whether women are seen as being in greater need of anesthesia because of their weak constitutions or as needing to go through the pain to make them better mothers.[64] As Robert Orsi suggested in his work on Catholic women's devotions to St. Jude, "The discourse on pain was gendered: to suffer pain well—which meant cheerfully, silently, submissively—was to suffer like a woman; conversely, the good woman had the same character as the person-in-pain."[65] Women seeking unmedicated birth today, however, have often proclaimed their pain as an act of defiance to medical protocol. Their defiance is rooted in a variety of views about what makes a good woman, and is made up of different combinations of surrender and agency. But in the midst of their differences was an important similarity—they were, for the most part, middle- and upper-middle-class women. Their embrace of pain, then, must be set in wider social contexts that take this similarity into account.

Social Locations of Pain and Control

Electing to have unmedicated childbirth in a home that a woman finds comforting and safe, while surrounded by caregivers she trusts (and can afford to pay), is a choice that is shaped by other experiences of pain that may not provide the same rewards as childbirth. If a woman lives with pain in the rest of her life, whether caused by biology, racism, or economic hardship, celebrating the pain of childbirth may not seem a path to personal fulfillment. As Emily Martin observed of her research, "Middle-class women . . . commonly said that they were seeking an aesthetically beautiful or spiritual experience of birth. In contrast, working-class women emphasize more often what they see as the substantial reality of birth: its extreme pain."[66] Like all interpretation, interpreting pain is a socially located practice.

Liza Rossiter, upper-middle-class and African-American, felt the pain of birth was "empowering" because "you are expected to want relief from it, [but] you are able to cope with it. To me, I felt very strong." For Liza, being at home and without drugs was the best way to give birth: "Even for as much as it hurts to have a baby, I think I was better off hurting at home than hurting in an unfamiliar setting, unfamiliar smells, or smells that are intimidating. . . . [A] hospital is an intimidating place, because once you walk in, you are essentially theirs unless you assert yourself.

You're surrendering your control to them." For Liza, control meant in part being able to birth without drugs, an episiotomy, or electronic fetal monitoring. To achieve all these goals without the stress of "asserting" oneself, especially as an African-American woman in a predominantly white institution, Liza felt that staying home with a direct-entry midwife who had already agreed with her philosophy of birth was the best strategy.

Control, like pain, can hold a variety of meanings. In a study of hospital births, anthropologist Ellen Lazarus has shown that for middle-class women choosing their own care providers, whether obstetricians or midwives, control was something that could be (somewhat) negotiated. Poor women, however, who often attended prenatal clinics where they saw a different doctor each visit and had little control over any aspect of their care, were most concerned not with control but with continuity and quality of care.[67] Even middle-class women's conceptions of control varied, as "for some women this meant few or no interventions. For others, it meant . . . not screaming or crying during labor and childbirth."[68] Home-birthing women I spoke with agreed more with the former conception, since what they primarily wanted to control was the environment of birth and the people in attendance. *Relinquishing* bodily control to forces, if not pains, of birth was an oft-stated goal.

Responses to pain are shaped by habitus—in this case, by ideas and practices about pain that the body incorporates as "second nature." Regarding the pain of childbirth, this point is put most forcefully by anthropologists Janice Morse and Caroline Park. In a study of attitudes and experiences of childbirth pain among Anglophone, East Indian, Hutterite, and Ukrainian Canadian women, they found that "not only are culturally appropriate pain behaviors communicated, but also the perceived intensity of the pain is taught. The expectations of the painfulness of childbirth are culturally determined."[69] In addition to class and habitus, a woman's past experiences of birth shape her attitude. Having control and being free to experience and deal with pain in the way she chooses does not always ensure that she will emerge from childbirth feeling either pleasure or power, as attested by the six women I interviewed who received episiotomies, epidurals, or cesareans in the hospital after long and difficult labors at home.

The pain of childbirth is thus open to a variety of socially and experientially located interpretations. In a psychological interpretation, David Bakan used childbirth as an example to explain his notion that pain is aversion to the other: "And perhaps the very pain of childbirth is functionally linked to getting rid of that which is causing the pain, so as to produce the new separated being, the child."[70] He further suggested that "the sacrifice of an affected limb is of essentially the same order psychologically as the sacrifice [i.e., birth] of a child."[71] Bakan did not make his pronouncements on the pain of childbirth from the standpoint of women's experiences. The comparison of the pain of childbirth to the pain of amputation—the pain of wounding and loss—was not one generally shared by home-birthing women. While birthing the baby was their goal, "getting rid" of the cause was not usually the way women spoke of their approaches to pain.

Some women's pleas to their midwives to "just get it out" may indicate that in the midst of pain some women would have assented to Bakan's analogy. However, Carrie Ryan asserted the "difference" of birth pain, and gave herself a more active role in its expression:

> Well, [the pain is] something that builds to a crescendo, and then it's totally gone, it's completely gone. It's not like a wound, where you'll feel the initial pain of it, and then you'll feel an ache or throbbing thereafter. When the body's done birthing, it's gone. I really don't know how otherwise to describe it. It's intense, but it's not anything that I thought that I would pass out from or lose consciousness because of, you know, [as] when people are really wounded. I didn't see it as a—like where you're injured and it's not a good thing, if you're cut or something breaks in your body. This wasn't anything like that. And . . . no matter what I thought about it, it was going to happen. And it was just a matter of realizing and keeping my mind on the fact that I was experiencing my body doing what it was designed to do, and opening up and allowing this life to come out, to come forth.

Focusing on her sense of the "rightness" of the process of birth, while also actively "opening up and allowing" her baby to emerge meant that Carrie positioned herself to the pain in an accepting way that she felt made not only the birth, but also her recovery, less arduous.

Visionary Pain

In Carrie's Christian tradition, life-bringing pain has its roots in the cross. That she has access to such narratives in which to place her experience helped her in some ways to bear the pain. Carrie's meaning-making aligns with David Morris's argument that there is more meaning to pain than the medical model has traditionally allowed.[72] Carrie's understanding of pain, along with that of many other home-birthing women—Christians, Jews, spiritual feminists—could be characterized, in Morris's terms, as "visionary pain," or pain that has an "otherworldliness [that] serves as an implicit critique of worldly power."[73] The worldly power that home-birthing women critique most unanimously is the medicalization of childbirth. Some extend this to a critique of patriarchy, others most emphatically do not. Taking their place alongside Morris's exemplars of visionary pain such as medieval women mystics and Romantic poets, many home-birthing women would assent to Morris's depiction: "Pain, especially when mixed inseparably with love and beauty, takes us out of our depth. It draws us toward a higher level of experience in which conventional false-hoods and evasions drop away."[74] As home-birther Nina Holly opined from her New Age perspective: "I don't see a lot of people who are really living their destiny in their lives; they're just kind of like plodding along, afraid to look pain in the face." According to Nina, without confronting pain, particularly in terms of childbirth, self-deception reigns.

Visionary pain, however, does not eliminate conventional falsehoods and evasions, but instead sets rival constructions of reality in their place. For example, birthing without drugs revalues a form of women's power denigrated in the wider society, many women argued. Joanna Katz, Adrienne's mother, averred that despite its trials, birth is a distinctly empowering act for women, since "it's something that a man could never do." Claiming power via the endurance and strength it takes to birth may seem like a dangerously essentialized view of female power, especially since not all women give birth. But this claim can also function as an inversion of a cultural emphasis on men's strength and women's passivity. For example, consider Sara Flaherty's earlier description of her husband's insistence to his friends that in terms of strength in childbirth, "Sara's the man." The rigors of birth in these women's experiences seemed not to accentuate female submission, but to evoke female power.

Some women constructed the power evoked by the pains of birth on another axis besides that of man versus woman; namely, in reference to women who gave birth in the hospital with drugs. With varying levels of discomfort, these women promulgated an "elitism of pain"[75] that considered home birth to result not only in healthier babies but in stronger women with better relationships to their partners and children. From Sara Flaherty's assertion that she had "respect for women who give birth without drugs, I mean it's a whole different ball game," to Brenda Matthews' insistence on the "supernatural bond" that comes from home birth (but her caveat that hospital birth was not "less of a birth"), these women often thought childbirth pain helped a woman to achieve moral, spiritual, and physical prowess. Many of these women had their own experiences of medicated hospital birth from which they made such judgments—their "elitism" did not stem from ignorance for the most part, but instead from a politically charged stance that they considered countercultural.

Visionary pain—a construction of pain that crosses between ecstasy and agony with political undertones—is perhaps an apt way to describe an aspect of the goal, if not experience, of home birth. Simone Taylor, who articulated a confluence between pain and pleasure, asserted that she was "not into glorifying pain, and I don't think that it's a sign of our sinfulness." Simone's meaning-making with her pain sounded less like masochism and more like the "self-possessed" body that feminist theologians Harrison and Heyward advocated. "I am creating," Simone asserted, not entirely alone, but in concert with her God. What turns pain into "creative possibility," in the words of one writer, is a resistance to "giv[ing] suffering final power."[76] For Simone (as for poet Sharon Olds), childbirth pain was not the end, but the means to find oneself at the powerful space where "two worlds collide."

Perhaps in contemporary America, where women are taught to be observers and critics of their own bodies from the outside, the pain of childbirth puts women back *in* their bodies. In this specific context, the countercultural force of pain holds an empowering and, for some, salvific dimension.[77] As historian Carolyn Walker Bynum asserted: "Our culture may finally need something of the medieval sense, reflected so clearly in the use of *birthing* and *nursing* as symbols for salvation, that generativity and suffering can be synonymous."[78] Many home-birthing women are working toward such a coupling. As they do, they enact a particular kind of agency that depends not so much on their conscious willing of something, but instead on their trusting an embodied knowledge that brings about not only a baby but a new constellation of relationships.

For these women who embraced unmedicated birth as the best way to birth their babies and as an uncertain path to unknown meanings, pain often (but not always) transformed and enhanced relationships, whether with God, their husbands, or their children. While remembering that pain can be gendered in harmful as well as emancipatory ways, writer Kimiko Hahn's version of the visionary pain of childbirth speaks to its transformative possibilities. Hahn wrote: "One of the most important 'moments' of my feminist education came in the contradictions of childbirth." Among these contradictions were physical ones, such as "the pain and the elation of seeing the child." More revealing to her, however, were the social contradictions, most specifically those arising from "the need to be self-absorbed and in complete partnership with my husband." As Hahn reflected: "My trust in him enabled me to relax. To focus the pain. To abandon pain. That depth of trust in the opposite sex is rare, profound, and ultimately necessary for political change."[79] Though the varieties of political change to which home-birthing women may aspire are many, relinquishing their pain not to medication but to pleasure and relationship, to trust in themselves and the other, are goals many women hold in common. The power in pain lies in its paradoxes: it destroys and creates life; it harms and heals.

Epilogue: The Miracle of Birth

OFFERING a provocative assessment of where women's power is most disputed, Emily Martin proclaimed the "three related domains in which there have . . . been ongoing struggles for control over women in western history: the mouth, the vagina, and the home." She continued: "Who or what gets in, and who or what comes out, as well as how such events are described and constructed, have been fiercely contested."[1] Home-birthing women have participated in this fierce contest as they have asserted verbally and corporeally, though with varying political and religious goals, their control over their homes and their bodies. This book, then, is a study of a "resistance" movement in which the motivations are many and the implications diverse.

Giving birth in contemporary America is an act laden with political meanings, whether a woman articulates them or not. Childbirth is political because it has to do with negotiations of power: a woman's power to bring forth new life and a midwife or doctor's power to help her do so (or hinder her). Furthermore, childbirth is embedded within a wider cultural and political discourse, including a legal discourse, that sanctions or censures a woman's decision about how best to accomplish her task of birth. Perhaps one of the most political dimensions of home birth in a society that consents to a predominantly medical model of birth is its advocates' insistence that childbirth is a life-shaping experience for the mother as well as for the baby. While all of these women profoundly desired healthy babies (or good "outcomes," in medical language), they also shared the conviction that when women feel empowered in birth, they will also feel empowered in mothering, making for healthy babies and mothers for the long term.

This attention to the mother's experience of birth runs counter to a late-twentieth-century trend described by legal theorist Janet Gallagher:

> The fetus becomes an icon, the object of a quasi-religious cult. And the woman within whose body that new object of devotion exists drops out of sight as an individual with hopes and plans and choices. She becomes instead the environment of the fetus, "the mother ship," or the "uterine capsule."[2]

The sharp distinction between the "fetus" and its "environment" has occluded what Gallagher called "the ethical and legal significance of the real geography of pregnancy."[3] In the name of "fetal rights," women and the tiny bodies growing within them are being set up as adversaries. At the same time, people ranging from prosecutors to doctors to biological fathers are claiming themselves to be the protectors of the innocent fetus against the purportedly irresponsible and ignorant women who "house" them.[4]

Home-birthing women, however, are not as willing as these others to make an icon of the fetus and a demon of the mother. While not all pro-choice in terms of abortion or a woman's right to decide, they are resolutely so when it comes to choosing methods of giving birth. They tie such decisions to considerations of their own physical and emotional health, and to the health of their babies, refusing to accept a model of maternal sacrifice that eclipses the mother in touting the virtues of a mother's love. As such, they disrupt the conventional expectations of motherhood, however unsuspectingly, as described by anthropologist Ellen Lewin in the context of her work on lesbian motherhood. Lewin wrote: "Motherhood is supposed to happen because women stand in a particular sexual and economic relationship to men, not because a woman determines that being a mother will meet her personal goals or be desirable in some other, less readily articulated, way."[5] Though some of these home-birthing women may profess little opposition to conventional patriarchal family structures, they do assert that becoming and being a mother is a choice that has distinctive significance to a woman's identity, aside from her relationship to a man. In this assertion lies common ground—perhaps narrow—between feminist and traditionalist women advocating home birth.

Is this common ground, between women of diverse political and religious perspectives to whom "choice" means different things, overshadowed when viewed next to the scope of reproductive politics at the dawn of a new millennium? At the same time that growing numbers of women are welcoming medical technology into their bodies as they struggle with infertility, home-birthing women are appealing to the "natural." They are proclaiming that birth is a potentially empowering rite of passage in a woman's life that transforms a woman into a mother in the most gentle and satisfying way.[6] New reproductive technologies and home birth are not mutually exclusive, as the one woman in my study who took fertility drugs showed. As the scope of these technologies widens, however, the biomedical "stealing" of women's power to give birth may seem like petty thievery.

Reproductive technologies have the potential to eclipse debates between feminists and traditionalists about what makes a mother: for example, brain-dead women are kept on life support until their fetuses mature enough to be "delivered," and uteruses are extracted from dead women and used experimentally to house fertilized eggs.[7] The "miraculous" qualities of birth, however defined, are put into question as scientists try to gestate goats in wombs that are altogether artificial—clear boxes made of acrylic.[8] As Carol Stabile suggested, the "proliferation of definitions of 'mother' is at once a site of intensifying oppression and of potential liberation."[9] The kinds of mothering promoted by home-birthing women are many—although not all would be considered liberating from a feminist perspective like Stabile's. But in their common assertion of an embodied knowledge and an ambivalent bodily autonomy, home-birthing women challenge the complex of notions of woman as a vessel, as a hostile adversary to her fetus, or as a disembodied mother, passive and brainless. Ironically, both feminist and traditionalist women find agency within surrender that for a time relinquishes control of their selves to multiple forces: nature, God, the energy of birth, their own bodies.

Given the small numbers of home-birthing women, however, what does this agency mean in the scope of twenty-first century reproductive politics? Are home-birthing women fighting a losing battle against increasing technological manipulation of women's reproductive powers? As anthropologist Faye Ginsburg has contended more generally regarding home-based female activism: "The issues that have mobilized women are not arbitrary. . . . [T]hey often represent those aspects of the domestic sphere thought to be most threatened by the expansion of the market at a given historical moment."[10] In the face of a rapidly paced and high-priced industry for new reproductive technologies, women's fight for their right to give birth under their own power in their own space seems almost like a struggle to return to a long-lost age. They raise their voices in an era where egg "harvesting" and in vitro fertilization now seem like simple (though not necessarily successful) procedures, and more complex processes like cloning are quickly progressing.

However, home-birthing women, though they may be swimming against some currents, are not Luddites: they evidence a certain "techno-pragmatism" in terms of both birth technology and other areas of their lives.[11] Throughout their pregnancies, they use pagers and cell-phones to call their midwives with questions. In giving birth, they consent to the use of hand-held fetal heart rate monitors and the injection of drugs to stop postpartum hemorrhage. Home-birth activists use their word processors to write newsletters, join e-mail chat groups on home birth, and design their own home pages with links to all the midwifery and birth-related information one could want. Most basically, almost all of them would welcome the technologies their midwives might have ready in case of complications, and most would welcome whatever the hospital offered in an emergency that they and/or their midwives believed necessary to attain a successful birth.

Alongside this technopragmatism, however, is a sense of its limits. Not wanting to abandon the process of childbirth to a technocratic model, many birthing women insist on a view of birth as an ethical and, often, religious action. Those who choose home birth construct and experience the religiousness of birth through a multiplicity of languages, evoking everything from Jesus, to midwives of the Hebrew Bible, to a nameless, powerful "energy" that fills their bodies and rooms. In their recourse to a range of differently spiritual reserves, they mediate wider religious institutions and messages in ways similar to women making other reproductive choices. As anthropologist Rayna Rapp has shown in her work on prenatal testing: "Religious identity provides one resource in the complex and often contradictory repertoire of possible identities a pregnant woman brings to her decision to use or reject amniocentesis. There is no definitive "Catholic," "Jewish," or "Protestant" position on reproductive technology, when viewed from the pregnant woman's point of view."[12] Similarly in home birth, while women draw from their religious traditions to make decisions about pregnancy and birth, they are usually creating their own local and contextual religious interpretations of childbirth. They give religious meaning to the home as a site of birth, to their bodies as the generative source of new life, and to their pain as a spark of both physical and spiritual power. The religious idioms they turn to in this meaning-making provide a persuasive moral language supporting a woman in her resistance to conventional biomedical approaches to birth.

Religious discourse, then, can be used as an oppositional language challenging biomedical perspectives, and not only in the case of religious groups typically thought of as antagonistic to biomedicine, such as Jehovah's Witnesses. In the case of home birth, however, this kind of religiously based opposition is often a hybrid of perspectives from religious, "alternative health," and sometimes feminist sources. In many instances, this hybridity even draws from biomedical discourse itself, utilizing the results of epidemiological studies or renegade doctors to show the benefits of such things as midwifery care or changing positions in labor. As such, religiously informed arguments for home birth bear similarities to what other anthropologists have discerned as laypeople's merging of multiple discourses to understand the mysteries of their bodies and those of their families.[13] The merging of biomedicine, religion, and alternative perspectives shows that despite the increasing kinds of knowledge that humans can have of their bodies, questions about what that knowledge consists of and how those bodies bear meaning remain puzzling.

In this book, I have pieced together some of that puzzle by showing the ways women's use of religious language and traditions shapes their embodiment, and vice versa, and how they thereby challenge conventional biomedical constructions of the birthing body. While childbirth in North America may be glossed over with vaguely religious sentiments in advice books, on cards, or in everyday parlance—called a "blessed event" or a "miracle"—a biomedical approach is dominant from the perspective of the actual practice of childbirth. Home-birthing women, however, employ the concepts of nature, spirituality, and religion to dispute the dominance of the Western biomedical habitus. They are part of a larger challenge to biomedical understandings of the body that is arising both within and outside biomedical circles. This challenge is shaping what I have called "postbiomedical" bodies—bodies in which the fusion of biomedicine, culture, and religion is increasingly accepted and explored.[14]

Postbiomedical bodies inhabit an age in which biomedical health care is growing increasingly costly and technical, while accessible and lower cost alternatives are gaining credibility and popularity. The nexus of religion, healing, gender, and commerce that shapes both biomedical and alternative forms of health needs further study. As a group of medical anthropologists stated, "The unstable boundaries between science and commercialism and between medicine and religion . . . are standard features of America on the brink of the new millennium."[15] It is no accident that these authors pair "science and commercialism" with "medicine and religion." To fully explore the ways religion and medicine shape each other in an increasingly "globalized" world and commercialized health care system is a task of both theoretical and practical importance.

Home birth is one example where religion, medicine, and commerce interact. The resistance enacted by home-birthing women blurs lines separating the "political," the "religious," and the "commercial," as women who choose direct-entry midwives (and in some cases certified nurse-midwives) show their willingness to step outside the bounds of care established by their health management organizations (HMOs) or insurance companies. In a time when HMOs favor practices formerly considered radical, such as quick discharge from the hospital after birth because it saves money (but then also takes away the option of women who want or need to stay longer), some HMOs are opposing midwifery practice in the home. For example, they are squeezing out certified nurse-midwives from home birth; and in one case, after pleased clients submitted the bill for a home birth, the insurance company betrayed the direct-entry midwives to legal authorities.[16]

Keeping in mind the interaction between religious, political, and economic dimensions of the "resistance" of home birth requires remembering the position of relative privilege that many home-birthing women enjoy. Forgoing insurance benefits in order to have a home birth demands the availability and willing expenditure of resources. Midwifery organizations stress that if choices about childbirth are to be truly available to all women in North America, not only do midwives have to be granted autonomy and the cooperation of doctors, but the structure for payment of health care also must be radically reworked. Anthropologist Ellen Lazarus voices one vision of how health-care reform could affect childbirth practices:

> A single payer approach, similar to those now followed by most Western European countries and Canada, does not have to limit choices for childbirth care. It could provide similar opportunities for care to all women. While poor women still would not come to childbirth with the same needs, beliefs, and knowledge as middle-class women, at the least the barrier of separate and unequal care could be reduced.[17]

Regardless of what kind of reform is enacted, it is clear that health-care choices motivated by religious or political commitments remain shaped in part by wider economic forces. As I have shown, even the needs and beliefs of middle-class women are diverse, but their class status affords them the ability to birth in accordance with these beliefs, though they may sometimes have to break the law to do so. The practice of religion is both curtailed and fostered by the economic and political structures with which it interacts—the practice of religion in childbirth is no different.

I came to this project wanting to be a sympathetic critic of home birth. At times I have felt my interpretations rankle my feminist sensibilities; at other times I have wondered if my analysis might be the subtle undoing of my sympathy. In the end, I hope to have offered an interpretation of home-birthing women that gives a vivid and respectful picture of their views and experiences of childbirth, while also setting this picture within a larger frame of the politics of religion, reproduction, and maternity in the United States.

When pondering the integrity of my representations of the women in this book, I take heart in historian Mary Poovey's assertion about her work on nineteenth-century women and obstetrics, where she was dependent on texts written only by men. She wrote: "Requiring interpretation, which can never be disinterested, representation can never completely contain or master its subject. Even the silenced body acts out a language that defies mastery, that resists such simple treatment."[18] While I hope that the bodies represented here are not silenced, I know that not all of what I write is the "true" interpretation in the eyes of those who read it. My wish is not to contain or master women's birthing bodies or their religious identities, but instead to provoke questions about the representations of childbirth that North American society condones and decries.

One simple answer to these provocations, regardless of which manner of birth one favors, is this: Childbirth is not merely a physiological process; therefore, a biomedical model is not sufficient to understand its many dimensions. In the practices of every culture, and in the embodied memories of every birthing woman, including those in North America, childbirth transforms women, babies, and their supporters through what many call—perhaps too easily—the "miracle of birth." In these pages, I have prodded the religious complexities of birth to reveal how women, together with the cultures of birth they inhabit, make such miracles come to pass.

Appendix A——————————————————————

Interview Guide

THESE QUESTIONS evolved somewhat over the course of my fieldwork. I strove for a casual atmosphere in our conversations, and did not always follow this order. Often I did not need to ask certain questions because women touched on the issues on their own. The guides were altered for interviews with pre- and postpartum mothers. I am indebted to Robbie Davis-Floyd's interview guide in *Birth as an American Rite of Passage* (1992) for some of these questions.

1. How did you decide to have a home birth? Why did you choose a CNM/lay midwife?

2. What was your relationship like with your caregiver during your pregnancy?

3. What did you know of your mother's experience of birth? What did you think of birth as a girl? Had you always wanted to have babies?

4. How old are you? How old are your children, and where were they born?

5. What kinds of books/videos did you read to prepare for birth?

6. Did you take prenatal classes? From whom? Did they make a difference?

7. Did you have an ultrasound or other test? Did you find out the sex of your baby?

8. What were your expectations for the birth, your visions of how it would proceed? Did you have any fears? How did you feel about not having technological support?

9. Were there any religious reasons in your choice to have a home birth?

10. How did your partner/extended family/friends react to your plan of a home birth?

11. Are you part of a religious community? If so, how did they react?

12. How did you prepare your home for the birth? How did you prepare yourself/ your partner/your birth attendants?

13. Did you dream about your birth before it happened?

14. Could you describe your labor(s) and birth(s) to me?

   When and how did it start? How long was it? Who was there? What did you do during early labor? What did you eat?

Did you want to be touched?

Did you have inhibitions? Did you feel you had to control yourself?

When did the midwives arrive?

How did you get along with the midwives/your partner/other attendants/ children?

What role did your husband play in the birth?

Were there any complications? Did the midwives act as you expected?

Where did you give birth? Is that where you expected to give birth?

Did you see the baby with a mirror?

Was the birth videotaped or photographed? By whom?

Did a pediatrician/doctor see the baby?

Did you do anything special during the birth, e.g., listen to certain music or have candles, smells, massage, visualizations, reading, etc.? What did you wear?

15. How would you describe the pain? How did you deal with the pain?

16. Why did you want to give birth without drugs?

17. What happened right after the birth? Did you welcome the baby in any particular way? Did you nurse?

18. Tell me about the days right after the birth. Did you have visitors? Who did the housekeeping/childcare?

19. When did you first leave the house? Where did you go? How did you feel?

20. Did you have a baptism/bris/religious or community ritual for your baby?

21. What do you think are the risks of home birth?

22. Do you think it takes any particular kind of faith to have a home birth?

23. Was giving birth a religious or spiritual experience for you?

24. How would you describe your religious and spiritual beliefs? Do you think that being [name religion] or the way you are [name religion] has anything to do with your choice to have a home birth?

25. Did religious ritual play a role in your birth (prayer, Bible, singing, meditating)?

26. Was your birth experience consistent with the way you live your life?

27. Did your birth experience change you? In what ways?

28. What did you like best about your birth? Least? What would you do differently if you were to give birth again?

29. Who do you feel had control or power during your birth?

30. What does your home mean to you? What do you think is a woman's role in the home? Do you have any regular religious practice in the home, such as Bible reading or prayer? What does the Bible mean to you?

31. How would you describe your body image; your relationship to your body?

32. What do you think of hospitals? What is your preferred mode of healing?

33. Did you have insurance for the birth? How much did it cost?

34. How do you feel about abortion?

35. Do you consider yourself a feminist? What do you think of feminism?

36. What do you make of the Genesis passage; the Virgin Birth?

37. Would you describe your primary occupation? Your husband/partner's? How long have you been together? What is your combined household income?

38. How would you describe your ethnic background?

39. What was the last level of education you attained? Spouse's?

Appendix B

The Women in the Study

ALL OF these names are pseudonyms, and the descriptions I give are of the women at the time that I interviewed them.

Meg Alexander, 37, had her first child in the hospital by cesarean section and her second at home with direct-entry midwives. She cares for her children at home and volunteers as a home-birth activist. She and her husband, an advertising executive who recently quit his job, were in the midst of preparing to move to a rural area, perhaps to an intentional community (where several families live in close proximity, sharing resources, such as schooling and sharing a common religious or political outlook). They are both Euro-American and had attended a Presbyterian church, but were considering other options, such as Unitarianism.

Valerie Auletta, 35, had her first two children in hospitals, the second by cesarean section. Her next two children were born at home with direct-entry midwives. She cares for her young children at home, and hopes to study at a direct-entry midwifery school. She and her husband are both Euro-American and occasionally attend a Unitarian church. Valerie also practices Goddess spirituality.

Suzanne Donato, 30, planned her first birth to be at home with direct-entry midwives, but was transported to the hospital for "failure to progress." Her second birth took place at home with the same direct-entry midwives. She cares for her children at home, and sometimes assists her husband in his chiropractic practice. They are both Italian-American Catholics, and were about to buy their first home in a suburban area.

Elizabeth Edwards, 30, has one child, born at home with certified nurse-midwives. While pregnant she converted to Catholicism, the faith of her husband of thirteen years. She has had some training in midwifery, but does not practice. She and her husband are Euro-American. Together, they attend a traditional Catholic church, and were in the process of deciding whether to join an intentional community based in anthroposophy. Anthroposophy is a movement based on the teachings of twentieth-century German author and mystic Rudolf Steiner, who merged theosophy and Christianity and applied his philosophy to a wide range of interests, including organic agriculture, homeopathy, and education (in the form of Waldorf Schools).

Olivia Eldrich, 37, gave birth to all three of her children at home, with certified nurse-midwives. She considers herself a "secular" Jew with New Age interests, and has worked in a number of jobs, including as a prenatal yoga instructor, childbirth educator, personal trainer, and aerobics instructor. Her husband is a chiropractor.

Mary Rose Erb, 35, is the mother of four children, aged 4 to 13. Her third baby was born in the hospital by scheduled cesarean section, and the other three were born at home with certified nurse-midwives. She is Old Order Amish and lives on a farm. Like all the other Amish women in my study, she and her husband are Euro-American.

Sara Flaherty, 36, gave birth to all her four children at home, the first three with direct-entry midwives, and the last one with certified nurse-midwives in order to be reimbursed by insurance. She has worked as a labor and delivery nurse. She has divorced and remarried (with two children from each marriage), and both she and her husband grew up in the Catholic church and are Irish-American.

Elise Gold, 40, gave birth to her first two sons in the hospital, and her last at home with certified nurse-midwives. Educated as an actuary, she now homeschools her children and is a leader in La Leche League. She and her husband, who works in telecommunications, own a home in the suburbs and go to a Reform Jewish synagogue. They are both Euro-American.

Judith Gordon, 40, is the mother of three children, aged 5 to 10. The first two were born in the hospital with doctors, and the last was to be born in a birth center with certified nurse-midwives, but ended up being born at home, because the labor progressed too quickly. She and her husband are both Conservative Jews and Euro-American.

Stefanie Harter, 34, has a 2-year-old son who was born at home with certified nurse-midwives. She came to the United States from Denmark in her early 20s. She cares for her son at her suburban town house, while also helping her husband (also Danish) with his home business. Together, they attend a Lutheran church, although Stefanie describes herself as a "born-again Christian." She is also active in La Leche League.

Eva Hechtel, 26, gave birth to her 3-year-old son in a birthing center and to her newborn at home with certified nurse-midwives. Neither she nor her husband, a photographer, are particularly religious. They are both Euro-American. She is a La Leche League leader and plans to study midwifery once her children are older.

Nina Holly, 30, has three children aged 1 to 5. The first was born in a hospital, the second at home with direct-entry midwives, and the third at home unassisted. She has written a variety of articles and booklets on pregnancy and birth, and has worked as a childbirth educator. She grew up in an Italian-American Catholic home, but now practices a range of New Age spiritualities. She was separating from her husband when we spoke.

Tina Hostetler, 27, has two children, aged 1 and 3, both born at home with certified nurse-midwives. She and her husband, a builder, are Amish Mennonites, and live in a new house on the outskirts of a town. She sells kitchen equipment from her home.

Alicia Jelten, 29, gave birth to her baby at home with certified nurse-midwives. She works as a chiropractor, together with her husband. They are both Euro-American and are not particularly religious.

Joanna Katz, 39, gave birth to her first three daughters in the hospital and her last at home with certified nurse-midwives. She has a master's degree and has taught, but now cares for her children at home. She is a La Leche League leader. Her husband, a former lawyer, is training to be an ultrasonographer. They live in a large suburban home and attend a Reform Jewish synagogue. They are both Euro-American.

Raina Lennox, 26, gave birth to her first child, now aged 4, in the hospital, and her second child, aged 1, at home with certified nurse-midwives. She was newly pregnant when we spoke, and was planning to give birth at home again, but this time with direct-entry midwives. She attends a midwifery study group and was planning to become a certified birth attendant, or "doula." She and her husband are both Seventh Day Adventists and African-American.

Debra Lensky is in her early 40s, and is the mother of six children. Her first two were born in the hospital (the first by cesarean section), her next two were born at home with direct-entry midwives, and her fifth child was born in the hospital by scheduled cesarean section. Her last child was born at home. She was active in a number of childbirth education and cesarean-prevention organizations and converted from secular Judaism to Orthodox Judaism after the birth of her fourth child. She and her husband are both Euro-American and live in a large house in a semiurban area.

Alison Lindt-Marliss, 40, is the mother of three children, aged 3 to 10. Her first child was born in a birth center and her subsequent two births took place at home with direct-entry midwives in attendance. She is a La Leche League leader and homeschools her children. She grew up as a Catholic and married a Jewish man. Together, they now go to a Reform synagogue. They are both Euro-American.

Larisa Marquez, 23, planned to give birth to her baby (3 months old when I met her) at home with direct-entry midwives, but she eventually went to the hospital to give birth after about two days of labor. Larisa came to the United States from Venezuela as a child, and is now married to a Euro-American man. She is attracted to Goddess spirituality and follows a vegan diet.

Marianne Martin, 38, gave birth to her first child in the hospital by emergency cesarean section after having planned a home birth. Her subsequent two births took place at home with direct-entry midwives. Her children are aged 1 to 8. She works part-time as a veterinarian and homeschools her children, together with her husband, a police officer. They are both traditional Catholics and Euro-American.

Kathy Martinelli, 34, gave birth to her son, now aged 1, at home with certified nurse-midwives. She works full-time as a special-education teacher. She and her husband, a postal carrier, recently began attending a Unity church. They are both Euro-American.

Brenda Matthews, 44, gave birth to all three of her children, aged 12 to 20, at home with direct-entry midwives. She became a Pentecostal Christian soon after marrying her husband of twenty-two years. She now sells herbal products and assists her husband in his home-based chiropractic clinic. They are both Euro-American.

Heather Monroe, 32, gave birth to her daughter, now aged 11, at home with direct-entry midwives. Her mother had given birth to her last daughter at home, and was a home-birth activist. When Heather gave birth to her daughter, she received a congratulatory note from the governor of her state at the time, William J. Clinton. She now works as a Christian Science nurse and is divorced. She is Euro-American.

Kathryn Morris, 31, planned to give birth to her baby at home with certified nurse-midwives, but eventually had a cesarean section in the hospital because of toxemia. She works as a video producer and was about to begin a master's program in social theory. She and her husband are both Catholic and Euro-American.

Connie Norris, 26, is the mother of three children, aged 1 month to 4 years. Her first child was born in the hospital with a doctor, and her subsequent two children were born at home with certified nurse-midwives. She works part-time at a catalogue sales company. Her husband, who works in computing, grew up in a family that practiced Americanized forms of Eastern mysticism, but now they both are unaffiliated religiously. They are both Euro-American.

Helen Otley, 36, gave birth to her first child in a birth center with certified nurse-midwives. Her subsequent two children were born at home with certified nurse-midwives. She has a Master of Arts degree in special education, and now stays home with her children. She and her husband have no religious affiliation and are both Euro-American.

Wendy Pearson, 25, gave birth to her first child in the hospital with a doctor and her second at home with direct-entry midwives. She worked part-time at a pet store before her second baby was born, but now stays at home caring for her children, aged 4 months and 3 years. She attends a United Methodist church with her children, where her husband, an electrician, occasionally joins them. She and her husband are both Euro-American.

Janice Pulaski, 38, planned to give birth to her baby at home with direct-entry midwives, but she went to the hospital after a long labor and gave birth with the help of vacuum extraction. Before becoming pregnant, she worked as a singer; her husband is an electrical designer. She grew up as a Baptist, but does not presently practice any particular faith.

Nell Reid, 37, planned to give birth to her first baby at home with direct-entry midwives, but after a long and unsuccessful pushing stage she went to the hospital where she received an episiotomy and quickly gave birth. She gave birth to her second child at home with the same direct-entry midwives. She worked as a special-education teacher before having children and now stays home to care for them. Her husband is a motivational speaker. Together, they go to a United Methodist church, and have attended "personal and spiritual growth" workshops together.

Liza Rossiter, 39, gave birth to her first child in a birth center with certified nurse-midwives and her second child at home with direct-entry midwives. Her children are aged 3 years and 4 months. She worked in a library prior to having children and now stays home with them. She also pursues painting and quilting. Neither she nor her husband, a computer programmer, are particularly religious. She is African-American, and he is Euro-American.

Charlene Roth, 33, is the mother of three children under 2 years of age. Her first and last child were born at home with certified nurse-midwives, and her second child was born prematurely in a hospital with a certified nurse-midwife. She has worked as a house cleaner and grew up in a Beachy Amish home. She and her husband, a fencing salesman, and formerly Old Order Amish, now attend a charismatic Mennonite church.

Natalie Ruppolo, 33, gave birth to her daughter, aged 9, at home with certified nurse-midwives. She works as a Christian Science practitioner. She and her husband, a retired police officer and now a taxi owner/driver, are both Euro-American.

Carrie Ryan, 36, gave birth to all four of her children at home with direct-entry midwives. She was trained as a dental hygienist, but now stays at home with her children. She was born again after the birth of her second child and now attends a Pentecostal church along with her husband, a builder. They are both Euro-American.

Miriam Shonovsky, 45, is the mother of five children, aged 3 to 16. Her first child was born in the hospital by cesarean section, her subsequent three children were born at home with direct-entry midwives, and her last child was born at home without assistance. She has worked as a childbirth educator, is active in a health food co-op, and plans to write a book about her birthing experiences. She laughingly called herself a "New Age Jew." She and her husband, a physicist, are both Euro-American.

Janet Stein, 44, gave birth to her baby, now 3 months old, at home without assistance. She worked as a spiritual counselor before marrying her husband two years ago, and now works part-time. She was born again while in college, and she and her husband (formerly a Jew) now attend a Pentecostal church. They are both Euro-American.

Annie Stoltzfus, 27, is the mother of five children under 6 years of age. Her first baby was born in a doctor's office, and the last four were born at home with certified nurse-midwives. She and her husband are Old Order Amish and live on a farm.

Sondra Tanner-Gordon, 31, gave birth to both of her children, aged 2 years and 3 months, respectively, at home with certified nurse-midwives. She works part-time as a lawyer. She and her husband are both Reconstructionist Jews and Euro-American.

Simone Taylor, 32, gave birth to her first child in the hospital with certified nurse-midwives. Her second child was born at home with certified nurse-midwives. She worked as a labor and delivery nurse and now is a seminary student. She and her husband are both Presbyterian and Euro-American.

Elaine Thatcher, 39, gave birth to her two children, aged 12 and 13, at home, the first with a doctor and the second with certified nurse-midwives. She and her husband both work as Christian Science nurses and are Euro-American.

Christina Upton, 42, is the mother of three children, aged 9 months to 8 years. Her first child was born in the hospital with certified nurse-midwives, and her last two children were born at home with certified nurse-midwives. She works part-time as a veterinarian and is active in La Leche League. She grew up as a Lutheran but now attends a Reconstructionist Jewish synagogue with her husband, also a veterinarian, who grew up as an Orthodox Jew. They are both Euro-American.

Michelle Varley, 31, gave birth to her baby, aged 9 months, at home with direct-entry midwives. She formerly worked as a special-education teacher and now does bookkeeping part-time from home. She is Catholic; her husband is not religiously affiliated. They are both Euro-American.

Gabriela Voth, 30, gave birth to her baby, 8 months old, at home with certified nurse-midwives. She and her husband are both graduate students. They are both vegetarians, and are of no particular religious affiliation. She is Euro-American, and her husband is Mexican-American.

Tessa Welland, 34, is the mother of four children, aged 4 to 10. Her first child was born in a birth center with certified nurse-midwives, and her subsequent three children were born at home with direct-entry midwives. She works as a childbirth educator and birth attendant, and plans to be a direct-entry midwife. She grew up as a Catholic but now practices Goddess spirituality. She and her husband, a civil engineer, are both Euro-American.

Judy Woodman, 39, has two children, aged 7 and 10. Her first child was born at home with a doctor, and her second child was born in a birth center with certified nurse-midwives. She works in the business office of a Christian Science health-care facility. She and her husband are both Christian Scientists and Euro-American.

Ruth Yoder, 24, is the mother of three children, aged 2 and under. She gave birth to her first baby in the hospital with a doctor and her subsequent two at home with certified nurse-midwives. After her last home birth she had to go to the hospital because of hemorrhaging. She cares for her children at home and sells household cleaning products from home. She and her husband, who builds storage sheds, are both Old Order Amish.

Notes

Preface
Motherhood Issues

1. I am grateful to Charles Hirschkind for helping me to formulate this point.

Chapter 1
Procreation Stories: An Introduction

1. Carole H. Poston, "Childbirth in Literature," *Feminist Studies* 4, no. 2 (1978): 18–31.

2. For only a few examples among many, see the work of Robbie Davis-Floyd, *Birth as an American Rite of Passage* (Berkeley: University of California Press, 1992); Ina May Gaskin, *Spiritual Midwifery*, 3d ed. (Summerton, Tenn.: Book Publishing Company, 1990); Ronald L. Grimes, *Marrying & Burying: Rites of Passage in a Man's Life* (Boulder, Colo.: Westview Press, 1995); Isabel Allende, *Paula* (New York: HarperCollins, 1995); and Katherine Martens and Heidi Harms, *In Her Own Voice: Childbirth Stories from Mennonite Women* (Winnipeg: University of Manitoba Press, 1997).

3. On Madonna, see Ingrid Sischy, "Madonna and Child," *Vanity Fair* 451 (March 1998): 204–212, 266–270. On Bobbi McCaughey, see Andrew Walsh, "The McCaughey Babies," *Religion in the News* 1, no. 1 (June 1988): 9–10.

4. For a range of approaches to religion and childbirth in the West, see Jacques Gélis, *History of Childbirth: Fertility, Pregnancy, and Birth in Early Modern Europe*, trans. Rosemary Morris (Cambridge: Polity Press, 1991 [1984]); Chava Weissler, "*Mizvot* Built into the Body: *Tkhines* for *Niddah*, Pregnancy, and Childbirth," in *People of the Body: Jews and Judaism from an Embodied Perspective*, ed. Howard Eilberg-Schwartz (Albany: State University of New York Press, 1992), 101–115. For feminist critiques of how male-dominated religions have used birth symbolism to usurp women's maternally based power, especially with regard to baptism in Christianity, see Marjorie Procter-Smith, *In Her Own Rite: Constructing Feminist Liturgical Tradition* (Nashville, Tenn.: Abingdon Press, 1990); Rosemary Radford Ruether, *Sexism and God-Talk* (Boston: Beacon Press, 1983), 260; and Susan Starr Sered, *Priestess, Mother, Sacred Sister: Religions Dominated by Women* (New York: Oxford University Press, 1994).

5. For arguments that support this view from both Jewish and Christian perspectives, see Lori Hope Lefkowitz, "Sacred Screaming: Childbirth in Judaism," in *Lifecycles: Jewish Women on Life Passages and Personal Milestones*, Vol. 1, ed. Rabbi Debra Orenstein (Woodstock, Vt.: Jewish Lights Publishing, 1994), 5–15; and Kathryn Allen Rabuzzi, *Mother with Child: Transformations through Childbirth* (Bloomington: Indiana University Press, 1994).

6. See also Brenda Waugh, "Repro-Woman: A View from the Labyrinth (from the Lithotomy Position)," *Yale Journal of Law and Feminism* 3 (1991): 9; and

Margaret Atwood, quoted in Paula Treichler, "Feminism, Medicine, and the Meaning of Childbirth," in *Body/Politics: Women and the Discourses of Science*, ed. Mary Jacobus, Evelyn Fox Keller, and Sally Shuttleworth (New York: Routledge, 1990), 113. Treichler quotes Atwood's story "Giving Birth," in which Atwood writes: "Who gives [birth]? And to whom is it given? Certainly it doesn't feel like giving, which implies a flow, a gentle handing over, no coercion. . . . Maybe the phrase was made by someone viewing the result only. . . . Yet one more thing that needs to be renamed."

7. See *www.mana.org/statechart.html*; updated 16 May 2000, accessed 4 January 2001.

8. Linda Blum used a similar methodology to mine in her research on ideologies of breast-feeding and offers a thoughtful reflection on method and the benefits of what she called "sociological dialogue." Linda Blum, *At the Breast: Ideologies of Breastfeeding and Motherhood in the Contemporary United States* (Boston: Beacon Press, 1999), 205.

9. Of the eighty planned home births among the 45 women in my study, the care was as follows: certified nurse-midwives, 38; direct-entry midwives, 37; unassisted birth, 3; and attended by a medical doctor, 2. No one openly denied my request to talk with her, although four women basically did so by asking me to keep calling back or by continually rescheduling interviews. In an effort to locate Muslim women, I called a local mosque to discover the Imam's wife had given birth at home, and he agreed to speak with me. While he was very forthcoming about Muslim perspectives on childbirth and invited me to talk to the women around the mosque one Friday, he was unwilling to let me speak with his wife. Ironically, the women he encouraged me to meet at the mosque (none of whom had given birth at home) thought the Imam's wife would be an ideal person with whom to speak, but I chose not to pursue the matter out of respect for the Imam.

10. All the women had explicitly chosen home birth, except one, who planned to go to a birthing center but had to give birth precipitously at home.

11. Labor assistants, also known as "doulas," are women who attend births to provide support for the birthing woman, but not as midwives. They attend both hospital and home births and often charge a fee.

12. All the names of these women are pseudonyms, as are those of family members or friends to whom the women refer.

13. Joshua Meyrowitz, *No Sense of Place: The Impact of Electronic Media on Social Behaviour* (New York: Oxford University Press, 1985).

14. For a variety of perspectives on the issue of ethnographic responsibility, see Lila Abu-Lughod, "Can There Be a Feminist Ethnography?" *Women and Performance: A Journal of Feminist Theory* 5 (1990): 7–27; Ruth Behar and Deborah A. Gordon, eds., *Women Writing Culture* (Berkeley: University of California Press, 1995); Karen McCarthy Brown, *Mama Lola: A Vodou Priestess in Brooklyn* (Berkeley: University of California Press, 1991); James Clifford and George Marcus, eds., *Writing Culture: The Poetics and Politics of Ethnography* (Berkeley: University of California Press, 1986); Judith Stacey, "Can There Be a Feminist Ethnography?" *Women's Studies* 11, no. 1 (1988): 21–27; Kamala Visweswaran, *Fictions of Feminist Ethnography* (Minneapolis: University of Minnesota Press, 1994); and Margery

Wolf, *A Thrice Told Tale: Feminism, Postmodernism & Ethnographic Responsibility* (Stanford: Stanford University Press, 1992).

15. Faye Ginsburg used the phrase "procreation stories" to describe life histories in which women "constitute[d] provisional solutions to disruptions in a coherent cultural model for the place of reproduction, motherhood, and work in the female life course in contemporary America." Faye Ginsburg, *Contested Lives: The Abortion Debate in an American Community* (Berkeley: University of California Press, 1989), 134.

16. For an example that shows further constraints on when childbirth is celebrated, however, see Anna Tsing's essay on "monster stories" about women who birthed alone and were charged with perinatal endangerment, in which she discusses how race and class shape notions of "good," "bad," and "unnatural" mothers. Anna Lowenhaupt Tsing, "Monster Stories: Women Charged with Perinatal Endangerment," in *Uncertain Terms: Negotiating Gender in American Culture*, ed. Faye Ginsburg and Anna Lowenhaupt Tsing (Boston: Beacon Press, 1990): 282–299.

17. For a considered discussion of the politics of breast-feeding, see Pamela Carter, *Feminism, Breasts, and Breast-feeding* (London: Macmillan, 1995).

18. Ironically, many of the "stay-at-home" mothers were also "working moms," since many of them had part-time jobs, but they defined themselves as "staying at home."

19. Some women did preface criticisms of certified nurse-midwives with apologies to me, because they knew I had chosen certified nurse-midwives as my birth attendants.

20. For a copy of the interview guide, see Appendix A.

21. I did interact with several of the women in different situations, such as the midwifery study group and the healing workshop.

22. I interviewed all the women in their own homes, with the exception of one whom I interviewed by phone, and one woman who came to my house, because she was in the midst of separating from her husband.

23. Compare this to Gertrude Fraser's work, in which she found the older African-American women she interviewed to be hesitant or unwilling to talk of birth and midwifery for reasons of both modesty and fear of retribution. Gertrude Fraser, "Afro-American Midwives, Biomedicine and the State: An Ethno-historical Account of Birth and Its Transformation in Rural Virginia" (Ph.D. diss., Johns Hopkins University, 1988), 233–235.

24. I follow Deborah Gordon in my use of "biomedicine" to describe Western medicine. In addition to cautioning that biomedicine is not a monolithic system and pointing out its social location, she argued that within its scientific claims lie unacknowledged spiritual ideals of "life beyond time and space." Deborah R. Gordon, "Tenacious Assumptions in Western Medicine," in *Biomedicine Examined*, ed. Margaret Lock and Deborah R. Gordon (Dordrecht: Kluwer Academic, 1988), 19, 22, 41.

25. For further analysis of the significance to women of narrating their stories of childbirth, see Teresa Frances Keeler, "Narrating, Attitudes, and Health: The Effects of Recounting Pregnancy and Childbirth Experiences on the Well-Being of the Participants" (Ph.D. diss., University Of California, Los Angeles, 1984).

26. Gordon, "Tenacious Assumptions in Western Medicine"; Paula A. Treichler, "Feminism, Medicine, and the Meaning of Childbirth," in *Body Politics: Women, Literature, and the Discourse of Science*, ed., Mary Jacobus, Evelyn Fox Keller, and Sally Shuttleworth (New York: Routledge, Chapman, and Hall, 1990), 121.

27. Habitus (a Latin word) is a concept developed by anthropologist Marcel Mauss in his 1935 essay "Techniques of the Body," trans. Ben Brewster, *Economy and Society* 2, no. 1 (1973): 70–88. Pierre Bourdieu elaborated upon it later in *Outline of a Theory of Practice*, trans. Richard Nice (Cambridge: Cambridge University Press, 1977), 124; and Pierre Bourdieu, *The Logic of Practice*, trans. Richard Nice (Stanford: Stanford University Press, 1990b), 80–81.

28. Karen McCarthy Brown, "Serving the Spirits: The Ritual Economy of Haitian Vodou," in *Sacred Arts of Haitian Vodou*, ed. Donald J. Cosentino (Los Angeles: UCLA Fowler Museum of Cultural History, 1995), 217.

29. Paula Treichler, "Feminism, Medicine, and the Meaning of Childbirth," 132; italics in the original.

Chapter 2
Cultural Contexts of Home Birth

1. For example, see Ina May Gaskin, *Spiritual Midwifery*, 3d ed. (Summertown, Tenn.: Book Publishing Company, 1990); and Sheila Kitzinger, *Home Birth: The Essential Guide to Giving Birth Outside the Hospital* (New York: Dorling Kindersley, 1991).

2. Janet Gallagher, "Collective Bad Faith: 'Protecting the Fetus,'" in *Reproduction, Ethics, and the Law: Feminist Perspectives*, ed. Joan C. Callahan (Bloomington: Indiana University Press, 1994), 349.

3. For a compendium of childbirth books, see Rosemary Cline Diulio, *Childbirth: An Annotated Bibliography and Guide* (New York: Garland, 1986).

4. Sandra E. Godwin, "Mothers on Pedestals: A Look at Childbirth Advice Books and Julia Kristeva" (M.A. thesis, Boston College, 1993), 50.

5. Barbara Ehrenreich and Deirdre English, *For Her Own Good: 150 Years of the Experts' Advice to Women* (Garden City, N.Y.: Anchor Books, 1979), 191.

6. Katherine Arnup, *Education for Motherhood: Advice for Mothers in Twentieth-Century Canada* (Toronto: University of Toronto Press, 1994), 6.

7. Ibid.

8. While midwives may be considered experts (and thus not to be trusted) in the eyes of those home-birth advocates committed to unassisted birth, in the eyes of the medical establishment they are not. For this view of midwives among advocates of unassisted birth, see Marilyn Moran, *Birth and the Dialogue of Love* (Leawood, Kans.: New Nativity Press, 1981); and Jeannine Parvati Baker, "The Shamanic Dimension of Childbirth," *Pre- and Peri-natal Psychology Journal* 7, no. 1 (1992): 5–20.

9. Tess Cosslett, *Women Writing Childbirth: Modern Discourses of Motherhood* (Manchester, U.K.: Manchester University Press, 1994), 15.

10. See, for example, Gaskin, *Spiritual Midwifery*.

11. See, for example, the women's birth stories in *Happy Birth Days*, in which the women consistently cite certain texts or authors as particularly important to their choice. Marilyn Moran, ed., *Happy Birth Days: Personal Accounts of Birth at Home the Intimate, Husband/Wife Way* (Leawood, Kans.: New Nativity Press, 1986).

12. Carol Shepherd McClain, "Some Social Network Differences between Women Choosing Home and Hospital Birth," *Human Organization* 46, no. 2 (1987): 149. Sargent and Stark complexified this portrait, however, in their study that found social networks of kin and friends to shape significantly the perspectives on birth of women who accepted the medical model. See Carolyn Sargent and Nancy Stark, "Childbirth Education and Childbirth Models: Parental Perspectives on Control, Anesthesia, and Technological Intervention in the Birth Process," *Medical Anthropology Quarterly* 3, no.1 (1989): 49.

13. Judith Pence Rooks, *Midwifery and Childbirth in America* (Philadelphia: Temple University Press, 1997), 148, 155. For a more detailed demographic description, see Rooks's book, which is an excellent and thorough analysis of the state of midwifery in twentieth-century America.

14. Judith Pence Rooks suggests that, given these factors, the "maximal estimate" of births attended by direct-entry midwives in 1994 is 17, 678, instead of the 11, 846 documented by birth certificate data. Rooks, *Midwifery and Childbirth in America*, 148.

15. Eugene R. Declercq, Lisa L. Paine, and Michael R. Winter, "Home Birth in the United States, 1989–1992: A Longitudinal Descriptive Report of National Birth Certificate Data," *Journal of Nurse-Midwifery* 40, no. 6 (1995): 480.

16. Ibid.

17. Ibid.

18. Gertrude Fraser, "Afro-American Midwives, Biomedicine and the State: An Ethno-historical Account of Birth and Its Transformation in Rural Virginia" (Ph.D. diss., Johns Hopkins University, 1988), 448. Fraser's study focused on women in the South. In other regions, such as the San Francisco Bay Area and urban centers in the Northeast, African-American women are often more critical of medical models of health care, and more supportive of home birth. Class also significantly shapes these views for both African- and Euro-American women. Donna Daniels, personal communication, Princeton, 6 June 1998.

19. Fraser, "Afro-American Midwives, Biomedicine and the State," 447.

20. For example, Ellen Lazarus found that middle-class women in the hospital had "more access to information than poor women, but it was never enough. No matter what they knew, it could not empower them within the medical system. Knowledge itself could not give them authority, nor could they know all the contingencies of the birth process or of institutional care." Ellen Lazarus, "What Do Women Want?: Issues of Choice, Control, and Class in Pregnancy and Childbirth," *Medical Anthropology Quarterly* 8, no. 1 (1994): 37–38.

21. African-American traditions of midwifery are continued in some form, however, by such groups as the American College of Nurse Midwives' Midwives of African Descent and (generally middle-class) African-American women who are consciously trying to restore their heritage of midwifery, albeit in a transformed

way. See Marsha E. Jackson and Alice J. Bailes, "Home Birth with Certified Nurse-Midwife Attendants in the United States," *Journal of Nurse-Midwifery* 40, no. 6 (1995): 497; Gertrude Fraser, "Modern Bodies, Modern Minds: Midwifery and Reproductive Change in an African American Community," in *Conceiving the New World Order: The Global Politics of Reproduction*, ed. Faye D. Ginsburg and Rayna Rapp (Berkeley: University of California Press, 1995), 51. Also, see Judith Rooks's brief discussion of African-American church women who attend the births of the women in their congregations, Rooks, *Midwifery and Childbirth in America*, 155.

22. Carol Shepherd McClain, "Women's Choice of Home or Hospital Birth," *Journal of Family Practice* 12, no. 6 (1981): 1036–1037; Beatrice A. Roeder, *Chicano Folk Medicine from Los Angeles, California*, University of California Publications: Folklore and Mythology Studies, vol. 34 (Berkeley: University of California Press, 1988), 98; Fraser, "Modern Bodies, Modern Minds," 51; Gaskin, *Spiritual Midwifery*; Rooks, *Midwifery and Childbirth in America*, 60–64.

23. Regi Teasley, "Birth and the Division of Labor: The Movement to Professionalize Nurse-Midwifery, and Its Relationship to the Movement for Home Birth and Lay Midwifery. A Case Study of Vermont" (Ph. D. diss., Michigan State University, 1983), 152, n. 1. We can still see an ironic version of this in that certified nurse-midwives have traditionally attended a large portion of Medicaid births in hospitals with very good results, although with changes in managed care some physicians are growing increasingly interested in attending Medicaid patients. See Rooks, *Midwifery and Childbirth in America*, 156, 221.

24. See Fraser, "Afro-American Midwives, Biomedicine and the State," 366.

25. Rooks, *Midwifery and Childbirth in America*, 156.

26. For the complexity of the New York situation regarding the legality of direct-entry midwifery, see Rooks, *Midwifery and Childbirth in America*, 236–237.

27. For other regional case studies of home birth, namely in Massachusetts, Vermont, and the San Francisco Bay area, see Christine Annette Johnson, "Normalizing Birth: The Home Birth Movement in Massachusetts" (Ph.D. diss., Boston University, 1987); Teasley, "Birth and the Division of Labor"; and Lester Dessez Hazell, *Birth Goes Home* (Seattle: Catalyst, 1974).

28. Altogether, there were 112 births among the 45 women. In addition to the planned home births, there were 24 hospital births, 6 birth-center births, one birth in a doctor's office, and one unplanned home birth. Of the hospital births, 22 were attended by doctors (6 were cesarean sections), and 2 were attended by certified nurse-midwives.

29. Rooks, *Midwifery and Childbirth in America*, 60.

30. I am not entirely comfortable with the moniker "New Age," but have not come across a more descriptive term, either in the sense of the eclectic religious sensibilities of such women, or in the sense of the "readable" labels scholars have given to such religions. See Appendix B for descriptions of all the women, including their religious identities.

31. Rooks, *Midwifery and Childbirth in America*, 155.

32. Annette Pollinger, "Diffusion of Innovations in Childbirth: An Analysis of Sociocultural Factors Associated with Traditional, Natural, and Home Birth," (Ph.D. diss., Fordham University, 1977), 137. Pollinger acknowledged that her results, dependent on a small sample, may have been skewed by the high propor-

tion of Catholic women in the region she was studying, most of whom gave birth in the hospital.

33. Spiritual beliefs came second to the desire for "no separation from family" as a reason for choosing home birth, in Naragon's study. In descending order, the women in her study identified themselves as liberal Protestants, no religion, Fundamentalist, Catholic, Eastern religions, and Jewish. Cynthia Ann Naragon, "Childbirth at Home: A Descriptive Study Of 675 Couples Who Chose Home Birth" (Ph.D. diss., California School Of Professional Psychology, 1980), 27, 38.

34. For example, see Keri Heitner Lipkowitz, "Interpretation and Critique of the Choice and Experience of Home Birth: Positive Home Birth Experiences of New York Women" (Ph.D. diss., City University Of New York, 1986), 84.

35. Sandra Vandam Anderson and Eleanor E. Bauwens, "An Ethnography of Home Birth," in *Anthropology of Human Birth*, ed. Margarita Artschwager Kay (Philadelphia: F. A. Davis, 1982), 301. Significant exceptions to this lack of attention to the role of religion in Western childbirth practices include the work of Gertrude Fraser on Afro-American midwives, Nancy Scheper-Hughes on Catholic women in Ireland, Sarah Stark on Mormon women in the United States, and Kimberly Hubbell on "Neo-Oriental Americans." All of these authors demonstrated that religious beliefs and practices had tangible (and not always positive) effects on how and where women chose to give birth and their bodily experiences of the process. See Fraser, "Afro-American Midwives, Biomedicine and the State"; Nancy Scheper-Hughes, "Virgin Mothers: The Impact of Irish Jansenism on Childbearing and Infant Tending in Western Ireland," in *Anthropology of Human Birth*, ed. Margarita Artschwager Kay (Philadelphia: F. A. Davis, 1982), 267–288; Sarah Stark, "Mormon Childbearing," in *Anthropology of Human Birth*, 341–361; and Kimberly Hubbell, "The Neo-Oriental American: Childbearing in the Ashram," in *Anthropology of Human Birth*, 267–288.

36. Robbie Davis-Floyd, *Birth as an American Rite of Passage*, 201.

37. Ibid., 160, 296. Davis-Floyd's 1992 study was not focused on home birth, and she interviewed only a small number of home-birthing women. Her later study addressed the views of this minority more directly. See Robbie Davis-Floyd, "The Technocratic Body and the Organic Body: Hegemony and Heresy in Women's Birth Choices," in *Gender and Health: An International Perspective*, ed. Carolyn F. Sargent and Caroline B. Brettell (Upper Saddle River, N.J.: Prentice-Hall, 1996), 123–166.

38. Davis-Floyd, *Birth as an American Rite of Passage*, 330, n. 2. In this distinction, Davis-Floyd characterized the holistic homeschoolers as those "who reject the educational system because they believe that it stifles individuality and creativity, teaches technocratic values they do not wish their children to absorb, and ignores the spiritual and emotional needs of the whole child."

39. See Barbara Katz Rothman, *In Labor: Women and Power in the Birthplace* (New York: W. W. Norton, 1982), 32; and Rooks, *Midwifery and Childbirth in America*, 155–156.

40. Hazell, *Birth Goes Home*, 8.

41. Richard W. Wertz and Dorothy C. Wertz, *Lying-In: A History of Childbirth in America*, expanded edition (New Haven: Yale University Press, 1989), 23; and Laurel Thatcher Ulrich, *A Midwife's Tale* (New York: Vintage, 1991), 203.

42. David D. Hall, *Worlds of Wonder, Days of Judgment: Popular Religious Belief in Early New England* (Cambridge: Harvard University Press, 1989), 100, 140. On the ambiguous religious stature of midwives throughout American history, also see Ulrich, *A Midwife's Tale*, 46–47.

43. Procter-Smith, discussing whether "Shakerism was feminist," argued that this stance toward childbearing was "emancipatory" for women, and allowed for a gynocentric religion. Her problematic formulation of childbirth as a "patriarchal institution imposed on women without their consent" potentially masks the difficulties some Shaker women had with celibacy as a practice that kept them from bearing children and from the forms of agency some women find in childbirth. Marjorie Procter-Smith, " 'In the Line of the Female': Shakerism and Feminism," in *Women's Leadership in Marginal Religions: Explorations Outside the Mainstream*, ed. Catherine Wessinger (Urbana: University of Illinois Press, 1993), 25, 27, 29.

44. Procter-Smith " 'In the Line of the Female': Shakerism and Feminism," 29.

45. Dorothy Day, *The Long Loneliness: An Autobiography* (New York: HarperCollins, 1981 [1952]), 139.

46. David Hall, *Worlds of Wonder*, 241.

47. Social childbirth was the phrase used by Wertz and Wertz to describe births in which "expectant women looked to friends and kin for aid and comfort." In the revolutionary period, doctors began to take their place in this circle of women friends and family. Richard W. Wertz and Dorothy C. Wertz, *Lying-In: A History of Childbirth in America*, 1.

48. Ibid., 26.

49. Janet Carlisle Bogdan, "Childbirth in America, 1650 to 1990," in *Women, Health, and Medicine in America*, ed. Rima D. Apple (New York: Garland, 1990), 114.

50. Accounts and analyses of the shift from home to hospital are many. For example, Angela D. Danzi, "From Home to Hospital: Jewish and Italian American Women and Childbirth, 1920–1940" (Ph.D. diss., New York University, 1993); Judith Walzer Leavitt, *Brought to Bed: Childbearing in America, 1750–1950* (New York: Oxford University Press, 1986); Gail Pat Parsons, "In Transition: Doctors, Disease, and the Decline of Home Birth" (Ph.D. diss., University of California, San Francisco, 1986); Catherine M. Scholten, *Childbearing in American Society, 1650–1850* (New York: New York University Press, 1985); Wertz and Wertz, *Lying-In*.

51. Paul Starr, *The Social Transformation of American Medicine* (New York: Basic Books, 1982), 50.

52. Charlotte Borst, *Catching Babies: The Professionalization of Childbirth, 1870–1920* (Cambridge: Harvard University Press, 1995); and Carol Schrom Dye, "History of Childbirth in America," *Signs* 6, no. 1 (1980): 103.

53. Wertz and Wertz, *Lying-In*, 139, 144. At the turn of the century, 95 percent of births occurred at home, decreasing to almost 21 percent by 1945, and stabilizing at around 1 percent by 1969. In the nineteenth century, poor Euro-American and African-American women (the latter sometimes slaves) were the "guinea pigs" for much of obstetrical "progress" in the United States, such as that achieved by Dr. J. Marion Sims. Joan J. Mathews and Kathleen Zadak, "The Alternative Birth

Movement in the United States: History and Current Status," *Women & Health* 17, no. 1 (1991): 41; and Wertz and Wertz, *Lying-In*, 101.

54. Leavitt, *Brought to Bed*, 176.

55. Ibid., 135.

56. Borst, *Catching Babies*, 203, 212; Wertz and Wertz, *Lying-In*, 145.

57. Wertz and Wertz *Lying-In*, 127.

58. Borst, *Catching Babies*, 210. Borst based this discussion on Pamela S. Summey and Marsha Hurst, "Ob/Gyn on the Rise: The Evolution of Professional Ideology in the Twentieth Century," *Women and Health*, Part 1: 11, no. 1 (1986): 133–145; Part 2: 11, no. 2 (1986): 102–122.

59. Wertz and Wertz *Lying-In*, 145.

60. Borst, *Catching Babies*, 213.

61. Robbie Davis-Floyd, *Birth as an American Rite of Passage*, 45; and Wertz and Wertz, *Lying-In*, 25. Wertz and Wertz asserted that in the United States Puritanism played a particular role in this "disenchantment" of birth, due to its condemnation of the magical and charismatic role of midwives. As well, they argued that a more general Protestant acceptance of science and the need to intervene in "nature" propelled women to turn to doctors in childbirth. However, for a view of early New England culture in which the occult continued to intermingle with official religion, see David Hall, *Worlds of Wonder*, 243. See also Margaret L. Hammer, *Giving Birth: Reclaiming Biblical Metaphor for Pastoral Practice* (Louisville, Ky.: Westminster/John Knox Press, 1994); and Margaret O'Brien Steinfels, "New Childbirth Technology: A Clash of Values," *Hastings Center Report* (February 1978): 12.

62. Jenna Weissman Joselit, *The Wonders of America: Reinventing Jewish Culture, 1880–1950* (New York: Hill and Wang, 1994), 66.

63. Ibid., 65. See also Danzi, "From Home to Hospital."

64. Fraser, "Afro-American Midwives, Biomedicine and the State," 340, 365.

65. Ibid., 451–453.

66. Ibid., 455.

67. Fraser described mother wit as "both a spiritual and material substance" that came from God and was "an intuitive capacity to adjust to unexpected circumstances . . . knowledge of nature and how to use it and . . . an ability to read signs or people's motivations/personality." Fraser, "Afro-American Midwives, Biomedicine and the State," 339. See also Fraser, "Modern Bodies, Modern Minds." For other perspectives on traditional African-American midwifery, see Molly C. Dougherty, "Southern Lay Midwives as Ritual Specialists," in *Women in Ritual and Symbolic Roles*, ed. Judith Hoch-Smith and Anita Spring (New York: Plenum Press, 1978), 151–164; Linda Holmes, "African American Midwives in the South," in *The American Way of Birth*, ed. Pamela Eakins (Philadelphia: Temple University Press, 1986); Onnie Lee Logan, as told to Katherine Clarke, *Motherwit: An Alabama Midwife's Story* (New York: Dutton, 1986); and Debra Ann Susie, *In the Way of Our Grandmothers: A Cultural View of Twentieth-Century Midwifery in Florida* (Athens: University of Georgia Press, 1988).

68. For example, obstetrician Joseph B. DeLee compared birth to a woman falling on a pitchfork and to a baby's head "caught in a door very lightly." DeLee was an influential obstetrician who developed the "prophylactic forceps opera-

tion," which made sedation, episiotomy, and forceps removal routine procedures. DeLee boasted that his episiotomies restored a woman's "virginal conditions," even making her perineum "better than new," while keeping the child from "brain damage and a life of crime." Wertz and Wertz, *Lying-In*, 141–142.

69. Judith Walzer Leavitt, "Birthing and Anesthesis: The Debate over Twilight Sleep," *Signs* 6, no. 1 (1980): 147–164; Margarete Sandelowski, *Pain, Pleasure, and American Childbirth: From the Twilight Sleep to the Read Method, 1914–1960* (Westport, Conn.: Greenwood Press, 1984). One of the foremost supporters of twilight sleep was a female doctor, Bertha van Hoosen. Leavitt, "Birthing and Anesthesis," 149.

70. Leavitt, "Birthing and Anesthesis," 153; Martin S. Pernick, *A Calculus of Suffering: Pain, Professionalism, and Anesthesia in Nineteenth-Century America* (New York: Columbia University Press, 1985), 153.

71. Ralph M. Beach, in Leavitt, "Birthing and Anesthesis," 156. Beach was an American physician writing in 1915.

72. The most famous blow to twilight sleep was the death in childbirth of Mrs. Francis X. Carmody, one of the greatest supporters of the procedure. Though Carmody's doctors and husband claimed that twilight sleep was not the cause of her death, their protestations did not quell rising fears regarding the safety of twilight sleep. Leavitt, "Birthing and Anesthesia," 163.

73. Borst, *Catching Babies*. For more on the interrelation between government and medical authorities in their regulation of childbirth, such as the politics surrounding the ill-fated 1921 Sheppard-Towner Act for maternal and child health, see Molly Ladd-Taylor, *Mother-Work: Women, Child Welfare, and the State, 1890–1930* (Urbana: University of Illinois Press, 1994); Sheila M. Rothman, *Woman's Proper Place: A History of Changing Ideals and Practices, 1870 to the Present* (New York: Basic Books, 1978), ch. 4; and Wertz and Wertz, *Lying-in*, ch. 7.

74. *Childbirth without Fear* went through two revised editions and several printings in English and eleven other languages. Grantly Dick-Read, *Childbirth without Fear: The Principles and Practice of Natural Childbirth*, 2d rev. ed. (New York: Harper and Row, 1959).

75. Ibid., 46.

76. Ibid., 102, 104.

77. Ibid., 52.

78. Ibid., 25.

79. Ibid., 48.

80. For examples of American obstetricians sympathetic to Dick-Read, see William Hazlett's claim that women, especially pregnant ones, were naturally close to God and his warning that a woman's "intellect splits off when woman is estranged from nature." William H. Hazlett, "The Advantages of Full Consciousness in Childbirth," in *Religion and Birth Control*, ed. John Clover Monsma (Garden City, N.Y.: Doubleday, 1963), 159. See also David Taber's reserved recommendation of "natural childbirth" for the Christian woman, in which he declared that God "expects bravery, a holy optimism, amidst all the hardships of giving birth." David L. Taber, "Natural Childbirth Recommended—with Reservations," in *Religion and Birth Control*, 165.

81. By the 1940s there were already some criticisms of obstetric practices by such anthropologists as Margaret Mead and such (problematic) psychoanalysts as Helene Deutsch, who considered the pain of childbirth to be particularly meaningful to women because of their supposedly innate masochism. Margaret Mead, *Blackberry Winter: My Earlier Years* (New York: Simon and Schuster, 1972); and Wertz and Wertz, *Lying-In*, 188.

82. The seven women who founded La Leche League met through the Christian Family Movement and their "common interest in natural childbirth and breast-feeding." Though in its official literature and group meetings, the league traditionally has not promoted other issues, including religion or home birth, specific groups can become oriented in this way. Lynn Y. Weiner, "Reconstructing Motherhood: The La Leche League in Postwar America," *Journal of American History* (March 1994): 1360, 1375.

83. Ibid., 1366.

84. Ibid., 1358.

85. For more on how La Leche League (LLL) has dealt with the challenges working mothers and poor mothers bring to the LLL philosophy, see Weiner "Reconstructing Motherhood," 1379–1380.

86. Carter lived in Titusville, Florida, and was married to an Army general (her second marriage). Patricia Cloyd Carter, *Come Gently, Sweet Lucina* (Titusville, Fla.: Patricia Cloyd Carter, 1957).

87. Marion Sousa suggests that *Come Gently Sweet Lucina* was the first home-birth advice book. Marion Sousa, *Childbirth at Home* (New York: Bantam, 1976), 129.

88. Carter, *Come Gently, Sweet Lucina*, 350. Drawing adoringly but critically from Dick-Read, Carter firmly stated that childbirth was an intricately psychological and physiological process in which the uterus "respond[s] to what we believe," and that fear (and doctors) caused unnecessary pain in this natural process. Carter, *Come Gently, Sweet Lucina*, 17–25, 361.

89. Ibid., 352–356.

90. Ibid., 51. In addition to some of her very peculiar and dangerous nutritional advice, such as cutting down on calcium to make one's pelvic bones softer, Carter had a curious and often contradictory mix of protofeminism and traditionalism. She could debunk the notion of penis envy by saying that "women do not envy the phallus per se . . . [but] what appears to be the broader lives that men can live not being tied down so biologically," but also argue that men, not women, should attend birthing women, that pregnant women should wear girdles to retain their figure, and that husbands should not see their wives in "dishabille." The last reason was partly why she chose to birth in total privacy, while her husband waited outside, "stand[ing] guard." Carter, *Come Gently, Sweet Lucina*, 54, 227, 224b, 226, 224.

91. Cynthia Huff, "Delivery: The Cultural Re-presentation of Childbirth," *Prose Studies: History, Theory, Criticism* 14, no. 2 (1991): 108–121.

92. For detailed attention both to the importance of Catholicism to La Leche League and to the suppression of this explicitly religious basis as the league grew in popularity, see Jule DeJager Ward, *La Leche League: At the Crossroads of Medicine, Feminism, and Religion* (Chapel Hill: University of North Carolina Press, 2000).

93. Wertz and Wertz, *Lying-In*, 187.

94. Helen S. Wessel, *Natural Childbirth and the Christian Family* (New York: Harper and Row, 1963).

95. Robert A. Bradley, *Husband-Coached Childbirth*, rev. ed. (New York: Harper and Row, 1974), 188.

96. For histories and analyses of the current state of the women's health movement both globally and in the United States, see Sheryl Burt Ruzek, "Feminist Visions of Health: An International Perspective," in *What Is Feminism?* ed. Juliet Mitchell and Ann Oakley (London: Basil Blackwell, 1986), 184–207; and Judy Norsigian, "The Women's Health Movement in the United States," in *Man-Made Medicine: Women's Health, Public Policy and Reform*, ed. Kary L. Moss (Durham: Duke University Press, 1996), 79–97.

97. Rothman, *In Labor*, 95.

98. Ronnie Lichtman, "Medical Models and Midwifery: The Cultural Experience of Birth," in *Childbirth in America: Anthropological Perspectives*, ed. Karen L. Michaelson (South Hadley, Mass.: Bergin and Garvey, 1988), 141, n. 2; Adrienne Rich, *Of Woman Born: Motherhood as Experience and Institution* (New York: Norton, 1986 [1976]); Deborah Goleman Wolf, "Lesbian Childbirth and Artificial Insemination: A Wave of the Future," in *Anthropology of Human Birth*, 321–340. For further discussion of how lesbian motherhood both draws on and resists conventional gendered norms of mothering, see Ellen Lewin, "On the Outside Looking In: The Politics of Lesbian Motherhood," in *Conceiving the New World Order: The Global Politics of Reproduction*, ed. Faye D. Ginsburg and Rayna Rapp (Berkeley: University of California Press, 1995), 103–121.

99. Rooks, *Midwifery and Childbirth in America*, 56.

100. For more on the history of traditional and nurse-midwifery in the United States, see, Jane B. Donegan, *Women and Men Midwives: Medicine, Morality, and Misogyny in Early America* (Westport, Conn.: Greenwood Press, 1978); Jean Donnison, *Midwives and Medical Men: A History of Inter-Professional Rivalries and Women's Rights* (New York: Schocken, 1977); and M. Theophane Shoemaker, *History of Nurse-Midwifery in the United States* (New York: Garland Publishing, 1984). For a comprehensive analysis of nurse-midwifery past and present, see Rooks, *Midwifery and Childbirth in America*.

101. Jackson and Bailes, "Home Birth with Certified Nurse-Midwife Attendants in the United States," 497. The American College of Nurse-Midwives (ACNM) was founded in 1955 and merged with the Kentucky-based American Association of Nurse-Midwives in 1968. In a joint statement with the American College of Obstetricians and Gynecologists, the ACNM declared certified nurse-midwives to be part of the "obstetrical team," meaning that they were to work in affiliation with an obstetrician.

102. Certified nurse-midwife Lea Rizack described her disputes with the ACNM over home birth in the 1970s. Lea Rizack, "Interview with Lea Rizack, CNM," interview by Ina May Gaskin, *Birth Gazette* 11, no. 3 (1995): 8.

103. Gaskin, *Spiritual Midwifery*; and Rahima Baldwin, *Special Delivery: The Complete Guide to Informed Birth* (Millbrae, Calif.: Les Femmes, 1979).

104. Suzanne Hope Suarez, "Midwifery Is Not the Practice of Medicine," *Yale Journal of Law and Feminism* 5 (1993): 332; Teasley, "Birth and the Division of Labor," 173–175.

105. Peggy O'Mara, *Midwifery and the Law: A* Mothering *Special Edition* (Santa Fe, N. Mex.: *Mothering*, 1990); Suarez, "Midwifery Is Not the Practice of Medicine," 355–357. Many direct-entry midwives began their practices in the 1970s by helping out a friend or family member, but as a glance through the journal *Birth Gazette* shows, there are now several independent midwifery schools where direct-entry midwives can receive both short-term and long-term training.

106. Jackson and Bailes, "Home Birth with Certified Nurse-Midwife Attendants in the United States," 497; Suarez, "Midwifery Is Not the Practice of Medicine," 333–335. Robbie Davis-Floyd is researching the relationship between these two professional organizations.

107. For an interesting reinvention of the doctor-run home-birth service, see Mayer Eisenstein, *Give Birth at Home with the Home Court Advantage* (Chicago: Mayer Eisenstein, 1988). Of home births between 1989 and 1992, for which the attendant was recorded, doctors attended about 20 percent, certified nurse-midwives attended 12.2 percent, and direct-entry midwives attended 30.5 percent. The remaining 37 percent were attended by neither physician nor midwife, though this number might be reduced if the attendant, particularly if a direct-entry midwife, did not record herself for fear of legal repercussions. Declercq, Paine, and Winter, "Home Birth in the United States," 476–477.

108. Johnson, "Normalizing Birth," 118, 123.

109. Rothman, *In Labor*, 96.

110. The range of groups involved in the alternative-birth movement is great, but most continue to be grassroots voluntary organizations dependent largely on the efforts of childbearing women who have become critical of the medical model through personal experience. Some of these groups include the International Childbirth Education Association (ICEA), Home Oriented Maternity Experience (HOME), Informed Homebirth, Birth Oriented Resource Network (BORN), and National Association of Parents and Professionals for Safe Alternatives in Childbirth (NAPSAC). Several magazines, including *The Birth Gazette*, *Mothering*, and *The Compleat Mother*, have also had formative influences on the alternative-birth movement. Mathews and Zadak, "The Alternative Birth Movement in the United States," 54; Teasley, "Birth and the Division of Labor," 152–155; Jackson and Bailes, "Home Birth with Certified Nurse-Midwife Attendants in the United States," 497.

111. Rothman, *In Labor*, 110.

112. American College of Nurse-Midwives (ACNM) and Sandra Jacobs, *Having Your Baby with a Nurse-Midwife* (New York: Hyperion and Jacobs, 1993), 7, 24–25.

113. Stephen Walzer and Allen Cohen, *Childbirth Is Ecstasy* (Albion, Calif.: Aquarius, 1971); Sousa, *Childbirth at Home*, 86; Wessel, *Natural Childbirth and the Christian Family*. A perusal of early editions of *Mothering* magazine shows the diversity of spiritualities called upon by home birthers, including Native American traditions, Christian traditions, and more eclectic blends like a confidence in "per-

fect Natural Law of Faith." Chuck Perry, in *Mothering* 4 (1977): 65; see also 57; and *Mothering* 3 (1976), 22.

114. Cosslett, *Women Writing Childbirth*, 37. Much of the feminist commentary on birth that considers religion has come in the form of fiction and poetry, as well as literary criticism, especially the work of those critics wanting to defy the "constraints of the Western narrative tradition with its long history of enforced maternal absence." Di Brandt, *Wild Mother Dancing: Maternal Narrative in Canadian Literature* (Winnipeg: University of Manitoba Press, 1993), 16. See also Alice E. Adams, *Reproducing the Womb: Images of Childbirth in Science, Feminist Theory, and Literature* (Ithaca: Cornell University Press, 1994), Alicia Ostriker, *The Mother/Child Papers*, repr. (Boston: Beacon Press, 1986); and Maureen T. Reddy, Martha Roth, and Amy Sheldon, eds., *Mother Journeys: Feminists Write about Mothering* (Minneapolis: Spinsters Ink, 1994).

115. For example, see Nina Barrett's description of "drug-free, intervention-free, painless labor" as "merely the newest utopian vision in a long line of fads dictating what a woman's labor *should* be like." She went on, however, only to describe hospital births using the Lamaze method, ignoring other perspectives on drugless birth that do not make claims for labor's "painlessness." Nina Barrett, *I Wish Someone Had Told Me: Comfort, Support and Advice for New Moms from More than 60 Real-life Mothers* (New York: Simon and Schuster, 1990), 2, 8.

116. Emily Martin, "The Ideology of Reproduction: The Reproduction of Ideology," in *Uncertain Terms: Negotiating Gender in American Culture*, ed. Faye Ginsburg and Anna Lowenhaupt Tsing (Boston: Beacon Press, 1990), 310.

117. Carol McClain suggested that the increased attention to childbirth came both from a disciplinary shift, in which "the study of whole cultures has given way to specialized interests," and the increase in female anthropologists, who overcame the lack of interest of male anthropologists in the subject and their inability to "gain access to women's domains." Carol Shepherd McClain, "Towards a Comparative Framework for the Study of Childbirth," in *Anthropology of Human Birth*, ed. Margarita Artschwager Kay (Philadelphia: F. A. Davis, 1982), 38.

118. Brigitte Jordan, *Birth in Four Cultures*, 4th ed. (Prospect Heights, Ill.: Waveland Press, 1993 [1978]); Margarita Artschwager Kay, ed., *Anthropology of Human Birth;* Carol P. MacCormack, ed., *Ethnography of Fertility and Birth* (Prospect Heights, Ill.: Waveland Press, 1994 [1982]); Carol Laderman, *Wives and Midwives: Childbirth and Nutrition in Rural Malaysia* (Berkeley: University of California Press, 1983).

119. For example, Vangie Bergum, *Woman to Mother: A Transformation* (Granby, Mass.: Bergin and Garvey, 1989); Barbara Ehrenreich and Deirdre English, *Witches, Midwives, and Nurses: A History of Women Healers* (Old Westbury, N.Y.: Feminist Press, 1973); Robbie Pfeufer Kahn, *Bearing Meaning: The Language of Birth* (Urbana: University of Illinois Press, 1995); Sheila Kitzinger, *Women as Mothers* (Oxford: Martin Robertson, 1978); Jacqueline Vincent Priya, *Birth Traditions and Modern Pregnancy Care* (Shaftesbury, U.K.: Element Books, 1992); Ann Oakley, *Women Confined: Toward a Sociology of Childbirth* (New York: Schocken Books, 1980); Adrienne Rich, *Of Woman Born: Motherhood as Experience and Institution* (New York: Norton, 1986 [1976]); Rothman, *In Labor;* Nancy

Stoller Shaw, *Forced Labor: Maternity Care in the United States* (New York: Pergamon Press, 1974).

120. For example, see Davis-Floyd, *Birth as an American Rite of Passage*; Emily Martin, *The Woman in the Body: A Cultural Analysis of Reproduction*, 2d ed. (Boston: Beacon Press, 1992 [1987]); Karen L. Michaelson and Barbara Alvin, "Technology and the Context of Childbirth: A Comparison of Two Hospital Settings," in *Childbirth in America*, ed. Karen Michaelson (South Hadley, Mass.: Bergin and Garvey, 1988), 142–152; Stacy Leigh Pigg, "Authority in Translation: Finding, Knowing, Naming, and Training 'Traditional Birth Attendants' in Nepal," in *Childbirth and Authoritative Knowledge*, ed. Robbie E. Davis-Floyd and Carolyn F. Sargent (Berkeley: University of California Press, 1997), 233–262; and Amara Jambai and Carol MacCormack, "Maternal Health, War, and Religious Tradition: Authoritative Knowledge in Pujehun District, Sierra Leone," in ibid., 421–440.

121. MacCormack, ed., *Ethnography of Fertility and Birth*, 1. MacCormack cited the World Health Organization as the source of these statistics.

122. The United States contains a microcosm of this inequality, since African-American babies and childbearing women have higher mortality and morbidity rates than do Euro-Americans, largely because of poverty and its attendant problems: poor nutrition and less access to quality health care. Ellen Lazarus, "Poor Women, Poor Outcomes: Social Class and Reproductive Health," in *Childbirth in America*, ed. Karen L. Michaelson (South Hadley, Mass.: Bergin and Garvey, 1988), 41; Wertz and Wertz, *Lying-In*, 271.

123. MacCormack, *Ethnography of Fertility and Birth*, 2. On the importance of global perspectives that analyze the effect of "multinational corporations, international development agencies, Western medicine, and religious groups as they construct the contexts within which local reproductive relations are played out," see the excellent review article by Faye Ginsburg and Rayna Rapp, "The Politics of Reproduction," *Annual Review of Anthropology* 20 (1991): 312.

124. While the majority of the world's women give birth at home, most of them do not have recourse to medical assistance should they require it. In their "middle ground" between medical and traditional birth practices, home-birthing women in the United States are joined by women from a variety of other Western nations where home birth is more accepted and common, especially Holland and, to a lesser degree, Great Britain and Canada. See Eva Abraham-Van der Mark, ed., *Successful Home Birth and Midwifery: The Dutch Model* (Westport, Conn.: Bergin and Garvey, 1993); Rona Campbell and Alison Macfarlane, "Recent Debate on the Place of Birth," in *The Politics of Maternity Care: Services for Childbearing Women in Twentieth-Century Britain*, ed. Jo Garcia, Robert Kilpatrick, and Martin Richards (Oxford: Clarendon Press, 1990), 217–237; and Brian Burtch, *Trials of Labor: The Re-emergence of Midwifery* (Montreal and Kingston: McGill–Queen's University Press, 1994).

125. Janet Gallagher, "The Fetus and the Law—Whose Life Is It Anyway?" *Ms. Magazine* 60, no. 8 (September 1984): 134; Wertz and Wertz, *Lying-In*, 293; Shelia Kitzinger, *Home Birth: The Essential Guide to Giving Birth Outside the Hospital* (New York: Dorling Kindersley, 1991).

126. Martin, *The Woman in the Body*; Davis-Floyd, *Birth as an American Rite of Passage*; Rothman, *In Labor*.

127. Here, Davis-Floyd adapted (among others) Barbara Katz Rothman's distinction between "medical" and "midwifery" models of childbirth. Rothman, *In Labor*, 34.

128. Davis-Floyd, *Birth as an American Rite of Passage*, 160–161. Some feminist advocates of home birth consider that the woman, not the family, should be the focus of care, since families can take all shapes and create both supportive and abusive environments. See Ronnie Lichtman, "Medical Models and Midwifery: The Cultural Experience of Birth," in *Childbirth in America: Anthropological Perspectives*, ed. Karen L. Michaelson (South Hadley, Mass.: Bergin and Garvey, 1988), 130–141.

129. Paula A. Treichler, "Feminism, Medicine, and the Meaning of Childbirth," in *Body Politics: Women, Literature, and the Discourse of Science*, ed. Mary Jacobus, Evelyn Fox Keller, and Sally Shuttleworth (New York: Routledge, Chapman, and Hall, 1990), 114.

130. Robbie Davis-Floyd and Elizabeth Davis, "Intuition as Authoritative Knowledge in Midwifery and Home Birth," in *Childbirth and Authoritative Knowledge: Cross-Cultural Perspectives*, ed. Robbie E. Davis-Floyd and Carolyn F. Sargent (Berkeley: University of California Press, 1997), 315–349; Rizack, "Interview with Lea Rizack, CNM," 9.

131. Davis-Floyd, *Birth as an American Rite of Passage*, 185; Phyllis A. Langton, "Obstetricians' Resistance to Independent, Private Practice by Nurse-Midwives in Washington, D.C., Hospitals," *Women & Health* 22, no. 1 (1994): 27–48; Lazarus, "What Do Women Want?" 40.

132. Davis-Floyd, *Birth as an American Rite of Passage*; Martin, *The Woman in the Body*; Margaret Nelson, "Birth and Social Class," in *The American Way of Birth*, ed. Pamela S. Eakins (Philadelphia: Temple University Press, 1986), 142–174.

133. Ginsburg and Rapp, "The Politics of Reproduction," 322. A similar analytical tension over women's agency exists among varying feminist analyses of women's experiences of ultrasound. See Barbara Duden, *Disembodying Women: Perspectives on Pregnancy and the Unborn* (Cambridge: Harvard University Press, 1993); and Janelle S. Taylor, "Image of Contradiction: Obstetrical Ultrasound in American Culture," in *Reproducing Reproduction: Kinship, Power, and Technological Innovation*, ed. Sarah Franklin and Helena Ragoné (Philadelphia: University of Pennsylvania Press, 1998), 15–45.

134. Barbara Katz Rothman, "Awake and Aware, or False Consciousness: The Cooption of Childbirth Reform in America," in *Childbirth: Alternatives to Medical Control*, ed. Shelly Romalis (Austin: University of Texas Press, 1981), 150–180.

135. Sylvia Bortin, Marina Alzugaray, Judy Dowd, and Janice Kalman, "A Feminist Perspective on the Study of Home Birth: Application of a Midwifery Care Framework," *Journal of Nurse-Midwifery* 39, no. 3 (1994): 148.

136. MacCormack, *Ethnography of Fertility and Birth*, 10. See also Davis-Floyd and Sargent, eds., *Childbirth and Authoritative Knowledge*, 28, n. 18.

137. Janice Boddy, *Wombs and Alien Spirits: Women, Men and the Zār Cult in Northern Sudan* (Madison: University of Wisconsin Press, 1989); Carol Delaney, *The Seed and the Soil: Gender and Cosmology in Turkish Village Society* (Berkeley:

University of California Press, 1991); Rita Gross, "Menstruation and Childbirth as Ritual and Religious Experience among Native Australians," in *Unspoken Worlds: Women's Religious Lives in Non-Western Cultures*, ed. Nancy Falk and Rita Gross (San Francisco: Harper and Row, 1980), 277–292; Carol Laderman, *Wives and Midwives: Childbirth and Nutrition in Rural Malaysia* (Berkeley: University of California Press, 1983); Carol P. MacCormack, "Health, Fertility, and Birth in Moyamba District, Sierra Leone," in *Ethnography of Fertility and Birth*, 115–130; Pigg, "Authority in Translation."

138. For example, Martin, *The Woman in the Body*; Michaelson, *Childbirth in America*; Shelly Romalis, ed., *Childbirth: Alternatives to Medical Control* (Austin: University of Texas Press, 1981).

139. Davis-Floyd, *Birth as an American Rite of Passage*; Hilary Graham, "The Social Image of Pregnancy: Pregnancy as Spirit Possession," *Sociological Review* N.S. 24, no. 2 (1976): 291–308; Hilary Homans, "Pregnancy and Birth as Rites of Passage for Two Groups of Women in Britain," in *Ethnography of Fertility and Birth*, ed. Carol P. MacCormack (Prospect Heights, Ill.: Waveland Press, 1984 [1982]), 221–258; Sheila Kitzinger, "The Social Context of Birth: Some Comparisons between Childbirth in Jamaica and Britain," in *Ethnography of Fertility and Birth*, 221–258. Exceptions to this include works by scholars or pastors who have written about childbirth in order to call their respective religious traditions to attention about the importance of childbirth to a woman's religious life, but their work is not ethnographic. For example, Margaret L. Hammer, *Giving Birth: Reclaiming Biblical Metaphor for Pastoral Practice* (Louisville, Ky.: Westminster/ John Knox Press, 1994); Tikva Frymer-Kensky, *Motherprayer: The Pregnant Woman's Spiritual Companion* (New York: Riverhead Books, 1995); Marjorie Procter-Smith, *In Her Own Rite: Constructing Feminist Liturgical Tradition* (Nashville, Tenn.: Abingdon Press, 1990).

140. Susan Starr Sered, "Childbirth as a Religious Experience?: Voices from an Israeli Hospital," *Journal for the Feminist Study of Religion* 7, no. 2 (1991): 7–18; Kathryn Rabuzzi, *Mother with Child: Transformations through Childbirth* (Bloomington: Indiana University Press, 1994); Bonnie J. Miller-McLemore, *Also a Mother: Work and Family as Theological Dilemma* (Nashville, Tenn.: Abingdon Press, 1994).

141. In a noteworthy parallel, Rita M. Gross found that scholars of Australian aborigines ignored the religious dimensions of childbirth, for both men *and* women, in their emphasis on men's rituals to the exclusion of women's. Gross, "Menstruation and Childbirth as Ritual and Religious Experience among Native Australians."

142. Robert A. Orsi, *Thank You, St. Jude: Women's Devotion to the Patron Saint of Hopeless Causes* (New Haven: Yale University Press, 1996), 66.

143. Judith Schott and Alix Henley, *Culture, Religion and Childbearing in a Multiracial Society: A Handbook for Health Professionals* (Oxford: Butterworth-Heinemann, 1996).

144. Meredith McGuire, "Religion and the Body: Rematerializing the Human Body in the Social Sciences of Religion," *Journal for the Scientific Study of Religion*. 29, no. 3 (1990): 283–296.

145. Ibid., 284–285.

146. The mindful body is drawn from Nancy Scheper-Hughes and Margaret Lock, "The Mindful Body: A Prolegomenon to Future Work in Medical Anthropology," *Medical Anthropology Quarterly* 1, no. 1 (1987): 6–41. See also Karen McCarthy Brown, "Serving the Spirits: The Ritual Economy of Haitian Vodou," in *Sacred Arts of Haitian Vodou*, ed. Donald J. Cosentino (Los Angeles: UCLA Fowler Museum of Cultural History, 1995), 205.

Chapter 3
Risk, Fear, and the Ethics of Home Birth

1. Preeclampsia, also know as toxemia and pregnancy-induced hypertension, is a type of high blood pressure peculiar to pregnancy that can lead to convulsions and organ damage in the mother. If it begins in the early stages of labor, as in Kathryn's case, the contractions are particularly strong and close together as the uterus tries to expel the fetus immediately. This severity of preeclampsia usually requires a cesarean section. Janet Balaskas and Yehudi Gordon, *The Encyclopedia of Pregnancy and Birth* (London: Little, Brown, 1992), 315.

2. For example, see the interview with Dr. Yvonne Thornton and midwife Ina May Gaskin on National Public Radio's "Talk of the Nation," on 31 March 1999.

3. John A. Robertson, quoted in Christine Overall, *Ethics and Human Reproduction: A Feminist Analysis* (Boston: Allen & Unwin, 1987), 98.

4. T. A. Wiegers, M.J.N.C. Keirse, J. van der Zee, and G.A.H. Berghs, "Outcome of Planned Home and Planned Hospital Births in Low Risk Pregnancies: Prospective Study in Midwifery Practices in the Netherlands," *British Medical Journal* 313 (23 November 1996): 1309–1313; and Ursula Ackerman-Liebrich et al., "Home versus Hospital Deliveries: Follow Up Study of Matched Pairs for Procedures and Outcomes," *British Medical Journal* 313 (23 November 1996): 1313–1318.

5. Carol P. MacCormack, "Risk, Prevention, and International Health Policy," in *Gender and Health: An International Perspective*, ed. Carolyn F. Sargent and Caroline B. Brettell (Upper Saddle River, N.J.: Prentice-Hall., 1996), 326–337.

6. On risk, see Mary Douglas, *Risk and Blame: Essays in Cultural Theory* (New York: Routledge, 1992).

7. Janelle S. Taylor, "Of Sonograms and Baby Prams: Prenatal Diagnosis, Pregnancy, and Consumption," *Feminist Studies* 26, no. 2 (2000): 391–418.

8. For example, most home-birthing women elect to forgo obstetrical ultrasound testing, out of both a concern about its safety and a desire to maintain the "mystery" of birth. See Eugene R. Declercq, Lisa L. Paine, and Michael R. Winter, "Home Birth in the United States, 1989–1992: A Longitudinal Descriptive Report of National Birth Certificate Data," *Journal of Nurse-Midwifery* 40, no. 6 (1995): 480.

9. Sara Ruddick, "Thinking Mothers/Conceiving Birth," in *Representations of Motherhood*, ed. Donna Basin, Margaret Honey, and Meryle Kaplan (New Haven: Yale University Press, 1994), 43.

10. Ibid., 44.

11. Carol Delaney, *Abraham on Trial: The Social Legacy of Biblical Myth* (Princeton: Princeton University Press, 1998), 7.

12. Ibid., 8.

13. Ibid., 7.

14. Susan L. Mizruchi, *The Science of Sacrifice: American Literature and Modern Social Theory* (Princeton: Princeton University Press, 1998), 210.

15. In Asad's words: "The concept of agency has been invoked, endorsed, and celebrated. It has not, to my knowledge, been systematically examined by analysts of culture." Talal Asad, "Agency and Pain: An Exploration" in *Culture and Religion* 1, no. 1 (2000): 29.

16. Ibid.

17. Ibid., 32–33.

18. Marsden Wagner, "Confessions of a Dissident," in *Childbirth and Authoritative Knowledge: Cross-Cultural Perspectives*, ed. R. E. Davis-Floyd and C. Sargent (Berkeley: University of California Press, 1997), 366–393. For a discussion of a medical perspective supportive of home birth, and the resistance it engenders, see Wagner's full article.

19. OMA Committee on Reproductive Care, "OMA Issues Revised Statement on Planned Home Births," *Ontario Medical Review* (May 1994): 36.

20. James W. Goodwin, "Where to Be Born Safely: Professional Midwifery and the Case against Home Birth," *Journal of the Society of Obstetricians and Gynecologists of Canada* 19, no. 11 (1997): 1187.

21. Ibid., 1186.

22. Sheryl Burt Ruzek, "Ethical Issues in Childbirth Technology," in *Birth Control and Controlling Birth: Women-Centered Perspectives*, ed. Helen B. Holmes, Betty B. Hoskins, and Michael Gross (Clifton, N.J.: Humana Press, 1980), 200.

23. American College of Nurse-Midwives Website, "ACNM Philosophy," 1989; accessed 21 May 1999: http://acnm.org.

24. Midwives Alliance of North America Website, "MANA Core Competencies for Basis Midwifery Practice," 1994; accessed 21 May 1999: http://www.mana.org/manacore.html

25. Judith Dickson Luce, "Ethical Issues Relating to Childbirth as Experienced by the Birthing Woman and Midwife," in *Birth Control and Controlling Birth*, 243.

26. See also Rebecca Sarah, "Power, Certainty and the Fear of Death," *Women & Health* 13, no. 1-2 (1987): 59–71.

27. Patricia Kaufert and John O'Neil, "Analysis of a Dialogue on Risks in Childbirth: Clinicians, Epidemiologists, and Inuit Women," in *Knowledge, Power, and Practice: The Anthropology of Medicine and Everyday Life*, ed. Shirley Lindenbaum and Margaret Lock (Berkeley: University of California Press, 1993), 46.

28. Ibid., 40.

29. Ibid., 47.

30. Paul A. Komesaroff, "Introduction," in *Troubled Bodies*, ed. Paul A. Komesaroff (Durham: Duke University Press, 1995), 4.

31. See also Valerie Hartouni, "Containing Women: Reproductive Discourse in the 1980s," in *Technoculture*, ed. Constance Penley and Andrew Ross (Minneapolis: University of Minnesota Press, 1991), 33.

32. Kathleen Norris, *The Cloister Walk* (New York: Riverhead Books, 1996), 24.

33. For several reflections on the religious meanings of birth, see the special issue of the *Scottish Journal of Religious Studies*, entitled "Beginning with Birth?" 19, no. 1 (1998).

34. Cotton Mather, *Ornaments for the Daughters of Zion*, reprint of the 3d ed. (Delmar, N.Y.: Scholars' Facsimiles and Reprints, 1978 [1741]). See also Nancy Cott's discussion of Mather's assertion in Nancy F. Cott, *The Bonds of Womanhood: "Woman's Sphere" in New England, 1780–1835* (New Haven: Yale University Press, 1977), 136. For a similar theme in Rabbinic Judaism, see also Daniel Boyarin, *Carnal Israel: Reading Sex in Talmudic Culture* (Berkeley: University of California Press, 1993), 92.

35. Phyllis Mack, personal communication, 23 June 1998. For Mack's analysis of the differences between this kind of "shamanic motherhood" and what she calls "spiritual motherhood" among eighteenth-century Methodists, see Phyllis Mack, "Giving Birth to the Truth," *Scottish Journal of Religious Studies* 19, no. 1 (1998): 19–30.

36. Blessing Way ceremonies are traditionally Navaho, but in Navaho communities they can be protective rituals for anyone from a pregnant woman about to birth to a man about to leave the community to join the army. Euro-American adaptations or appropriations of the Blessing Way may have little to do with the tradition as practiced among Navahos. See Clyde Kluckhohn and Dorothea Leighton, *The Navaho* (Cambridge: Harvard University Press, 1974), 212; and Louise Lamphere, *To Run After Them: Cultural and Social Bases of Cooperation in a Navajo Community* (Tucson: University of Arizona Press, 1977), 28.

37. Jeannine Parvati Baker, "The Shamanic Dimension of Childbirth," *Pre- and Perinatal Psychology Journal* 7, no. 1 (1992): 7.

38. For example, see Sheila Kitzinger, *Home Birth: The Essential Guide to Giving Birth Outside the Hospital* (New York: Dorling Kindersley, 1991), 100–101.

39. Jeannine Parvati Baker, "Shamanic Midwifery: Every Mother a Midwife," paper (Junction, Utah: Freestone Publishing, n.d.), 3.

40. Nancy Wainer Cohen, *Open Season: Survival Guide for Natural Childbirth and VBAC in the 90s* (New York: Bergin and Garvey, 1991), 212.

41. Beth C. Junker, "Transition in Childbirth: Claiming our own Death and Resurrection," *Daughters of Sarah* 18, no. 4 (1992): 7.

42. On women fearing more for the lives of their babies than their own, see Susan Starr Sered "Childbirth as a Religious Experience?: Voices from an Israeli Hospital," *Journal for the Feminist Study of Religion* 7, no. 2 (1991): 14.

43. U.S. Bureau of the Census, *Statistical Abstract of the United States: 1996*. 116th ed. (Washington, D.C.: U.S. Government, 1996), 92; and Marsha E. Jackson and Alice J. Bailes, "Home Birth with Certified Nurse-Midwife Attendants in the United States," *Journal of Nurse-Midwifery* 40, no. 6 (1995): 500.

44. Rondi E. Anderson and Patricia Aikins Murphy, "Outcomes of 11,788 Planned Home Births Attended by Certified Nurse-Midwives: A Retrospective

Descriptive Study," *Journal of Nurse-Midwifery* 40, no. 6 (1995): 483; see also Wiegers et al., "Outcome of Planned Home and Planned Hospital Births in Low Risk Pregnancies."

45. Only 3 of the 45 women I spoke with initiated contact in this way.

46. Kathryn had chosen to have an ultrasound during her pregnancy, but the doctors analyzing the results did not detect her baby's condition.

47. Kathryn put the rate of naturally occurring miscarriage at 25 percent of all fertilized eggs, but nature is even less of a life-lover than she thought: only about 25 percent of fertilizations result in the *birth* of a live child. Many of these miscarriages are not even noticed, since the egg does not implant in the uterus. Balaskas and Gordon, *The Encyclopedia of Pregnancy and Birth*, 323.

48. Rebecca Sarah offers a similar view as a direct-entry midwife critical of both medical and midwifery tendencies to want complete power over life and death: "Unrealistic expectations of reproductive technologies among some doctors, technicians and childbearing women are matched by unrealistic expectations of nature and women's bodies by others, including people in the feminist and women's health movement." Sarah, "Power, Certainty and the Fear of Death," 60–61.

49. Rosi Braidotti, *Nomadic Subjects: Embodiment and Sexual Difference in Contemporary Feminist Theory* (New York: Columbia University Press, 1994), 81.

50. Ellen M. Umansky, "Finding God: Women in the Jewish Tradition," *Cross Currents* 41, no. 4 (1991): 528. Olivia Eldrich also remembered learning that "God was in everything" during her childhood days in Hebrew School.

51. Umansky, "Finding God," 533.

52. Norma Swenson, "Childbirth Overview," in *Birth Control and Controlling Birth: Women-Centered Perspectives*, ed. Helen B. Holmes, Betty B. Hoskins, and Michael Gross (Garden City, N.J.: Humana Press, 1980), 146.

53. Marion Sousa, *Childbirth at Home* (New York: Bantam, 1976), 98; and Ina May Gaskin, *Spiritual Midwifery*, 3d ed. (Summertown, Tenn.: Book Publishing Company, 1990), 14.

54. David Stewart and Lee Stewart, in Paula A. Treichler, "Feminism, Medicine, and the Meaning of Childbirth," in *Body Politics: Women, Literature, and the Discourse of Science*, ed. Mary Jacobus, Evelyn Fox Keller, and Sally Shuttleworth (New York: Routledge, Chapman, and Hall, 1990), 121. David and Lee Stewart are home-birth activists involved in NAPSAC.

55. Treichler, "Feminism, Medicine, and the Meaning of Childbirth," 115.

56. Many Amish women, though not those with whom I spoke, also choose direct-entry midwives. Louise Acheson, "Perinatal, Infant, and Child Death Rates among the Old Order Amish," abstracted in *Birth Gazette* 11, no. 3 (1995), 36; and Karla Campanella, Jill E. Korbin, and Louise Acheson, "Pregnancy and Childbirth among the Amish," *Social Science and Medicine* 36, no. 3 (1993): 333.

57. Vitamin K injections given to the infant to prevent hemorrhage are another such procedure. Robbie Davis-Floyd argued that the standardization of these procedures, instead of deciding upon them case by case, has meant that "these postpartum procedures form the modern structural equivalent of baptism: they symbolically enculturate the newborn, removing her step-by-step from the natural realm through restructuring her very physiology in accordance with technocratic

standardization." Robbie Davis-Floyd, *Birth as an American Rite of Passage* (Berkeley: University of California Press, 1992), 139.

58. A key argument in such cases is that "midwifery is not the practice of medicine" and thus midwives should not be prosecuted for practicing medicine without a license. Suzanne Hope Suarez, "Midwifery Is Not the Practice of Medicine," *Yale Journal of Law and Feminism* 5 (1993).

59. Jessica. Mitford, "Afterword," in Mitford, *The American Way of Birth*, reprinted in Birth Gazette 9, no. 3 (1993): 16.

60. Davis-Floyd, *Birth as an American Rite of Passage*, 160. I deal with the family in terms of the "nuclear family" here, since most of the women I interviewed lived in such arrangements. Some lived within communities, like the Amish and Christian Scientists, but their homes still comprised a mother, a father, and children. In addition, one woman was divorced and not remarried, and another woman had her grandmother living with her.

61. Jane Collier, Michelle Z. Rosaldo, and Sylvia Yanagisako, "Is There a Family?" in *Rethinking the Family: Some Feminist Questions*, 2d ed., ed. Barrie Thorne with Marilyn Yalom (Boston: Northeastern University Press, 1992), 43.

62. Linda J. Nicholson, *Gender and History: The Limits of Social Theory in the Age of the Family* (New York: Columbia University Press, 1986), 114.

63. Ibid., 106, 112.

64. The allegiances among what Mitchell Stevens calls "earth-based" and "heaven-based" homeschoolers, however, are also beset by some serious disagreements. See Mitchell Stevens, *Kingdom of Children: Culture and Controversy in the Homeschooling Movement* (Princeton: Princeton University Press, forthcoming), especially ch. 4.

65. Cynthia Ann Naragon, "Childbirth at Home: A Descriptive Study of 675 Couples Who Chose Home Birth" (Ph.D. diss., California School of Professional Psychology, 1980), 51.

66. Brenda Waugh, "Repro-Woman: A View of the Labyrinth (from the Lithotomy Position)," *Yale Journal of Law and Feminism*. 3, no. 9 (1991).

67. Faye D. Ginsburg, *Contested Lives: The Abortion Debate in an American Community* (Berkeley: University of California Press, 1989), 215.

68. Ibid., 144, 219.

69. Quoted in Margaret L. Hammer, *Giving Birth: Reclaiming Biblical Metaphor for Pastoral Practice* (Louisville, Ky.: Westminster/John Knox Press, 1994), 197, n. 18.

70. Robbie Davis-Floyd pointed to tensions within MANA, the national direct-entry midwives association, between Christian midwives and those espousing feminist spirituality and repudiating homophobia (personal communication, 30 October 1995). For a perspective on religious diversity within the parallel nurse-midwife association, the ACNM, see Gwendolyn V. Spears, "Melting Pot vs. Salad Bowl," *Quickening: Bimonthly Publication of the American College of Nurse-Midwives* 26, no. 4 (1995): 5.

71. Jan Thomas. "Politics and Pregnancy: The Contested Terrain of Childbirth in Ohio," paper presented at the American Sociological Association Annual Meeting, San Francisco, August 1998.

72. MANA, in contrast to the American College of Nurse-Midwives, is home to many "spiritual midwives" of all stripes, and its constituency and publications make liberal use of spirituality in describing midwifery and in advocating its benefits. For example, see Agneta Bergenheim, "Spiritual Emergency Treatment of the Newborn," *Birth Gazette* 11, no. 3 (1995): 14–15; and Gaskin, *Spiritual Midwifery.*

73. Midwives Alliance of North America (MANA), "Statement of Core Values and Ethics." *MANA News* 10, no. 4 (1992): 10–12.

74. MANA member, personal communication, 2 November 1998.

75. Ginsburg, *Contested Lives,* 213.

76. On the effects of ultrasound, see Barbara Duden, *Disembodying Women: Perspectives on Pregnancy and the Unborn* (Cambridge: Harvard, 1993); on court-ordered Caesareans see George Annas, "Forced Cesareans: The Most Unkindest Cut of All," *Hastings Center Report* 12, no. 3 (1982): 16–17, 45; and Janet Gallagher, "Prenatal Invasions & Interventions: What's Wrong with Fetal Rights," *Harvard Women's Law Journal* 10 (1987): 9–58. On gestational substance abuse, see Julia Epstein, *Altered Conditions: Disease, Medicine, and Storytelling* (New York: Routledge, 1995), 124; and Janet Gallagher, "Collective Bad Faith: 'Protecting the Fetus,'" in *Reproduction, Ethics, and the Law: Feminist Perspectives,* ed. Joan C. Callahan (Bloomington: Indiana University Press, 1994), 343–379.

77. Judy Pasternak, "Custody of Unborn Child Faces Court Test," *Los Angeles Times,* 2 February 1997. I thank Sherrill Cohen for this reference and for providing me with Janet Gallagher's work.

78. Gallagher, "Collective Bad Faith," 345.

79. Viviana A. Zelizer, *Pricing the Priceless Child: The Changing Social Value of Children* (Princeton: Princeton University Press, 1994), 11. Zelizer's broader argument asserts that children were "sacralized" as they shifted from useful laborers to "useless" children in the nineteenth and twentieth centuries.

80. Ibid., 227.

81. I thank Bob Gibbs for helping me to clarify this point.

82. Caroline Walker Bynum, *Fragmentation and Redemption: Essays on Gender and the Human Body in Medieval Religion* (New York: Zone Books, 1991), 297.

83. Stacey Pigg, "Authority in Translation: Finding, Knowing, Naming, and Training 'Traditional Birth Attendants' in Nepal," *Childbirth and Authoritative Knowledge: Cross-Cultural Perspectives,* ed. Robbie E. Davis-Floyd and Carolyn F. Sargent (Berkeley: University of California Press, 1997), 233–262.

84. For an eloquent analysis of the ironies and complexities of the connections between Western and non-Western ways of childbirth that pays attention to questions of religion, fear, and death, see Janice Boddy, "Remembering Amal: On Birth and the British in Northern Sudan," in *Pragmatic Women and Body Politics,* ed. M. Lock and P. A. Kaufert (Cambridge: Cambridge University Press, 1998), 28–57.

Chapter 4
Procreating Religion: Spirituality, Religion,
and the Transformations of Birth

1. Quoted in Lesley A. Northup, *Ritualizing Women: Patterns of Spirituality* (Cleveland: Pilgrim Press, 1997), 17.

2. Lori Hope Lefkowitz, "Sacred Screaming: Childbirth in Judaism" in *Lifecycles: Jewish Women on Life Passages and Personal Milestones*, vol. 1, ed. Rabbi Debra Orenstein (Woodstock, Vt.: Jewish Lights Publishing, 1994), 5. For a parallel Christian perspective, see Kari Sandhaas, "Birth, Choice, and the Abuse of the Sacred: A Personal Story of Resistance," *Daughters of Sarah* 18, no. 4 (1992): 8–11.

3. Linda Layne, "Of Fetuses and Angels: Fragmentation and Integration in Narratives of Pregnancy Loss," *Knowledge and Society: The Anthropology of Science and Technology* 9 (1992): 29–58; and Rayna Rapp, "Accounting for Amniocentesis," in *Knowledge, Power, and Practice: The Anthropology of Medicine and Everyday Life*, ed. S. Lindenbaum and M. Lock (Berkeley: University of California Press, 1993), 55–78. See also Rayna Rapp, *Testing Women, Testing the Fetus: The Social Impact of Amniocentesis in America* (New York and London: Routledge, 1999).

4. Tikva Frymer-Kensky, author of *Motherprayer*, is a Reconstructionist rabbi and a scholar of the Hebrew Bible. Margaret Hammer, author of *A Spiritual Guide through Pregnancy*, is a Lutheran pastor.

5. For an analysis of this contemporary turn to spirituality, see Robert Wuthnow, *After Heaven: Spirituality in America since the 1950s* (Berkeley: University of California Press, 1998).

6. Though using both terms (religion and spirituality) in this question may have set up a dichotomy in the minds of some women, I did not want to use only one of the terms in case the one I chose had little meaning for the woman. Our conversations often turned to the very question of the nature of the difference between religion and spirituality.

7. Stephanie Kirkwood Walker, *This Woman in Particular: Contexts for the Biographical Image of Emily Carr* (Waterloo, Ont.: Wilfrid Laurier University Press, 1996), 126.

8. Catherine Albanese, "Religion and the American Experience: A Century After," *Church History* 57 (September 1988): 337–351; Wade Clark Roof, *A Generation of Seekers: The Spiritual Journeys of the Baby Boom Generation* (San Francisco: HarperSanFrancisco, 1993).

9. Roof, *A Generation of Seekers*, 76–77. Roof's examples here are perhaps ill-chosen, since lighting Hanukkah candles is an act of institutionally sanctioned domestic piety, but one that, given its location in the home, has been transformed in many ways by the women who practice it. Furthermore, Roof's terminology is confusing at times as he simultaneously asserts that *religion* in America is "deeply personal . . . and against any kind of organizational involvement." Roof, *A Generation of Seekers*, 105. As well, his figures show that the majority of people consider themselves both religious *and* spiritual.

10. Amanda Porterfield, in Jody Shapiro Davie, *Women in the Presence* (Philadelphia: University of Pennsylvania Press, 1995), 12. See also Amanda Porterfield,

Feminine Spirituality in America: From Sarah Edwards to Martha Graham (Philadelphia: Temple University Press, 1980). As well, Margaret Chatterjee described
spirituality as the "desire to avoid the reified concept of religion per se, a stress on
ambience rather than on belief, and a wish to point up the experiential." Margaret
Chatterjee, "The Smorgasbord Syndrome: Availability Reexamined," in *Modern
Spiritualities: An Inquiry*, ed. Laurence Brown, Bernard C. Farr, and R. Joseph
Hoffman (Oxford: Prometheus, 1997), 29.

11. Roof, *A Generation of Seekers*, 68.

12. Ibid., 105.

13. T. J. Jackson Lears, "From Salvation to Self-Realization," in *The Culture of
Consumption: Critical Essays in American History*, ed. Richard W. Fox and T. J.
Jackson Lears (New York: Pantheon, 1983), 4.

14. Ibid., 4.

15. Ibid., 8.

16. See also Una Kroll, "A Womb-Centered Life," in *Sex and God: Some Varieties of Women's Religious Experience*, ed. Linda Hurcombe (New York: Routledge
and Paul Kegan, 1987), 92.

17. A common warning in home-birth literature, however, is to avoid choosing
home birth just because it is less expensive. In this view, a woman must want to
give birth at home for more than economic reasons if she is to feel safe and be
successful. Tracy Leal, "Consumerism and Birth Care," *New Jersey Friends of Midwives Newsletter* (Holiday Issue) 8-9 (1995); Helen Wessel, *Under the Apple Tree:
Marrying, Birthing, Parenting* (Fresno, Calif.: Bookmates International, 1981).

18. Robert Wuthnow, *Acts of Compassion: Caring for Others and Helping Ourselves* (Princeton: Princeton University Press, 1991), 153, 156.

19. About half of the women in this study were involved in La Leche League
as participants and as league leaders. LLL leaders are required to give only breast-
feeding advice and not to promote other issues, such as home birth, at meetings.
But given the conversational structure of meetings, many women spoke of learning
there about home birth and practicing midwives. One woman reported first thinking seriously about home birth when at an LLL meeting where all the women told
their birth stories, and more than half of the women had given birth at home,
with midwives.

20. On the uses of "energy," see David J. Hess, *Science in the New Age: The
Paranormal, Its Defenders and Debunkers, and American Culture* (Madison: University of Wisconsin Press, 1993).

21. Peter H. Van Ness, "Introduction: Spirituality and the Secular Quest," in
Spirituality and the Secular Quest, ed. Peter Van Ness (New York: Crossroad,
1996), 1.

22. I would hazard that Van Ness's link between viewing sex as sacred and
being distant from biblical tenets is a particularly Christian assumption. One of
the main differences between Jewish and Christian views of childbirth in particular lies in their divergent appreciation of sexuality and fertility. Generally speaking,
while Christianity has a long tradition valuing asceticism and virginity, Judaism
has historically (both because of its persecuted status and because of its attitudes
to the body and sexuality) celebrated the birth of children. Daniel Boyarin pointed
to late antique examples within both Christianity and Judaism where "autonomy

and power are bought for women at the cost of their sexuality," but he also noted the overwhelming support of sexuality within marriage in rabbinic Judaism. Daniel Boyarin, *Carnal Israel: Reading Sex in Talmudic Culture* (Berkeley: University of California Press, 1993), 75, 168.

23. For an example of a home-birth activist who ties childbirth, sexuality, and Scripture together from a Catholic perspective, see Marilyn Moran, *Birth and the Dialogue of Love* (Leawood, Kans.: New Nativity Press, 1981).

24. Sherry B. Ortner, *Making Gender: The Politics and Erotics of Culture* (Boston: Beacon Press, 1996), 184.

25. For a discussion of the centrality of marriage and motherhood to women in Orthodox Judaism, see Lynn Davidman, *Tradition in a Rootless World: Women Turn to Orthodox Judaism* (Berkeley: University of California Press, 1991), esp. ch. 5.

26. Ina May Gaskin, *Spiritual Midwifery*, 3d ed. (Summertown, Tenn.: Book Publishing Company, 1990).

27. Generally speaking, when referring to birth, women usually meant childbirth in which women were awake, aware, and respected during the process.

28. Marsha G. Witten, *The Secular Message in American Protestantism* (Princeton: Princeton University Press, 1993), 53.

29. Frederick Leboyer, *Birth without Violence* (New York: Alfred A. Knopf, 1978). Agneta Bergenheim, a Swedish midwife, felt that giving physical and eye contact and talking to the newborn were ways to "ground" an infant as he or she makes the transition to life on earth. Agneta Bergenheim, "Spiritual Emergency Treatment of the Newborn," *Birth Gazette* 11, no. 3 (1995): 15.

30. The Shema is a daily prayer drawn from Deuteronomy 6:4–9, and begins "Hear, O Israel: The Lord is our God, the Lord alone." Verse 7 is particularly relevant in this case: "Recite [these words] to your children and talk about them when you are at home and when you are away, when you lie down and when you rise." The prayer as a whole affirms monotheism and God's creativity.

31. Though I asked all the women whether the Virgin Mary was significant for their experiences of childbirth, only a couple assented, and they said her humanity and motherly qualities made her attractive. Traditional Catholic Marianne Martin said Mary was not important to her births because she had not actually suffered in childbirth, since Jesus had passed through her as a "ray of light." While the notion of Mary's postpartum virginity was the subject of much medieval poetry and song, and was affirmed by the sixteenth-century Council of Trent, it was not proclaimed an article of faith by the Second Vatican Council in 1964 (for whose reforms Marianne had little respect). Marina Warner, *Alone of All Her Sex: The Myth and the Cult of the Virgin Mary* (London: Picador, 1976), 45.

32. Gayatri Chakravorty Spivak, *Outside in the Teaching Machine* (New York: Routledge, 1993), 3.

33. Albanese, "Religion and the American Experience," 347.

34. Ibid., 349–350.

35. Copeland is the author of over twenty books, a number of which deal with healing. Historian Grant Wacker situated Copeland as a leader in "prosperity evangelism, or the 'Faith Confession' movement," which holds that "there are foundational spiritual laws in the world which, like the laws of physics, are universal and

immutable." Grant Wacker, "The Pentecostal Tradition," in *Caring and Curing: Health and Medicine in the Western Religious Traditions*, ed. Ronald L. Numbers and Darrel W. Amundsen (New York: MacMillan, 1986), 528. While Wacker discussed generous returns on extravagant financial giving to televangelists as one of these laws, the sense of the body following spiritual laws was most important to these women in the context of birth.

36. This book, written by Gladys West Hendrick, advised parents to rigidly schedule their babies' feeding times so that they would sleep through the night at a few weeks of age. Most home-birthing women (and others who breast-feed) would be aghast at such advice, given their practice of breast-feeding their infants "on demand." See Gladys West Hendrick. *My First 300 Babies* (Santa Ana, Calif.: Vision House Publishers, 1978).

37. Lois Paul and B. Paul, "The Maya Midwife as a Sacred Specialist: A Guatemalan Case," *American Ethnologist* 2 (1975): 707–726; Molly C. Dougherty, "Southern Lay Midwives as Ritual Specialists," in *Women in Ritual and Symbolic Roles*, ed. Judith Hoch-Smith and Anita Spring (New York: Plenum Press, 1978), 151–164; Gaskin, *Spiritual Midwifery*; Carol Balizet, *Born in Zion*, 3d ed. (Grapevine, Tex.: Perazim House, 1996).

38. I say this based on interviews with four midwives and on the stories their clients told me.

39. Arthur Kleinman, *Patients and Healers in the Context of Culture* (Berkeley: University of California Press, 1980).

40. Even women who decried the negative effects of biomedicine used it to some degree in understanding the physiology of birth.

41. Susan Starr Sered, *Priestess, Mother, Sacred Sister: Religions Dominated by Women* (New York: Oxford University Press, 1994), 117.

42. Ibid., 110.

43. Talal Asad, *Genealogies of Religion: Discipline and Reasons of Power in Christianity and Islam* (Baltimore: Johns Hopkins University Press, 1993), 45.

44. Ibid., 54.

45. Ibid., 43.

46. For more reflection on the history of "religion" as a second-order category and not necessarily a native term, see Jonathan Z. Smith, "Religion, Religions, Religious," in *Critical Terms for Religious Studies*, ed. Mark C. Taylor (Chicago: University of Chicago Press, 1998), 269- 284.

47. For examples of other scholars who analyze religion in unconventional settings, see Rebecca Kneale Gould, "Getting (Not Too) Close to Nature: Modern Homesteading as Lived Religion in America," in *Lived Religion in America: Toward a History of Practice*, ed. David D. Hall (Princeton: Princeton University Press, 1997), 217–242; and Michelle Mary Lelwica, *Starving for Salvation: The Spiritual Dimensions of Eating Problems among American Girls and Women* (New York: Oxford University Press, 1999).

48. For an example of the former view, see Van Ness, "Introduction," 5.

49. For a clear argument that discusses how sacrificial religions supplant childbirth, see the work of Nancy Jay, *Throughout Your Generations Forever: Sacrifice, Religion, and Paternity* (Chicago: University of Chicago Press, 1992), 147.

50. Margaret Hammer, in her appeal for Christian clergy to develop a "birthing ministry," argued that clergy in hospitals generally do not attend to healthy births. Instead, they focus on "providing 'pastoral care and grief services in the hospital for people who are experiencing a high-risk pregnancy' or other childbearing difficulty or tragedy." Margaret L. Hammer, *Giving Birth: Reclaiming Biblical Metaphor for Pastoral Practice* (Louisville, Ky.: Westminster/John Knox Press, 1994), 182. While some women in my study spoke of their ministers (particularly female ones) as supportive of their home birth, most said their clergy had nothing to do with the birth. Within Judaism two radically different approaches to childbirth are found in the work of Tikva Frymer-Kensky, a Reconstructionist Jew, and that of Baruch Finkelstein and Michal Finkelstein, who, from an Orthodox perspective, compiled a "halachic guide" to childbirth that warns against home birth. Baruch Finkelstein and Michal Finkelstein, *B'Sha'ah Tovah: The Jewish Woman's Clinical and Halachic Guide to Pregnancy and Childbirth* (Jerusalem and New York: Feldheim Publishers, 1993); Frymer-Kensky, *Motherprayer*.

51. Regarding women's health more generally, Susan Sered argues that "in many cultural situations the male-dominated religion does not offer women adequate responses to suffering." Sered, *Priestess, Mother, Sacred Sister*, 111.

52. Susan Starr Sered, "Childbirth as a Religious Experience?: Voices from an Israeli Hospital," *Journal for the Feminist Study of Religion* 7, no. 2 (1991): 15.

53. Kari Sandhaas, a Christian feminist, described her own hospital birth experience as an "abuse of the sacred" that was "akin to rape." She castigated both medical models of birth and "theological assumptions and acquiescence which have allowed this system to develop and our bodies to be treated as cadavers." Sandhaas, "Abuse of the Sacred," 8–9, 11. For the perspectives of a Catholic and a Mormon woman who described both the difficulties and possibilities of making one's hospital birth a religious experience, see Leonie Caldecott, "Inner Anatomy of a Birth," in *Sex and God: Some Varieties of Women's Religious Experience*, ed. Linda Hurcombe (New York: Routledge and Kegan Paul, 1987), 147–160; and Maureen Ursenbach Beecher, "Birthing," in *Mormon Women Speak*, ed. May Lythgoe Bradford (Salt Lake City: Olympus, 1982), 45–55.

54. Nancy Scheper-Hughes, *Death without Weeping: The Violence of Everyday Life in Brazil* (Berkeley: University of California Press, 1992), 356. Scheper-Hughes discussed women living in extreme poverty with little means to nourish their babies (especially since they had given up breast-feeding due to complex social, cultural, and economic effects of industrialization). These women deemed their sickly infants, who seemed unlikely to survive, babies who were "born already *wanting* to die," but cared assiduously for those babies seen to have *forca*, or a desire to live. Scheper-Hughes characterized the "maternal practices" of these women as based in a social context where "mortal selective neglect *and* intense maternal attachment coexist." Scheper-Hughes, *Death without Weeping*, 315, 356.

55. As Faye Ginsburg and Rayna Rapp phrased it, "The Western propensity to conflate biological and social parenthood" has significantly shaped anthropological preoccupations with "theories of kinship and the search for the universal nuclear family" and deflected attention from the wide variety of childcare practices used in North America as well as elsewhere. Faye D. Ginsburg and Rayna Rapp, "The Politics of Reproduction," *Annual Review of Anthropology* 20 (1991): 329.

56. Arnold Van Gennep, *The Rites of Passage* (Chicago: University of Chicago Press, 1960 [1908]), 13.

57. Ibid., 11.

58. Caroline Walker Bynum, *Fragmentation and Redemption: Essays on Gender and the Human Body in Medieval Religion* (New York: Zone Books, 1991), 48.

59. I am grateful to Karen McCarthy Brown for this insight, as well as for the reference to a parallel example of a woman enclosing herself in her home in order to achieve self-knowledge, found in Carol Christ's discussion of Doris Lessing's character, Martha Quest. Carol P. Christ, *Diving Deep and Surfacing: Women Writers on Spiritual Quest*, 2d ed. (Boston: Beacon Press, 1986), 67.

60. Van Gennep, *Rites of Passage*, 46.

61. Ibid., 12. Van Gennep does not make clear what the sacred means to him—whether it is a positive designation or simply a condition of being "set apart"—but he does provide a brief definition of religion. For him, religion is the combination of dynamistic (impersonal) and animistic (personalized) theories of power, and the techniques (ceremonies, rites, services) of this power are magic. He felt that theory and technique could not be separated, so preferred to use the term "magico-religious." Van Gennep, *Rites of Passage*, 13.

62. Robbie E. Davis-Floyd, *Birth as an American Rite of Passage* (Berkeley: University of California Press, 1992), 305.

63. Ibid., 65, 68.

64. Ibid., 72.

65. Ibid., 280. Davis-Floyd notes that there is a range of types of obstetricians in practice today, from "conservative" to "radical." One of her "radical" interviewees corroborated her view of "transcendence through technology" by stating that the majority of medical students who succeed emerge from their training with an "adoration of technology." Davis-Floyd, *Birth as an American Rite of Passage*, 269. See also Deborah Gordon on biomedicine as a religious worldview with its own claims to transcendence. Deborah R. Gordon, "Tenacious Assumptions in Western Medicine," in *Biomedicine Examined*, ed. Margaret Lock and Deborah R. Gordon (Dordrecht: Kluwer Academic, 1988), 19–56.

66. Jay, *Throughout Your Generations Forever*, 147.

67. Davis-Floyd, *Birth as an American Rite of Passage*, 137.

68. The ease with which many women talked of birth as a miracle puts a different, perhaps American, spin on Susan Sered's finding that birth is not considered a miracle in women's religions, because women's bodies are considered normative. Sered argued that such religions are not concerned with bodies or biological facts, but with social ties, so women's biological functions are not seen as "unique." Sered, *Priestess, Mother, Sacred Sister*, 139. In my research it was not spiritual feminists, but a Pentecostal woman (Carrie Ryan, see ch. 4) and Amish women who argued that birth was not really a miracle, but a process designed by God.

69. Starhawk, in Sered, *Priestess, Mother, Sacred Sister*, 140.

70. Husband-attended or husband-directed birth advocates, like Moran and Balizet, would point to Eva's comments as a troubling sign of displaced affections, dangerously close to homoeroticism. In this view, Eva's husband should have brought the flowers, and her love should have gone to him.

71. As religion scholar Catherine Bell noted about ritual more generally, "some ritualized practices distinguish themselves by their deliberate informality, although usually in contrast to a known tradition or style of ritualization." Catherine Bell, *Ritual Theory, Ritual Practice* (New York: Oxford University Press, 1992), 220.

72. Joanna felt that her husband was much more involved with her home birth than with her hospital birth, and that being at home allowed her daughters to be supportive of her in a way unlikely in the hospital (see ch. 7).

73. On these varieties of women's "ritualizing," see Northup, *Ritualizing Women*, 45.

74. Bell, *Ritual Theory, Ritual Practice*, 220, 223.

75. On the ways the midwifery model contests the pace of hospital birth, see Barbara Katz Rothman, "Midwives in Transition: The Structure of a Clinical Revolution," *Social Problems* 30, no. 3 (1983): 262–271.

76. On the ways space shapes the birthing body, see Margaret E. MacDonald, "Expectations: The Cultural Construction of Nature in Midwifery Discourses in Ontario," (Ph.D. diss., York University, Toronto, 1999).

77. Bell, *Ritual Theory, Ritual Practice*, 107. In her explication of ritual mastery, Bell borrowed significantly from Bourdieu and his notion of having a "feel for the game."

78. Ibid., 218.

79. Ibid., 99.

80. The phrase "echoes in the body" was used by Robert Orsi during a presentation to the Center for the Study of American Religion, 14 March 1997.

81. For the former opinion, see Barry A. Kosmin and Seymour P. Lachman, *One Nation Under God: Religion in Contemporary American Society* (New York: Harmony Books, 1993), 231. For the latter opinion, see Roof, *A Generation of Seekers*, 169.

82. For a useful summary of the contentiousness of life-cycle theories, especially in relation to gender, see Adele E. Clarke, "Women's Health: Life-Cycle Issues," in *Women, Health, and Medicine in America*, ed. Rima D. Apple (New York: Garland, 1990), 37. She specifically addressed problems of normativity and biological determinism embedded in such constructs.

83. Sered, "Childbirth as a Religious Experience," 11.

84. Ibid.

85. For example, Sered found that only the American-born women in her study "treated natural childbirth as a persuasive set of symbols and symbolic acts." Sered, "Childbirth as a Religious Experience," 10.

86. Ibid., 7.

87. Lynn Davidman found a similar dynamic in her study of women converts to Orthodox Judaism. Davidman, *Tradition in a Rootless World*, 133, 195.

88. Nancy F. Cott, *The Bonds of Womanhood: "Woman's Sphere" in New England, 1780–1835* (New Haven: Yale University Press, 1977), 200.

89. The idea that an infant's character can be shaped in the womb is not unique to home-birth advocates, but the notion that the process of birth itself has significance for a baby's personality is more so. For example, see the reference to the work of Janet Di Pietro, in Natalie Angier, "Baby in a Box," *New York Times Magazine*, 16 May 1999, pp. 86–90, 154.

90. See also Sered, *Priestess, Mother, Sacred Sister*, 111.

91. Sheilaism is a term coined by Bellah et al. to describe an approach to religion holding that each individual has his or her own version of faith. Robert N. Bellah et al., *Habits of the Heart: Individualism and Commitment in American Life* (New York: Harper and Row, 1985), 221. That a woman's name became synonymous with this approach, often disdained in academic circles, strikes me as a not-coincidentally sexist metonymy.

92. R. Marie Griffith, *God's Daughters: Evangelical Women and the Power of Submission* (Berkeley: University of California Press, 1997), 208. For a parallel example in the context of debates about abortion, see Faye D. Ginsburg, *Contested Lives: The Abortion Debate in an American Community* (Berkeley: University of California Press, 1989).

93. For examples, see Karen McCarthy Brown, *Mama Lola: A Vodou Priestess in Brooklyn* (Berkeley: University of California Press, 1991); and Sered, *Priestess, Mother, Sacred Sister.*

Chapter 5
A Sense of Place: Meanings of Home

1. For an important analysis of this "placelessness," from which I adapt my chapter title, see Joshua Meyrowitz, *No Sense of Place: The Impact of Electronic Media on Social Behaviour* (New York: Oxford University Press, 1985).

2. Orsi discussed the centrality of the mother to the Italian-American "domus," in Robert A. Orsi, *The Madonna of 115ᵗʰ Street: Faith and Community in Italian Harlem, 1880–1950* (New Haven: Yale University Press, 1985). Bachelard writes: "All really inhabited space bears the essence of the notion of home," and he describes the beginnings of life in the "bosom of the home." Gaston Bachelard, *The Poetics of Space*, trans. Maria Jolas (Boston: Beacon, 1964 [1958]). I was alerted to the Bachelard reference by Annemarie Klassen, "Human Dimensions of Space: Home," *Anima* 21, no. 1 (1994): 14–29.

3. For a cross-cultural perspective that cautions against universalizing Western "denigrations" of women and domesticity, see Marilyn Strathern, "Domesticity and the Denigration of Women," in *Rethinking Women's Roles: Perspectives from the Pacific*, ed. Denise O'Brien and Sharon W. Tiffany (Berkeley: University of California Press, 1984), 13–31.

4. Susan Starr Sered, *Priestess, Mother, Sacred Sister: Religions Dominated by Women* (New York: Oxford University Press, 1994), 150. On the importance of home to feminist ritualizing, see Lesley A. Northrup, *Ritualizing Women: Patterns of Spirituality* (Cleveland: Pilgrim Press, 1997).

5. Carol A. Stabile, *Feminism and the Technological Fix* (Manchester, UK: Manchester University Press, 1994), 134.

6. See also Robbie Davis-Floyd, *Birth as an American Rite of Passage* (Berkeley: University of California Press, 1992), 206.

7. Deborah A. Sullivan and Rose Weitz, *Labor Pains: Modern Midwives and Home Birth* (New Haven: Yale University Press, 1988), 133. In another example, a 1973 birth advice book written by a doctor called home birth "cultist, ignorant, and magical"—the latter being a negative term. Cherry, in Sandra E. Godwin,

"Mothers on Pedestals: A Look at Childbirth Advice Books and Julia Kristeva" (M.A. thesis, Boston College, 1993), 73.

8. Stanley K. Peck, in George Judson, "The Trials of an American Midwife," *New York Times*, 4 November 1995, 25, 29. In the popular press, home birth receives scattered attention. For example, an article on "medical vs. natural" childbirth in a parenting newspaper discussed certified nurse-midwives (cautioning readers to distinguish them from direct-entry midwives) but said nothing about home birth. Melanie Dhondt, "Birthing: Medical or Natural?" *Suburban Parent* 4–5 (4 January 1996): 4. More "alternative" publications, such as *Mothering* magazine, frequently publish articles on the benefits of home birth and midwifery.

9. For examples of home-birth activists' criticism of the pathologizing of birth, see Suzanne Arms, *Immaculate Deception: A New Look at Women and Childbirth in America* (New York: Bantam, 1977 [1975]), 64; Sheila Kitzinger, *Home Birth: The Essential Guide to Giving Birth Outside the Hospital* (New York: Dorling Kindersley, 1991), 15.

10. For a discussion of the religious dimensions of purity and pollution, see Mary Douglas, *Purity and Danger: An Analysis of the Concepts of Pollution and Taboo* (London and New York: Ark Paperbacks, 1984 [1966]).

11. Dr. Felix J. Underhill, in Sullivan and Weitz, *Labor Pains*, 11. Underhill was the director of the Mississippi Bureau of Child Hygiene.

12. Sullivan and Weitz, *Labor Pains*, 133. For an example of a midwife advising her colleagues to contest this stereotype through dressing "professionally," see Elizabeth Davis, *A Guide to Midwifery: Heart and Hands* (New York: Bantam, 1983). Phyllis Langton details the ongoing conflict between obstetricians and nurse-midwives, especially those who attend home births. Phyllis A. Langton, "Obstetricians' Resistance to Independent, Private Practice by Nurse-Midwives in Washington, D.C., Hospitals," *Women & Health*, 22, no. 1 (1994): 27–48.

13. Davis-Floyd, *Birth as an American Rite of Passage*, 182. For studies of the relative safety of home birth, see Rondi E. Anderson and Patricia Aikins Murphy, "Outcomes of 11,788 Planned Home Births Attended by Certified Nurse-Midwives: A Retrospective Descriptive Study," *Journal of Nurse-Midwifery* 40, no. 6 (1995): 483–492; Carol A. Sakala, "Midwifery Care and Out-of-Hospital Birth Settings: How Do They Reduce Unnecessary Cesarean Section Births?" *Social Science and Medicine* 37, no. 10 (1993): 1233–1250; and Suzanne Hope Suarez, "Midwifery Is Not the Practice of Medicine," *Yale Journal of Law and Feminism*, 5 (1993): 315–364.

14. Davis-Floyd, *Birth as an American Rite of Passage*, 184.

15. Ibid., 160.

16. Insurance is a troublesome issue for certified nurse-midwives, as the insurance industry and medical authorities have tried to restrict the ability of certified nurse-midwives to take out their own liability insurance. They have also ostracized or levied insurance premiums on doctors who have agreed to work with midwives, and have made it difficult for midwives to be reimbursed directly, instead of through a doctor. Certified nurse-midwives who attend home births sometimes do not even take out insurance, because suits against them are rare. American College of Nurse-Midwives (ACNM) and Sandra Jacobs, *Having Your Baby with a Nurse-Midwife* (New York: Hyperion, 1993):250; Judy Norsigian, "The Women's

Health Movement in the United States," in *Man-Made Medicine: Women's Health, Public Policy and Reform*, ed. Kary L. Moss (Durham: Duke University Press, 1996), 88.

17. See Jessica Mitford, *The American Way of Birth* (London: V. Gollancz, 1992).

18. Leslie Reagan, "Linking Midwives and Abortion in the Progressive Era," *Bulletin of the History of Medicine* 69 (1995): 573. I thank John Gager for alerting me to this reference.

19. For example, Balizet made a parallel between doctors' "naturally" unclean hands, as the cause of puerperal fever in the late nineteenth century, and their "spiritually" unclean hands, because of their abortion practices, as the cause of "contaminated" births today. Carol Balizet, *Born in Zion*, 3d ed. (Grapevine, Tex.: Perazim House, 1996), 67. For a similar position, in which he advised women to ask their obstetricians whether they performed abortions and to switch doctors if they did, see William Sears, *Christian Parenting and Child Care* (Nashville, Tenn.: Thomas Nelson, 1985), 383.

20. Balizet, *Born in Zion*, 59. Here Balizet referred to the entire medical system, which she considered "paganizing" and "dangerous," not only because of abortion practices, but also because of the widespread use of drugs and blood transfusions. Ibid., 177.

21. Ibid., 85

22. For a discussion of how romanticism continues to nurture a range of critiques of modernity, many of which women such as Meg would likely agree to, see Charlene Spretnak, *The Resurgence of the Real: Body, Nature and Place in a Hypermodern World* (Reading, Mass.: Addison Wesley, 1997).

23. On the importance of being on one's own turf during childbirth, see Brigitte Jordan, *Birth in Four Cultures*, 4th ed. (Prospect Heights, Ill.: Waveland Press, 1993 [1978]).

24. Nancy F. Cott, *The Bonds of Womanhood: "Woman's Sphere" in New England, 1780–1835* (New Haven: Yale University Press, 1977); Colleen McDannell, *The Christian Home in Victorian American, 1840–1900* (Bloomington: Indiana University Press, 1986).

25. Cott, *The Bonds of Womanhood*, 67; Barbara Leslie Epstein, *The Politics of Domesticity: Women, Evangelism, and Temperance in Nineteenth Century America* (Middletown, Conn.: Wesleyan University Press, 1981), 20. Cott nuances this view in a parenthetical remark that the practice of the "given-out" market, or what we now call "cottage industries," showed that the market was not necessarily so distinct from the home. Cott, *The Bonds of Womanhood*, 70. For a perspective on women's "homework" in postwar America, see Eileen Boris, "Mothers Are Not Workers: Homework Regulation and the Construction of Motherhood, 1948–1953," in *Mothering: Ideology, Experience, Agency*, ed. Evelyn Nakano Glenn, Grace Chang, and Linda Rennie Forcey (New York: Routledge, 1994), 32–54.

26. Barbara Epstein's work is an example of the former view. Epstein, *The Politics of Domesticity*, 149. Carroll Smith-Rosenberg's work is an example of the latter. Carroll Smith-Rosenberg, *Disorderly Conduct: Visions of Gender in Victorian America* (New York: Oxford University Press, 1985), 71.

27. Cott, *The Bonds of Womanhood*, 159; Patricia R. Hill, *The World Their Household: The American Woman's Foreign Mission Movement and Cultural Transformation, 1870–1920* (Ann Arbor: University of Michigan Press, 1985).

28. Ann Taves, *The Household of Faith: Roman Catholic Devotions in Mid-Nineteenth-Century America* (Notre Dame: University of Notre Dame Press, 1986); and Colleen McDannell, *The Christian Home*.

29. McDannell, *The Christian Home*, 154.

30. Sylvia D. Hoffert, *Private Matters: American Attitudes toward Childbearing and Infant Nurture in the Urban North, 1800–1860* (Urbana: University of Illinois Press, 1989), 9.

31. On support networks for childbirth, see Smith-Rosenberg, *Disorderly Conduct*, 70.

32. For a comprehensive summary of the uses historians have made of the metaphor of "separate spheres," see Linda K. Kerber, "Separate Spheres, Female Worlds, Woman's Place: The Rhetoric of Women's History," *Journal of American History* 75, no. 1 (1988): 9–39.

33. Ibid., 39.

34. Charlotte Borst, *Catching Babies: The Professionalization of Childbirth, 1870–1920* (Cambridge: Harvard University Press, 1995), 147.

35. Kerber, "Separate Spheres," 31. Robert Orsi's work on Italian Catholics in New York City offers the type of rich detail of home life that Kerber names, specifically focused on how religion is practiced in the home. For Orsi, drawing from historian Emmanuel LeRoy Ladurie, the domus—namely the family in its extended form including non–blood members and the physical space the family inhabits—was the moral and religious center of Italian Catholics in the first half of the twentieth century. In his analysis, however, separate spheres did not describe the gendered family patterns of Italian-Americans—instead, "the life of the domus spilled out into closely watched streets and hallways." Robert A. Orsi, *The Madonna of 115th Street: Faith and Community in Italian Harlem, 1880–1950* (New Haven: Yale University Press, 1985), xx, 92.

36. Homeschooling, also with nineteenth-century roots, is a growing movement in which parents teach their children at home, often with the help of curricula from a centralized organization, be it secular or Christian. For more on Christian homeschooling, see Colleen McDannell, "Creating the Christian Home: Home Schooling in Contemporary America," in *American Sacred Space*, ed. David Chidester and Edward T. Linenthal (Bloomington: Indiana University Press, 1995a), 187–219; and Mitchell Stevens, *Kingdom of Children: Culture and Controversy in the Homeschooling Movement* (Princeton: Princeton University Press, forthcoming).

37. McDannell's binary between Protestant and Catholic obscures the nuances within both of these enveloping categories. For more on Jewish practices of the home, see Jenna Weissman Joselit, *The Wonders of America: Reinventing Jewish Culture, 1880–1950* (New York: Hill and Wang, 1994).

38. The amalgamation of religion and alternative health care also has nineteenth-century precursors in what Catherine Albanese called "nature religion." Catherine Albanese, *Nature Religion in America* (Chicago: University of Chicago Press, 1990).

39. John Hostetler offers a detailed description of how Amish homes are transformed for the "preaching service." John A. Hostetler, *Amish Society*, 4th ed. (Baltimore: Johns Hopkins University Press, 1993), 210–219.

40. It is likely that for an Amish woman living on a farm without electricity "natural" has different meanings from that held by an urban-dwelling woman. For example, where many of the urban or suburban women talked about the importance of feeding their children "natural" foods, several of the Amish women liberally fed their young children from bowls of candies and chocolates while we talked. I more fully address the meanings of "natural" in the next chapter.

41. Ironically, Charlene Roth, who grew up Beachy Amish, a relatively more liberal type of Amish than Old Order, thought that Old Order Amish women were pampered after birth because they hired maids to do the housework for several weeks after a woman gave birth.

42. Hostetler, *Amish Society*, 191. For a portrayal of an "English" home-birth midwife's relationship to an Amish community in Pennsylvania, see Penny Armstrong and Sheryl Feldman, *A Midwife's Story* (New York: Arbor House, 1986).

43. Hostetler, *Amish Society*, 326.

44. While it is beyond the scope of this research to fully investigate the historical trend in Amish home births, the specific process of the medicalization of Amish birth would be a worthy topic of study. Why were the Amish willing to embrace the technology of birth when they were unwilling to accept the technology of agriculture or electricity?

45. For more on the history and practice of ceremonies surrounding birth in Judaism, see David Novak, "Be Fruitful and Multiply: Issues Related to Birth in Judaism," in *Celebration and Renewal: Rites of Passage in Judaism*, ed. Rela M. Geffen (Philadelphia: Jewish Publication Society, 1993), 12–31; Michael Strassfeld and Sharon Strassfeld, *The First Jewish Catalog* (Philadelphia: Jewish Publication Society, 1973); and Chava Weissler, "*Mizvot* Built into the Body: *Tkhines* for *Niddah*, Pregnancy, and Childbirth," in *People of the Body: Jews and Judaism from an Embodied Perspective*, ed. Howard Eilberg-Schwartz (Albany: State University of New York Press, 1992), 101–115.

46. On domestic rituals in Jewish women's lives, see Susan Starr Sered, *Women as Ritual Experts: The Religious Lives of Elderly Jewish Women in Jerusalem* (New York: Oxford University Press, 1992).

47. See Baruch Finkelstein and Michal Finkelstein, *B'Sha'ah Tovah: The Jewish Woman's Clinical and Halachic Guide to Pregnancy and Childbirth* (Jerusalem and New York: Feldheim Publishers, 1993), 145–146.

48. The story of Shiphrah and Puah is found in Exodus 1:15–22. They were Hebrew midwives who refused the pharaoh's orders to kill all Hebrew baby boys, and who justified their disobedience by telling the pharaoh: "The Hebrew women are not like the Egyptian women; for they are vigorous and give birth before the midwife comes to them."

49. A "halachic" guide to pregnancy and childbirth that Debra owned tried to dissuade Orthodox women from home birth, arguing that it is a "potentially life-threatening situation" and possibly counter to halacha. Finkelstein and Finkelstein, *B'Sha'ah Tovah*, 105.

50. For examples of Jewish women's childbirth rituals historically, see Weissler, "*Mizvot* Built into the Body," and Tikva Frymer-Kensky, *Motherprayer: The Pregnant Woman's Spiritual Companion* (New York: Riverhead Books, 1995). Susan Sered described the wealth of birthing rituals from which contemporary Jewish women can draw from the various cultural traditions of Judaism. Susan Starr Sered, "Childbirth as a Religious Experience?: Voices from an Israeli Hospital," *Journal for the Feminist Study of Religion* 7, no. 2 (1991):7–18.

51. Anthroposophy is a movement based on the philosophy and teachings of the German writer Rudolf Steiner, who wrote between 1883 and 1925. Steiner blended theosophy and Christianity in an applied philosophy that encompassed organic agriculture, homeopathy, and education (in the form of Waldorf Schools). Despite their new commitment to traditional Catholicism and questions from members of the anthroposophical community, Elizabeth and her husband saw no contradictions between joining the community and remaining Catholic.

52. On the churching of women, see William Coster, "Purity, Profanity, and Puritanism: The Churching of Women," in *Women in the Church*, ed. W. Sheils and Diana Wood (Cambridge: Basil Blackwell, 1990), 377–387; Cheryl Kristolaitis, "From Purification to Celebration: The History of the Service for Women after Childbirth," *Journal of the Canadian Church Historical Society* 28, no. 2 (1986): 53–62; David Tripp and James Cameron, "Churching: A Common Problem of the English Churches," *Church Quarterly* 3, no. 2 (1970): 125–133; and Walter von Arx, "The Churching of Women after Childbirth: History and Significance," in *Liturgy and Human Passage*, ed. David Power and Luis Maldonado (New York: Seabury Press, 1979), 63–71. Both von Arx and Coster saw churching in its Catholic and early Protestant forms as a rite of purification for the woman who was seen to be impure and particularly susceptible to demon possession during and after childbirth. Coster, however, argued that the Puritan rejection of churching may have been a form of protofeminism that affirmed the "naturalness" of the body and sexuality. Both of these authors espoused an interpretation of churching as remnant within Christianity of a Jewish antipathy to the body. For a contrasting view on Jewish approaches to the body, see Daniel Boyarin, *Carnal Israel: Reading Sex in Talmudic Culture* (Berkeley: University of California Press, 1993).

53. Colleen McDannell, "Catholic Domesticity, 1860–1960," in *American Catholic Women: A Historical Exploration*, ed. Karen Kennelly (New York: Macmillan, 1989), 80. McDannell argued that in the 1940s and 1950s, Catholic writers urged men to take a more active role in home devotions as the family patriarch, in response to the rise of a suburban domesticity that assumed that "women were the head of the home and men the head of the workplace." McDannell, "Catholic Domesticity," 76. Given their turn to Catholic traditionalism, Mark's role as domestic priest echoes these midcentury laments over men's diminishing authority.

54. Orsi, "Madonna of 115th Street," 227. For more on Marian devotions, see Sandra L. Zimdars-Swartz, "The Marian Revival in American Catholicism: Focal Points and Features of the New Marian Enthusiasm," in *Being Right: Conservative Catholics in America*, ed.Mary Jo Weaver and R. Scott Appleby (Bloomington: Indiana University Press, 1995), 213–240.

55. Ina May Gaskin, *Spiritual Midwifery*, 3d ed. (Summertown, Tenn.: Book Publishing Company, 1990), 361.

56. Arms, *Immaculate Deception*, 6.

57. See also Robbie Davis-Floyd's albeit brief reference to Blessing Way ceremonies, in which she does not problematize the cross-cultural power issues involved. Robbie Davis-Floyd, *Birth as an American Rite of Passage*, 294.

58. I wrote to Jeannine Parvati Baker asking her how she understood her borrowing from native culture, but she responded by offering to send me more of her writings, or to call her for a phone consultation at $90 per hour. For more on the ethics of cross-cultural borrowing within the feminist spirituality movement, see Cynthia Eller, *Living in the Lap of the Goddess: The Feminist Spirituality Movement in America* (New York: Crossroad, 1993), 74–82.

59. See Smith-Rosenberg, *Disorderly Conduct*, 70. Of course, even in eighteenth-century New England midwives charged fees, as Ulrich shows. See Laurel Thatcher Ulrich, *A Midwife's Tale* (New York: Vintage, 1991), 198–199.

60. For differing perspectives on the commodification of religion, see R. Laurence Moore, *Selling God: American Religion in the Marketplace of Culture* (New York: Oxford University Press, 1994); and Leigh E. Schmidt, *Consumer Rites: The Buying and Selling of American Holidays* (Princeton: Princeton University Press, 1995).

61. Pierre Bourdieu, *Distinction: A Social Critique of the Judgement of Taste* (Cambridge: Harvard University Press, 1984).

62. For an example of these treatments of domesticity, see Barbara Leslie Epstein, "The Politics of Domesticity," 149, and Wendy Kozol, "Fracturing Domesticity: Media, Nationalism, and the Question of Feminist Influence," *Signs* 20, no. 3 (1995): 647.

63. Bonnie Smith, "Havens No More? Discourses of Domesticity," *Gender and History* 2, no. 1 (1990): 99.

64. Ibid., 102.

65. Michel Foucault, *The Archaeology of Knowledge and the Discourse on Language* (New York: Pantheon, 1972), 49. I was alerted to this reference by Abu-Lughod and Lutz, who provide a very helpful discussion of the use of the category of "discourse" in anthropology. Lila Abu-Lughod and Catherine A. Lutz, eds., *Language and the Politics of Emotion* (Cambridge: Cambridge University Press, 1990), 9.

66. In a 1977 comparative study, Annette Pollinger found similar sentiments about feminism among home-birthing women: they professed support of many feminist goals, but found their particular lifestyles not recognized by the feminist movement. Annette Pollinger, "Diffusion of Innovations in Childbirth: An Analysis of Sociocultural Factors Associated with Traditional, Natural, and Home Birth" (Ph.D. diss., Fordham University, 1977), 185.

67. See also Judith Stacey, *Brave New Families: Stories of Domestic Upheaval in Late Twentieth Century America* (New York: Basic Books, 1991), 19.

68. Biddy Martin and Chandra Talpade Mohanty, "Feminist Politics: What's Home Got to Do with It?" in *Feminist Studies/Critical Studies*, ed. Teresa De Lauretis (Bloomington: Indiana University Press, 1986), 193.

69. Ibid., 206.

70. Ibid., 197, 199.

71. Ibid., 206.

72. For a concise analysis of the diversity of mothering practices in the United States, both historically and currently, see Evelyn Nakano Glenn, "Social Constructions of Mothering: A Thematic Overview," in *Mothering: Ideology, Experience & Agency*, ed. Evelyn Nakano Glenn, Grace Change, and Linda Rennie Forcey (New York: Routledge, 1994), 1–32.

73. bell hooks, *Yearning: Race, Gender, and Cultural Politics* (Boston: South End Press, 1990), 46.

74. Ibid., 47.

75. Ibid., 48.

76. Ibid., 47.

77. Nancy Hewitt, "The Economics of Family Life," *National Women's Studies Association Journal* 1, no. 1 (1998): 114. Though with wide influence, this professionalization affected women differently according to race and class. See Molly Ladd-Taylor, *Mother-Work: Women, Child Welfare, and the State, 1890–1930* (Urbana: University of Illinois Press, 1994), 18.

78. Hewitt, "The Economics of Family Life," 116. Joanne Meyerowitz's assertion, that Friedan's critique of the "feminine mystique" was not so much a radical disjuncture from her social conditions as an encapsulation of wider currents of opinion, supports Hewitt's analysis of Friedan. Joanne Meyerowitz, "Beyond the Feminine Mystique: A Reassessment of Postwar Mass Culture, 1946–1958," *Journal of American History* (March 1993): 1455–1482.

79. In her analysis of "intensive mothering" (that sometimes seems disingenuously puzzled by women's devotion to their children), Sharon Hays argued that even paid working mothers who continue to hold their children as first priority before work enact an "active rejection of market logic." Sharon Hays, *The Cultural Contradictions of Motherhood* (New Haven: Yale University Press, 1996), 171.

80. Micaela di Leonardo, "Morals, Mothers, and Militarism: Antimilitarism and Feminist Theory," *Feminist Studies* 11, no. 3 (1985): 613; Iris Marion Young, "Humanism, Gynocentrism, and Feminist Politics," in *Hypatia Reborn: Essays in Feminist Philosophy*, ed. Azizah Y. al-Hibri and Margaret A. Simons (Bloomington: Indiana University Press, 1990), 231–269; Regina Morantz-Sanchez, "Feminist Theory and Historical Practice: Rereading Elizabeth Blackwell," in *Feminists Revision History*, ed. Ann-Louise Shapiro (New Brunswick: Rutgers University Press, 1994), 98; and Judith Stacey, "Are Feminists Afraid to Leave Home?: The Challenge of Conservative Pro-Family Feminism," in *What Is Feminism?*, ed. Juliet Mitchell and Ann Oakley (London: Basil Blackwell, 1986), 219–248.

81. Young, "Humanism, Gynocentrism, and Feminist Politics," 247.

Chapter 6
Natural Women: Bodies and the Work of Birth

1. Mary Poovey, " 'Scenes of an Indelicate Character': The Medical 'Treatment' of Victorian Women," in *The Making of the Modern Body: Sexuality and Society in the Nineteenth Century*, ed. Catherine Gallagher and Thomas Laqueur (Berkeley: University of California Press, 1987), 137–168.

2. For example, see Helen Callaway, "'The Most Essentially Female Function of All': Giving Birth," in *Defining Females: The Nature of Women in Society,* ed. Shirley Ardener (Oxford: Berg, 1993), 146–167; and Brigitte Jordan, *Birth in Four Cultures,* 4th ed. (Prospect Heights, Ill.: Waveland Press, 1993 [1978]).

3. For a specific study of the relationship between embodiment and language focusing on emotions, see Lila Abu-Lughod and Catherine A. Lutz, eds., *Language and the Politics of Emotion* (Cambridge: Cambridge University Press, 1990).

4. Pierre Bourdieu, *In Other Words: Essays Towards a Reflexive Sociology,* trans. Matthew Adamson (Stanford: Stanford University Press, 1990a), 63.

5. Ibid., 87.

6. For a helpful critique and expansion of Bourdieu's notion of the field in terms of gender, see Toril Moi, "Appropriating Bourdieu: Feminist Theory and Pierre Bourdieu's Sociology of Culture," *New Literary History* 22 (1991): 1017–1049.

7. Judith Butler, *Bodies that Matter: On the Discursive Limits of "Sex"* (New York: Routledge, 1993), xi.

8. Ibid., 10.

9. Ibid., xi.

10. For example, see Nancy Wainer Cohen's description of natural childbirth as "purebirth." Nancy Wainer Cohen, *Open Season: A Survival Guide for Natural Childbirth and VBAC in the 90s* (New York: Bergin and Garvey, 1991), 290–291.

11. For a critique of the use of the "primitive" in "natural childbirth" literature, see Tess Cosslett, *Women Writing Childbirth: Modern Discourses of Motherhood* (Manchester, U.K.: Manchester University Press, 1994).

12. Suzanne Arms, *Immaculate Deception: A New Look at Women and Childbirth in North America* (New York: Bantam, 1977) Carol P. MacCormack, "Risk, Prevention, and International Health Policy," in *Gender and Health: An International Perspective,* ed. Carolyn F. Sargent and Caroline B. Brettell (Upper Saddle River, N.J.: Prentice-Hall, 1996), 328, 330.

13. Ibid., 331. A 1996 UNICEF report stated that 600,000 women per year die from pregnancy and childbirth-related problems, with the highest rate of maternal mortality in sub-Saharan Africa. One of the solutions to this tragedy, according to UNICEF, is not more hospitals, but more trained midwives with proper equipment and medication. (John Stackhouse, "Maternal Mortality a Neglected Tragedy, UN Report Says," *The Globe and Mail,* Tuesday, 11 June 1996, A12.) For a poet's portrayal of the experience of childbirth in the "Third World," see Meena Alexander's poem, "Passion," in *The Shock of Arrival: Reflections on Postcolonial Experience* (Boston: South End Press, 1996), 17–20; see also Kathryn S. March, "Childbirth with Fear," in *Mother Journeys: Feminists Write about Mothering,* ed. Maureen T. Reddy, Martha Roth, and Amy Sheldon (Minneapolis: Spinsters Ink, 1994), 145–154; and Nancy Scheper-Hughes, *Death without Weeping: The Violence of Everyday Life in Brazil* (Berkeley: University of California Press, 1992).

14. MacCormack, "Risk, Prevention, and International Health Policy," 331.

15. The women who made recourse to such portrayals spanned a range of religious and class identities, from a New Order Amish woman who had been a missionary in Haiti, to a "born again Lutheran" who had emigrated from Denmark. However, during her "healing workshop," Nancy Wainer Cohen lamented the

spread of biomedical approaches to childbirth to nonindustrialized countries, complicating this romantic portrayal.

16. Donna J. Haraway, *Simians, Cyborgs and Women: The Reinvention of Nature* (New York: Routledge, 1991), 151, 176.

17. George Lakoff and Mark Johnson, *Metaphors We Live By* (Chicago: University of Chicago Press, 1980), 193.

18. George Lakoff, *Women, Fire, and Dangerous Things: What Categories Reveal about the Mind* (Chicago: University of Chicago Press, 1987), xii.

19. Emily Martin, *The Woman in the Body: A Cultural Analysis of Reproduction*, 2d ed. (Boston: Beacon Press, 1992 [1987]), 146; see also Robbie Davis-Floyd, *Birth as an American Rite of Passage* (Berkeley: University of California Press, 1992), 51.

20. Davis-Floyd, *Birth as an American Rite of Passage*, 52.

21. Martin, *The Woman in the Body*, 157.

22. Ibid., 159. For an intriguing attempt to find new words for childbirth, see Robbie Pfeufer Kahn, *Bearing Meaning: The Language of Birth* (Urbana and Chicago: University of Illinois Press, 1995).

23. Mary O'Brien, *The Politics of Reproduction* (London: Routledge and Kegan Paul, 1981), 9; see also Helena Michie and Naomi R. Cahn, "Unnatural Births: Cesarean Sections in the Discourse of the Natural Childbirth Movement," in *Gender and Health: An International Perspective*, ed. Carolyn F. Sargent and Caroline B. Brettell (Upper Saddle River, N.J.: Prentice-Hall, 1996), 46; and Iris Marion Young's critique of Simone de Beauvoir's understanding of pregnancy as an "ordeal." Iris Marion Young, "Humanism, Gynocentrism, and Feminist Politics," in *Hypatia Reborn: Essays in Feminist Philosophy*, ed. Azizah Y. al-Hibri and Margaret A. Simons (Bloomington: Indiana University Press, 1990), 236.

24. Robert A. Bradley, *Husband-Coached Childbirth*, rev. ed. (New York: Harper and Row, 1974), 12; Michel Odent, *Birth Reborn* (New York: Pantheon Books, 1984), 46. For feminist critiques of both turn-of-the-century understandings of women as more closely related to animals than men, and the contemporary animal metaphors used by "natural" childbirth doctors like Odent, see Rosalind Rosenberg, *Beyond Separate Spheres: Intellectual Roots of Modern Feminism* (New Haven: Yale University Press, 1982), 9; and Martin, *The Woman in the Body*, 164.

25. "Traditional Catholics" are those who attend a church that offers the Mass in Latin, and are overtly critical of the reforms of Vatican II. For more on Catholic traditionalism as a twentieth-century movement, see William D. Dinges, "'We Are What You Were': Roman Catholic Traditionalism in America," in *Being Right: Conservative Catholics in America*, ed. R. Scott Appleby and Mary Jo Weaver (Bloomington: Indiana University Press, 1995), 241–269.

26. Placenta praevia is a condition in which the placenta grows too low in the uterus, blocking the way for the baby's birth. It shows itself through heavy bleeding, generally prior to the onset of labor, and requires an emergency cesarean.

27. In a parallel story of "intervening" in nature, only one woman I interviewed told me of taking fertility drugs to become pregnant, and she worried later that she may have been manipulating nature unduly.

28. Margarete Sandelowski and Linda Corson Jones, " 'Healing Fictions': Stories of Choosing in the Aftermath of the Detection of Fetal Anomalies," *Social Science and Medicine* 42, no. 3 (1996): 357.

29. For a fascinating analysis of the diverse and perhaps unexpected ways women negotiate prenatal testing and religious beliefs, see Rayna Rapp, "Accounting for Amniocentesis," in *Knowledge, Power, and Practice: The Anthropology of Medicine and Everyday Life*, ed. S. Lindenbaum and M. Lock (Berkeley: University of California Press, 1993), 55–78.

30. Natural family planning, or the "rhythm" method, is a method of birth control based on determining a woman's fertile and nonfertile days, by charting a woman's menstrual cycle. It is the only method of birth control that has received papal sanction, which it gained in 1951. For more on the history and reception of natural family planning among Catholics, see Patricia M. Lennon, "Conceiving Catholicism: Nature, Rhythm, and the Christian Family Movement Survey, 1965–66," paper presented at the AAR Annual Meeting, New Orleans, 1996. There are a variety of other "natural" methods of birth control, including some with feminist roots, and thus very different philosophies, such as the "Justisse Method."

31. Michel Odent, *Birth Reborn*, 13.

32. Ibid.

33. Valerie described a stork pin as being a pin received by emergency personnel who caught babies outside the hospital.

34. Barbara Katz Rothman, *In Labor: Women and Power in the Birthplace* (New York: W. W. Norton, 1982), 79; see also Cohen, *Open Season*, 290.

35. For examples of the "sacralizing" of childbirth advocated by spiritual feminists, see Riane Eisler, *Sacred Pleasure: Sex, Myth, and the Politics of the Body* (San Francisco: HarperSanFrancisco, 1995), 297–98; and Vicki Noble, *Shakti Woman: Feeling Our Fire, Healing Our World* (San Francisco: HarperSanFrancisco, 1991), 3, 216–223.

36. A hysterotomy is the removal of the fetus through surgical incision.

37. Even in Emily Martin's work, where religion was not a category of analysis, several of the women she quoted spoke of God's purpose in designing women's bodies for birth. Martin, *The Woman in the Body*, 191, 194.

38. La Leche League International, *The Womanly Art of Breastfeeding*, 4th rev. ed. (New York: New American Library, 1987), 20.

39. For a popular and a scholarly treatment of the evolutionary design of women's birthing bodies, see Natalie Angier, "Why Babies Are Born Facing Backward, Helpless and Chubby," *New York Times*, 23 July 1996, C1, C11; and Wenda R. Trevathan, *Human Birth: An Evolutionary Perspective* (New York: Aldine De Gruyter, 1987).

40. A practitioner is a formal category within Christian Science, which denotes a healer trained in Christian Science methods of prayer. Practitioners have their roots in nineteenth-century Christian Science, in which the healer mentally took on the worries or ills of the patients and thus cured them. They are paid for their services, and now offer their services to cure everything from drug addiction to marital problems. For more on the history of practitioners, see Rennie B. Schoepflin, "The Christian Science Tradition," in *Caring and Curing: Health and Medi-*

cine in the Western Religious Traditions, ed. Ronald L. Numbers and Darrel W. Amundsen (New York: Macmillan, 1986), 421–446.

41. For Judy, however, the dilemmas of a matter-denying faith arose once her children were older and had health problems or accidents, and she had to decide whether she would take them to the hospital or not. In several instances her faith was flexible enough to allow her to provide her children with medical care, but such situations always demanded a great deal of prayer and a subtlety of interpretation.

42. Mary Baker Eddy, *Science and Health with a Key to the Scriptures* (Boston: First Church of Christ, Scientist, 1994 [1875]), 171.

43. Ibid., 111, 162.

44. An 1888 incident in Boston, in which a Christian Science "metaphysical midwife" was charged with manslaughter in the death of a mother and baby whom she was attending, created a scandal for Mary Baker Eddy, who ended up not defending the midwife. Instead, she adapted Christian Science practice to the situation by instructing that in childbirth women were to work with physicians. This incident provoked a third of her Boston followers to leave the church and prompted Eddy to withdraw from public life for a period of two years, after which she returned to reorganize Christian Science institutions; see Schoepflin, "The Christian Science Tradition," 436. Accommodation to medicalized models of childbirth continues, in that Christian Science women generally seek the care of obstetricians or certified nurse-midwives. As can be seen in Natalie's case, however, tensions still remain between Christian Science and medical approaches to the birthing body, over such issues as vitamin supplements and testing.

45. As Susan Sered ironically noted, "Christian Science draws attention to the physical through spiritual cures of bodily ailments." Susan Starr Sered, *Priestess, Mother, Sacred Sister: Religions Dominated by Women* (New York: Oxford University Press, 1994), 148.

46. Writing of Christianity more generally, Colleen McDannell stated, "Even though Christian theology may deny that the body is more significant than the spirit, Christian practice accentuates the relevance of the physical self." Colleen McDannell, *Material Christianity: Religion and Popular Culture in America* (New Haven: Yale University Press, 1995b), 275.

47. On interpreting women's approaches to healing as "pragmatic," see Margaret Lock and Patricia Kaufert, eds., *Pragmatic Women and Body Politics* (Cambridge: Cambridge University Press, 1998).

48. Isaiah 66:9.

49. Joanne Carlson Brown and Carole R. Bohn, eds., *Christianity, Patriarchy, and Abuse: A Feminist Critique* (New York: Pilgrim Press, 1989).

50. Though scholars of the Hebrew Bible would not all agree with Carrie's interpretation of Elohim, for my purposes the important issue is her interpretation of the word, which was shaped by what she learned from her female pastor in church. For more on the breasts of God, see Stephen Moore, *God's Gym: Divine Male Bodies of the Bible* (New York: Routledge, 1996), 93.

51. Agnes N. Ozman LaBerge, *What God Hath Wrought: Life and Work of Mrs. Agnes N. O. LaBerge* (New York: Garland, 1985), 63. I am grateful to Marie Griffith for directing me to LaBerge's autobiography.

52. In her antimedical stance, Janet seems to run contrary to Grant Wacker's portrayal of contemporary Pentecostals, in which he asserts that "physicians [are] highly esteemed." Grant Wacker, "The Pentecostal Tradition," in *Caring and Curing: Health and Medicine in the Western Religious Traditions*, ed. Ronald L. Numbers and Darrel W. Amundsen (New York: MacMillan, 1986), 530. However, Janet remarked that in her own church a number of members were medical professionals and that home birth was not the dominant method of childbirth within the congregation. For more on Pentecostal approaches to medicine, see Margaret M. Poloma, *The Assemblies of God at the Crossroads: Charisma and Institutiona.: Dilemmas* (Knoxville: University of Tennessee Press, 1989), esp. ch. 4.

53. Institute for Basic Life Principles (IBLP), "Basic Concepts in Understanding and Treating Morning Sickness" (n.p.: IBLP, n.d), 6.

54. Ibid., 14. The main impetus for the booklet seemed to be the propagation of a pronatalist message. The booklet repeatedly referred to women whose pregnancies had been so unbearable that their husbands had undergone vasectomies in order to avoid future pregnancies. Happily, however, in the eyes of these authors, these men had also reversed their vasectomies once they realized that it was God's will for them to bring more children into the world.

55. Ibid., 6, italics original.

56. Due to the inexactitude of calculating conception, this prayer was to be prayed retroactively.

57. IBLP, "Basic Concepts," 8.

58. For examples among feminist theologians, see Paula Cooey, "The Redemption of the Body," in *After Patriarchy: Feminist Transformations of the World Religions*, ed. Paula M. Cooey, William R. Eakin, and Jay B. McDaniel (Maryknoll, N.Y.: Orbis, 1991), 106–130; Linda Hogan, *From Women's Experience to Feminist Theology* (London: Sheffield Press, 1995), 42; and Elisabeth Moltman-Wendel, *I Am My Body: A Theology of Embodiment* (New York: Continuum, 1995). For a more ambivalent celebration from a Catholic perspective, see Susan A. Ross, " 'Then Honor God in Your Body': Feminist and Sacramental Theology on the Body," in *Horizons on Catholic Feminist Theology*, ed. Joann Wolski Conn and Walter E. Conn (Georgetown: Georgetown University Press, 1992), 109–132. Helen Callaway offered a parallel critique in her caution against romanticizing traditions of female midwifery, saying that just because women attend births does not mean that the symbols and rituals of childbirth will be emancipatory for women; Helen Callaway, " 'The Most Essentially Female Function of All,' " in *Defining Females: The Nature of Women in Society* (Oxford: Berg: 1993), 156.

59. On the models of sacralization and emancipation in women's religions, see Lesley A. Northrup's discussion of the work of Susan Sered and Marjorie Proctor-Smith, in Northrup, *Ritualizing Women* (Cleveland: Pilgrim Press, 1997), 93–94.

60. Folklorists Joan Newlon Radner and Susan Lanser describe coding as "covert expressions of ideas, beliefs, experiences, feelings, and attitudes that the dominant culture—and perhaps even the dominated group—would find disturbing or threatening if expressed in more overt forms." See Radner and Lanser, "Strategies of Coding in Women's Cultures," in *Feminist Messages: Coding in Women's Folk Culture*, ed. Joan Newlon Radner (Urbana and Chicago: University of Illinois Press, 1993), 4.

61. For a collection that sets this type of pragmatic action in a wide cultural context, see Margaret Lock and Patricia Kaufert, eds., *Pragmatic Women and Body Politics* (Cambridge: Cambridge University Press, 1998).

62. See, for example, Carolyn Merchant, *The Death of Nature: Women, Ecology, and the Scientific Revolution* (San Francisco: Harper and Row, 1980).

63. Haraway, *Simians, Cyborgs, and Women*, 149.

64. Ibid., 150.

65. Ibid., 174.

66. Ibid., 180.

67. Ibid., 181.

68. Ibid., 176.

69. As exemplars of "holistic feminism," Haraway listed Adrienne Rich, Susan Griffin, and Audre Lorde. See Haraway, *Simians, Cyborgs, and Women*, 174, 181.

70. Ibid., 149. The tension within feminist theory between considering birth and mothering as sources of women's power or sources of women's oppression has been long-standing. For a diversity of perspectives, see Shulamith Firestone, *The Dialectic of Sex* (New York: Bantam, 1972); Adrienne Rich, *Of Woman Born: Motherhood as Experience and Institution* (New York: Norton, 1986 [1976]); Nel Noddings, *Caring: A Feminine Approach to Ethics* (Berkeley: University of California Press, 1984); Sara Ruddick, *Maternal Thinking* (Boston: Beacon Press, 1989); Maureen T. Reddy, Martha Roth, and Amy Sheldon, eds., *Mother Journeys: Feminists Write about Mothering* (Minneapolis: Spinsters Ink, 1994).

71. Ynestra King, "Healing the Wounds: Feminism, Ecology, and Nature/Culture Dualism," in *Gender/Body/Knowledge: Feminist Reconstructions of Being and Knowing*, ed. Alison M. Jaggar and Susan R. Bordo (New Brunswick: Rutgers University Press, 1992), 121.

72. Carol P. Christ, *Diving Deep and Surfacing: Women Writers on Spiritual Quest*, 2d ed. (Boston: Beacon Press, 1986), 53.

73. Debate over the value of women "controlling" their sexuality more generally has led some ecofeminist critics to argue that "the language of controlling our bodies does not necessarily challenge masculinist power and can easily become a principle of regulation which sustains that power." See Irene Diamond, *Fertile Ground: Women, Earth, and the Limits of Control* (Boston: Beacon Press, 1994), 88. To this charge, however, Rosalind Pollack Petchesky wrote that for "women's movements around the globe, the idea of women owning their bodies is . . . not an individualist, exclusionary interest but rather a fundamental condition for women's development and strength as a social group and thus for their full participation as citizens." Rosalind Pollack Petchesky, "The Body as Property: A Feminist Revision," in *Conceiving the New World Order: The Global Politics of Reproduction*, ed. Faye D. Ginsburg and Rayna Rapp (Berkeley: University of California Press, 1995), 403.

74. An important part of Brenda's sense of God's control over her body resided in her belief in the imminence of the Second Coming. As a young girl of 6, while looking at a cemetery from a window in her church basement, she had a vision in which Jesus came to her and told her that her body would never be buried in the ground. She forgot this vision until she was 16, when her parents bought cemetery

plots and she grew angry with them, saying, "You don't need those!" Her mother (whom she had told about the vision) then said to her that Jesus might be coming back for her, but that he might not come in time for them. At this point she remembered her vision, and ever since has been assured that he will return for her family, as well as for her.

75. Haraway, *Simians, Cyborgs and Women*, 162.

76. For a parallel analysis of the "flexibility" of bodily metaphors, see Emily Martin, *Flexible Bodies: Tracking Immunity in American Culture—From the Days of Polio to the Age of AIDS* (Boston: Beacon Press, 1994).

77. David Hess describes a similar process of drawing on common images in his discussion of the similarities between New Age thinkers and their scientific debunkers. David J. Hess, *Science in the New Age: The Paranormal, Its Defenders and Debunkers, and American Culture* (Madison: University of Wisconsin Press, 1993).

78. Haraway, *Simians, Cyborgs and Women*, 172.

79. Sandra Lee Bartky, *Femininity and Domination: Studies in the Phenomenology of Oppression* (New York: Routledge, 1990), 80.

80. In New Jersey, battles over a bill that would clarify that nursing a baby is not an indecent act show once again how public breast-feeding is often considered inappropriate and embarrassing by both men and women. New York State has actually declared breast-feeding a civil right. See Natalie Pompilio, "In New Jersey, Second Thoughts on Breastfeeding," *Philadelphia Inquirer*, 18 November 1996, A1, A7. That the right to breast-feed even needs to be codified in law shows the extent of the discomfort the culture has with the nursing mother.

81. That the goal of such sensuality is to attract male attention is not a given, despite Bartky's comment about "presumed heterosexuality." However, some (male) breast-feeding advocates hasten to assure husbands that nursing a baby need not be a disruption of heterosexuality. In response to a man who declared his wife's breasts belonged to him and not his baby, Dr. Bradley calmly asserted, "As men, we must admit that breasts make lovely sweater decorations. However, as doctors, we remind you that their primary purpose is a source of food for babies." Robert A. Bradley, *Husband-Coached Childbirth*, rev. ed. (New York: Harper and Row, 1974), 179. In Bradley's objectifying interpretation, a woman's breasts have "purpose" and function only in relation to others, not to herself.

82. The Beachy Amish emerged from the Old Order Amish in Pennsylvania in 1927, and are a loosely organized group that have accepted a variety of "worldly" goods, such as automobiles, electricity, and relaxed dress standards. See John A. Hostetler, *Amish Society*, 4th ed. (Baltimore: Johns Hopkins University Press, 1993), 283. Like other Beachy Amish women, Charlene continues to cover her head with a head scarf, a biblically based cultural tradition symbolizing women's submission to men.

83. For a parallel analysis of the use of the word "family" in the 1950s, see Warren Susman, cited in Suzanne Danuta Walters, *Lives Together, Worlds Apart: Mothers and Daughters in Popular Culture* (Berkeley: University of California Press, 1992), 72.

84. See Michie and Cahn, "Unnatural Births."

85. As Nancy Wainer Cohen suggested, "You can bring your foremothers to your births with you . . . [o]n both a spiritual and a physical plane. . . ." Cohen, *Open Season*, 291.

86. Emily Martin alluded to the critical edge in women's alternative uses of nature when she wrote, "When women derive their view of experience from their bodily processes as they occur in society, they are not saying 'back to nature' in any way. They are saying on to another kind of culture, one in which our current rigid separations and oppositions are not present." Martin, *The Woman in the Body*, 200. In the context of my discussion of home birth, I would not agree with Martin's assertion that women are not saying "back to nature" in *any* way, but would agree that their uses of the "natural" are profoundly cultural.

87. Lila Abu-Lughod, "Can There Be a Feminist Ethnography?" *Women and Performance: A Journal of Feminist Theory* 5 (1990): 7–27; Ellen Lewin, "Wives, Mothers, and Lesbians: Rethinking Resistance in the U.S.," in *Pragmatic Women and Body Politics*, ed. M. Lock and P. A. Kaufert (Cambridge: Cambridge University Press, 1998), 164–177; and Ellen Gruenbaum, "Resistance and Embrace: Sudanese Rural Women and Systems of Power," in *Pragmatic Women and Body Politics*, ed. Margaret Lock and Patricia Kaufert (Cambridge: Cambridge University Press, 1998), 74.

88. As Marie Griffith has shown in her work on the Women's Aglow prayer movement in North America, women's submission is often a complex negotiation engaging power from many different angles. See R. Marie Griffith, *God's Daughters: Evangelical Women and the Power of Submission* (Berkeley: University of California Press, 1997).

89. Butler, *Bodies that Matter*.

90. Rich, *Motherhood*, xii.

91. Davis-Floyd, *Birth as an American Rite of Passage*, 299.

92. For examples of conservative religious women who insist on the sexuality of birth, see Marilyn Moran, *Birth and the Dialogue of Love* (Leawood, Kans.: New Nativity Press, 1981); and Helen Wessel, *Natural Childbirth and the Christian Family* (New York: Harper and Row, 1963).

93. Butler, *Bodies that Matter*, 247.

94. As Sheila Kitzinger shows, home birth also affords greater possibilities for women to have a diversity of people at their birth, including women friends or partners, thus disrupting the presumed heterosexuality of the birthing woman. Sheila Kitzinger, *Home Birth: The Essential Guide to Giving Birth Outside the Hospital* (New York: Dorling Kindersley, 1991), 115.

95. J. Boddy, "Remembering Amal: On Birth and the British in Northern Sudan," in *Pragmatic Women and Body Politics*, ed. M. Lock and P. A. Kaufert (Cambridge: Cambridge University Press, 1998), 28–57.

96. Haraway, *Simians, Cyborgs, and Women*, 151, 176.

97. See J. Boddy, "Remembering Amal," 28–57.

98. On the importance of recognizing class when judging the effects of childbirth reform, see Rich, *Motherhood*, xii.

99. Haraway, *Simians, Cyborgs, and Women*, 180.

100. Carol Laderman, *Wives and Midwives: Childbirth and Nutrition in Rural Malaysia* (Berkeley: University of California Press, 1983); Janice Boddy, *Wombs*

and Alien Spirits: Women, Men and the Zār Cult in Northern Sudan (Madison: University of Wisconsin Press, 1989).

101. Robin Blaetz, "In Search of the Mother Tongue: Childbirth and the Cinema," *Velvet Light Trap* 29 (1992): 15–20.

Chapter 7
Sliding between Pain and Pleasure: Home Birth and Visionary Pain

1. I was alerted to this poem by Martin S. Pernick, *A Calculus of Suffering: Pain, Professionalism, and Anesthesia in Nineteenth-Century America* (New York: Columbia University Press, 1985), 62.

2. Mary Poovey, " 'Scenes of an Indelicate Character': The Medical 'Treatment' of Victorian Women," in *The Making of the Modern Body: Sexuality and Society in the Nineteenth Century,* ed. Catherine Gallagher and Thomas Laqueur (Berkeley: University of California Press, 1987), 137–168.

3. Talal Asad, "On Torture, or Cruel, Inhuman, and Degrading Treatment," in *Social Suffering,* ed. Arthur Kleinman, Veena Das, and Margaret Lock (Berkeley: University of California Press, 1997), 290.

4. See Beverly Wildung Harrison and Carter Heyward, "Pain and Pleasure: Avoiding the Confusions of Christian Tradition in Feminist Theory," in *Sexuality and the Sacred: Sources for Theological Reflection,* ed. James B. Nelson and Sandra P. Longfellow (Louisville, Ky.: Westminster/John Knox Press, 1984), 131–147; and Elaine Scarry, *The Body in Pain: The Making and Unmaking of the World* (Oxford: Oxford University Press, 1985).

5. Lana Hartman Landon, "Suffering over Time: Six Varieties of Pain," *Soundings* 72, no. 1 (1989): 82.

6. From 1960 to 1964 the fertility rate in the U.S. was approximately 3.5 children per woman; from 1975 to 1979 it was 1.7; and in 1993 it was 2.0. African-American women have had consistently higher fertility rates than Euro-American women. U.S. Bureau of the Census, *Statistical Abstract of the United States: 1996,* 116th ed. (Washington, D.C.: U.S. Government, 1996), 77.

7. The fruit diet was meant to keep the fetus's bones in a soft and gristly state, so that the baby would emerge more easily. Upon giving birth, the nursing mother was to commence eating foods that would cause the baby's bones to harden. Martin Luther Holbrook, *Parturition without Pain; A Code of Directions for Escaping from the Primal Curse* (New York: Wood and Holbrook, 1871), 58.

8. Ibid., 15.

9. Ibid., 25, 92.

10. This is the version of the antianesthesia argument that later "natural-childbirth" doctors like Dick-Read and Bradley scorned and upbraided.

11. Pernick, *A Calculus of Suffering,* 51.

12. For more on perfectionist arguments among health reformers, see Catharine Albanese, *Nature Religion in America* (Chicago: University of Chicago Press, 1990), 124–125.

13. Pernick, *A Calculus of Suffering,* 79.

14. Mary Poovey, " 'Scenes of an Indelicate Character,' " 14.

15. Margarete Sandelowski, *Pain, Pleasure, and American Childbirth: From the Twilight Sleep to the Read Method, 1914–1960* (Westport, Conn.: Greenwood Press, 1984), 10.

16. Judith Walzer Leavitt, "Birthing and Anesthesis: The Debate over Twilight Sleep," *Signs* 6, no. 1 (1980): 164.

17. Charlotte Tell, in Richard W. Wertz and Dorothy C. Wertz, *Lying-In: A History of Childbirth in America*, expanded edition (New Haven: Yale University Press, 1989 [1977]), 105–106.

18. Elaine Tyler May, *Homeward Bound: American Families in the Cold War Era* (New York: Basic Books, 1988), 9.

19. Sandelowski, *Pain, Pleasure, and American Childbirth*, 114.

20. Ironically, in the nineteenth century, some doctors argued *against* obstetric anesthesia for the same reason, namely, that if a woman was relieved of the pain of birth she might feel a pleasure that could come dangerously close to a sexual experience. Mary Poovey, "'Scenes of an Indelicate Character,'" 137–168.

21. Sandelowski, *Pain, Pleasure, and American Childbirth*, 120.

22. Ibid., 134; John A. Robertson (a professor of law at the University of Texas), in Brenda Waugh, "Repro-Woman: A View of the Labyrinth (from the Lithotomy Position)," *Yale Journal of Law and Feminism* 3, no. 4 (1991): 37.

23. Robbie E. Davis-Floyd, *Birth as an American Rite of Passage* (Berkeley: University of California Press, 1992), 99. Yvonne Brackbill, Karen McManus, and Lynn Woodward, *Medication in Maternity: Infant Exposure and Maternal Information*, International Academy for Research in Learning Disabilities, Monograph Series, Number 2 (Ann Arbor: University of Michigan Press, 1985), 109. In a study of 602 women who gave birth in hospitals, birth centers, and homes, Brackbill, McManus, and Woodward found that, compared to the other two groups, the home-birthing women were significantly better informed about drugs used in pregnancy and childbirth and consumed less of them; Brackbill, McManus, and Woodward, *Medication in Maternity*, 127.

24. Davis-Floyd, *Birth as an American Rite of Passage*, 97, 114; Penny Simkin, "Epidural Epidemic," *Birth Gazette* 10, no. 4 (1994): 28–34. For a parallel example of biomedical approaches that result in increasing suffering, see Meredith McGuire, with Debra Kantor, *Ritual Healing in Suburban America* (New Brunswick: Rutgers University Press, 1988), 242.

25. Many Amish Mennonites, as is true in the case of Tina's family, have left more conservative Old Order communities to embrace a more worldly lifestyle that includes cars, telephones, electricity, and overseas missionary work. For a particular example of this, whereas Tina and Charlene (see below) allowed me to tape-record our conversations, the three Old Order women preferred that I take written notes.

26. Transition is the stage before the mother pushes out the baby, during which the cervix stretches to its greatest width and the baby prepares to move down the birth canal. The contractions of transition are often the most intense and closest together during this period.

27. Wertz and Wertz asserted that "natural childbirth" in the hospital "put a premium on silence during labor; the 'successful' patient was the silent one, who thereby demonstrated relaxation. Screaming . . . was forbidden, by use of anaesthesia if necessary." Wertz and Wertz, *Lying-In*, 197. While being at home did not

keep Stefanie from worrying about disturbing her neighbors, it did allow her to let go of those worries when necessary.

28. The idea that the pain a woman feels in labor is tied into her relationships, either in the past or the present, is widely held in midwifery circles (though less so in medical opinions). See Emily Martin, *The Woman in the Body: A Cultural Analysis of Reproduction*, 2d ed. (Boston: Beacon Press, 1992), 62.

29. In the *Iliad*, Homer compares Agamemnon's pain on the battlefield to a woman in travail; see Robbie Pfeufer Kahn, *Bearing Meaning: The Language of Birth* (Urbana: University of Illinois Press, 1995), 31. On Simone de Beauvoir, see Margaret A. Simons, "Motherhood, Feminism and Identity," in *Hypatia Reborn: Essays in Feminist Philosophy*, ed. Azizah Y. al-Hibri and Margaret A. Simons (Bloomington: Indiana University Press, 1990), 162; and Simone de Beauvoir, *The Second Sex*, trans. H. M. Parshley (New York: Knopf, 1953).

30. On generativity and motherhood, see Bonnie J. Miller-McLemore, *Also a Mother: Work and Family as Theological Dilemma* (Nashville, Tenn.: Abingdon Press, 1994), 142.

31. Elaine referred me to Revelation 12:2, which reads: "And she being with child cried, travailing in birth, and pained to be delivered." Eddy's commentary is as follows: "Also the spiritual idea is typified by a woman in travail, waiting to be delivered of her sweet promise, but remembering no more her sorrow for joy that the birth goes on; for great is the idea, and the travail portentous." Mary Baker Eddy, *Science and Health with a Key to the Scriptures* (Boston: First Church of Christ, Scientist, 1994 [1875]), 562.

32. Christian Science principles can sometimes generate animosity in health-care providers, as Judy's story of her friend showed, in which Judy recounted that "it was almost like this midwife was out to prove that it was going to be painful." In Judy's telling of it, her friend was to give birth at a birthing center but ended up birthing at home, because she was sent home from the birthing center when she first arrived by a midwife who thought she was not ready to birth.

33. Padanaram Settlement published a booklet in 1987 entitled *Faith Babies*, which described pregnancy and childbirth as women's "divine right and privilege." Though there is no reference to Jesus, and the Scriptures alluded to in the booklet are mostly from the Hebrew Bible, the emphasis on "a new day" being "above the curse" and on spiritual rebirth give a decidedly Christian cast to the group. I was unable to reach anyone when I called the number on the back of the booklet to speak with a community member.

34. In addition to these more spiritual practices, the birth code contained some strict requirements on the physical plane: "Your temple [body?] is the temple of God, and you must keep it holy. You will eat no fattening or starchy foods, but you will be very mindful to eat healthy foods. You will watch your diet and weight very carefully." Padanaram Settlement, *Faith Babies* (Williams, Ind.: Padanaram Settlement, 1987), 8. In this disciplinary attitude, the Birth Code was more akin to mainstream pregnancy-advice books (e.g., *What to Expect When You're Expecting*) than to alternative approaches to pregnancy, which, while concerned about nutrition, place less emphasis on weight control. Arlene Eisenberg, Heidi E. Murkoff, and Sandee E. Hathaway, *What to Expect When You're Expecting*, 2d rev. ed. (New York: Workman, 1991), 81, 148.

35. Padanaram Settlement, *Faith Babies*, 21.

36. Ibid.

37. This is the New Revised Standard Version (NRSV) translation. It was Carrie's understanding that in the original Hebrew the word was not "infirmities" but "pains."

38. Though she did not birth entirely without pain, Carrie does attribute the painless nature of the crowning of her baby's head to God, (see ch. 6).

39. On medieval women mystics' use of birthing imagery to describe their suffering, see Caroline Walker Bynum, *Holy Feast and Holy Fast* (Berkeley: University of California Press, 1987), 300.

40. Waugh, "Repro-Woman," 42. Ironically, the Roe v. Wade decision is used in such cases, specifically the assertion that "the state's interests are paramount over the woman's privacy rights in the final trimester of pregnancy," therefore also in labor and birth. Suzanne Hope Suarez, "Midwifery Is Not the Practice of Medicine," *Yale Journal of Law and Feminism* 5 (1993): 357.

41. Sharon Olds, "The Moment When Two Worlds Meet," in *Mother Journeys: Feminists Write about Mothering*, ed. Maureen T. Reddy, Martha Roth, and Amy Sheldon (Minneapolis: Spinsters Ink, 1994), 47.

42. For a discussion of how hospital birth has desexualized birth and to read more testimonies to birth as a sexual experience, see Davis-Floyd, *Birth as an American Rite of Passage*, 69–71.

43. See, for example, David Bakan, *Disease, Pain & Sacrifice: Toward a Psychology of Suffering* (Chicago: University of Chicago Press, 1966), 67; Joseph Fichter, *Religion and Pain: The Spiritual Dimensions of Health Care* (New York: Crossroad, 1981), 30; Mary S. Sheridan, *Pain in America* (Tuscaloosa: University of Alabama Press, 1992), 3. In his discussion, Bakan argues that "one of the major psychological uses of Christianity has been to overcome the essential loneliness and privacy of pain." Bakan, *Disease, Pain & Sacrifice*, 67.

44. Elaine Scarry, *The Body in Pain: The Making and Unmaking of the World* (Oxford: Oxford University Press, 1985), 4.

45. Ibid., 12.

46. Ibid., 310.

47. Ibid., 190.

48. Ibid., 188–89. I was aided in my reading of Scarry by David B. Morris, "How to Read *The Body in Pain*," *Literature and Medicine* 6 (1987): 139–155.

49. For an account of a more ritualized version of male suffering in childbirth, see Nor Hall and Warren R. Dawson, *Broodmales* (Dallas: Spring Publications, 1989), which discusses the custom of "couvade," in which men enact the process of childbirth.

50. None of the women I interviewed had women partners. There is little analysis explicitly regarding the experience of childbirth for lesbians, but on lesbian motherhood, see Ellen Lewin, "On the Outside Looking In: The Politics of Lesbian Motherhood," in *Conceiving the New World Order: The Global Politics of Reproduction*, ed. Faye D. Ginsburg and Rayna Rapp (Berkeley: University of California Press, 1995), 103–121. On childbirth, see Deborah Goleman Wolf, "Lesbian Childbirth and Artificial Insemination: A Wave of the Future," in *Anthropology of*

Human Birth, ed. Margarita Artschwager Kay (Philadelphia: F. A. Davis, 1982), 321–340.

51. Stripping the membrane can be a painful procedure, meant to weaken the amniotic sac and to stimulate labor less dramatically than amniotomy, which actually punctures the amniotic sac.

52. Although interviewing fathers would have made an interesting comparison, both for reasons of time and research interest I chose not to. For a moving and provocative reflection on a father's experience of home and hospital birth, see Ronald L. Grimes, *Marrying & Burying: Rites of Passage in a Man's Life* (Boulder, Colo.: Westview Press, 1995), 155–185. For more on fathers and childbirth, see Dennis Kulpa, "The Father's Experience of Childbirth" (Ph.D. diss., Union Institute, 1992); Joel Richman and W. O. Goldthorp, "Fatherhood: The Social Construction of Pregnancy and Birth," in *The Place of Birth*, ed. Sheila Kitzinger and John Davis (Oxford: Oxford University Press, 1978), 157–173; Max Philip Shapiro, "Fathers' Experiences of Childbirth" (Ph.D. diss., Boston University, 1980).

53. Sondra's dismay at the interventions of her midwives points to the dilemmas certified nurse-midwives face in walking the line between "medical" and "holistic" approaches. Sondra and her husband, who specifically chose certified nurse-midwives because of their medical training, had requested that the umbilical cord not be cut immediately and that the baby not be suctioned after birth. Both of these things happened, and while Sondra and her husband agreed that they were necessary procedures, Sondra wished the midwives would have told her what they were doing at the time. Instead they acted quickly, and Sondra felt "tricked."

54. Tikva Frymer-Kensky, *Motherprayer: The Pregnant Woman's Spiritual Companion* (New York: Riverhead Books, 1995), 190.

55. Ibid.

56. Parvati Baker, in Davis-Floyd, *Birth as an American Rite of Passage*, 71.

57. Mary S. Sheridan, *Pain in America* (Tuscaloosa: University of Alabama Press, 1992), 109.

58. Ibid.

59. Eisenberg, Murkoff, and Hathaway, *What to Expect When You're Expecting*, 232, 227. The denial that women may prove their strength or endurance in childbirth and the assertion that medication is natural show how mainstream childbirth literature self-consciously places itself in opposition to alternative approaches—which do sometimes consider childbirth a feat of strength or endurance.

60. Marina Warner makes this comment in her discussion of the Virgin Mary's milk, and was writing specifically of "Christian affirmations" of "natural" childbirth and breast-feeding, Marina Warner, *Alone of All Her Sex: The Myth and the Cult of the Virgin Mary* (London: Picador, 1976,), 204–205.

61. Kathleen Barry, in Mary Daly, *Gyn/ecology: The Metaethics of Radical Feminism* (Boston: Beacon Press, 1990), 285.

62. Harrison and Heyward, "Pain and Pleasure," 134; emphasis in original.

63. Ibid., 138; emphasis in original.

64. Martin S. Pernick, *A Calculus of Suffering*, 186; Sandelowski, *Pain, Pleasure, and American Childbirth*, 114. Pernick also showed how race and class affected the use of anesthesia, with doctors generally thinking that lower-class and non-European people were better able to handle pain and in less need of anesthesia.

65. Robert A. Orsi, *Thank You, St. Jude: Women's Devotion to the Patron Saint of Hopeless Causes* (New Haven: Yale University Press, 1996), 165.

66. Emily Martin, "The Ideology of Reproduction: The Reproduction of Ideology," in *Uncertain Terms: Negotiating Gender in American Culture*, ed. Faye Ginsburg and Anna Lowenhaupt Tsing (Boston: Beacon Press, 1990), 309.

67. Ellen Lazarus, "What Do Women Want?: Issues of Choice, Control, and Class in Pregnancy and Childbirth," *Medical Anthropology Quarterly* 8, no. 1 (1994): 32, 36.

68. Ibid., 34.

69. Janice M. Morse and Caroline Park, "Differences in Cultural Expectations of the Perceived Painfulness of Childbirth," in *Childbirth in America: Anthropological Perspectives*, ed. Karen L. Michaelson (South Hadley, Mass.: Bergin and Garvey, 1988), 129.

70. Bakan, *Disease, Pain & Sacrifice*, 77.

71. Ibid., 79.

72. David Morris, *The Culture of Pain* (Berkeley: University of California Press, 1991), 12, 143.

73. Ibid., 138.

74. Ibid., 208.

75. Orsi, *Thank you, St. Jude*, 158.

76. Pamela A. Smith, "Chronic Pain and Creative Possibility: A Psychological Phenomenon Confronts Theologies of Suffering" in *Broken and Whole: Essays on Religion and the Body*, ed. Maureen A. Tilley and Susan A. Ross (Lanham, Md.: University Press of America, 1993), 179.

77. I am grateful to Karen McCarthy Brown for this insight.

78. Bynum, *Holy Feast, Holy Fast*, 301.

79. Kimiko Hahn, "A Feminist Moment," in *Mother Journeys: Feminists Write about Mothering*, ed., Maureen T. Reddy, Martha Roth, and Amy Sheldon (Minneapolis: Spinsters Ink, 1994), 61.

Epilogue
The Miracle of Birth

1. Emily Martin, "The Ideology of Reproduction: The Reproduction of Ideology," in *Uncertain Terms: Negotiating Gender in American Culture*, ed. Faye Ginsburg and Anna Lowenhaupt Tsing (Boston: Beacon Press, 1990), 300.

2. Janet Gallagher, "Collective Bad Faith: 'Protecting the Fetus,'" in *Reproduction, Ethics, and the Law: Feminist Perspectives*, ed. Joan C. Callahan (Bloomington: Indiana University Press, 1994), 350.

3. Ibid.

4. Brenda Waugh, "Repro-Woman: A View of the Labyrinth (from the Lithotomy Position)," *Yale Journal of Law and Feminism* 3, no. 5–61 (1991): 34.

5. Ellen Lewin, "On the Outside Looking In: The Politics of Lesbian Motherhood," in *Conceiving the New World Order: The Global Politics of Reproduction*, ed. Faye D. Ginsburg and Rayna Rapp (Berkeley: University of California Press, 1995), 117.

6. Further research on the birth choices and experiences of women who have used new reproductive technologies is necessary. For a personal and a scholarly account of the complexities of "assisted reproduction," see Lila Abu-Lughod, "A Tale of Two Pregnancies," in *Women Writing Culture*, ed. Ruth Behar and Deborah A. Gordon (Berkeley: University of California Press, 1995), 339–349; and Sarah Franklin, "Postmodern Procreation: A Cultural Account of Assisted Reproduction," in *Conceiving the New World Order: The Global Politics of Reproduction*, ed. Faye D. Ginsburg and Rayna Rapp (Berkeley: University of California Press, 1995), 323–345.

7. Valerie Hartouni, "Containing Women: Reproductive Discourse in the 1980s," in *Technoculture*, ed. Constance Penley and Andrew Ross (Minneapolis: University of Minnesota Press, 1991), 48.

8. Natalie Angier, "Baby in a Box," *New York Times Magazine*, 16 May 1999 p. 88.

9. Carol A. Stabile, *Feminism and the Technological Fix* (Manchester, U.K.: Manchester University Press, 1994), 93.

10. Faye D. Ginsburg, *Contested Lives: The Abortion Debate in an American Community* (Berkeley: University of California Press, 1989), 204.

11. Stabile, *Feminism and the Technological Fix*, 94.

12. Rayna Rapp, "Accounting for Amniocentesis," in *Knowledge, Power, and Practice: The Anthropology of Medicine and Everyday Life*, ed. S. Lindenbaum and M. Lock (Berkeley: University of California Press, 1993), 65.

13. Linda Layne, "Of Fetuses and Angels: Fragmentation and Integration in Narratives of Pregnancy Loss," *Knowledge and Society: The Anthropology of Science and Technology* 9 (1992): 31.

14. For another perspective on this fusion, see Emily Martin, *Flexible Bodies: Tracking Immunity in American Culture—From the Days of Polio to the Age of AIDS* (Boston: Beacon Press, 1994).

15. Mary-Jo DelVecchio Good et al, eds., *Pain as Human Experience: An Anthropological Perspective* (Berkeley: University of California Press, 1992), 205.

16. American College of Nurse-Midwives (ACNM) and Sandra Jacobs, *Having Your Baby with a Nurse-Midwife* (New York: Hyperion, 1993); George Judson, "The Trials of an American Midwife," *New York Times*, 4 November 1995, pp. 25, 29.

17. Ellen Lazarus, "What Do Women Want?: Issues of Choice, Control, and Class in Pregnancy and Childbirth," *Medical Anthropology Quarterly* 8, no. 1 (1994): 42. Regarding calls for a version of socialized medicine among home-birth advocates, see Ina May Gaskin's editorial in the fall 1994 issue of *Birth Gazette*; and Sheryl Burt Ruzek, "Ethical Issues in Childbirth Technology," in *Birth Control and Controlling Birth: Women-Centered Perspectives*, ed. Helen B. Holmes, Betty B. Hoskins, and Michael Gross (Clifton, N.J.: Humana Press, 1980), 197–202.

18. Mary Poovey, "'Scenes of an Indelicate Character': The Medical 'Treatment' of Victorian Women," in *The Making of the Modern Body: Sexuality and Society in the Nineteenth Century*, ed. Catherine Gallagher and Thomas Laqueur (Berkeley: University of California Press, 1987), 156.

Bibliography

Abraham-Van der Mark, Eva, ed. 1993. *Successful Home Birth and Midwifery: The Dutch Model*. Westport, Conn.: Bergin and Garvey.

Abu-Lughod, Lila. 1990. "Can There Be a Feminist Ethnography?" *Women and Performance: A Journal of Feminist Theory* 5:7–27.

———. 1995. "A Tale of Two Pregnancies." In *Women Writing Culture*. Ed. Ruth Behar and Deborah A. Gordon. Berkeley: University of California Press.

Abu-Lughod, Lila, and Catherine A. Lutz, eds. 1990. *Language and the Politics of Emotion*. Cambridge: Cambridge University Press.

Acheson, Louise. 1995. "Perinatal, Infant, and Child Death Rates among the Old Order Amish." Abstracted in *Birth Gazette* 11, no. 3:36.

Ackerman-Liebrich, Ursula, et al. 1996. "Home versus Hospital Deliveries: Follow Up Study of Matched Pairs for Procedures and Outcomes." *British Medical Journal* 313 (23 November): 1313–1318.

Adams, Alice E. 1994. *Reproducing the Womb: Images of Childbirth in Science, Feminist Theory, and Literature*. Ithaca: Cornell University Press.

Albanese, Catherine L. 1988. "Religion and the American Experience: A Century After." *Church History* 57:337–351.

———. 1990. *Nature Religion in America*. Chicago: University of Chicago Press.

Alexander, Meena. 1996. *The Shock of Arrival: Reflections on Postcolonial Experience*. Boston: South End Press.

Allende, Isabel. 1995. *Paula*. New York: HarperCollins.

American College of Nurse-Midwives (ACNM) and Sandra Jacobs. 1993. *Having Your Baby with a Nurse-Midwife*. New York: Hyperion.

Anderson, Rondi E., and Patricia Aikins Murphy. 1995. "Outcomes of 11,788 Planned Home Births Attended by Certified Nurse-Midwives: A Retrospective Descriptive Study." *Journal of Nurse-Midwifery* 40, no. 6:483–492.

Anderson, Sandra Vandam, and Eleanor E. Bauwens. 1982. "An Ethnography of Home Birth." In *Anthropology of Human Birth*. Ed. Margarita Artschwager Kay. Philadelphia: F. A. Davis.

Angier, Natalie. 1996. "Why Babies Are Born Facing Backward, Helpless and Chubby." *New York Times*. 23 July, C1, C11.

———. 1999. "Baby in a Box." *New York Times Magazine*. 16 May, 86–90, 154.

Annas, George. 1982. "Forced Cesareans: The Most Unkindest Cut of All." *Hastings Center Report* 12, no. 3:16–17, 45.

Arms, Suzanne. 1977 [1975]. *Immaculate Deception: A New Look at Women and Childbirth in America*. New York: Bantam.

Armstrong, Penny, and Sheryl Feldman. 1986. *A Midwife's Story*. New York: Arbor House.

Arnup, Katherine. 1994. *Education for Motherhood: Advice for Mothers in Twentieth-Century Canada*. Toronto: University of Toronto Press.

Asad, Talal. 1993. *Genealogies of Religion: Discipline and Reasons of Power in Christianity and Islam*. Baltimore: Johns Hopkins University Press.

———. 1997. "On Torture, or Cruel, Inhuman, and Degrading Treatment," in *Social Suffering*, 285–308. Ed. Arthur Kleinman, Veena Das, and Margaret Lock. Berkeley: University of California Press.

———. 2000. "Agency and Pain: An Exploration." In *Culture and Religion*, vol. 1, no. 1: 33–52, 58–60.

Bachelard, Gaston. 1964 [1958]. *The Poetics of Space*. Trans. Maria Jolas. Boston: Beacon Press.

Bakan, David. 1966. *Disease, Pain & Sacrifice: Toward a Psychology of Suffering*. Chicago: University of Chicago Press.

Balaskas, Janet, and Yehudi Gordon. 1992. *The Encyclopedia of Pregnancy and Birth*. London: Little, Brown.

Baldwin, Rahima. 1979. *Special Delivery: The Complete Guide to Informed Birth*. Millbrae, Calif.: Les Femmes.

Balizet, Carol. 1996. *Born in Zion*. 3d ed. Grapevine, Tex.: Perazim House.

Barrett, Nina. 1990. *I Wish Someone Had Told Me: Comfort, Support and Advice for New Moms from More than 60 Real-life Mothers*. New York: Simon and Schuster.

Bartky, Sandra Lee. 1990. *Femininity and Domination: Studies in the Phenomenology of Oppression*. New York: Routledge.

Beecher, Maureen Ursenbach. 1982. "Birthing." In *Mormon Women Speak*. Ed. May Lythgoe Bradford. Salt Lake City: Olympus.

Behar, Ruth, and Deborah A. Gordon, eds. 1995. *Women Writing Culture*. Berkeley: University of California Press.

Bell, Catherine. 1992. *Ritual Theory, Ritual Practice*. New York: Oxford University Press.

Bellah, Robert N., et al. 1985. *Habits of the Heart: Individualism and Commitment in American Life*. New York: Harper and Row.

Bergenheim, Agneta. 1995. "Spiritual Emergency Treatment of the Newborn." *Birth Gazette* 11, no. 3:14–15.

Bergum, Vangie. 1989. *Woman to Mother: A Transformation*. Granby, Mass.: Bergin and Garvey.

Blaetz, Robin. 1992. "In Search of the Mother Tongue: Childbirth and the Cinema." *Velvet Light Trap* 29:15–20.

Blum, Linda M. 1999. *At the Breast: Ideologies of Breastfeeding and Motherhood in the Contemporary United States*. Boston: Beacon Press.

Boddy, Janice. 1989. *Wombs and Alien Spirits: Women, Men and the Zār Cult in Northern Sudan*. Madison: University of Wisconsin Press.

———. 1998. "Remembering Amal: On Birth and the British in Northern Sudan." In *Pragmatic Women and Body Politics*. Ed. M. Lock and P. A. Kaufert. Cambridge: Cambridge University Press.

Bogdan, Janet Carlisle. 1990. "Childbirth in America 1650 to 1990." In *Women, Health, and Medicine in America*. Ed. Rima D. Apple. New York: Garland.

Boris, Eileen. 1994. "Mothers Are Not Workers: Homework Regulation and the Construction of Motherhood, 1948–1953." In *Mothering: Ideology, Experience, Agency*. Ed. Evelyn Nakano Glenn, Grace Chang, and Linda Rennie Forcey. New York: Routledge.

Borst, Charlotte. 1990. "The Professionalization of Obstetrics: Childbirth Becomes a Medical Specialty." In *Women, Health, and Medicine in America*. Ed. Rima D. Apple. New York: Garland.

———. 1995. *Catching Babies: The Professionalization of Childbirth, 1870–1920*. Cambridge: Harvard University Press.

Bortin, Sylvia, Marina Alzugaray, Judy Dowd, and Janice Kalman. 1994. "A Feminist Perspective on the Study of Home Birth: Application of a Midwifery Care Framework." *Journal of Nurse-Midwifery* 39, no. 3:142–149.

Bourdieu, Pierre. 1977. *Outline of a Theory of Practice*. Trans. Richard Nice. Cambridge: Cambridge University Press.

———. 1984. *Distinction: A Social Critique of the Judgement of Taste*. Cambridge: Harvard University Press.

———. 1990a. *In Other Words: Essays Towards a Reflexive Sociology*. Trans. Matthew Adamson. Stanford: Stanford University Press.

———. 1990b. *The Logic of Practice*. Trans. Richard Nice. Stanford: Stanford University Press.

Boyarin, Daniel. 1993. *Carnal Israel: Reading Sex in Talmudic Culture*. Berkeley: University of California Press.

Brackbill, Yvonne, Karen McManus, and Lynn Woodward. 1985. *Medication in Maternity: Infant Exposure and Maternal Information*. International Academy for Research in Learning Disabilities, Monograph Series, Number 2. Ann Arbor: University of Michigan Press.

Bradley, Robert A. 1974. *Husband-Coached Childbirth*, rev. ed. New York: Harper and Row.

Braidotti, Rosi. 1994. *Nomadic Subjects: Embodiment and Sexual Difference in Contemporary Feminist Theory*. New York: Columbia University Press.

Brandt, Di. 1993. *Wild Mother Dancing: Maternal Narrative in Canadian Literature*. Winnipeg: University of Manitoba Press.

Brown, Joanne Carlson, and Carole R. Bohn, eds. 1989. *Christianity, Patriarchy, and Abuse: A Feminist Critique*. New York: Pilgrim Press.

Brown, Karen McCarthy. 1991. *Mama Lola: A Vodou Priestess in Brooklyn*. Berkeley: University of California Press.

———. 1995. "Serving the Spirits: The Ritual Economy of Haitian Vodou." In *Sacred Arts of Haitian Vodou*. Ed. Donald J. Cosentino. Los Angeles: UCLA Fowler Museum of Cultural History.

Burtch, Brian. 1994. *Trials of Labor: The Re-emergence of Midwifery*. Montreal and Kingston: McGill–Queen's University Press.

Butler, Judith. 1993. *Bodies that Matter: On the Discursive Limits of "Sex."* New York: Routledge.

Bynum, Caroline Walker. 1987. *Holy Feast and Holy Fast*. Berkeley: University of California Press.

———. 1991. *Fragmentation and Redemption: Essays on Gender and the Human Body in Medieval Religion*. New York: Zone Books.

Caldecott, Leonie. 1987. "Inner Anatomy of a Birth." In *Sex and God: Some Varieties of Women's Religious Experience*. Ed. Linda Hurcombe. New York: Routledge and Kegan Paul.

Callaway, Helen. 1993. "The Most Essentially Female Function of All': Giving Birth." In *Defining Females: The Nature of Women in Society*. Ed. Shirley Ardener. Oxford: Berg.

Campanella, Karla, Jill E. Korbin, and Louise Acheson. 1993. "Pregnancy and Childbirth among the Amish." *Social Science and Medicine* 36, no. 3:333–342.

Campbell, Rona, and Alison Macfarlane. 1990. "Recent Debate on the Place of Birth." In *The Politics of Maternity Care: Services for Childbearing Women in Twentieth-Century Britain*. Ed. Jo Garcia, Robert Kilpatrick, and Martin Richards. Oxford: Clarendon Press.

Carter, Pamela. 1995. *Feminism, Breasts, and Breast-feeding*. London: MacMillan.

Carter, Patricia Cloyd. 1957. *Come Gently, Sweet Lucina*. Titusville, Fla.: Patricia Cloyd Carter.

Chatterjee, Margaret. 1997. "The Smorgasbord Syndrome: Availability Reexamined." In *Modern Spiritualities: An Inquiry*. Ed. Laurence Brown, Bernard C. Farr, and R. Joseph Hoffman. Oxford: Prometheus.

Christ, Carol P. 1986. *Diving Deep and Surfacing: Women Writers on Spiritual Quest*. 2d ed. Boston: Beacon Press.

Clarke, Adele E. 1990. "Women's Health: Life-Cycle Issues." In *Women, Health, and Medicine in America*. Ed. Rima D. Apple. New York: Garland.

Clifford, James, and George Marcus, eds. 1986. *Writing Culture: The Poetics and Politics of Ethnography*. Berkeley: University of California Press.

Cohen, Nancy Wainer. 1991. *Open Season: A Survival Guide for Natural Childbirth and VBAC in the 90s*. New York: Bergin and Garvey.

Cohen, Nancy Wainer, and Lois Estner. 1982. *Silent Knife: Cesarean Prevention and Vaginal Birth after Cesarean*. New York: Bergin and Garvey.

Collier, Jane, Michelle Z. Rosaldo, and Sylvia Yanagisako. 1992. "Is There a Family?" In *Rethinking the Family: Some Feminist Questions*, 2d ed. Ed. Barrie Thorne, with Marilyn Yalom. Boston: Northeastern University Press.

Cooey, Paula. 1991. "The Redemption of the Body." In *After Patriarchy: Feminist Transformations of the World Religions*. Ed. Paula M. Cooey, William R. Eakin, and Jay B. McDaniel. Maryknoll, N.Y.: Orbis.

Cosslett, Tess. 1994. *Women Writing Childbirth: Modern Discourses of Motherhood*. Manchester, U.K.: Manchester University Press.

Coster, William. 1990. "Purity, Profanity, and Puritanism: The Churching of Women." In *Women in the Church*. Ed. W. Sheils and Diana Wood. Cambridge, Mass.: Basil Blackwell.

Cott, Nancy F. 1977. *The Bonds of Womanhood: "Woman's Sphere" in New England, 1780–1835*. New Haven: Yale University Press.

Daly, Mary. 1990. *Gyn/ecology: The Metaethics of Radical Feminism*. Boston: Beacon Press.

Danzi, Angela D. 1993. "From Home to Hospital: Jewish and Italian American Women and Childbirth, 1920–1940." Ph.D. diss., New York University.

Davidman, Lynn. 1991. *Tradition in a Rootless World: Women Turn to Orthodox Judaism*. Berkeley: University of California Press.

Davie, Jody Shapiro. 1995. *Women in the Presence.*. Philadelphia: University of Pennsylvania Press.

Davis, Elizabeth. 1983. *A Guide to Midwifery: Heart and Hands.* New York: Bantam.

Davis-Floyd, Robbie E. 1992. *Birth as an American Rite of Passage.* Berkeley: University of California Press.

———. 1996. "The Technocratic Body and the Organic Body: Hegemony and Heresy in Women's Birth Choices." In *Gender and Health: An International Perspective.* Ed. Carolyn F. Sargent and Caroline B. Brettell. Upper Saddle River, N.J.: Prentice Hall.

Davis-Floyd, Robbie E., and Elizabeth Davis. 1997. "Intuition as Authoritative Knowledge in Midwifery and Home Birth." In *Childbirth and Authoritative Knowledge: Cross-Cultural Perspectives.* Ed. Robbie E. Davis-Floyd and Carolyn F. Sargent. Berkeley: University of California Press.

Day, Dorothy. 1981 [1952]. *The Long Loneliness: An Autobiography.* New York: HarperCollins.

De Beauvoir, Simone. 1953. *The Second Sex.* Trans. H. M. Parshley. New York: Knopf.

Declercq, Eugene R., Lisa L. Paine, and Michael R. Winter. 1995. "Home Birth in the United States, 1989–1992: A Longitudinal Descriptive Report of National Birth Certificate Data." *Journal of Nurse-Midwifery* 40, no. 6: 474–482.

Delaney, Carol. 1998. *Abraham on Trial: The Social Legacy of Biblical Myth.* Princeton: Princeton University Press.

———. 1991. *The Seed and the Soil: Gender and Cosmology in Turkish Village Society.* Berkeley: University of California Press.

Dhondt, Melanie. 1996. "Birthing: Medical or Natural?" *Suburban Parent,* 4–5, 4 January.

Diamond, Irene. 1994. *Fertile Ground: Women, Earth, and the Limits of Control.* Boston: Beacon Press.

Dickinson, Emily. 1955. *The Poems of Emily Dickinson.* Ed. Thomas H. Johnson. Cambridge: Belknap Press of Harvard University Press.

Dick-Read, Grantly. 1959. *Childbirth without Fear: The Principles and Practice of Natural Childbirth.* 2d rev. ed. New York: Harper and Row.

Di Leonardo, Micaela. 1985. "Morals, Mothers, and Militarism: Antimilitarism and Feminist Theory." *Feminist Studies* 11, no. 3:599–617.

Dinges, William D. 1995. "'We Are What You Were': Roman Catholic Traditionalism in America." In *Being Right: Conservative Catholics in America.* Ed. R. Scott Appleby and Mary Jo Weaver. Bloomington: Indiana University Press.

Diulio, Rosemary Cline. 1986. *Childbirth: An Annotated Bibliography and Guide.* New York: Garland.

Donegan, Jane B. 1978. *Women and Men Midwives: Medicine, Morality, and Misogyny in Early America.* Westport, Conn.: Greenwood Press.

Donnison, Jean. 1977. *Midwives and Medical Men: A History of Inter-Professional Rivalries and Women's Rights.* New York: Schocken.

Dougherty, Molly C. 1978. "Southern Lay Midwives as Ritual Specialists." In *Women in Ritual and Symbolic Roles.* Ed. Judith Hoch-Smith and Anita Spring. New York: Plenum Press.

Douglas, Mary. 1984 [1966]. *Purity and Danger: An Analysis of the Concepts of Pollution and Taboo.* London and New York: Ark Paperbacks.

Douglas, Mary. 1992. *Risk and Blame: Essays in Cultural Theory.* New York: Routledge.

Duden, Barbara. 1993. *Disembodying Women: Perspectives on Pregnancy and the Unborn.* Cambridge: Harvard University Press.

Dye, Carol Schrom. 1980. "History of Childbirth in America." *Signs* 6, no. 1 97–108.

Eakins, Pamela S., ed. 1986. *The American Way of Birth.* Philadelphia: Temple University Press.

Eddy, Mary Baker. 1994 [1875]. *Science and Health with a Key to the Scriptures.* Boston: First Church of Christ, Scientist.

Eggebroten, Anne. 1989. "The Cost of Life: A Mother Experiences Incarnation." *The Other Side* 25, no. 3: 46.

Ehrenreich, Barbara, and Deirdre English. 1973. *Witches, Midwives, and Nurses: A History of Women Healers.* Old Westbury, N.Y.: Feminist Press.

———. 1979. *For Her Own Good: 150 Years of the Experts' Advice to Women.* Garden City, N.Y. Anchor Books.

Eisenberg, Arlene, Heidi E. Murkoff, and Sandee E. Hathaway. 1991. *What to Expect When You're Expecting.* 2d rev. ed. New York: Workman.

Eisenstein, Mayer. 1988. *Give Birth at Home with the Home Court Advantage.* Chicago: Mayer Eisenstein.

Eisler, Riane. 1995. *Sacred Pleasure: Sex, Myth, and the Politics of the Body.* San Francisco: HarperSanFrancisco.

Eller, Cynthia. 1993. *Living in the Lap of the Goddess: The Feminist Spirituality Movement in America.* New York: Crossroad.

Epstein, Barbara Leslie. 1981. *The Politics of Domesticity: Women, Evangelism, and Temperance in Nineteenth Century America.* Middletown, Conn.: Wesleyan University Press.

Epstein, Julia. 1995. *Altered Conditions: Disease, Medicine, and Storytelling.* New York: Routledge.

Fichter, Joseph. 1981. *Religion and Pain: The Spiritual Dimensions of Health Care.* New York: Crossroad.

Finkelstein, Baruch, and Michal Finkelstein. 1993. *B'Sha'ah Tovah: The Jewish Woman's Clinical and Halachic Guide to Pregnancy and Childbirth.* Jerusalem and New York: Feldheim Publishers.

Firestone, Shulamith. 1972. *The Dialectic of Sex.* New York: Bantam.

Foucault, Michel. 1972. *The Archaeology of Knowledge and the Discourse on Language.* New York: Pantheon.

Franklin, Sarah. 1995. "Postmodern Procreation: A Cultural Account of Assisted Reproduction." In *Conceiving the New World Order: The Global Politics of Reproduction.* Ed. Faye D. Ginsburg and Rayna Rapp. Berkeley: University of California Press.

Fraser, Gertrude J. 1988. "Afro-American Midwives, Biomedicine and the State: An Ethno-historical Account of Birth and Its Transformation in Rural Virginia." Ph.D. diss., Johns Hopkins University.

———. 1995. "Modern Bodies, Modern Minds: Midwifery and Reproductive Change in an African American Community." In *Conceiving the New World*

Order: The Global Politics of Reproduction. Ed. Faye D. Ginsburg and Rayna
Rapp. Berkeley: University of California Press.

Frymer-Kensky, Tikva. 1995. *Motherprayer: The Pregnant Woman's Spiritual Companion.* New York: Riverhead Books.

Gallagher, Janet. 1984. "The Fetus and the Law—Whose Life Is It Anyway?" *Ms. Magazine* 66, no. 8 (September) 66–68:134–135.

———. 1987. "Prenatal Invasions & Interventions: What's Wrong with Fetal Rights." *Harvard Women's Law Journal* 10:9–58.

———. 1989. "Fetus as Patient." In *Reproductive Laws for the 1990s.* Ed. Sherrill Cohen and Nadine Taub. Clifton, N.J.: Humana Press.

———. 1994. "Collective Bad Faith: 'Protecting the Fetus.'" In *Reproduction, Ethics, and the Law: Feminist Perspectives.* Ed. Joan C. Callahan. Bloomington: Indiana University Press.

Gaskin, Ina May. 1975. *Spiritual Midwifery.* 1st ed. Summertown, Tenn.: Book Publishing Company.

———. 1990. *Spiritual Midwifery.* 3d ed. Summertown, Tenn.: Book Publishing Company.

———. 1995. "Review of *Born in Zion.*" *Birth Gazette* 11, no. 3:41–42.

Gélis, Jacques. 1991 [1984]. *History of Childbirth: Fertility, Pregnancy, and Birth in Early Modern Europe.* Trans. Rosemary Morris. Cambridge: Polity Press.

Ginsburg, Faye, D. 1989. *Contested Lives: The Abortion Debate in an American Community.* Berkeley: University of California Press.

Ginsburg, Faye, D. and Rayna Rapp. 1991. "The Politics of Reproduction." *Annual Review of Anthropology* 20:311–343.

Ginsburg, Faye D., and Rayna Rapp, eds. 1995. *Conceiving the New World Order: The Global Politics of Reproduction.* Berkeley: University of California Press.

Glenn, Evelyn Nakano. 1994. "Social Constructions of Mothering: A Thematic Overview." In *Mothering: Ideology, Experience & Agency.* Ed. Evelyn Nakano Glenn, Grace Change, and Linda Rennie Forcey. New York: Routledge.

Godwin, Sandra E. 1993. "Mothers on Pedestals: A Look at Childbirth Advice Books and Julia Kristeva." M.A. thesis, Boston College.

Good, Mary-Jo DelVecchio, et al., eds. 1992. *Pain as Human Experience: An Anthropological Perspective.* Berkeley: University of California Press.

Goodwin, James W. 1997. Where to Be Born Safely: Professional Midwifery and the Case against Home Birth. *Journal of the Society of Obstetricians and Gynecologists of Canada* 19, no. 11:1179–1188.

Gordon, Deborah R. 1988. "Tenacious Assumptions in Western Medicine." In *Biomedicine Examined.* Ed. Margaret Lock and Deborah R. Gordon. Dordrecht: Kluwer Academic.

Gould, Rebecca Kneale. 1997. "Getting (Not Too) Close to Nature: Modern Homesteading as Lived Religion in America." In *Lived Religion in America: Toward a History of Practice.* Ed. David D. Hall. Princeton: Princeton University Press.

Graham, Hilary. 1976. "The Social Image of Pregnancy: Pregnancy as Spirit Possession." *Sociological Review* N.S. 24, no. 2:291–308.

Griffith, R. Marie. 1997. *God's Daughters: Evangelical Women and the Power of Submission.* Berkeley: University of California Press.

Grimes, Ronald L. 1995. *Marrying & Burying: Rites of Passage in a Man's Life*. Boulder, Colo.: Westview Press.

Gross, Rita. 1980. "Menstruation and Childbirth as Ritual and Religious Experience among Native Australians." In *Unspoken Worlds: Women's Religious Lives in Non-Western Cultures*. Ed. Nancy Falk and Rita Gross. San Francisco: Harper and Row.

Gruenbaum, Ellen. 1998. "Resistance and Embrace: Sudanese Rural Women and Systems of Power." In *Pragmatic Women and Body Politics*. Ed. Margaret Lock and Patricia Kaufert. Cambridge: Cambridge University Press.

Hahn, Kimiko. 1994. "A Feminist Moment." In *Mother Journeys: Feminists Write about Mothering*. Ed. Maureen T. Reddy, Martha Roth, and Amy Sheldon. Minneapolis: Spinsters Ink.

Hall, David D. 1989. *Worlds of Wonder, Days of Judgment: Popular Religious Belief in Early New England*. Cambridge: Harvard University Press.

Hall, Nor and Warren R. Dawson. 1989. *Broodmales*. Dallas: Spring Publications.

Hammer, Margaret L. 1994. *Giving Birth: Reclaiming Biblical Metaphor for Pastoral Practice*. Louisville, Ky.: Westminster/John Knox Press.

———. 1997. *A Spiritual Guide to Pregnancy*. Minneapolis: Augsburg.

Haraway, Donna J. 1991. *Simians, Cyborgs and Women: The Reinvention of Nature*. New York: Routledge.

Harrison, Beverly Wildung, and Carter Heyward. 1984. "Pain and Pleasure: Avoiding the Confusions of Christian Tradition in Feminist Theory." In *Sexuality and the Sacred: Sources for Theological Reflection*. Ed. James B. Nelson and Sandra P. Longfellow. Louisville, Ky.: Westminster/John Knox Press.

Hartouni, Valerie. 1991. "Containing Women: Reproductive Discourse in the 1980s." In *Technoculture*. Ed. Constance Penley and Andrew Ross. Minneapolis: University of Minnesota Press.

Hays, Sharon. 1996. *The Cultural Contradictions of Motherhood*. New Haven: Yale University Press.

Hazell, Lester Dessez. 1974. *Birth Goes Home*. Seattle: Catalyst.

Hazlett, William H. 1963. "The Advantages of Full Consciousness in Childbirth." In *Religion and Birth Control*. Ed. John Clover Monsma. Garden City, N.Y.: Doubleday.

Heggenhougen, H. K. 1980. "Father and Childbirth: An Anthropological Perspective." *Journal of Nurse-Midwifery* 25, no. 6:21–26.

Hendrick, Gladys West. 1978. *My First 300 Babies*. Santa Ana, Calif.: Vision House Publishers.

Hess, David J. 1993. *Science in the New Age: The Paranormal, Its Defenders and Debunkers, and American Culture*. Madison: University of Wisconsin Press.

Hewitt, Nancy. 1988. "The Economics of Family Life." *National Women's Studies Association Journal* 1, no. 1:114–119.

Hill, Patricia, R. 1985. *The World Their Household: The American Woman's Foreign Mission Movement and Cultural Transformation, 1870–1920*. Ann Arbor: University of Michigan Press.

Hoffert, Sylvia D. 1989. *Private Matters: American Attitudes toward Childbearing and Infant Nurture in the Urban North, 1800–1860*. Urbana: University of Illinois Press.

Hogan, Linda. 1995. *From Women's Experience to Feminist Theology.* London: Sheffield Press.

Holbrook, Martin Luther. 1871. *Parturition without Pain: A Code of Directions for Escaping from the Primal Curse.* New York: Wood and Holbrook.

Holmes, Helen B., Betty B. Hoskins, and Michael Gross, eds. 1980. *Birth Control and Controlling Birth: Women-Centered Perspectives.* Clifton, N.J.: Humana Press.

Holmes, Linda. 1986. "African American Midwives in the South." In *The American Way of Birth.* Ed. Pamela Eakins. Philadelphia: Temple University Press.

Homans, Hilary. 1994. "Pregnancy and Birth as Rites of Passage for Two Groups of Women in Britain." In *Ethnography of Fertility and Birth.* Ed. Carol P. MacCormack. Prospect Heights, Ill.: Waveland Press. Original edition, London: Academic Press, 1982.

hooks, bell. 1990. *Yearning: Race, Gender, and Cultural Politics.* Boston: South End Press.

Hostetler, John A. 1993. *Amish Society.* 4th ed. Baltimore: Johns Hopkins University Press.

Hubbell, Kimberly. 1982a. "The Neo-Oriental American: Childbearing in the Ashram." In *Anthropology of Human Birth.* Ed. Margarita Kay. Philadelphia: F. A. Davis.

Huff, Cynthia. 1991. "Delivery: The Cultural Re-presentation of Childbirth." *Prose Studies: History, Theory, Criticism* 14, no. 2:108–121.

Institute for Basic Life Principles. N.d. *Basic Concepts in Understanding and Treating Morning Sickness.* N.p.: IBLP.

Jackson, Marsha E., and Alice J. Bailes. 1995. "Home Birth with Certified Nurse-Midwife Attendants in the United States." *Journal of Nurse-Midwifery* 40, no. 6:493–507.

Jacobs, Sandra. 1993. *Having Your Baby with a Nurse-Midwife.* New York: Hyperion and Jacobs.

Jambai, Amara, and Carol McCormack. 1997. "Maternal Health, War, and Religious Tradition: Authoritative Knowledge in Pujehun District, Sierra Leone." In *Childbirth and Authoritative Knowledge: Cross-Cultural Perspectives.* Ed. R. E. Davis-Floyd and C. F. Sargent. Berkeley: University of California Press.

Jay, Nancy. 1992. *Throughout Your Generations Forever: Sacrifice, Religion, and Paternity.* Chicago: University of Chicago Press.

Johnson, Christine Annette. 1987. "Normalizing Birth: The Home Birth Movement in Massachusetts." Ph.D. diss., Boston University.

Jordan, Brigitte. 1993 [1978]. *Birth in Four Cultures.* 4th ed. Prospect Heights, Ill.: Waveland Press.

Joselit, Jenna Weissman. 1994. *The Wonders of America: Reinventing Jewish Culture, 1880–1950.* New York: Hill and Wang.

Judson, George. 1995. "The Trials of an American Midwife." *New York Times.* 4 November, 25, 29.

Junker, Beth C. 1992. "Transition in Childbirth: Claiming Our Own Death and Resurrection. *Daughters of Sarah* 18, no. 4: 4–7.

Kahn, Robbie Pfeufer. 1995. *Bearing Meaning: The Language of Birth.* Urbana: University of Illinois Press.

Kaufert, Patricia, and John O'Neil. 1993. "Analysis of a Dialogue on Risks in Childbirth: Clinicians, Epidemiologists, and Inuit Women." In *Knowledge, Power, and Practice: The Anthropology of Medicine and Everyday Life*. Ed. Shirley Lindenbaum and Margaret Lock. Berkeley: University of California Press.

Kay, Margarita Artschwager, ed. 1982. *Anthropology of Human Birth*. Philadelphia: F. A. Davis.

Keeler, Teresa Frances. 1984. "Narrating, Attitudes, and Health: The Effects of Recounting Pregnancy and Childbirth Experiences on the Well-Being of the Participants." Ph.D. diss., University of California, Los Angeles.

Kerber, Linda K. 1988. "Separate Spheres, Female Worlds, Woman's Place: The Rhetoric of Women's History." *Journal of American History* 75, no. 1:9–39.

Kern, Louis. 1993. "Pronatalism, Midwifery, and Synergistic Marriage: Spiritual Enlightenment and Sexual Ideology on The Farm (Tennessee)." *Women in Spiritual and Communitarian Societies in the United States*. Ed. Wendy E. Chmielewski, Louis J. Kern, and Marlyn Klee-Hartzell. Syracuse: Syracuse University Press.

King, Ynestra. 1992. "Healing the Wounds: Feminism, Ecology, and Nature/Culture Dualism." In *Gender/Body/Knowledge: Feminist Reconstructions of Being and Knowing*. Ed. Alison M. Jaggar and Susan R. Bordo. New Brunswick: Rutgers University Press.

Kitzinger, Sheila. 1978. *Women as Mothers*. Oxford: Martin Robertson.

———. 1991. *Home Birth: The Essential Guide to Giving Birth Outside the Hospital*. New York: Dorling Kindersley.

———. 1994 [1982]. "The Social Context of Birth: Some Comparisons between Childbirth in Jamaica and Britain." In *Ethnography of Fertility and Birth*. Ed. Carol P. MacCormack. Prospect Heights, Ill.: Waveland Press. Original edition, London: Academic Press, 1982.

Klassen, Annemarie. 1994. "Human Dimensions of Space: Home." *Anima* 21, no. 1:14–29.

Kleinman, Arthur. 1980. *Patients and Healers in the Context of Culture*. Berkeley: University of California Press.

Kluckhohn, Clyde, and Dorothea Leighton. 1974. *The Navaho*. Cambridge: Harvard University Press.

Komesaroff, Paul A. 1995. "Introduction." In *Troubled Bodies*. Ed. Paul A. Komesaroff. Durham: Duke University Press.

Kosmin, Barry A., and Seymour P. Lachman. 1993. *One Nation Under God: Religion in Contemporary American Society*. New York: Harmony Books.

Kozol, Wendy. 1995. "Fracturing Domesticity: Media, Nationalism, and the Question of Feminist Influence." *Signs* 20, no. 3:646–667.

Kristolaitis, Cheryl. 1986. "From Purification to Celebration: The History of the Service for Women after Childbirth." *Journal of the Canadian Church Historical Society* 28, no. 2:53–62.

Kroll, Una. 1987. "A Womb-Centered Life." In *Sex and God: Some Varieties of Women's Religious Experience*. Ed. Linda Hurcombe. New York: Routledge and Kegan Paul.

Kulpa, Dennis. 1992. "The Father's Experience of Childbirth." Ph.D. diss., Union Institute.

LaBerge, Agnes N. Ozman. 1985. *What God Hath Wrought: Life and Work of Mrs. Agnes N. O. LaBerge.* New York: Garland.

Ladd-Taylor, Molly. 1994. *Mother-Work: Women, Child Welfare, and the State, 1890–1930.* Urbana: University of Illinois Press.

Laderman, Carol. 1983. *Wives and Midwives: Childbirth and Nutrition in Rural Malaysia.* Berkeley: University of California Press.

Lakoff, George. 1987. *Women, Fire, and Dangerous Things: What Categories Reveal about the Mind.* Chicago: University of Chicago Press.

Lakoff, George, and Mark Johnson. 1980. *Metaphors We Live By.* Chicago: University of Chicago Press.

La Leche League International. 1987 [1958]. *The Womanly Art of Breastfeeding.* 4th rev. ed. New York: New American Library.

Lamphere, Louise. 1977. *To Run After Them: Cultural and Social Bases of Cooperation in a Navajo Community.* Tucson: University of Arizona Press.

Landon, Lana Hartman. 1989. "Suffering over Time: Six Varieties of Pain." *Soundings* 72, no. 1:75–82.

Langton, Phyllis A. 1994. "Obstetricians' Resistance to Independent, Private Practice by Nurse-Midwives in Washington, D.C., Hospitals." *Women & Health* 22, no. 1:27–48.

Lawless, Elaine J. 1991. "Women's Life Stories and Reciprocal Ethnography as Feminist and Emergent." *Journal of Folklore Research* 28, no. 1:35–60.

Layne, Linda. 1992. "Of Fetuses and Angels: Fragmentation and Integration in Narratives of Pregnancy Loss." *Knowledge and Society: The Anthropology of Science and Technology* 9:29–58.

Lazarus, Ellen S. 1988. "Poor Women, Poor Outcomes: Social Class and Reproductive Health." In *Childbirth in America.* Ed. Karen L. Michaelson. South Hadley, Mass.: Bergin and Garvey.

———. 1994. "What Do Women Want?: Issues of Choice, Control, and Class in Pregnancy and Childbirth." *Medical Anthropology Quarterly* 8, no. 1:25–46.

Leal, Tracy. 1995. "Consumerism and Birth Care." *New Jersey Friends of Midwives Newsletter* (holiday issue): 88, no. 9.

Lears, T. J. Jackson. 1983. "From Salvation to Self-Realization." In *The Culture of Consumption: Critical Essays in American History.* Ed. Richard W. Fox and T. J. Jackson Lears. New York: Pantheon.

Leavitt, Judith Walzer. 1980. "Birthing and Anesthesis: The Debate over Twilight Sleep." *Signs* 6, no. 1:147–164.

———. 1986. *Brought to Bed: Childbearing in America, 1750–1950.* New York: Oxford University Press.

———. 1987. "The Growth of Medical Authority: Technology and Morals in Turn-of-the-Century Obstetrics." *Medical Anthropology Quarterly* 1:230–255.

Leboyer, Frederick. 1978. *Birth without Violence.* New York: Alfred A. Knopf.

Lefkowitz, Lori Hope. 1994. "Sacred Screaming: Childbirth in Judaism." In *Lifecycles: Jewish Women on Life Passages and Personal Milestones,* vol. 1. Ed. Rabbi Debra Orenstein. Woodstock, Vt.: Jewish Lights Publishing.

Lelwica, Michelle Mary. 1999. *Starving for Salvation: The Spiritual Dimensions of Eating Problems among American Girls and Women.* New York: Oxford University Press.

Lennon, Patricia M. 1996. "Conceiving Catholicism: Nature, Rhythm, and the Christian Family Movement Survey, 1965–66." Paper presented at the AAR Annual Meeting, New Orleans, La.

Lewin, Ellen. 1995. "On the Outside Looking In: The Politics of Lesbian Mother-hood." In *Conceiving the New World Order: The Global Politics of Reproduction.* Ed. Faye D. Ginsburg and Rayna Rapp. Berkeley: University of California Press.

———. 1998. "Wives, Mothers, and Lesbians: Rethinking Resistance in the U.S." In *Pragmatic Women and Body Politics.* Ed. M. Lock and P. A. Kaufert. Cambridge: Cambridge University Press.

Lichtman, Ronnie. 1988. "Medical Models and Midwifery: The Cultural Experience of Birth." In *Childbirth in America: Anthropological Perspectives.* Ed. Karen L. Michaelson. South Hadley, Mass.: Bergin and Garvey.

Lipkowitz, Keri Heitner. 1986. "Interpretation and Critique of the Choice and Experience of Home Birth: Positive Home Birth Experiences of New York Women." Ph. D. diss., City University of New York.

Lock, Margaret. 1993. "Cultivating the Body: Anthropology and the Epistemologies of Bodily Practice and Knowledge." *Annual Review of Anthropology* 22:133–155.

Lock, Margaret, and Patricia Kaufert, eds. 1998. *Pragmatic Women and Body Politics.* Cambridge: Cambridge University Press.

Logan, Onnie Lee, as told to Katherine Clarke. 1986. *Motherwit: An Alabama Midwife's Story.* New York: Dutton.

Luce, Judith Dickson. 1980. "Ethical Issues Relating to Childbirth as Experienced by the Birthing Woman and Midwife." In *Birth Control and Controlling Birth.* Ed. Helen B. Holmes, Betty B. Hoskins, and Michael Gross. Clifton, N.J.: Humana Press.

MacCormack, Carol P. 1994. "Health, Fertility, and Birth in Moyamba District, Sierra Leone." In *Ethnography of Fertility and Birth.* Ed. Carol P. MacCormack. Prospect Heights, Ill.: Waveland Press. Original edition, London: Academic Press, 1982.

———. 1996. "Risk, Prevention, and International Health Policy." In *Gender and Health: An International Perspective.* Ed Carolyn F. Sargent and Caroline B. Brettell. Upper Saddle River, N.J.: Prentice-Hall.

MacCormack, Carol P., ed. 1994. *Ethnography of Fertility and Birth.* Prospect Heights, Ill.: Waveland Press. Original edition, London: Academic Press, 1982.

MacDonald, Margaret E. 1999. "Expectations: The Cultural Construction of Nature in Midwifery Discourses in Ontario." Ph.D. diss., York University.

Mack, Phyllis. 1998. "Giving Birth to the Truth." *Scottish Journal of Religious Studies* 19, no. 1:19–30.

March, Kathryn S. 1994. "Childbirth with Fear." In *Mother Journeys: Feminists Write about Mothering.* Ed. Maureen T. Reddy, Martha Roth, and Amy Sheldon. Minneapolis: Spinsters Ink.

Martens, Katherine, and Heidi Harms. 1997. *In Her Own Voice: Childbirth Stories from Mennonite Women.* Winnipeg: University of Manitoba Press.

Martin, Biddy, and Chandra Talpade Mohanty. 1986. "Feminist Politics: What's Home Got to Do with It?" In *Feminist Studies/Critical Studies.* Ed. Teresa De Lauretis. Bloomington: Indiana University Press.

Martin, Emily. 1990a. "The Ideology of Reproduction: The Reproduction of Ideology." In *Uncertain Terms: Negotiating Gender in American Culture*. Ed. Faye Ginsburg and Anna Lowenhaupt Tsing. Boston: Beacon Press.

————. 1990b. "Science and Women's Bodies: Forms of Anthropological Knowledge." In *Body Politics: Women, Literature, and the Discourse of Science*. Ed. Mary Jacobus, Evelyn Fox Keller, and Sally Shuttleworth. New York: Routledge, Chapman, and Hall.

————. 1992 [1987]. *The Woman in the Body: A Cultural Analysis of Reproduction*. 2d ed. Boston: Beacon Press.

————. 1994. *Flexible Bodies: Tracking Immunity in American Culture—From the Days of Polio to the Age of AIDS*. Boston: Beacon Press.

Mathews, Joan J., and Kathleen Zadak. 1991. "The Alternative Birth Movement in the United States: History and Current Status." *Women & Health* 17, no. 1:39–56.

Mather, Cotton. 1978 [1741]. *Ornaments for the Daughters of Zion*. Reprint of 3d ed. Delmar, NY: Scholars' Facsimiles and Reprints.

Mauss, Marcel. 1973. "Techniques of the Body." Trans. Ben Brewster. *Economy and Society* 2, no. 1:70–88.

May, Elaine Tyler. 1988. *Homeward Bound: American Families in the Cold War Era*. New York: Basic Books.

McClain, Carol Shepherd. 1981. "Women's Choice of Home or Hospital Birth." *Journal of Family Practice* 12, no. 6:1033–1038.

————. 1982. "Towards a Comparative Framework for the Study of Childbirth." In *Anthropology of Human Birth*. Ed. Margarita Artschwager Kay. Philadelphia: F. A. Davis.

————. 1987. "Some Social Network Differences between Women Choosing Home and Hospital Birth." *Human Organization* 46, no. 2:146–152.

McDannell, Colleen. 1986. *The Christian Home in Victorian American, 1840–1900*. Bloomington: Indiana University Press.

————. 1989. "Catholic Domesticity, 1860–1960." In *American Catholic Women: A Historical Exploration*. Ed. Karen Kennelly. New York: Macmillan.

————. 1995a. "Creating the Christian Home: Home Schooling in Contemporary America." In *American Sacred Space*. Ed. David Chidester and Edward T. Linenthal. Bloomington: Indiana University Press.

————. 1995b. *Material Christianity: Religion and Popular Culture in America*. New Haven: Yale University Press.

McGuire, Meredith. 1990. "Religion and the Body: Rematerializing the Human Body in the Social Sciences of Religion." *Journal for the Scientific Study of Religion* 29, no. 3:283–296.

McGuire, Meredith, with Debra Kantor. 1988. *Ritual Healing in Suburban America*. New Brunswick: Rutgers University Press.

Mead, Margaret. 1972. *Blackberry Winter: My Earlier Years*. New York: Simon and Schuster.

Merchant, Carolyn. 1980. *The Death of Nature: Women, Ecology, and the Scientific Revolution*. San Francisco: Harper and Row.

Meyerowitz, Joanne. 1993. "Beyond the Feminine Mystique: A Reassessment of Postwar Mass Culture, 1946–1958." *Journal of American History* (March): 1455–1482.

Meyrowitz Joshua. 1985. *No Sense of Place: The Impact of Electronic Media on Social Behaviour*. New York: Oxford University Press.

Michaelson, Karen L., ed. 1988. *Childbirth in America: Anthropological Perspectives*. South Hadley, Mass.: Bergin and Garvey.

Michaelson, Karen L., and Barbara Alvin. 1988. "Technology and the Context of Childbirth: A Comparison of Two Hospital Settings." In *Childbirth in America*. Ed. Karen Michaelson. South Hadley, Mass.: Bergin and Garvey.

Michie, Helena, and Naomi R. Cahn. 1996. "Unnatural Births: Cesarean Sections in the Discourse of the Natural Childbirth Movement." In *Gender and Health: An International Perspective*. Ed. Carolyn F. Sargent and Caroline B. Brettell. Upper Saddle River, N.J.: Prentice-Hall.

Midwives Alliance of North America (MANA). 1992. "Statement of Core Values and Ethics." *MANA News* 10, no. 4:10–12.

Miller-McLemore, Bonnie J. 1994. *Also a Mother: Work and Family as Theological Dilemma*. Nashville, Tenn.: Abingdon Press.

Mitford, Jessica. 1992. *The American Way of Birth*. London: V. Gollancz.

———. 1993. "Afterword." In *The American Way of Birth*. Reprinted in *Birth Gazette* 9, no. 3:15–17.

Mizruchi, Susan L. 1998. *The Science of Sacrifice: American Literature and Modern Social Theory*. Princeton: Princeton University Press.

Moi, Toril. 1991. "Appropriating Bourdieu: Feminist Theory and Pierre Bourdieu's Sociology of Culture." *New Literary History* 22:1017–1049.

Moltman-Wendel, Elisabeth. 1995. *I Am My Body: A Theology of Embodiment*. New York: Continuum.

Moore, R. Laurence. 1994. *Selling God: American Religion in the Marketplace of Culture*. New York: Oxford University Press.

Moore, Stephen, 1996. *God's Gym: Divine Male Bodies of the Bible*. New York: Routledge.

Moran, Marilyn. 1981. *Birth and the Dialogue of Love*. Leawood, Kans.: New Nativity Press.

———, ed. 1986. *Happy Birth Days: Personal Accounts of Birth at Home the Intimate, Husband/Wife Way*. Leawood, Kans.: New Nativity Press.

Morantz-Sanchez, Regina. 1994. "Feminist Theory and Historical Practice: Rereading Elizabeth Blackwell." In *Feminists Revision History*. Ed. Ann-Louise Shapiro. New Brunswick: Rutgers University Press.

Morris, David B. 1987. How to Read The Body in Pain. *Literature and Medicine* 6:139–155.

———. 1991. *The Culture of Pain*. Berkeley: University of California Press.

Morse, Janice M., and Caroline Park. 1988. "Differences in Cultural Expectations of the Perceived Painfulness of Childbirth." In *Childbirth in America: Anthropological Perspectives*. Ed. Karen L. Michaelson. South Hadley, Mass.: Bergin and Garvey.

Naragon, Cynthia Ann. 1980. "Childbirth at Home: A Descriptive Study of 675 Couples Who Chose Home Birth. Ph.D. diss., California School Of Professional Psychology.

Nelson, Margaret. 1986. "Birth and Social Class." In *The American Way of Birth.* Ed. Pamela S. Eakins. Philadelphia: Temple University Press.

Nicholson, Linda J. 1986. *Gender and History: The Limits of Social Theory in the Age of the Family.* New York: Columbia University Press.

Noble, Vicki. 1991. *Shakti Woman: Feeling Our Fire, Healing Our World.* San Francisco: HarperSanFrancisco.

Noddings, Nel. 1984. *Caring: A Feminine Approach to Ethics.* Berkeley: University of California Press.

———. 1989. *Women and Evil.* Berkeley: University of California Press.

Norris, Kathleen. 1996. *The Cloister Walk.* New York: Riverhead Books.

Norsigian, Judy. 1996. "The Women's Health Movement in the United States." In *Man-Made Medicine: Women's Health, Public Policy and Reform.* Ed. Kary L. Moss. Durham: Duke University Press.

Northrup, Lesley A. 1997. *Ritualizing Women: Patterns of Spirituality.* Cleveland: Pilgrim Press.

Novak, David. 1993. Be Fruitful and Multiply: Issues Related to Birth in Judaism. In *Celebration and Renewal: Rites of Passage in Judaism.* Ed. Rela M. Geffen. Philadelphia: Jewish Publication Society.

Oakley, Ann. 1980. *Women Confined: Toward a Sociology of Childbirth.* New York: Schocken Books.

———. 1984. *The Captured Womb: A History of the Medical Care of Pregnant Women.* Oxford: Basil Blackwell.

O'Brien, Mary. 1981. *The Politics of Reproduction.* London: Routledge and Kegan Paul.

Odent, Michel. 1984. *Birth Reborn.* New York: Pantheon Books.

Olds, Sharon. 1994. "The Moment When Two Worlds Meet." In *Mother Journeys: Feminists Write about Mothering.* Ed. Maureen T. Reddy, Martha Roth, and Amy Sheldon. Minneapolis: Spinsters Ink.

OMA Committee on Reproductive Care. 1994. OMA Issues Revised Statement on Planned Home Births. *Ontario Medical Review* (May) 36–37.

O'Mara, Peggy. 1990. *Midwifery and the Law: A* Mothering *Special Edition.* Santa Fe, N. Mex.: Mothering.

Orsi, Robert A. 1985. *The Madonna of 115th Street: Faith and Community in Italian Harlem, 1880–1950.* New Haven: Yale University Press.

———. 1996. *Thank You, St. Jude: Women's Devotion to the Patron Saint of Hopeless Causes.* New Haven: Yale University Press.

Ortner, Sherry B. 1994. "Theory in Anthropology Since the Sixties." In *Culture/Power/History: A Reader in Contemporary Social Theory.* Ed. Nicholas B. Dirks, Geoff Eley, and Sherry B. Ortner. Princeton: Princeton University Press.

———. 1996. *Making Gender: The Politics and Erotics of Culture.* Boston: Beacon Press.

Ostriker, Alicia. 1980. *The Mother/Child Papers.* Santa Monica, Calif.: Momentum Press. Reprinted by Beacon Press, 1986.

Overall, Christine. 1987. *Ethics and Human Reproduction: A Feminist Analysis.* Boston: Allen & Unwin.

Padanaram Settlement. 1987. *Faith Babies.* Williams, Ind.: Padanaram Settlement.

Parsons, Gail Pat. 1986. "In Transition: Doctors, Disease, and the Decline of Home Birth." Ph.D. diss., University of California, San Francisco.

Parvati Baker, Jeannine. 1992. "The Shamanic Dimension of Childbirth." *Pre- and Peri-natal Psychology Journal* 7, no. 1:5–20.

———. N.d. "Shamanic Midwifery: Every Mother a Midwife," paper. Junction, Utah: Freestone Publishing.

Pasternak, Judy. 1997. "Custody of Unborn Child Faces Court Test." *Los Angeles Times*, 2 February.

Paul, Lois. 1978. "Careers of Midwives in a Mayan Community." In *Women in Ritual and Symbolic Roles.* Ed. Anita Hoch-Smith and Judith Spring. New York: Plenum Press.

Paul, Lois, and B. Paul. 1975. "The Maya Midwife as a Sacred Specialist: A Guatemalan Case." *American Ethnologist* 2:707–726.

Pernick, Martin S. 1985. *A Calculus of Suffering: Pain, Professionalism, and Anesthesia in Nineteenth-Century America.* New York: Columbia University Press.

Perry, Chuck. 1976. *Mothering* 3:22.

———. 1977. *Mothering* 4:57, 65.

Perry, Ronald James. 1986. An In-Depth Understanding of Parents Who Choose Home Birth and Their Experience. Ph. D. diss., Boston University.

Petchesky, Rosalind Pollack. 1995. "The Body as Property: A Feminist Re-vision." In *Conceiving the New World Order: The Global Politics of Reproduction.* Ed. Faye D. Ginsburg and Rayna Rapp. Berkeley: University of California Press.

Pigg, Stacey Leigh. 1997. "Authority in Translation: Finding, Knowing, Naming, and Training 'Traditional Birth Attendants' in Nepal." In *Childbirth and Authoritative Knowledge: Cross-Cultural Perspectives.* Ed. Robbie E. Davis-Floyd and Carolyn F. Sargent. Berkeley: University of California Press.

Pollinger, Annette. 1977. "Diffusion of Innovations in Childbirth: An Analysis of Sociocultural Factors Associated with Traditional, Natural, and Home Birth." Ph.D. diss., Fordham University.

Poloma, Margaret M. 1989. *The Assemblies of God at the Crossroads: Charisma and Institutional Dilemmas.* Knoxville: University of Tennessee Press.

Pompilio, Natalie. 1996. "In New Jersey, Second Thoughts on Breastfeeding." *Philadelphia Inquirer*, 18 November, A1, A7.

Poovey, Mary. 1987. "Scenes of an Indelicate Character': The Medical 'Treatment' of Victorian Women." In *The Making of the Modern Body: Sexuality and Society in the Nineteenth Century.* Ed. Catherine Gallagher and Thomas Laqueur. Berkeley: University of California Press.

Porterfield, Amanda. 1980. *Feminine Spirituality in America: From Sarah Edwards to Martha Graham.* Philadelphia: Temple University Press.

Poston, Carol H. 1978. "Childbirth in Literature." *Feminist Studies* 4, no. 2:18–31.

Pratt, Minnie Bruce. 1984. "Identity: Skin Blood Heart." In *Yours in Struggle: Three Feminist Perspectives on Anti-Semitism and Racism.* Ed. Elly Bulkin, Minnie Bruce Pratt, and Barbara Smith. Brooklyn, N.Y.: Long Haul Press.

Priya, Jacqueline Vincent. 1992. *Birth Traditions and Modern Pregnancy Care.* Shaftesbury, U.K.: Element Books

Procter-Smith, Marjorie. 1990. *In Her Own Rite: Constructing Feminist Liturgical Tradition.* Nashville, Tenn.: Abingdon Press.

Procter-Smith, Marjorie. 1993. "'In the Line of the Female': Shakerism and Feminism." In *Women's Leadership in Marginal Religions: Explorations Outside the Mainstream.* Ed. Catherine Wessinger. Urbana: University of Illinois Press.

Rabuzzi, Kathryn Allen. 1994. *Mother with Child: Transformations through Childbirth.* Bloomington: Indiana University Press.

———. 1988. *Motherself: A Mythic Analysis of Motherhood.* Bloomington: Indiana University Press.

Radner, Joan Newlon, and Susan Lanser. 1993. "Strategies of Coding in Women's Cultures." In *Feminist Messages: Coding in Women's Folk Culture.* Ed. Joan Newlon Radner. Urbana and Chicago: University of Illinois Press.

Rapp, Rayna. 1993. "Accounting for Amniocentesis." In *Knowledge, Power, and Practice: The Anthropology of Medicine and Everyday Life.* Ed. S. Lindenbaum and M. Lock. Berkeley: University of California Press.

———. 1999. *Testing Women, Testing the Fetus: The Social Impact of Amniocentesis in America.* New York and London: Routledge.

Reagan, Leslie. 1995. "Linking Midwives and Abortion in the Progressive Era." *Bulletin of the History of Medicine* 69:569–598.

Reddy, Maureen T., Martha Roth, and Amy Sheldon, eds. 1994. *Mother Journeys: Feminists Write about Mothering.* Minneapolis: Spinsters Ink.

Reynolds, Vernon, and Ralph Tanner. 1995. *The Social Ecology of Religion.* Oxford: Oxford University Press.

Rich, Adrienne. 1986 [1976]. *Of Woman Born: Motherhood as Experience and Institution.* New York: Norton.

Richman, Joel, and W. O. Goldthorp. 1978. "Fatherhood: The Social Construction of Pregnancy and Birth." In *The Place of Birth.* Ed. Sheila Kitzinger and John Davis. Oxford: Oxford University Press.

Rizack, Lea. 1995. "Interview with Lea Rizack, CNM." Interview by Ina May Gaskin. *Birth Gazette* 11, no. 3:6–12.

Roeder, Beatrice A. 1988. *Chicano Folk Medicine from Los Angeles, California.* University of California Publications: Folklore and Mythology Studies, vol. 34. Berkeley: University of California Press.

Romalis, Shelly, ed. 1981. *Childbirth: Alternatives to Medical Control.* Austin: University of Texas Press.

Roof, Wade Clark. 1993. *A Generation of Seekers: The Spiritual Journeys of the Baby Boom Generation.* San Francisco: HarperSanFrancisco.

Rooks, Judith Pence. 1997. *Midwifery and Childbirth in America.* Philadelphia: Temple University Press.

Rosenberg, Rosalind. 1982. *Beyond Separate Spheres: Intellectual Roots of Modern Feminism.* New Haven: Yale University Press.

Ross, Susan A. 1992. "'Then Honor God in Your Body': Feminist and Sacramental Theology on the Body." In *Horizons on Catholic Feminist Theology.* Ed. Joann Wolski Conn and Walter E. Conn. Georgetown: Georgetown University Press.

Rothman, Barbara Katz. 1981. "Awake and Aware, or False Consciousness: The Cooption of Childbirth Reform in America." In *Childbirth: Alternatives to Medical Control.* Ed. Shelly Romalis. Austin: University of Texas Press.

———. 1982. *In Labor: Women and Power in the Birthplace.* New York: W. W. Norton. (Reprinted in paperback as *Giving Birth: Alternatives in Childbirth.* New York: Penguin Books, 1885.)

———. 1983. "Midwives in Transition: The Structure of a Clinical Revolution." *Social Problems* 30, no. 3:262–271.

———. 1994. "Beyond Mothers and Fathers: Ideology in a Patriarchal Society." In *Mothering: Ideology, Experience, Agency.* Ed. Evelyn Nakano Glenn, Grace Chang, and Linda Rennie Forcey. New York: Routledge.

Rothman, Sheila M. 1978. *Woman's Proper Place: A History of Changing Ideals and Practices, 1870 to the Present.* New York: Basic Books.

Ruddick, Sara. 1989. *Maternal Thinking.* Boston: Beacon Press.

———. 1994. "Thinking Mothers/Conceiving Birth." In *Representations of Motherhood.* Ed. Donna Basin, Margaret Honey, and Meryle Kaplan. New Haven: Yale University Press.

Ruether, Rosemary Radford. 1983. *Sexism and God-Talk.* Boston: Beacon Press.

Ruzek, Sheryl Burt. 1980. "Ethical Issues in Childbirth Technology." In *Birth Control and Controlling Birth: Women-Centered Perspectives.* Ed. Helen B. Holmes, Betty B. Hoskins, and Michael Gross. Clifton, N.J.: Humana Press.

———. 1986. "Feminist Visions of Health: An International Perspective." In *What Is Feminism?.* Ed. Juliet Mitchell and Ann Oakley. London: Basil Blackwell.

Sakala, Carol A. 1993. "Midwifery Care and Out-of-Hospital Birth Settings: How Do They Reduce Unnecessary Cesarean Section Births?" *Social Science and Medicine* 37, no. 10: 1233–1250.

Sandelowski, Margarete. 1984. *Pain, Pleasure, and American Childbirth: From the Twilight Sleep to the Read Method, 1914–1960.* Westport, Conn.: Greenwood Press.

Sandelowski, Margarete, and Linda Corson Jones. 1996. "'Healing Fictions': Stories of Choosing in the Aftermath of the Detection of Fetal Anomalies." *Social Science and Medicine* 42, no. 3:353–361.

Sandhaas, Kari. 1992. "Birth, Choice, and the Abuse of the Sacred: A Personal Story of Resistance." *Daughters of Sarah* 18, no. 4: 8–11.

Sarah, Rebecca. 1987. "Power, Certainty and the Fear of Death." *Women & Health* 13, no. 1-2:59–71.

Sargent, Carolyn. 1989. *Maternity, Medicine, and Power: Reproductive Decisions in Urban Benin.* Berkeley: University of California Press.

Sargent, Carolyn, and Nancy Stark. 1989. "Childbirth Education and Childbirth Models: Parental Perspectives on Control, Anesthesia, and Technological Intervention in the Birth Process." *Medical Anthropology Quarterly* 3, no. 1:36–51.

Scarry, Elaine. 1985. *The Body in Pain: The Making and Unmaking of the World.* Oxford: Oxford University Press.

Scheper-Hughes, Nancy. 1982. "Virgin Mothers: The Impact of Irish Jansenism on Childbearing and Infant Tending in Western Ireland." In *Anthropology of Human Birth.* Ed. Margarita Artschwager Kay. Philadelphia: F. A. Davis.

————. 1992. *Death without Weeping: The Violence of Everyday Life in Brazil.* Berkeley: University of California Press.

Scheper-Hughes, Nancy, and Margaret Lock. 1987. "The Mindful Body: A Prolegomenon to Future Work in Medical Anthropology." *Medical Anthropology Quarterly* 1, no. 1:6–41.

Schmidt, Leigh E. 1995. *Consumer Rites: The Buying and Selling of American Holidays.* Princeton: Princeton University Press.

Schoepflin, Rennie B. 1986. "The Christian Science Tradition." In *Caring and Curing: Health and Medicine in the Western Religious Traditions.* Ed. Ronald L. Numbers and Darrel W. Amundsen. New York: Macmillan.

Scholten, Catherine M. 1985. *Childbearing in American society, 1650–1850.* New York: New York University Press.

Schott, Judith, and Alix Henley. 1996. *Culture, Religion and Childbearing in a Multiracial Society: A Handbook for Health Professionals.* Oxford: Butterworth-Heinemann.

Sears, William. 1985. *Christian Parenting and Child Care.* Nashville, Tenn.: Thomas Nelson.

Sered, Susan Starr. 1991. "Childbirth as a Religious Experience?: Voices from an Israeli Hospital." *Journal for the Feminist Study of Religion* 7, no. 2:7–18.

————. 1992. *Women as Ritual Experts: The Religious Lives of Elderly Jewish Women in Jerusalem.* New York: Oxford University Press.

————. 1994. *Priestess, Mother, Sacred Sister: Religions Dominated by Women.* New York: Oxford University Press.

Shapiro, Max Philip. 1980. "Fathers' Experiences of Childbirth." Ph.D. diss., Boston University.

Shaw, Nancy Stoller. 1974. *Forced Labor: Maternity Care in the United States.* New York: Pergamon Press.

Sheridan, Mary S. 1992. *Pain in America.* Tuscaloosa: University of Alabama Press.

Shoemaker, M. Theophane. 1984. *History of Nurse-Midwifery in the United States.* New York: Garland Publishing.

Simkin, Penny. 1994. "Epidural Epidemic." *Birth Gazette* 10, no. 4:28–34.

Simons, Margaret A. 1990. "Motherhood, Feminism and Identity." In *Hypatia Reborn: Essays in Feminist Philosophy.* Ed. Azizah Y. al-Hibri and Margaret A. Simons. Bloomington: Indiana University Press.

Sischy, Ingrid. 1998. Madonna and Child. *Vanity Fair* 451 (March): 204–212, 266–270.

Smith, Bonnie. 1990. Havens No More? Discourses of Domesticity. *Gender and History* 2, no. 1:98–102.

Smith, Jonathan Z. 1998. "Religion, Religions, Religious." In *Critical Terms for Religious Studies.* Ed. Mark C. Taylor. Chicago: University of Chicago Press.

Smith, Pamela A. 1993. "Chronic Pain and Creative Possibility: A Psychological Phenomenon Confronts Theologies of Suffering." In *Broken and Whole: Essays on Religion and the Body.* Ed. Maureen A. Tilley and Susan A. Ross. Lanham, Md.: University Press of America.

Smith-Rosenberg, Carroll. 1985. *Disorderly Conduct: Visions of Gender in Victorian America.* New York: Oxford University Press.

Sousa, Marion. 1976. *Childbirth at Home*. New York: Bantam.

Spears, Gwendolyn V. 1995. Melting Pot vs. Salad Bowl. *Quickening: Bimonthly Publication of the American College of Nurse-Midwives* 26, no. 4:5.

Spivak, Gayatri Chakravorty. 1993. *Outside in the Teaching Machine*. New York: Routledge.

Spretnak, Charlene. 1997. *The Resurgence of the Real: Body, Nature and Place in a Hypermodern World*. Reading, Mass.: Addison Wesley.

Stabile, Carol A. 1994. *Feminism and the Technological Fix*. Manchester, U.K.: Manchester University Press.

Stacey, Judith. 1986. "Are Feminists Afraid to Leave Home?: The Challenge of Conservative Pro-Family Feminism." In *What Is Feminism?* Ed. Juliet Mitchell and Ann Oakley. London: Basil Blackwell.

———. 1988. "Can There Be a Feminist Ethnography?" *Women's Studies* 11, no. 1:21–27.

———. 1991. *Brave New Families: Stories of Domestic Upheaval in Late Twentieth Century America*. New York: Basic Books.

Stackhouse, John. 1996. "Maternal Mortality a Neglected Tragedy, UN Report Says." *The Globe and Mail*. 11 June, A12.

Stark, Sarah. 1982. "Mormon Childbearing." In *Anthropology of Human Birth*. Ed. Margarita Artschwager Kay. Philadelphia: F. A. Davis.

Starr, Paul. 1982. *The Social Transformation of American Medicine*. New York: Basic Books.

Steinfels, Margaret O'Brien. 1978. "New Childbirth Technology: A Clash of Values." *Hastings Center Report* (February): 9–12.

Stevens, Mitchell. Forthcoming. *Kingdom of Children: Culture and Controversy in the Homeschooling Movement*. Princeton: Princeton University Press.

Strassfeld, Michael, and Sharon Strassfeld. 1973. *The First Jewish Catalog*. Philadelphia: Jewish Publication Society.

Strathern, Marilyn. 1984. "Domesticity and the Denigration of Women." In *Rethinking Women's Roles: Perspectives from the Pacific*. Ed. Denise O'Brien and Sharon W. Tiffany. Berkeley: University of California Press.

Suarez, Suzanne Hope. 1993. "Midwifery Is Not the Practice of Medicine." *Yale Journal of Law and Feminism* 5:315–364.

Sullivan, Deborah A., and Rose Weitz. 1988. *Labor Pains: Modern Midwives and Home Birth*. New Haven: Yale University Press.

Summey, Pamela S., and Marsha Hurst. 1986. "Ob/Gyn on the Rise: The Evolution of Professional Ideology in the Twentieth Century." *Women and Health*, pt. 1: 11, no. 1:133–45; pt. 2: 11, no. 2:102–122.

Susie, Debra Anne. 1988. *In the Way of Our Grandmothers: A Cultural View of Twentieth-Century Midwifery in Florida*. Athens: University of Georgia Press.

Swenson, Norma. 1980. "Childbirth Overview." In *Birth Control and Controlling Birth: Women-Centered Perspectives*. Ed. Helen B. Holmes, Betty B. Hoskins, and Michael Gross. Clifton, N.J.: Humana Press.

Taber, David L. 1963. "Natural Childbirth Recommended—with Reservations." In *Religion and Birth Control*. Ed. John Clover Monsma. Garden City, N.Y.: Doubleday.

Taves, Ann. 1986. *The Household of Faith: Roman Catholic Devotions in Mid-Nineteenth-Century America*. Notre Dame: University of Notre Dame Press.

Taylor, Janelle S. "Of Sono-grams and Baby Prams: Prenatal Diagnosis, Pregnancy, and Consumption." *Feminist Studies* 26, no. 2 (2000): 391–418.

———. 1998."Image of Contradiction: Obstetrical Ultrasound in American Culture." In *Reproducing Reproduction: Kinship, Power, and Technological Innovation*. Ed. Sarah Franklin and Helena Ragoné. Philadelphia: University of Pennsylvania Press.

Teasley, Regi. 1983. "Birth and the Division of Labor: The Movement to Professionalize Nurse-Midwifery, and Its Relationship to the Movement for Home Birth and Lay Midwifery. A Case Study of Vermont." Ph. D. diss., Michigan State University.

———. 1986. "Nurse and Lay Midwifery in Vermont." In *The American Way of Birth*. Ed. Pamela S. Eakins. Philadelphia: Temple University Press.

Thomas, Jan. 1998. "Politics and Pregnancy: The Contested Terrain of Childbirth in Ohio." Paper presented at the American Sociological Association Annual Meeting, San Francisco.

Treichler, Paula A. 1990. "Feminism, Medicine, and the Meaning of Childbirth." In *Body Politics: Women, Literature, and the Discourse of Science*. Ed. Mary Jacobus, Evelyn Fox Keller, and Sally Shuttleworth. New York: Routledge, Chapman, and Hall.

Trevathan, Wenda R. 1987. *Human Birth: An Evolutionary Perspective*. New York: Aldine De Gruyter.

Tripp, David, and James Cameron. 1970. "Churching: A Common Problem of the English Churches." *Church Quarterly* 3, no. 2:125–133.

Tronto, Joan C. 1989. "Women and Caring: What Can Feminists Learn about Morality from Caring?" In *Gender/Body/Knowledge*. Ed. Alison M. Jaggar and Susan R. Bordo. New Brunswick: Rutgers University Press.

Tsing, Anna Lowenhaupt. 1990. "Monster Stories: Women Charged with Perinatal Endangerment." In *Uncertain Terms: Negotiating Gender in American Culture*. Ed. Faye Ginsburg and Anna Lowenhaupt Tsing. Boston: Beacon.

Turkel, Kathleen Doherty. 1988. "Technology, Authority, and Childbirth: A Case Study of the Control of Birthing in Delaware." Ph.D.diss., University of Delaware.

Turner, Victor. 1969. *The Ritual Process: Structure and Anti-Structure*. Ithaca: Cornell University Press.

Ulrich, Laurel Thatcher. 1991. *A Midwife's Tale*. New York: Vintage.

Umansky, Ellen M. 1991. "Finding God: Women in the Jewish Tradition." *Cross Currents* 41, no. 4:521–537.

Umansky, Lauri. 1996. *Motherhood Reconceived: Feminism and the Legacies of the Sixties*. New York: New York University Press.

U.S. Bureau of the Census. 1996. *Statistical Abstract of the United States: 1996*. 116th ed. Washington, D.C.: U.S. Government.

Van Gennep, Arnold. 1960 [1908]. *The Rites of Passage*. Chicago: University of Chicago Press.

Van Ness, Peter H. 1996. "Introduction: Spirituality and the Secular Quest." In *Spirituality and the Secular Quest*. Ed. Peter Van Ness. New York: Crossroad.

Visweswaran, Kamala. 1994. *Fictions of Feminist Ethnography.* Minneapolis: University of Minnesota Press.

Von Arx, Walter. 1979. "The Churching of Women after Childbirth: History and Significance." In *Liturgy and Human Passage.* Ed. David Power and Luis Maldonado. New York: Seabury Press.

Wacker, Grant. 1986. "The Pentecostal Tradition." In *Caring and Curing: Health and Medicine in the Western Religious Traditions.* Ed. Ronald L. Numbers and Darrel W. Amundsen. New York: MacMillan.

Wagner, Marsden. 1997. "Confessions of a Dissident." In *Childbirth and Authoritative Knowledge: Cross-Cultural Perspectives.* Ed. R. E. Davis-Floyd and C. Sargent. Berkeley: University of California Press.

Walker, Stephanie Kirkwood. 1996. *This Woman in Particular: Contexts for the Biographical Image of Emily Carr.* Waterloo, Ont.: Wilfrid Laurier University Press.

Walsh, Andrew. 1988. "The McCaughey Babies."*Religion in the News* 1, no. 1 (June 1988): 9–10.

Walters, Suzanne Danuta. 1992. *Lives Together, Worlds Apart: Mothers and Daughters in Popular Culture.* Berkeley: University of California Press.

Walzer, Stephen, and Allen Cohen. 1971. *Childbirth Is Ecstasy.* Albion, Calif.: Aquarius.

Ward, Jule DeJager. 2000. *La Leche League: At the Crossroads of Medicine, Feminism, and Religion.* Chapel Hill: University of North Carolina Press.

Warner, Marina. 1976. *Alone of All Her Sex: The Myth and the Cult of the Virgin Mary.* London: Picador.

Waugh, Brenda. 1991. "Repro-Woman: A View of the Labyrinth (from the Lithotomy Position)." *Yale Journal of Law and Feminism* 3, no. 4:5–61.

Weiner, Lynn Y. 1994. "Reconstructing Motherhood: The La Leche League in Postwar America." *Journal of American History* (March): 1357–1381.

Weissler, Chava. 1992. "*Mizvot* Built into the Body: *Tkhines* for *Niddah,* Pregnancy, and Childbirth. In *People of the Body: Jews and Judaism from an Embodied Perspective.* Ed. Howard Eilberg-Schwartz. Albany: State University of New York Press.

Wertz, Richard W., and Dorothy C. Wertz. 1989 [1977]. *Lying-In: A History of Childbirth in America.* Expanded Edition. New Haven: Yale University Press.

Wessel, Helen S. 1963. *Natural Childbirth and the Christian Family.* New York: Harper and Row.

———. 1981. *Under the Apple Tree: Marrying, Birthing, Parenting.* Fresno, Calif.: Bookmates International.

———. 1983. *Natural Childbirth and the Christian Family,* 4th rev. ed. New York: Harper and Row.

Wiegers, T. A., M.J.N.C. Keirse, J. van der Zee, and G.A.H. Berghs. 1996. "Outcome of Planned Home and Planned Hospital Births in Low Risk Pregnancies: Prospective Study in Midwifery Practices in the Netherlands." *British Medical Journal* 313 (23 November): 1309–1313.

Witten, Marsha G. 1993. *The Secular Message in American Protestantism.* Princeton: Princeton University Press.

Wolf, Deborah Goleman. 1982. "Lesbian Childbirth and Artificial Insemination: A Wave of the Future." In *Anthropology of Human Birth*. Ed. Margarita Artschwager Kay. Philadelphia: F. A. Davis.

Wolf, Margery. 1992. *A Thrice Told Tale: Feminism, Postmodernism & Ethnographic Responsibility*. Stanford: Stanford University Press.

Wuthnow, Robert. 1991. *Acts of Compassion: Caring for Others and Helping Ourselves*. Princeton: Princeton University Press.

———. 1994. *Producing the Sacred: An Essay on Public Religion*. Urbana and Chicago: University of Illinois Press.

———. 1998. *After Heaven: Spirituality in America since the 1950s*. Berkeley: University of California Press.

Young, Iris Marion. 1990. "Humanism, Gynocentrism, and Feminist Politics." In *Hypatia Reborn: Essays in Feminist Philosophy*. Ed. Azizah Y. al-Hibri and Margaret A. Simons. Bloomington: Indiana University Press.

Zelizer, Viviana A. 1994. *Pricing the Priceless Child: The Changing Social Value of Children*. Princeton: Princeton University Press.

Zimdars-Swartz, Sandra L. 1995. "The Marian Revival in American Catholicism: Focal Points and Features of the New Marian Enthusiasm." In *Being Right: Conservative Catholics in America*. Ed. Mary Jo Weaver and R. Scott Appleby. Bloomington: Indiana University Press.

Index